Childhood Matters

Report of the
National Commission of Inquiry
into the Prevention of
Child Abuse

Chairman: Lord Williams of Mostyn

Volume 1: The Report

London: The Stationery Office

ISBN 011 321997 0

Published by The Stationery Office and available from:

The Stationery Office Publications Centre
(mail, telephone and fax orders only)
PO Box 276, London SW8 5DT
General enquiries 0171 873 0011
Telephone orders 0171 873 9090
Fax orders 0171 873 8200

The Stationery Office Bookshops
49 High Holborn, London WC1V 6HB
(counter service only and fax orders only)
Fax 0171 831 1326
68–69 Bull Street, Birmingham B4 6AD
0121 236 9696 Fax 0121 236 9699
33 Wine Street, Bristol BS1 2BQ
01179 264 306 Fax 01179 294 515
9–21 Princess Street, Manchester M60 8AS
0161 834 7201 Fax 0161 833 0634
16 Arthur Street, Belfast BT1 4GD
01232 238 451 Fax 01232 235 401
71 Lothian Road, Edinburgh EH3 9AZ
0131 479 3141 Fax 0131 479 3142
The Stationery Office Oriel Bookshop
The Friary, Cardiff CF1 4AA
01222 395 548 Fax 01222 384 347

The Stationery Office's Accredited Agents
(see Yellow Pages)

and through good booksellers

Printed in the UK for The Stationery Office
Dd 303371   C20   10.96

Contents

*Report of the
National
Commission of
Inquiry into the
Prevention of
Child Abuse*

Report of the
National
Commission of
Inquiry into the
Prevention of
Child Abuse

The National Commission of Inquiry Into The Prevention of Child Abuse

Membership

Chairman
Lord Williams of Mostyn QC

Members

Elaine Arnold

Professor Stewart Asquith

Michael Grade

Sir Peter Newsam

Deidre Sanders

Professor Jo Sibert

Sir Roger Sims, JP MP

Professor Daphne Statham, CBE

Christine Walby

Commission Secretariat

Secretary
Christopher Cloke

Research Assistant
Sarah King

Press Managers
Henrietta Bond
Judith Tavanyar

Administrative/Secretarial Support
Fenella Davidson
Katharine Peake

Acknowledgements

*Report of the
National
Commission of
Inquiry into the
Prevention of
Child Abuse*

Many individuals and organisations have contributed to the work of the Commission and I am grateful to them all for their help and support. A number of companies have welcomed us with great hospitality. A full list of everyone who has supported the Commission is included in Appendix 19.

I am particularly grateful to the NSPCC for having the vision to set up the Commission and fund the bulk of our work, including our secretariat, to Channel Four for financing several projects, and to *Community Care* for collaborating on two national conferences and a survey of social workers' attitudes.

Ours has been a highly committed Commission and all members have worked unstintingly in addressing what at times have been very painful issues. We have been supported by a small but able staff team which ensured the efficient running of our work. I am grateful to them all.

Most important, we have constantly heard the voices of many people who have experienced abuse themselves and who found the courage to speak about what happened in the hope that it would make a difference for other children. To them we owe the greatest debt; and I would like to reassure them that their contribution has been a constant source of inspiration and help in our endeavour to ensure that *childhood matters*.

vii

Lord Williams of Mostyn QC
Chairman, National Commission

Foreword

*Report of the
National
Commission of
Inquiry into the
Prevention of
Child Abuse*

Most of today's thirteen million children in the United Kingdom are brought up healthily and happily. That is what we want for all our children.

Against this background, however, too many children do not have such a secure start to life. They encounter adverse, sometimes terrifyingly adverse, situations which are detrimental to them and to their healthy development into adulthood. In extreme cases, this leads not only to damaged children but, at huge cost to themselves and society, to children who may become damaging to others.

There is every human and practical reason for preventing harm of this kind, rather than having to cope with it after it has occurred. That is why prevention - the prevention of harm to children - was chosen as the subject of this Inquiry.

Under the general heading of "abuse", the Commission has taken a wide view of the forms of damage to which children are subjected. The main responsibility for preventing that abuse lies with the family or those with direct responsibility for a child's upbringing. That is why this Report emphasises the importance of good parenting and support for it. We wish to build on the commitment that most parents have to being good parents. But there is also a wider responsibility, incorporated into law and included in the work of a range of public and other bodies, to support parents.

ix

This Report is concerned with the better provision of all forms of preventive support. That must include the help provided to those who have been abused. Unless that is effectively provided, abused children face continuing difficulties, which in time may affect their relationships with their own children.

During the course of its work, the Commission has received evidence from a wide range of people and agencies. These are listed in Appendix 1 to the Report but that cannot do justice to the richness of the evidence and the commitment and concern, sometimes amounting to anguish, of those who came forward. Child and adult alike, they have told us what they believe should now be done.

The weight of testimony has left the Commission in no doubt that most of the abuse children now suffer is preventable.

In formulating its recommendations, the Commission has found itself supporting measures already proposed by others, as well as making new proposals of its own. Throughout, it has worked to ensure that its main recommendations could rapidly be put into effect. It is not a revolution in preventive action that is required; it is a realistic reappraisal of present efforts, a sharper focus, a strengthened emphasis.

The prevention of child abuse requires action from a wide range of individuals and agencies. The Commission's recommendations reflect this and are directed at those different bodies

*Report of the
National
Commission of
Inquiry into the
Prevention of
Child Abuse*

who have responsibility for policies and practices in the care and protection of children. We hope that each of these agencies will share our belief that *childhood matters*.

Finally, as chairman of the Commission, I should like to place on record our thanks to the NSPCC for its financial and administrative support of the Commission's work and for providing this in a way that guaranteed the Commission's independence.

Lord Williams of Mostyn QC
Chairman of the Commission

x

*Report of the
National
Commission of
Inquiry into the
Prevention of
Child Abuse*

Introduction
The Commission

- Over 10,000 people contributed to the work of the Commission

- Over 450 written submissions were received

- Special studies were commissioned from leading experts on key issues, including finance and the law

- More than 1,000 letters were received from individuals, most of whom were abused as children

The Status of the Commission

The National Commission of Inquiry into the Prevention of Child Abuse was established and funded by the NSPCC to consider the different ways in which children are harmed, how this can best be prevented, and to make recommendations for developing a national strategy for reducing the incidence of child abuse. Since it was established in the autumn of 1994, the Commission has operated as an independent body.

Membership

If child abuse is to be prevented, a broad range of individuals and organisations needs actively to be engaged. This was reflected in the Commission's membership which included individuals from differing backgrounds and professions. They served in their own right, and not as representatives of any organisation, discipline, or interest group. Their biographical details are given in Appendix 2.

Terms of Reference

The terms of reference, originally suggested by the NSPCC, were subsequently amended and developed by the Commission and agreed as follows:

> *"The Commission will consider current provision and make recommendations for a national strategy for the prevention of child abuse and neglect in the United Kingdom. It will give prime consideration to law and social policy provisions, service provision, professional practice, and the role of parenting. It will look at the external factors which impinge upon child abuse and neglect and recognise that the prevention of abuse involves all sectors of the community."*

In inviting submissions from individuals and a wide range of voluntary and statutory organisations, the Commission also identified a number of areas relevant to its inquiry. These are described in Appendix 3.

*Report of the
National
Commission of
Inquiry into the
Prevention of
Child Abuse*

The Scope of the Inquiry

The inquiry concerned the whole of the United Kingdom. Evidence was received from and hearings held in England, Wales, Scotland and Northern Ireland, and the differences and similarities between them were noted. Details were also sought of the experiences of other countries.

Throughout, the Commission was concerned with child abuse at a general level. Individual cases of abuse were not addressed. It drew on positive experiences and good professional practice.

The terms of reference cover the prevention of the abuse of children in the United Kingdom. It is recognized, however, that if UK citizens abuse children overseas they may place children in the UK at risk on their return. It is for that reason, quite apart from any general abhorrence of such behaviour, that the Commission supports government proposals to ensure that offences against children committed outside the UK are regarded in the same manner as those committed within the UK.

The Method of Working

The focus of the work was on the *prevention* of child abuse. Large numbers of people share that concern and this influenced the Commission's way of working. There was widespread consultation and evidence from a wide variety of sources. As well as meeting on more than 20 occasions to review the evidence and consider its response, the Commission:

○ took written evidence from organisations, community groups, professionals, and researchers. Over 450 written submissions were received. The individuals and organisations who gave evidence are listed in Appendix 1. In addition there were letters from more than 1,000 people, most of whom were themselves abused as children.

○ received oral evidence from more than 40 people and conducted telephone interviews with survivors of child abuse who wanted to speak about their experiences.

○ held consultation meetings and focus-group discussions, including meetings with educationalists, health professionals, legal professionals, researchers, media representatives, advice columnists and young people in care.

○ paid field visits to projects in different parts of the United Kingdom.

○ took part in a number of conferences, including national conferences in London and in Glasgow, organised jointly with the journal *Community Care*.

○ reviewed the research on issues affecting the prevention of child abuse.

○ made a short video of survivors of child abuse speaking about their experiences and discussing how they thought child abuse could be prevented.

Work Commissioned

To widen the scope of the evidence available, work was commissioned from external advisers in the following areas:

○ **The law and child abuse prevention:** prepared by Kathleen Marshall, a solicitor and

Report of the
National
Commission of
Inquiry into the
Prevention of
Child Abuse

Fellow in Children's Rights, University of Glasgow, and Professor Christina Lyon, University of Liverpool.

o **The cost of child abuse.** The **Institute of Public Finance (CIPFA)** undertook detailed work on the costing of services and **International Computer Limited** conducted a two-day workshop on the allocation of resources between agencies.

o **Survivors of child abuse:** more than 1,000 letters from individuals, most of whom were abused as children, were analysed by **Corinne Wattam** and **Clare Woodward, University of Lancaster.**

o **Children and young people's views:** a questionnaire survey was carried out involving 1,000 children and young people.

o **A review of recent research into child abuse** was carried out **Dr David Gough** and **Dr Kathleen Murray.**

o **The impact of race and culture and racism on the response to child abuse** was considered in a paper by **Ratna Dutt** and **Melanie Phillips,** of the **Race Equality Unit.**

o **Social workers' attitudes:** in collaboration with the journal *Community Care*, market research was conducted among more than 1,000 social workers.

o **The impact of employment policies on family support and the prevention of child abuse** were examined by **Dr Alma Erlich,** psychologist.

o **Attitudes of parliamentarians:** there were interviews with 38 MPs and peers and meetings with the **All Party Parliamentary Group for Children** and the **All Party Parliamentary Group on Parenting.**

o **The media and child abuse:** the **Communications Research Group, University of Aston,** analysed the portrayal of young people on British terrestrial television and the **Glasgow Media Group, University of Glasgow** conducted research on the handling of child sexual abuse in the Channel Four soap opera Brookside.

The Commission was impressed by the range and quality of the submissions it received, both from the main agencies dealing with the prevention of abuse and the protection of children, and from the public at large. Well over 2,000 people provided evidence directly and many more were involved in its preparation. It is estimated that more than 10,000 people have contributed to the work of the Commission. A notable feature of the views expressed has been the degree to which there is general agreement on the urgent need for renewed efforts, nationally and locally, to prevent the abuse of children. The urgency of that need is reflected in the Commission's recommendations.

Access to Documents

The evidence the Commission received provides a wide-ranging view of child abuse and how it is perceived in the United Kingdom at the end of the twentieth century. This report does not have the space to record or do full justice to the wealth of information and insights that was amassed. Copies of the written submissions and transcripts of the oral hearings are lodged with the NSPCC archives and those that are not confidential may be viewed by appointment. It is hoped that this rich source of material will be widely used.

Chapter 1
Defining Child Abuse

*Report of the
National
Commission of
Inquiry into the
Prevention of
Child Abuse*

- **Professionals, researchers and the public have different views of what constitutes child abuse**

- **The Commission supports a broad definition of child abuse**

- **This broad definition should form the basis of all policies and practices affecting children**

- **Within that broad definition, professionals need technical definitions, which can be consistently interpreted, to assist their formal procedures**

1.1   Agreed definitions of child abuse are important for two reasons. The first is to establish a general framework within which policies designed to prevent child abuse can be developed and assessed. The second is to provide a set of technical definitions for identifying actions or circumstances which are taken to be abusive to children. These technical definitions are needed for statutory, legal, statistical, procedural and research purposes.

1.2   At present that there is some uncertainty or, in some instances, disagreement among professionals and the public over what constitutes child abuse. In addition, different professional disciplines do not always work to the same definitions of abuse. Despite the fact that there may be broad agreement at the extremes over what is harmful to children, there is a sizeable grey area about which there is confusion. For example, should a single instance of harm, which appears unlikely to be repeated, be regarded as abusive in the absence of evidence that any long-term damage has been or is likely to be done? These considerations have important implications for assessing whether a child is at risk, the "diagnosis" of abuse, and the appropriateness of official intervention.

1.3   Differences of emphasis are inevitable when people with strongly held views are dealing with such an emotive issue as child abuse. With that in mind, the Commission concluded that a single definition of abuse, however extended, could not meet the twin requirements of providing a general framework for the common understanding of abuse and a set of technical terms for identifying abusive acts. Accordingly, it has established a broad definition of abuse for general use; within that, it has considered technical definitions for professional use.

> "As a child I never felt loved by my mother. I was always told by my mother that I was thick, stupid, hopeless and useless. I was never praised for what I could do, only put down for what I could not do."
> **Letter to the Commission**

*Report of the
National
Commission of
Inquiry into the
Prevention of
Child Abuse*

The broad definition of abuse

1.4   The broad definition adopted by the Commission is as follows:

*"Child abuse consists of anything which individuals, institutions, or processes do or
fail to do which directly or indirectly harms children or damages their prospects of
safe and healthy development into adulthood."* (1)

1.5   The broad definition is designed to ensure that the promotion of a "safe and healthy development" for children is the primary aim of all policies affecting them and to stress that institutions and processes can be quite as abusive as individuals to any particular child. To that extent, this will require policy-makers to consider broad social and economic issues which run far wider than the particular needs of children but which nevertheless profoundly affect them. The adoption of a broad definition of abuse is also intended to encourage everyone to consider how *all* aspects of their behaviour affect children but does not, of course, imply that most of that behaviour is abusive.

1.6   The broad definition adopted in this Report reflects the principles set down in the United Nations Convention on the Rights of the Child(2), ratified by the United Kingdom government in 1991. Such an approach was proposed in much of the evidence received by the Commission. The Articles of the Convention relevant to the prevention of child abuse are set out in Appendix 4.

2

> "I realise that when some people use the expression "child abuse" they mean only sexual abuse. That of course, is a horrific crime. Some would take the view that physical abuse is "nothing" compared with it. I don't take that view because from experience I know that it damages, especially when verbal abuse accompanies the beatings."
> **Letter to the Commission**

1.7   The Commission defines a child as aged from birth until eighteen. Some who fall within this age range will consider themselves, and be considered by others, to be "young people".

> "The range and extent of the unkindness, cruelty, violence and wrongdoing to which children are subjected is shocking... Instances of gross or sadistic abuse are acutely distressing but so also is the extent to which children's lives are impoverished by lack of affection or care, by intrusive sexual contacts, relentless verbal abuse, ongoing physical assault, and constant fear."
> **ChildLine**

Technical definitions of abuse

1.8   Within the broad definition, technical definitions which relate to specific forms of abuse or to specific areas of professional practice are needed for statutory, statistical, procedural and research purposes. An account of definitions currently in use is in Appendix 5.

1.9   Two of the most important technical definitions deriving from legislation are those of *"significant harm"* and *"children in need"*. The Children Act 1989, which covers England and Wales, the Children (Northern Ireland) Order 1995, and the Children (Scotland) Act 1995 make similar provisions. Section 31 of the Children Act 1989 deals with "harm" as follows:

> *"harm" means ill-treatment or the impairment of health or development;*
> *"development" means physical, intellectual, emotional, social or behavioural development;*
> *"health" means physical or mental health; and*
> *"ill-treatment" includes sexual abuse and forms of ill-treatment which are not physical.*

The Children Act 1989 defines a child as being "in need" if:

> *"(a)   he is unlikely to achieve or maintain, or have the opportunity of achieving or maintaining, a reasonable standard of health or development without the provision for him of services by the local authority;*
>
> *(b)   his health or development is likely to be significantly impaired, or further impaired, without the provision of such services; or*
>
> *(c)   he is disabled."*

The Children (Scotland) Act 1995 includes a fourth criterion which is not contained in the English and Welsh legislation:

> *"the child is affected adversely by the disability of another family member."*

The definitions of "significant harm" and "children in need" overlap to some extent, and both come within the broad definition of abuse adopted by the Commission.

1.10   For operational purposes, social services departments and other agencies use criteria to help them determine how best to provide services for children "in need". Table 1 below sets out the main criteria(3) used but it must be recognised that not all local authorities use all these criteria in assessing children's needs, and even when they do, that there is no guarantee that the appropriate services will be provided.

Table 1.1   *"Children in need" criteria*
(Adapted from Aldgate and Tunstill, 1996)

○ Child at risk of abuse	○ Child at risk of offending
○ Child at risk of neglect	○ Child with developmental problems
○ Child with a disability	
○ Child who has offended	○ Child is drug abusing
○ Child who is HIV+	○ Child is homeless
○ Child in a low income family	○ Child lives in bad housing
○ Child with behaviour problems (for example, child is truanting; is excluded from school; is being bullied or is a bully)	○ Parents have marital/ relationship problems
	○ Focus of problems is with parents (for example, domestic violence, drug or alcohol abuse)

3

*Report of the
National
Commission of
Inquiry into the
Prevention of
Child Abuse*

1.11 The legal definitions of "significant harm" are complemented by government guidance on child protection criteria and procedures. The key guidance on inter-agency working in relation to child abuse for England and Wales is *Working Together* (4), issued by the Department of Health in 1991. Equivalent guidance, which is likely to be similar, is being developed for Scotland and Northern Ireland. *Working Together* adopts a set of narrowly defined categories of abuse which is broken down into *neglect*, *physical injury*, *sexual abuse*, and *emotional abuse*. These definitions (see Appendix 5), are intended for professionals making decisions about placing children's names on child protection registers but are generally accepted as the "official" definitions of *child abuse*. While all child protection professionals should be working to these definitions, the evidence received by the Commission indicates wide disparities in interpretation, due in part to availability of resources and the different priorities of various disciplines.

Table 2   *Definitions of child abuse: non-statutory guidance*

Neglect	The persistent or severe neglect of a child or the failure to protect a child from exposure to any kind of danger, including cold or starvation, or extreme failure to carry out important aspects of care, resulting in the significant impairment of the child's health or development, including non-organic failure to thrive.
Physical Injury	Actual or likely physical injury to a child, or failure to prevent physical injury (or suffering) to a child, including deliberate poisoning, suffocation, and Munchausen's syndrome by proxy.
Sexual Abuse	Actual or likely sexual exploitation of a child or adolescent. The child may be dependent and/or developmentally immature.
Emotional Abuse	Actual or likely severe adverse effect on the emotional and behavioural development of a child caused by persistent or severe emotional ill-treatment or rejection. All abuse involves some emotional ill-treatment.

Source: *Working Together*, Department of Health, 1991

The adequacy of definitions currently used

1.12   The technical definitions now in operational use need to be interpreted consistently across different professional disciplines. Such consistency would be helped by revising the categories of abuse given in *Working Together* so that they relate more closely to the definition of "significant harm" given in the Children Act 1989.

1.13   Greater coherence could be also brought to these technical definitions through interdisciplinary training, including that of judges and advocates, and the effective monitoring of the interpretation of official definitions of abuse by professonals concerned with child protection. Effective working relationships between professional practitioners depend upon a common language and use of terminology. It is important that practice guidance to different professional groups reflects a common interpretation of the nature of "significant harm".

1.14   Child protection agencies tend to work to narrow legal and technical definitions of abuse, partly because of fears of widening the net for formal intervention or actions and partly because of the need to allocate scarce resources. These issues are discussed later in the Report. In the opinion of the Commission, definitions of abuse should not be governed by availability of resources. Moreover, if society is to become less tolerant of the abuse of children, there is a need for a wider definition of abuse than is generally accepted.

Abuse by systems

1.15   One form of abuse which requires greater recognition and more precise definition is that of *system abuse*. The definition recommended by the Commission is as follows:

"System abuse may be said to occur whenever the operation of legislation, officially sanctioned procedures or operational practices within systems or institutions is avoidably damaging to children and their families."

1.16   System abuse occurs where:

(i)   children's needs are not recognised or understood and so they are not considered specifically and separately from those of adults, for example, as witnesses or victims in the criminal justice system, or as children of parents in receipt of punitive or harsh treatment in the penal, refugee or asylum systems;

(ii)   services are unavailable because they do not exist, are inadequate, with restrictive criteria for access, or inaccessible through lack of information, location, or through insensitivity to race, culture or gender;

(iii) services are so poorly organised, managed, monitored or resourced that they permit unskilled and unsafe environments in day, residential and family care settings; they permit repressive and abusive regimes to develop; and they do not detect and deal with abusive individuals who infiltrate organisations and services for children;

(iv)   services for children with emotional and behavioural disorders are so poorly defined and co-ordinated that organisations can avoid or shift responsibilities on to others or define problems so narrowly that the proposed "solution" is inadequate and partial;

(v)   there are unnecessarily intrusive procedures or practices which undermine children or their families.(5)

Public understanding and perceptions of child abuse

1.17   The Commission was aware that, whatever broad or technical definitions of abuse might have legal force, the general public principally see child abuse in terms of gross physical or sexual assault.

1.18   Some researchers have analysed how the public perceive child abuse, focusing particularly on perceptions of acceptable and unacceptable behaviour. The Creighton and Russell(6) survey of childhood experiences and attitudes to child rearing, for example, found that many respondents believed that physical punishment was justified in certain circumstances. The researchers concluded that what is understood as abuse depends on a range of factors including social norms and the parenting styles associated with them.

1.19   Recent research commissioned by the Department of Health addressed similar issues in its analysis of "normal" family behaviour and the long-term outcomes of different styles

5

Report of the
National
Commission of
Inquiry into the
Prevention of
Child Abuse

of parenting. The overview provided in *Messages from Research*(7) notes that "in assessing the long-term effects of different parenting styles, the severity and endurance of particular incidents can be important. In a warm, supportive environment, children who have been hit once or twice seldom suffer long-term negative effects." It suggests that abuse should be considered in terms both of the severity of the incident and of the general care of the child. An event of severe abuse in the context of a negative parenting style may, it is suggested, have a more damaging effect than a similar event which occurs in a more positive parenting context. Families who are "low on warmth and high on criticism", where "negative incidents accumulate as if to remind a child that he or she is unloved", is considered to be particularly harmful to children. It is suggested that in these families, "although parents behave badly or are unavailable to their children, they seldom, if ever, commit acts of deliberate cruelty. However, punishment, physical neglect and very occasionally child sexual abuse, are probably more likely to occur to children in low-warmth, high-criticism situations." Child abuse is here defined in terms of the longer-term impact of the individual incident or the cumulative impact of incidents, and it falls to the professional to judge when abuse has occurred. The process of making that judgement is further complicated by the fact that taking a long-term view can be dangerous: an apparently isolated and minor injury to a very young child has proved in some cases to be the precursor to major injury or death as a result of abuse.

1.20   The lack of shared understanding between individuals who have been abused, professionals, and policy-makers is apparent in the study of letters, mainly from survivors of abuse, sent to the Commission and analysed at Lancaster University. They expressed the view that professionals do not fully understand what constitutes child abuse. Wattam and Woodward(8) conclude from their study of the letters, (summarised in Appendix 6), that while correspondents' definitions of child abuse included the more conventional descriptive terms (ie. sexual, physical, and emotional abuse and neglect), they also addressed a broader range of potentially harmful actions, such as bullying, the deliberate subjection of a child to danger, and lack concern for children's rights. Many placed greater emphasis on the longer-term emotional consequences of abuse than on the immediate effect of physical injury or sexual assault. They also linked abuse to its impact on personal relationships within the family, partly defined by what sense the child makes of what is happening to him or her. In other words, their definition of child abuse related not only to the abuse itself, but also to its context and its longer-term impact on the individual and the family concerned. This is a key component of the wide definition of abuse proposed by the Commission. Evidence from families against whom allegations of abuse have been made testifies to the often severe and lasting impact on family life and relationships which result from the inquiries or investigations, particularly when the allegations are not proven. Research, including that by June Thoburn, University of East Anglia(9), confirms this.

> "All my life I had been filled with abuse of one kind or another, so for many years, although I knew it was wrong, I thought it was normal and that everybody had secrets."
> **Letter to the Commission**

*Report of the
National
Commission of
Inquiry into the
Prevention of
Child Abuse*

1.21 The definitions and perceptions of child abuse held by people who wrote of their experiences do not relate neatly to the definitions provided in legislation and in government guidance. The importance these survivors attached to the emotional impact of abuse is not reflected in child protection registrations. Their letters demonstrate that, in terms of defining abuse, greatest weight is generally given to the views of professionals. They also show how "official definitions" exclude certain forms of abuse that can have damaging consequences. For example, the emotional impact on children who witness violence was mentioned many times but is not acknowledged in official definitions. These differences in perception need to be addressed in policy and professional practice.

Conclusion

1.22 How abuse is defined and how the definitions are then put into operation is crucial to strategies for preventing child abuse. The Commission has reviewed the definitions of child abuse which derive from legislation and government guidance. It has also considered the perceptions held by professionals, policy makers and the general public, including those who have been abused. It has concluded that the wide definition of abuse set out in 1.4 above should be supplemented by a set of technical definitions revised in the manner described in 1.12 to 1.16 above.

7

References

1. Derived from Gil D G, 1970, Violence Against Children, Harvard University Press

2. United Nations, 1989, UN Convention on the Rights of the Child, New York: United Nations

3. Algate J, Tunstill J, 1995, Making Sense of Section 17: a study for the Department of Health, Implementing Services for Children in Need within the Children Act 1989, London: HMSO

4. Home Office, Department of Health, Department of Education and Science and Welsh Office, 1991, Working Together Under The Children Act 1989: A Guide to Arrangements for Inter-Agency Co-operation for the Protection of Children from Abuse, London: HMSO

5. Derived from Cashman J, Dolby R, Brennan D (1994), Systems Abuse: problems and solutions, Sydney: New South Wales Child Protection Council

6. Creighton S, Russell N, 1995, Voices from Childhood: A Survey of childhood experiences and attitudes to child rearing among adults in the United Kingdom, NSPCC

7. Child Protection: Messages From Research, 1995, Department of Health, London: HMSO

8. Wattam C, Woodward C, 1996, And Do I Abuse my Children? No! Learning about prevention from people who have experienced child abuse, *in* National Commission of Inquiry into the Prevention of Child Abuse, 1996, Childhood Matters, Volume 2, London: HMSO

9. Thoburn J, Lewis A, and Shemmings D, 1995, Paternalism or Partnership? Family Involvement in the Child Protection Process, London: HMSO

Chapter 2
The Extent of Abuse

*Report of the
National
Commission of
Inquiry into the
Prevention of
Child Abuse*

- On the basis of the Commission's broad definition, at least one million children and young people are harmed each year

- At least 150,000 children annually suffer severe physical punishment

- Up to 100,000 children each year have a potentially harmful sexual experience

- 350-400,000 children live in an environment which is consistently low in warmth and high in criticism

- 450,000 children are bullied at school at least once a week

- In 1992 there were 4.3 million children living in poverty, one in three of all children in the UK

- Many of the effects of child abuse are long lasting and persist into adulthood

2.1   Children can be harmed by a wide range of events - from an isolated incident to systematic and long-term maltreatment. Inevitably, as abuse arises between individuals or individuals and institutions, with much remaining hidden and unreported, estimating the extent of abuse in its different forms, relies only partly on official statistics. They need to be supplemented by information from surveys of the experience of adults and children, and from other sources.

2.2   The Commission's definition of abuse covers a wide spectrum of damage: at one extreme there are actions resulting in criminal convictions; at the other, the broader effects of poverty and deprivation. However, problems of definition and of making decisions about the point at which society must take action should not be allowed to influence assessments of the scale of abuse. The numbers of children significantly harmed by abuse and of adults suffering the effects of their abuse as children are likely to be far greater than has been recognised because many children do not tell anyone about what is happening to them. Surveys among adults who were abused as children have consistently shown that less than half had told anybody at the time. Most children are abused by individuals known to them, which can increase the difficulty of telling, especially when the alleged abuser is a close family member. The situation may be improving with access to children's helplines and more open discussion about abuse. Yet the problem remains: far too many children and young people still feel unable to seek support and help.

> "I cannot remember a day of my childhood when I was not abused. It was not until I reached secondary school that I realised that this sort of thing doesn't happen to everybody"
> Letter to the Commission

Report of the
National
Commission of
Inquiry into the
Prevention of
Child Abuse

Official estimates of abuse

2.3   Official statistics record cautions and convictions for crimes against children, and list the number of children who are considered sufficiently at risk of significant harm from abuse that they are placed on a local authority child protection register.

2.4   **Criminal convictions** represent cases of severe abuse where the evidence is so strong that prosecution has succeeded. However, since the victim's age is not recorded by the police for some sexual crimes, such as rape, and for most offences involving physical violence, the total number of such cases where the victim was under 16 is not known.

In 1994, in English courts, more than 2,300 people were convicted, and a further 1,700 admitted guilt and were cautioned, for sexual offences involving children under 16. Of these, 274 were for "gross indecency with a child" and 2,204 for "indecent assault on a female person under 16." For most violent crimes there is no separate category of offence where the victim is under the age of 16. Convictions and cautions are, therefore, at just under 500 in 1994, much lower than for sexual offences. However, as official figures exclude most violent crimes, they severely underestimate the number of people found guilty of, or cautioned for, violent offences against children.(1)

Since 1988/9, there has been a steady decline in the number of successful prosecutions for sexual offences against children. This has occurred in spite of an increase in the numbers notified to the police. Some attribute the decline in convictions and cautions to an attempt to keep young people out of a potentially traumatic court experience. Others, however, argue that it is due to an increasing reluctance on the part of the Crown Prosecution Service to prosecute such cases due to the difficulty of securing a conviction.

2.5   **Child deaths from abuse** are recorded in different ways: in criminal statistics; by the Office of Population Censuses and Surveys; through child abuse death inquiries; in local studies; and by confidential inquiry into stillbirths and deaths in infancy. The problems of collating these statistics, and the reluctance of professionals to make a diagnosis of death by abuse, results in an under-representation of such deaths in official statistics. There are very few deaths recorded as infanticide. Figures show, in 1992, 38 infants under one year died through abuse. They are six times as likely to be killed in this way as children aged one to four years.(2)

Very young children are most at risk of physical injury through abuse. The highest rates of deaths from abuse and rates of registration are among infants under the age of one, of whom, in England, six in every thousand were placed on the register before their first birthday in 1994/5.

2.6   **Child protection registers** cover children considered to be at risk of abuse if there already is, or is likely to be, significant harm, and for whom a protection plan has been developed by the relevant local agencies. At the end of March 1995, 40,746 children were on UK registers because they were considered to be at risk of significant harm from one or more of the specified forms of abuse: physical, sexual or emotional abuse, or neglect. In England, that amounted to just under 35,000, approximately one in every 300. A similar proportion were registered in Northern Ireland (1,523 children). In Wales and Scotland, the chances of a child being on a register were lower, at one in 400 (1,668 in Wales; 2,601 in Scotland). (3)(4)(5)(6)

2.7   The figures on child protection registers are often quoted as if they gave an estimate of the true extent of abuse. These figures, however, record the child protection process, *not* the number of children who are abused. Not all children on registers have been abused. Some are registered because they are deemed to be "at risk". Registers mainly record cases of abuse within the family, where urgent action is needed and generally exclude abuse by people outside the family when the family can protect the child. Additionally, the fact that a child is not placed on the register does not mean that no abuse has occurred. It may be that the child is no longer considered to be at risk, for example, because either the child or the abuser has left the home, and registration is no longer regarded as necessary. Inevitably, registers exclude the large numbers of children who do not come to the attention of social workers but who have exactly the same experience as those who are registered.

2.8   The chance that a child will be placed on the register depends on definitions and interpretations which vary in different parts of the UK and on thresholds determined by local circumstances, practice and resources. The registration rate for 1994/5 in Sunderland and Tyneside is four times higher than in Gloucestershire and Hampshire, for example.(3)

2.9   In England at 31 March, 1995, fewer than one in five (18 per cent) of registered children were living in foster homes, community or voluntary homes or hostels.(3) Most of them continue to live in the parental home. There is, however, a high level of mobility. In Farmer and Owen's study (1995), two-fifths of the children who had suffered physical or emotional abuse or neglect were being looked after away from their own home twenty months after registration.(7)

2.10   Most children stay on the register for less than a year. One consequence of this is that, many more children are registered for some of the time than are counted at the time returns are made. During the year to 31 March 1995, for example, more than 60,000 children were on English registers, although on 31 March there were under 35,000.(3)

2.11   The children who are registered represent only a minority of those referred to the authorities. In 1991-2, an estimated 160,000 children were referred to social services in England, with up to 120,000 family visits and 40,000 social services case conferences, resulting in around 24,500 children and young people being placed on English registers.(8)

In addition to the children referred to social services, many more are involved in the situation: both close family and a wider circle of family and friends are affected, sometimes profoundly, by suspicions of abuse.

2.12   Much of this effort by social services seems to be concentrated on the same families. A review of child protection practices in English local authorities found that in two-thirds of the referrals the families were already known to social services departments. Just under half of them had been investigated previously for suspected maltreatment of their children.(9)

11

Report of the
National
Commission of
Inquiry into the
Prevention of
Child Abuse

Most children and families drop out of the child protection process before registration but many of them do not then receive the support they need because they do not meet the local criteria that would make them eligible for services.

2.13   In England, Scotland and Wales, physical abuse or injury is the most common reason for registration (around two in five of those on registers), followed by neglect and sexual abuse, with emotional abuse the smallest category in each country. The pattern in Northern Ireland is different with "grave concern" the most common reason for registration (two in five), a category not used in the rest of the United Kingdom.

Table 2.1   *UK Child Protection Registers*
Reasons for Registration
at 31 March 1995

	England	Scotland(a)	Wales	N Ireland
Total Children	34,954	2601 (1532)	1,668	1,523
Physical abuse	-	-	44%	10%
Physical injury	37%	48%	-	-
Physical neglect	-	22%	-	-
Neglect	32%	-	30%	25%
Failure to thrive	-	1%	-	-
Sexual abuse	26%	21%	19%	12%
Emotional abuse	13%	9%	15%	10%
Grave concern	-	-	-	41%
Categories not recommended	*	-	-	-
Other	*	-	-	4%
More than 1 category	9%	0%	7%	2%

NB: - indicates category not specified in statistics.   * = very low

a: The percentages shown for categories for abuse for Scotland are based on those registered during the year to 31 March 1995 in all regions except Grampian (1532 cases: there were 162 registrations in Grampian). Only the main category is recorded. Source: (3),(4),(5),(6)

2.14   These figures do not accurately reflect patterns of abuse, even among registered children. In most cases, only one type of abuse is recorded. This practice, which appears to be for administrative convenience, reduces the apparent extent of emotional abuse in comparison with other types of abuse and may influence the level of resources available for emotional and psychological support for children and their families.

2.15   Official statistics underestimate abuse, and they also divert attention from important issues. Their focus on an alleged incident or risk, with a single cause, masks the complex social, economic and personal problems which may have contributed to the abuse occurring, and which may not be addressed in child protection procedures.

Towards more realistic estimates

2.16   Official statistics on offences and registrations cover only a small part of abuse. Information based on surveys provides a basis for more realistic, and higher, estimates. The Commission does not wish to suggest that every child at risk of harm should be on a register.

Report of the
National
Commission of
Inquiry into the
Prevention of
Child Abuse

Its aim is rather to assess the size of the problem and underline the importance of adopting more realistic and effective strategies for preventing harm to children in the first place. Whatever the mechanism, children who are being harmed in exactly the same way as those currently on a register should be offered the same support. This does not happen.

Physical injury and abuse

2.17   In its extreme form, physical abuse can lead to death or permanent disability. For approximately 25,000 children, physical abuse was the main reason for their being on child protection registers during the 12 months to March 1995. In most cases, this is a result of excessive physical punishment, usually reflecting parents' inability to cope with the child's behaviour.[1] Evidence from UK surveys suggests that the extent of severe physical harm within the home is much greater. Each year an estimated 150,000 children are harmed by severe physical assault (ie. bruised or marked).

2.18   Physical punishment is widespread in the UK. Most children are occasionally hit by their parents. In a 1994 survey three in four parents claimed to have smacked a child at some time.(10) One study estimated that 91 per cent of children aged 11 or under had been hit at some point in their lives, 77 per cent in the past year. Thirty-eight per cent of children aged four were hit more than once a week. Boys were more likely to be punished by hitting than girls, and younger children were more likely to be hit than older children.(11)

2.19   A significant minority of children are severely punished; more than one million children have been severely hit at some time in their lives.(11) In a 1994 survey of adults(10), one in 12 said they had frequently or occasionally suffered bruising or marking following physical punishment as a child; nine per cent felt they had suffered long-term effects - more than three million adults.

Sexual abuse

2.20   The problems in defining the boundaries of sexual abuse reflect some of our society's uncertainties about what is acceptable behaviour towards children and young people. This in turn creates problems in measuring the extent of sexual abuse. However, a 1995 overview of a large number of UK and (mainly) US studies of sexual abuse concluded:

"Taken as a whole the prevalence studies indicate the significant numbers of people who have experienced abuse and who are willing to disclose aspects of these abusive experiences."(12)

> "Daddy's in bed with me and R...He does a lady and man kiss. He's got no clothes on. I don't like it. I told mum but she said Daddy doesn't," said a nine year old girl.
> **Caller to ChildLine**

2.21   This is certainly borne out by British research. Based on UK student samples, Kelly estimated that childhood sexual abuse, defined broadly to include flashing, had been experienced by more than one in two young women and one in four young men. Using a very narrow definition, to include only some form of penetration or forced masturbation,

13

*Report of the
National
Commission of
Inquiry into the
Prevention of
Child Abuse*

one in 25 young women and one in 50 young men had been abused.(13) Other UK estimates for females lie between these figures - from one in four in a 1994 survey(10) to one in eight in a 1985 MORI survey(14). For adult males both these surveys report just under one in ten.

Based on a special sample of young people, the British Crime Survey estimated that one in ten girls aged 12 to 15 had been sexually harassed in the past six to eight months by adult men; one in fifty of the boys had had a similar experience; half of the victims had been "very frightened."(15)

2.22   The consequences for the individual, and the types of help they need, may change over time. Emotional damage may remain long after physical scars have healed. Anxiety and depression, anger and guilt, poor self image, difficulties in functioning at school and later at work, problems with personal relationships and parenting, sexual problems, and physical effects - these are all increasingly recognised as among the long-term consequences of child sexual abuse.(16)

Overall, one in six of the adults who were sexually abused as children (three per cent of all adults) report a lasting and permanent effect(10). Survivors' letters to the Commission described the trauma they suffered through long-term sexual abuse by a close relation, which often remained undetected and unreported.

2.23   Official figures in England show approximately 4,000 convictions and cautions for sexual offences against children and 17,000 children on the registers for sexual abuse. However, the above survey information suggests that up to 100,000 children each year have a harmful sexual experience and that over a million adults may still be suffering the consequences of sexual abuse.

2.24   Most sexual abuse of children is committed by adult males. However, surveys of child protection register statistics in the UK indicate that approximately one in three sexually abused children is assaulted by an adolescent or pre-adolescent. (17)(18) Criminal Statistics in the UK (Home Office, 1990) covering offences reported during 1989 show that out of the 10,729 individuals found guilty or cautioned for sexual offences, one third were aged 20 years or younger. Research suggests that between two and seven per cent of adolescent sexual offenders are female.(19)(20)(21)

2.25   Large numbers of children and young people are sexually exploited through child pornography, organised paedophile rings and child prostitution but it is impossible to give accurate estimates. There is no reliable national figure, for example, of the number of young people under the age of 18 used for prostitution. It is estimated, however, that at least 5,000 British children under the age of 16 are involved. Approximately a third of the children and young people exploited through prostitution come from residential care.(22)

Research has indicated that factors particularly associated with child prostitution are: sexual abuse; neglect; school problems; parental unemployment; and running away from

Report of the
National
Commission of
Inquiry into the
Prevention of
Child Abuse

home or residential care. In addition, financial problems often cause young people leaving care to be vulnerable to involvement in prostitution.

Emotional abuse and neglect

2.26   Emotional abuse and neglect are less tangible than physical or sexual abuse, and are correspondingly more difficult to quantify. Attention is increasingly focused on the harm to a child from emotional neglect, or emotional maltreatment.(8) At any time 350,000-400,000 children (three per cent) live in a home environment which is consistently low in warmth and high in criticism. Many more children experience such an environment at some time in their lives.

2.27   A significant minority of adults describe their childhood relationships with their parents in negative terms: as many as one in three did not feel close to either parent, and one in five recalled constant criticism from or rejection by parents. Most adults, however, describe relationships with parents positively and feel they experienced love, affection, respect and understanding, especially from their mothers.(10)

> "Dad is beating me with a belt...it leaves bruises and marks...my sisters get beaten too...my mum knows but she doesn't stop it...I get on well with Dad other than the beatings...I want to go in a children's home."
>
> Children talk about smacks, slaps, pinches, squeezes, punches, kicks; being kicked out, thrown downstairs or at walls or wardrobes; being scratched, bitten, shaken, crushed, strangled; being locked in rooms and cupboards, having toys broken, their things torn, their rooms trashed or wrecked.
> **ChildLine**

2.28   Violence between parents or carers is not uncommon and has an emotionally disturbing effect on children, especially if they love both parties. In Creighton's survey(10), nearly one in two adults (45 per cent) said that as a child they saw at least some physical violence of this type and one in ten witnessed it constantly or frequently. These children may develop behavioural and other problems. They are themselves vulnerable to physical violence and other abuse; in two studies, in about one in four cases of child abuse there was also domestic violence(9). Another study demonstrated that in three out of five cases where children had suffered physical or emotional abuse or neglect, their mothers were also subjected to violence by their male partners.(7)

> "I didn't know any different. I didn't *know* a life with a loving mother and so I didn't miss it. Because you don't know to compare it to something else, it doesn't hurt as much as people might think. It's only afterwards ... It's only then that you really start to become messed up and pay for what you went through all those years ago."
> **Letter to the Commission.**

2.29   Alcohol and drug abuse are often factors in domestic violence. Children whose parents or carers abuse alcohol or drugs have been shown to be at increased risk of abuse

15

Report of the
National
Commission of
Inquiry into the
Prevention of
Child Abuse

and neglect.(9) In many cases of physical abuse one or both parents often have a history of alcohol and/or drug abuse. The care of children in households where the adults have such a dependency is often of a lower standard than in other homes and can manifest itself in poor standards of cleanliness, a lack of interest in child development and education, and a general lack of capacity to meet a child's physical and emotional needs.

2.30   Family disharmony takes many forms, almost all of which can have damaging effects on children, whether the family remains together or whether the problems lead to separation and divorce. Over the past two decades, divorces in England and Wales have doubled: in 1993 in England and Wales, there were 176,000 children involved in divorce cases. Twenty-five per cent of children now under 16 will suffer family disruption through divorce and by the year 2000 some three million children in the United Kingdom will be growing up in stepfamilies.(23) The distress caused to children by the break-up of the family is often compounded by consequent financial hardship. During periods of family disharmony and especially when problems lead to separation and divorce, children need support, if necessary from outside the family, when the problems of carers render them unable to meet the emotional needs of their children.

2.31   Neglect is the reason recorded for approximately three in ten children on registers in England and Wales - about 18,500 children in the year to March 1995. Many practitioners and researchers have expressed concern that this significantly underestimates the real extent of neglect. This "neglect of neglect"(24) can be explained partly by problems of definition and partly that, because of this uncertainty, thresholds for intervention may be changed in line with available resources. Whatever the reason, the indications are that many more children than are registered for neglect are left "bumping along the bottom" until something assessed as a higher risk, such as physical or sexual abuse, stimulates action.

2.32   Among all ages, children with disabilities are at greater risk of all types of abuse. The most significant study, in the United States, demonstrated that disabled children are more than one and a half times as likely to be abused in any one year as other children.(25) There is no comparable information for the United Kingdom. However, a 1989 study of deaf children found very high levels of suspected and confirmed physical, emotional and sexual abuse.(26)

> "Touching is very important in the development of close relationships with visually impaired children but the boundaries between acceptable and unacceptable touching may be less easy to distinguish... Everyday bruises and signs of physical abuse may be confused...alternatively children and young people who are used to being touched may not recognise some types of touch as abuse, making them particularly vulnerable."
> **Royal National Institute for Blind People**

2.33   Children who are disabled in some way are also particularly vulnerable to bullying at school, especially verbal abuse, with damaging effects on education and social activities.

Beyond official definitions

Report of the
National
Commission of
Inquiry into the
Prevention of
Child Abuse

2.34   The definitions used by statutory agencies derive from legislation and focus on a fairly narrow definition of risk. The Commission's broad definition of abuse includes many other factors which inhibit the safe and healthy development of children into adulthood, which are included in the following table.

Table 2.2   *Estimates of Total Numbers of Children at Risk of Harm Annually*

In the legal system	
Convictions/cautions (England)	4,500
In child protection system	
On register at risk of abuse or neglect	70,000
Not on register but in process family visit/conference (England)	100,000
Referred to social services, no visit (England)	40,000
Harmful experiences similar to registration categories	
Severe physical punishment	150,000
Witness violence between parents/carers	250,000
Sexual	100,000
Living in homes which are low in warmth/high in criticism	350,000
Other 'in need' categories	
Poverty	4.3 million
Disability in private homes	171,000
Record of offending	130,000
Parents' marital problems/divorce	250,000
Homeless	250,000
Other harm/risk	
School:	
bullied	600,000
permanent exclusions	11,181
Institutions/care (LA)	62,000
Child carers	40,000

Note: the figures cannot be added across groups as one child may appear under several headings.
UK figures unless otherwise indicated.

Poverty and Homelessness

2.35   An internationally recognised measure of poverty - living on less than half the average national income - includes more than four million children in the UK, one in three. Many of these live in poor housing conditions. The Joseph Rowntree Foundation's *Inquiry into Income and Wealth* (1995)(27) demonstrated increasing polarisation over the past 15 years, which has dramatically affected families with children. Poverty among children has trebled since 1979, a much faster rate than in the adult population. Over the same period, social and economic disadvantage has tended to build up in particular geographical areas, typically those that suffer from low-quality health and education services and lack of cheap, local amenities.

2.36   The harmful effects of socio-economic deprivation on children are well established. Poverty is associated with postnatal and infant mortality, malnutrition and ill-health, low

*Report of the
National
Commission of
Inquiry into the
Prevention of
Child Abuse*

educational attainment, delinquency and teenage pregnancy. It is a question not simply of material deprivation, but also of social and cultural exclusion as is recognised in the European Community definition of those living in poverty as:

*"persons, families and groups of persons whose resources (material, cultural and
social) are so limited as to exclude them from the minimal acceptable way of life in
the Member States in which they live"*

Article 27 of the UN Convention on the Rights of the Child indicates what is a "minimal acceptable way of life" in its provision that every child is entitled to a "standard of living adequate for the child's physical, mental, spiritual, moral and social development", including proper nutrition, adequate housing, an environment not detrimental to health, safe places to play, and access to good quality health and education services. In addition, children are entitled to a standard of living that enables them to participate in the activities of the society of which they form a part. Shortage of money can mean they are excluded from opportunities taken for granted by most parents and children in our society, such as school trips, leisure activities, holidays, birthday presents.

2.37   Most of the children on child protection registers are from low income families. It would be inappropriate, however, to conclude that there is a direct link between narrowly defined forms of child abuse and poverty. Abuse occurs across all social classes and involves a combination of social, psychological, economic and environmental factors. When parents are under stress, for whatever reason and in whatever circumstances, children are vulnerable. The pressures associated with a low or unpredictable income may increase the likelihood of family tension and breakdown. The most commonly identified stress factors in all registered cases of child abuse - unemployment and debt - are closely related to poverty.(28)

2.38   Children from some ethnic minorities are particularly disadvantaged. The black and ethnic minority population are twice as likely as those classified as white to be in the poorest fifth of the population, and in an NCH Action for Children study in London, Asian, black African and Caribbean families were twice as likely to be living in overcrowded accommodation as white European families.(29)

2.39   Similarly, there has been a steady increase in the number of homeless families. In 1994, almost 140,000 households were found temporary accommodation by local authorities. Of these, 59 per cent were families with children.(30) Such families suffer from overcrowded, often unhealthy conditions and the disruption of multiple moves. Children living in temporary accommodation are at increased risk of health problems, lack safe places to play, and suffer disruption to education and social relationships.

A 1996 inquiry into youth homelessness conducted by CHAR calculated that between 200,000 and 300,000 young people aged 17 and under experienced homelessness in the UK in 1995.(31) In a 1995 Surrey University study(32), about half of young homeless had been in local authority care. The withdrawal of income support from 16 to 17-year-olds has been a significant factor in the increase of homelessness in this age group.

2.40   Families who come to the notice of child protection agencies tend to be those with a young single parent, or where children are not living with both natural parents, who are living on a low income in poorer areas, where social workers are more likely to concentrate their efforts. This is reflected in their represention on child protection registers. Children from the most disadvantaged sectors of society are more likely to be removed from their families and taken into care than other children.

Children living away from home

2.41   Large numbers of children are looked after away from home in a variety of settings which include residential care, boarding schools, secure accommodation, young offenders' institutions or hospitals. None of these has been exempt from evidence of abuse. The particular vulnerability to abuse of children and young people in residential institutions has become apparent over the past ten years: a number of establishments and regimes have allowed children and young people, in large numbers, to be maltreated. Several major inquiries have prompted a series of measures to combat abuse in these institutions; for example, the inquiries into the "Pindown" regime in Staffordshire Children's Homes (1991)(33), Castle Hill School (1991)(34), Ty Mawr former approved school in Gwent (1992)(35), Feltham Young Offenders' Institution (1993), Leicestershire children's homes (1993)(36), Kincora boys' hostel in East Belfast (1989)(37), and Crookham Court Independent Boarding School in Berkshire (1988). Recent revelations of abuse over long periods in residential homes in North Wales and the North West of England have confirmed that the problem is even more widespread than had previously been recognised and involves establishments run by central and local government, the independent and voluntary sectors, encompassing educational, social services, health and penal provision.

19

2.42   The catalogue of abuse in residential institutions is appalling. It includes physical assault and sexual abuse; emotional abuse; unacceptable deprivation of rights and privileges; inhumane treatment; poor health care and education. This is especially disturbing because many of the children in residential institutions have already been deeply harmed: it is estimated that between a third and two-thirds of those in residential care have been abused before being taken into residential institutions.

2.43   The dramatic decline in the number of children looked after by social services departments in England over the past 15 years (from 92,270 in 1981 to 49,000 in 1995) has been accompanied by an even steeper reduction in the numbers in residential care (down from 37,069 in 1981 to 8,200 in 1994). The percentage of children placed with foster carers has steadily increased.

2.44   A significant minority of fostered children - around one in four - report problems with: poor relationships with carers; multiple placements, which have adverse effects on educational and social opportunities and weaken links with family and home locality; and inadequate consultation and poor complaints procedures.(38)

A small minority of children are abused while in foster care, either by foster parents or by their relatives, including their children.

Report of the
National
Commission of
Inquiry into the
Prevention of
Child Abuse

Children in secure accommodation

2.45   Some children have to be placed in secure accommodation for their own and others' safety. However, they may be at increased risk of bullying and violence. There are no comprehensive annual statistics on what *behaviour* has caused children to be placed in secure accommodation. The most recent survey of children in secure accommodation suggested that one in three were locked up unnecessarily.(39)

2.46   Research into the backgrounds of convicted juvenile offenders shows that the majority have suffered abuse and/or loss as children. A 1995 study(40) of 200 offenders sentenced as juveniles to long-term detention (half of them convicted of murder) found that 72% had suffered emotional, sexual, physical or organized abuse, and 53% had lost a significant figure to whom they were emotionally attached, as a result of bereavement or cessation of contact. In total, 91% had experienced abuse or loss, and 35% had suffered both. Most had not received effective help to enable them to come to terms with their experiences.

School: bullying and exclusions

2.47   Bullying may take the form of physical attacks, such as hitting, kicking, taking or damaging belongings; verbal assaults, including name-calling, insults, repeated teasing, racist remarks; or it may take more indirect forms, such as spreading malicious rumours or excluding someone from social groups. Bullying at school is a more serious problem than is sometimes realised. It is widespread and there is increasing evidence of immense distress caused by bullying, with a small number of children being driven to suicide every year. A 1990 study in Sheffield showed that approximately ten per cent of primary school pupils and four per cent of secondary school pupils reported being bullied at least once a week: this translates to 350,000 school children aged 8 to 12 and more than 100,000 secondary school children. Other surveys indicate that up to two in five secondary school pupils have been bullied.(41)

2.48   A survey published in 1996 by Exeter University showed that, among 12 to 13-year-olds, more than 26 per cent of the boys and more than 34 per cent of the girls feared bullying. The number who said they were "often" or "very often" afraid dropped to just over five per cent and six per cent respectively, but that still suggests a large number of frightened children.(42)

2.49   Bullying is a particular problem in children's residential institutions, particularly young offenders' institutions which are notoriously violent.(43)

2.50   Procedures that lead to exclusion, permanent or for a limited period, are well established. Increasing numbers of children are being excluded and these inevitably suffer some disadvantage. The figures for England and Wales show an increase between 1991/2 and 1993/4, from 3,833 to 11,181(44). Most exclusions are of secondary pupils, although there has also been a significant increase among primary schoolchildren. Boys are four to five times more likely to be excluded than girls. Local and national research also points to a disproportionate number of black African and Caribbean boys among those excluded, up to four times the national average.

Racial harassment of children

2.51   Racial harassment ranges from serious violence to name calling. There is no UK system for recording racial harassment and no national research has been undertaken. Nevertheless, racial harassment is recognised as being widespread. For some children there is no escape from it at school, on the journey to and from school or in the family's immediate neighbourhood. This can seriously constrain social and leisure activities and creates additional pressures on family relationships. In spite of substantial efforts, some organisations and staff within them remain ineffective in dealing with racial harassment or the impact of policies which unwittingly exclude or disadvantage children from ethnic minorities. This creates distrust of those organisations and individuals and reduces willingness to seek help or support from them.

Young Carers

2.52   A young carer has been defined(45) as a child or young person "who is carrying out significant caring tasks and assuming a level of responsibility for another person, which would usually be taken by an adult." These children and young people provide care for a parent, sibling or other relative because there are no other resources available to provide the support and personal assistance the parent needs. They are distinguished from other children involved in family caring and household tasks by the extent to which their responsibilities and circumstances restrict their childhood.

2.53   It is not known for certain how many young carers there are in Britain, although estimates suggest that in 1993 there were about 10,000 child carers, with a further 30,000 children regularly sharing caring tasks with adult carers. As a result of their responsibilities, young carers may suffer reduced access to educational and recreational opportunities, compounded by an absence of established friendships and other supportive networks.

Children and employment

2.54   A number of recent studies have raised concerns that legal restrictions on the hours worked by children and the nature of the jobs they undertake are not being observed. A survey of Birmingham school children in 1991(46) showed that 75 per cent of those studied were working illegally: more than 200 were working below the minimum legal age, one third were doing prohibited jobs and an even higher proportion were working illegal hours. Research in Strathclyde(47) found more than 495 children working illegal hours, nearly half of them working in prohibited environments or illegal employment. Both surveys showed a high incidence of accidents at work among children and young people.

Conclusion

It is difficult to produce precise figures on the extent of child abuse in the UK. Under-reporting is likely to continue and there will always be judgements to be made about what, in any one instance, qualifies as abuse. However, it is clear that the number of children involved in harmful or potentially harmful situations is large and that there are no obvious

Report of the
National
Commission of
Inquiry into the
Prevention of
Child Abuse

signs of those numbers diminishing. There is an urgent need, therefore, to improve the statistical information on which effective policies for preventing abuse can be based.

Recommendations

1. Data on the condition of children in the UK should be systematically collected, published annually and presented to Parliament either through a Children's Commissioner (see Chapter 6) or through some other agency statutorily required to carry out this function.

2. The data, reflecting a wide definition of abuse, should include information on poverty, health, and an assessment of the numbers of children "in need" as well as providing information under the statutorily defined categories of abuse.

3. The age of the victim and the relationship of the victim to the alleged offender should be recorded by the police for all crimes, including sexual and violent crimes.

4. Crime statistics should separately report the extent of crimes against children under the age of 16.

References

1. Statistics from Crime and Criminal Justice Unit, Home Office and Home Office Research and Statistics

2. UK Child Homicides in 1992 (Central Statistical Office)

3. Department of Health: Children and Young People on Child Protection Registers Year Ending 31 March 1995, England

4. The Scottish Office: Statistical Bulletin, Social Work Series: Child Protection Management Information 1993-94 November 1995

5. Northern Ireland: Information from Regional Information Branch (DHSS)

6. Welsh Office: Child Protection Register Statistics at 31 March 1995

7. Farmer E, Owen M, 1995, Child Protection Practice : Private Risks and Public Remedies, London : HMSO

8. Child Protection: Messages From Research, 1995, Department of Health, London : HMSO

9. Gibbons J, Conroy S, Bell C, 1995, Operating the Child Protection System, London : HMSO

10. Creighton S, Russell N, 1995, Voices from Childhood: A Survey of childhood experiences and attitudes to child rearing among adults in the United Kingdom, London, NSPCC

11. Smith M A, A Community Study of Physical Violence to Children in the Home and Associated Variables: poster presented at International Society for the Prevention of Child Abuse and Neglect: V European Conference May 1995, Oslo, Norway

12. Pilkington B, Kremer J, 1995, A Review of the Epidemiological Review on Child Sexual Abuse, Child Abuse Review, vol 4 pp 84-98, 191-205

13. Kelly L, Regan L, Burton S, 1991 An Exploratory Study of the Prevalence of Sexual Abuse in a Sample of 16-21 Year Olds, University of North London

*Report of the
National
Commission of
Inquiry into the
Prevention of
Child Abuse*

14. Baker A W, Duncan S P, 1985, Child Sexual Abuse: A Study of Prevalence in Great Britain, Child Abuse and Neglect 9, pp 457-467

15. Aye Maving N, 1995, Young people, victimisation and the police, British Crime Survey findings on experiences and attitudes of 12-15 year olds, Home Office Research and Statistics 140, London: HMSO

16. Smith D, Pearce L, Pringle M, Caplan R, 1995, Adults with a history of child sexual abuse: evaluation of a pilot therapy service, British Medical Journal, 6 May 1995, vol 310 pp 1175-1178

17. Northern Ireland Social Services Inspectorate, 1994, An Abuse of Trust (Huston Report)

18. Horne L, Glasgow D, Cox A & Calam R, 1991, Sexual Abuse of Children by Children *in* Journal of Child Law 314: 147-151

19. Mathews R, 1987, Female Sexual Offenders: Treatment and Legal Issues, Report by Phase Programme, Genesis II, Minneapolis

20. Fehrenback P, Smith W Monastersky C & Deisher R, 1986, Adolescent Sex Offenders: Offenders and Offence Characteristics *in* American Journal of Orthopsychiatry 56: 225-233

21. The Utah Report on Juvenile Sex Offenders, 1989

22. Kelly L, Wingfield R, Burton S & Regan L, Splintered Lives: Sexual exploitation of children in the context of children's rights and child protection, 1995

23. Walker J, Hornick J P, Communication in Marriage and Divorce: A Consultation on Family Law, London, 1996

24. Professor Olive Stevenson, University of Nottingham

25. Crosse S B, Kaye E & Ratnofsky, A C, A Report on the Maltreatment of Children with Disabilities, 1993, Washington, DC: National Center on Child Abuse and Neglect

26. Kennedy M, The Abuse of Deaf Children *in* Child Abuse Review, 3(1), 3-7

27. Joseph Rowntree Foundation Inquiry into Income and Wealth, Vols 1 & 2, 1995

28. Creighton S J 1992, Child Abuse Trends in England and Wales 1988-1990 and an Overview from 1973-1990, London NSPCC

29. NCH Action for Children, Factfile, 1996

30. Ibid.

31. We Don't Choose to be Homeless: Inquiry into Preventing Youth Homelessness, CHAR, 1996

32. Young People on the Move, Psychology Department, Surrey University 1993

33. Levy A, Kahan B, The Pindown Experience and the Protection of Children: Report of the Staffordshire Child Care Inquiry, 1990

34. Brannan C, Jones J D, Murch, J D, Castle Hill Report: practice guide, Shropshire County Council, 1993

35. Williams, G, McCreadie J, Ty Mawr Community Home Inquiry, Gwent County Council, 1992

36. Foster D, Inquiry into police investigation of complaints of child and sexual abuse in Leicestershire children's homes: a summary, 1993

37. Report of the Committee of Inquiry into Children's Homes and Hostels (Kincora Inquiry), HMSO, Belfast, 1989

38. So Who Are We Supposed to Trust Now? Responding to Abuse in Care: the Experiences of Young People, NSPCC/Safe and Sound Partnership, 1995

23

*Report of the
National
Commission of
Inquiry into the
Prevention of
Child Abuse*

39. Safe to Let Out? The current and future of secure accommodation for children and young people, National Children's Bureau, 1995

40. Boswell, G, Violent Victims: the prevalence of abuse and loss in the lives of Section 53 offenders, The Prince's Trust, 1995

41. Sharp P K, & Sharp S, School Bullying: insights and perspectives, Routledge, London, 1994

42. Balding J, Regis D, Wise A, Bish D & Muirden J, Bully Off: Young people that fear going to school, University of Exeter, 1996

43. Kennedy, H, Banged Up, Beaten Up, Cutting Up: Report of the Howard League Commission of Inquiry into violence in penal institutions for young people, Howard League for Penal Reform, London, 1995

44. National Survey of local education authorities' policies and procedures for the identification of, and provision for, chldren who are out of school by reason of exclusion or otherwise, Canterbury Christ Church College, 1995

45. Dearden C & Becker S, Young Carers: the Facts, Community Care, 1996

46. Pond C, Searle A, The Hidden Army: Children at Work in the 1990s, Low Pay Unit, London, 1991

47. Lavalette M, McKechnie J and Hobbs S, The Forgotten Workforce: Scottish Children at Work, Glasgow: Scottish Low Pay Unit, 1991

Children in Society

*Report of the
National
Commission of
Inquiry into the
Prevention of
Child Abuse*

- As a society we do not recognise and make sufficient provision for children

- Many of our institutions and systems operate against children's interests

- There is a general reluctance to accept that children are being harmed in significant numbers

- Most abusers are members of, or known to, the family of those abused

- There is a widespread belief that no one is entitled to "interfere" between parents and children, except in extreme circumstances

3.1   It makes obvious sense to prevent problems from arising rather than having to cope with them once they have developed. The Commission has identified a number of reasons why efforts to prevent child abuse have been less energetic than is required. These include the position of children and those who work with them; the financial, legal and structural arrangements affecting children; and, finally, the absence of research on which preventive measures are most effective.

The position of children and those who work with them

3.2   The Commission received extensive evidence that within the UK there is still a general reluctance to accept the fact that children suffer abuse or are harmed in such damaging ways and in such numbers. This reluctance may be because to do so can be overwhelmingly distressing, particularly when it awakens painful memories that some adults would prefer to keep buried.

> "Maybe if it was spoken about more, accepted that this type of thing does happen in all walks of life by men and women, then this subject would not be 'taboo'! I think if more people were open and stopped burying their heads in the sand we could start to prevent it."
>
> **Letter to the Commission**

3.3   There is also a widely held view that abuse is only perpetrated by people who are in some way abnormal or intractably evil. The reality is different. Although some abusers are indeed evil, the evidence is that most are apparently ordinary people, nearly all of them a member of, or known to, the family of the abused child.

3.4   One view commonly expressed is that those abused must have provoked their ill-treatment. Such attitudes and blame, combined with a lack of understanding of children's behaviour, reflect and reinforce the widespread perception of children as the possessions of their parents and the view that no one but their parents is entitled to "interfere", except in extreme circumstances. One effect of this is to make the public reluctant to intervene in order to secure a child's well-being.

*Report of the
National
Commission of
Inquiry into the
Prevention of
Child Abuse*

3.5   If prevention of abuse is to be effective, it needs to be widely recognised that all parents face stresses at some time and may need, and welcome, help and support. The welfare of children is, of course, primarily the responsibility of their parents. But there is a general obligation on all members of society to do what they properly can, without behaving unnecessarily intrusively, to share in that responsibility when the need arises.

> "In some ways our system helps to support abuse. Children are not always brought up to value themselves. They are forced to be pliant and people pleasers, instead of encouraging them to speak up if things are bothering them...They are not taught how to listen to and value their inner feelings."
> **Letter to the Commission**

3.6   Children do not vote and their interests appear to be accorded little political weight. This leads to the attention of politicians and welfare agencies, with expenditure similarly weighted, being predominantly directed towards the needs of the adult population. The NHS and Community Care Act 1993 and the Children Act 1989 together represent one of the most significant reviews in welfare legislation since the establishment of the welfare state. It has been noticeable, however, that the former has received considerably more public, media and political attention and been supported by much greater resources.

3.7   The Commission believes that attitudes which lead to children not being valued need to be tackled through education, including public education, and also through more enlightened social policy and professional practice.

> What is the thing you would most like to change about grown ups?
> "Make them listen to what you are saying and to make them think that children are just the same as adults, just younger and smaller."
> **10 year old girl, in Commission Questionnaire**

3.8   Evidence to the Commission has also suggested that professional practice itself is being affected by an increasing emphasis on formalised systems of accountability. In the aftermath of the inquiry into the death of seven-year-old Maria Colwell in 1973 at the hands of her stepfather - when professional mismanagement was seen as partly to blame - attention and resources have been directed almost exclusively towards filling gaps in the system and avoiding professional error with the attendant blame. Such over-emphasis on procedures has led to a stifling of the exercise of professional judgement, because of the fear of exposure to formal censure if the rules are not followed to the letter. Practitioners are tending to work within the protection of their own discipline, rather than undertake more demanding inter-professional work. At the same time, some professionals do not have sufficient training, development and support to enable them to exercise professional judgement with confidence and skill, or to work with other professional disciplines.

3.9   The low priority accorded to children has meant that, in general, work with children and people who work with children are undervalued and not properly supported by the community. This manifests itself in recruitment and retention difficulties and in the marginalisation of institutions for children within their local communities. Residential and

*Report of the
National
Commission of
Inquiry into the
Prevention of
Child Abuse*

day institutions can and do provide beneficial environments for children, but may become isolated from normal society and develop cultures and practices of their own which are conducive to the interests of neither staff nor children. One way of preventing the abuse of children in such situations is by ensuring that children's homes, day care facilities and schools are part of the local community and accessible to families and friends.

3.10   The way in which society undervalues professionals who work with children is also apparent in attitudes towards parents and parenting. This is evident in the commonly held assumptions that parenting skills do not need to be learnt since they are naturally found in parents, that parents learn to be good parents from their own parents, and that parenting is not demanding. The Commission has heard many descriptions which disprove these assumptions. The devaluing of parents is shown by the lack of support services for them, such as nursery and other forms of day care, and in the lack of workplace facilities and support for working parents.

3.11   The UK's entrenched systems and structures concerning finance, the legal system, central and local government structures, and research priorities are a barrier to promoting prevention. Each are dealt with in the chapters that follow.

The financial, legal and structural arrangements affecting children

3.12   **Finance:** Patterns of expenditure of money and time are proving difficult to shift from the measurable - dealing with a child on a child protection register, for example - to the unmeasurable, such as ensuring that the problem does not arise in the first place. Prevention costs money and, in a context of scarce resources, pragmatic managers will always invest most heavily, or exclusively, in high-priority work such as protecting children in dangerous situations. Managers cannot move funding from this work without exposing children to unacceptable danger unless, first, those dangers have been removed and, second, cheaper and more flexible ways can be found of protecting children who are at risk.

3.13   **The legal system:** In the last decade, there have been improvements in the law affecting children, in particular with the passing of recent child care legislation in all UK jurisdictions, and ratification of the United Nations Convention on the Rights of the Child. The main problem is the way the legal system *operates*. It is found threatening to children subject to abuse.

3.14   **Structure and organisation:** Both locally and nationally, there is a lack of coherence in the way policies relating to children are devised and implemented. At national level, several major government departments, or even parts of departments, produce legislation, regulation and guidance directly affecting children's services, much of which does not appear to be in harmony and does not facilitate a "whole child" approach. This fragmentation is echoed at local level.

Research into effective preventive measures

3.15   Partly because there have been few such initiatives and also because funding bodies give a low priority to children's issues, the efficacy of support and preventive strategies has not been thoroughly tested, so there is a lack of strong evidence-based practice models of "what works". This is despite the Children and Young Persons Act 1963, the 1975 Children

Report of the
National
Commission of
Inquiry into the
Prevention of
Child Abuse

Act and the 1989 Children Act - where the optimistic moves towards prevention have never been matched with sufficient funding of services or research.

3.16   The chapters that follow deal with areas where the Commission wishes to see a shift of emphasis towards the prevention of child abuse: finance, the law, national and local structures, children's place in society and the research required to ensure cost-effective outcomes to a renewed effort to provide a more secure future for the nation's children.

*Report of the
National
Commission of
Inquiry into the
Prevention of
Child Abuse*

- The current cost of child abuse to statutory and voluntary agencies is £1 billion a year. Most of this is spent dealing with the aftermath of abuse rather than its prevention

- The total cost of abuse far exceeds this estimate. Individuals and families bear most of the consequences, sometimes for the rest of their lives at an incalculable cost

- National and local government expenditure does not give sufficient priority to preventing abuse

- Funding arrangements across all relevant services which focus on the prevention of abuse would make possible a more effective use of resources.

- National and local Children's Business Plans should be developed

4.1   Child abuse is costing the nation more than £1 billion a year. Most of this money is spent on providing limited support and services *after* abuse has occurred rather than on initiatives to stop abuse happening. This cannot be an effective use of resources. Not only should investing in prevention save money in the long term, but there are also added benefits in terms of reducing the human and financial costs of delinquency, crime, and poor parenting. Many young offenders, for example, are reacting to abuse in childhood (see 2.46). The total cost of dealing with offenders aged between 10 and 20 in 1993-94 was approximately £650 million. Child abuse also lies behind a large proportion of mental health problems among adults. Expenditure on community and hospital mental health services in England amounted to £2.4 bn in 1994-5 (DoH). An extremely conservative estimate would be that at least 10 per cent of these costs are attributable to the effects of abuse.

Importantly, a direction of resources towards prevention will also stop some young people themselves becoming abusers. Additional resources are needed in the short term to ensure that an effective system for meeting children's needs is established.

4.2   Much evidence to the Commission emphasised the need for a more intelligent and better co-ordinated investment in preventive and supportive services. There was also a strong common perception of services, characterised by unintegrated, expensive and late investment in a variety of remedial, punitive and legal responses to children in need. This was also apparent in parts of the Audit Commission Report *Seen But Not Heard* (1994)(1) and the Department of Health's *Messages from Research* (1995)(2).

4.3   To clarify these resourcing issues, the Commission undertook three practical exercises. The first, by the Institute of Public Finance (IPF), the commercial arm of the Chartered Institute of Public Finance and Accountancy (CIPFA), analysed the broad national pattern of investment in services for children and attempted to quantify the expenditure upon other services, such as adult mental health care, needed as a direct result of avoidable trauma and deprivation in childhood (see Appendix 7). The result was to

Report of the
National
Commission of
Inquiry into the
Prevention of
Child Abuse

provide a "map" of investment in services and to highlight the financial consequences of unco-ordinated service provision.

The second exercise, conducted by International Computer Ltd (ICL), modelled some of the practical implications of a shift in the pattern of investment within and between services for children in one local authority area (see Appendix 8). A third piece of work examined actual case studies and analysed the costs incurred. (See Appendix 9).

> "I was in and out of hospital with depression being given tablets every time, when all I needed was someone to look that little bit closer, little bit harder."
> **Letter to the Commission**

4.4   The first exercise involved the identification and analysis of available national statistical information. The second derived from an analysis of expenditure on programmes in one local authority area, based upon actual services, departments and budgets, with decisions on reallocating that expenditure made by the relevant managers. The third exercise was designed to analyse and illuminate the detailed cost elements involved in specific cases of abuse.

4.5   The purpose of the three exercises was to illustrate the nature and extent of the financial issues involved in child abuse. Although, in some instances, further work would be needed to establish expenditure with greater precision, the factual information and methodologies are sufficiently robust to indicate how some of the Commission's recommendations might be achieved.

> "If services are to be rationed, children must not be discriminated against. There is evidence that children are not receiving a fair share despite the fact that, of all the age groups, children arguably have the highest claim on resources."
> **National Children's Bureau**

National expenditure

4.6   The findings of the IPF study are set out in full in Appendix 7. In brief, they are as follows:

○ there is a lack of hard data about the extent of child abuse and costs to all the agencies involved.

○ the cost of child abuse to the public purse is *at least* £700 million per annum, or £12 per head of the UK population (and probably much more, see para 4.7). The IPF calculation is shown in Table 4.1.

○ there is no funding mechanism which specifically addresses child abuse.

○ the funding mechanisms which do exist do not seem to be related to actual demand and costs; this applies in health, social services, education and police funding.

○ the main agencies involved in preventing and investigating child abuse neither know what they spend on it at local and national levels, nor what return they get for their investment and effort.

○   the voluntary sector contributes ten per cent to the total child protection programme.

Table 4.1   *Child Abuse - Costs to the public purse*

*Report of the
National
Commission of
Inquiry into the
Prevention of
Child Abuse*

Estimated Costs for United Kingdom	Estimated Cost £M			Proportion of total costs
	Preventive Services	Intervention Services	Total	
Personal social services:				
Care for children in homes/foster placement	12	107	119	16%
Initial case conferences (all services)	8	25	33	5%
Reviewing cases (all services)	-	25	25	3%
Intermediate treatment	101	116	217	30%
Direct preventive action	116	-	116	16%
Management overheads (SSR)	4	5	9	1%
Total	241	278	519	71%
Other welfare services:				
Homelessness	3	5	8	1%
Education	4	6	10	1%
Total	7	11	18	2%
Health services:				
General practice	2	3	5	1%
Paediatrics	3	5	8	1%
Child & adolescent psychiatry	13	20	33	4%
Total	18	28	46	6%
Home office services:				
Probation	-	19	19	3%
Magistrates & crown courts	-	22	22	3%
Police	24	49	73	10%
Prisons	-	38	38	5%
Total	24	128	152	21%
Total services	290	445	735	100%

Note: The cost of attending case conferences for all services is shown under the personal social services.

4.7   It is clear from the IPF study that comprehensive data about investment in child protection, whether in a specific or broadly based sense, is neither readily available nor consistently gathered and analysed. It is equally clear that expenditure across a range of services and within a fairly narrow definition of child protection is extremely high. Annual expenditure by the public services is likely to exceed the £700 million quoted by IPF. This is because the calculation does not include the costs to, say, the prison service or adult mental health services, or the costs in special education, child psychiatric services or secure residential care for young people, which are a consequence of avoidable deprivation or trauma to younger children.

For example, if the problems of a mere 10 per cent of adults in mental health care or prison are attributable to childhood abuse, the annual costs of child abuse would increase by £348 million. A similar calculation could be made for a relevant proportion of the children receiving expensive special education, special residential care and psychiatric services.

*Report of the
National
Commission of
Inquiry into the
Prevention of
Child Abuse*

In addition, the analysis of costs attributed to health visiting and community health services generally are almost certainly too low because they are difficult to isolate. Thus, the full cost of child abuse to the public purse easily exceeds £1 billion a year.

4.8   From the evidence available, the Commission has drawn three conclusions. First, not only are ill-defined and substantial sums of money spent in a largely unco-ordinated fashion, but there is no funding mechanism which specifically directs resources towards the prevention of child abuse. There are no specific indicators in the police services to identify funding for child protection; and the formulae for health services resources gives low priority to the five to 14 years age group in the "age/cost adjustment" of hospital and community health service allocations. Moreover, funding allocations to family health services make no allowance for the impact of child abuse cases on GP consultation times.

4.9   Second, as there are no systems of information for collecting data on the resources devoted to preventing abuse, it seems unlikely those agencies dealing with the prevention of abuse and the protection of children are aware of the levels of investment each makes, either nationally or locally. Similarly, there has been no financial analysis of the costs of current procedures, compared with the return for that investment.

4.10   Finally, it seems at least likely that, at a very simple level, better information more consistently recorded, together with a co-ordinated and focused programme of action, could lead to greater benefits for the same investment of resources. The voluntary sector shares this responsibility for, as preliminary information suggests, it contributes approximately ten per cent to the total expenditure responses on to child abuse. It is clearly important that it is involved in any new framework developed for data exchange, recording and financial analysis.

> "As soon as he was allowed back into the house it all started up again. For years I was rebelling against everything and everyone to the extent I was taken away from home and placed in the care of the county. A period of time in Holloway prison doing borstal and still everyone thought I was just a crazy kid trying to get attention all the time by whatever means I could."
> **Letter to the Commission**

Local expenditure

4.11   Some of the issues raised in the national mapping exercise were developed in the second exercise, ICL's Decisions Conferencing Workship, which looked at the implications of a shift in the pattern of investment within and between services to children. It was based upon a local authority area and its two health authorities. A full report of the workshop and methodology is found in Appendix 8, but some key facts, shared opinions and conclusions are summarised here. The two-day workshop - involving budget holders/senior managers from health, education and social services and two external advisers on policy and research - aimed to: identify the key issues impacting upon the prevention of child abuse in the area; reach a shared understanding of the options available within and between the relevant services for children; evaluate these options against agreed criteria; and generate a set of alternatives leading to a pattern of investment with more emphasis on prevention.

Report of the
National
Commission of
Inquiry into the
Prevention of
Child Abuse

4.12   The lack of certain financial information identified in the IPF exercise was apparent. There was difficulty in producing a base line of current spending on children's services in health, because this spending was often aggregated into much more broadly based budgets, such as community services.

4.13   From the outset, there was consensus that:

o   the Children Act 1989 had not been adequately funded and the main casualty had been Section 17, Provision of Services for Children in Need, their Families and Others. Managers had no option but to give priority to high-risk child protection work, children in local authority care and the expensive prescriptive demands of criminal and civil court systems.

o   low resources breed reaction, not promotion or prevention. There are initial costs associated with shifting the bias into more cost-effective prevention.

o   the policies and practices of government departments tend to create conflict and perverse incentives, leading to cost shunting, blame shunting and work shunting. Key indicators, monitoring systems, and national directives and changing policies tend to be service-based not child-centred and do not assist co-operation.

o   there is a lack of interest and enthusiasm for children's services among most politicians and very senior managers, which is not redressed by formal government initiatives and requirements.

o   there is an inability to exert full influence over health and education because of independent NHS trusts, general practitioners and locally managed schools.

o   local government reforms divert management time and energy to the change process itself. Change was seen to imply further loss of funding because of dis-economies of scale and the problem of forging new working relationships with another "key player".

o   different agencies have different perceptions of need and priority.

o   there is particular concern about increasing numbers of children out of school during the day and at risk.

4.14   The varied backgrounds, roles and perspectives of participants created some predictable initial difficulties in identifying criteria, reaching shared understandings of terminology and relating different concepts and approaches. However, there was a strong convergence of thinking about necessary and desirable developments and a shared understanding of relative values. This consensus underlined many issues about which the Commission was becoming concerned and had received extensive comment. These included: the impact of year-on-year public sector reductions in services; the apparent lack of co-ordination between government departments about legislation, guidance, funding initiatives and priorities, all of which affect co-ordination at local level; the need to recognise the relationship between child abuse and environmental factors; the varying and unsatisfactory interpretations of definitions of child abuse; the heavy focus on adult services in both health and social services, as a result of political emphasis; the relative absence of national targets and key indicators for children's services; and the perverse incentive for locally managed schools to exclude difficult and demanding children.

4.15   The lack of research identifying effective preventive interventions was a problem and it was recognised that some of the proposals made were more in the nature of articles of faith

33

Report of the
National
Commission of
Inquiry into the
Prevention of
Child Abuse

or practice wisdom than based on evidence. This lack of sufficient appropriate research and the absence of relevant national key indicators relating to children in general and their social well-being in particular, are related issues which have important implications for government if there is to be a true shift to an emphasis on prevention.

4.16   However, even within those limitations, and taking a cautious approach, there were resources that could be redirected to preventive work without jeopardising current investment in formal child protection. All three agencies spent resources on the same client group, had overlapping responsibilities and some similar services. The workshop participants demonstrated a refreshing willingness to think laterally, to "give up" some resources and projects, and even to contemplate transferring some resources to other agencies, had this been legally and technically feasible. Some of this flexibility may be attributable to the fact that participants already had good working relationships within developing joint commissioning mechanisms in the local authority studied. It is probably not untypical, however, of the kinds of relationships, open-mindedness and flexibility built upon trust and experience that exist in many local authority areas.

4.17   The exercise also revealed that some service provisions were regarded as sacrosanct, making them difficult to change. This was perceived as a product of political and managerial resistance to loss of "empires", and anxiety about the implications of changing outmoded patterns of provision which enjoyed the support of vociferous sectors of the electorate.

4.18   Importantly, the exercise demonstrated that children at high risk could continue to be adequately protected, even given some shifts in expenditure. It emphasised that identified needs should be met as early as possible in as normal a way as possible, and that facilitating communication between workers, speed of response and access to providers of support were critical factors. It also highlighted that there must be corporate awareness of the financial implications of internal decisions across service boundaries. All of these factors required openness in dealings between all key players.

4.19   The exercise produced a model which evaluated a wide range of possible options. It took into account value for money, in terms of protection and prevention, and indicated an optimal package of measures. This was a mixture of health, education and social services-led initiatives, offset by reductions in each of the services. If technical and political impediments to a whole-child approach could be removed or reduced, the options would be even greater.

> "There is massive motivation among many who have been abused and then helped to work through their abuse. A small investment to assist voluntary services can provide real value for money."
> **Dunfermline Incest Survivors Group**

The cost of abuse: some case histories

4.20   The analysis of case histories (see Appendix 9) in the third exercise confirmed some of the conclusions already drawn from the other two exercises: for example, lack of readily available unit costing, particularly for preventive and investigative services; the "spin off"

Report of the
National
Commission of
Inquiry into the
Prevention of
Child Abuse

from child abuse into hidden and often costly demands for services for adults; and the high cost of reactive institutional response.

4.21   The case histories also highlighted cost demands which are rarely considered, such as treatment for physical illness caused or exacerbated by the stress of abusive situations, additional demands upon welfare services because of diminished ability to function adequately, and compensation for criminal injuries or negligence. What the case histories also exposed was the poignancy of lost opportunities and the personal, and community, tragedy involved. They demonstrated the cost to victims, their near relatives, and to society as a whole, of individuals unable, because of damage to their physical and/or psychological health, to reach their potential in terms of healthy, happy and productive lives. The case histories and the letters from survivors show that it is often left to individuals and their families to find the resources to meet some of these costs - for example, counselling, therapy and self help initiatives. Many small community groups provide much needed support but are often dependent on funding provided by their own members.

4.22   The IPF financial study and the ICL workshop were complementary in their main themes and findings, and these were endorsed and enriched by the case history study. Similar themes emerged from evidence to the Commission and from work undertaken by bodies such as the Audit Commission and the Association of Directors of Social Services. As a result, the Commission has concluded that:

○   additional short-term investment is needed to facilitate change and to keep the most high-risk children safe during the process of change.

○   the present system of allocating resources makes it difficult to establish whether additional long-term investment is needed.

○   that ways must be found to work across organisational and service boundaries at national and local levels, to develop a child and family-centred approach and to facilitate more co-ordinated and rational financial investment. Ideally, this would include transferring some investment from relevant adult services, such as penal and mental health services, although additional short-term investment would be needed to protect those services and vulnerable adults.

○   that a long-term strategic approach is essential if there is to be a realistic hope of achieving a change in the balance of preventive and child protection services and of making a real impact upon the present and next generations of children.

○   that there are, inadvertently, procedures within existing formal systems which militate implicitly or explicitly against the prevention of child abuse. These have a direct bearing upon financial investment.

35

> "Resources are a key issue in implementing a national strategy for children and a national strategy for preventing child abuse. The key to resources is political will. Without a political mandate making children a priority, and the attendant resources that follow from such a mandate, any national strategy will fail."
> **NSPCC**

Report of the
National
Commission of
Inquiry into the
Prevention of
Child Abuse

Recommendations

5. Government departments should co-operate to develop a "business plan for children" designed to shift investment to a preventive approach to child abuse while maintaining proper protection of those most at risk. Such plans should include the following measures:

   (a) Central government resource allocation formulae for health, education, social services and the penal system should be reviewed and factors introduced to give an emphasis to preventive services for children.

   (b) National performance indicators produced by government departments, the Audit Commission and other relevant bodies should be revised and co-ordinated to give greater emphasis to the well-being of all children, including those who have problems or who are under-achieving, and to managerial/organisational targets which demonstrate effective preventive work.

6. To accompany the children's services plan, local statutory agencies should be required to produce a financial plan. This should identify the funding invested in present services for children. In particular, there should be a requirement that the National Health Service identifies those proportions of the community health, family health services and acute services budgets that are allocated to children. Voluntary sector agencies should be encouraged to participate in this approach.

7. Government departments should stimulate joint planning and purchasing of local services through providing incentives, such as short-term funding, and removing technical and legal barriers to joint budgets and funding transfers.

8. The major child care voluntary organisations should co-ordinate their plans and funding priorities with each other and with the relevant local authorities and agencies.

9. Government, in co-operation with the main statutory and voluntary agencies, should develop a medium to long-term funding strategy designed to achieve greater investment in preventive services while continuing to protect high-risk children and families. The strategy should include an analysis of whether there is sufficient funding in the system to achieve this and identify any shortfall.

10. Government should reassess the balance of funding between children's and adults' services in the public sector.

References

1. Audit Commission, 1994, Seen But Not Heard, Co-ordinating Community Child Health and Social Services for Children in Need, London: HMSO

2. Child Protection: Messages From Research, 1995, Department of Health, London: HMSO

Report of the
National
Commission of
Inquiry into the
Prevention of
Child Abuse

Chapter 5
The Law, Regulation and Legal Practice

- Children, their families and professionals who work with them frequently find the law hostile, confusing, and incoherent

- The adversarial nature of the UK legal system and associated evidential and procedural requirements operate against the interests of children and families

- Law, regulation, and legal practice could make a more positive contribution to the prevention of child abuse

- Changes are needed in the substantive law and its administration

- Legislation based on the UN Convention on the Rights of the Child should be introduced to support the overall rights and needs of children

5.1   Legal processes have a profound effect on children and families whom they directly involve. In relation to the abuse of children, the Commission has considered the substantive law, the legal process and the way the law is administered, and identified the changes that it believes are necessary.

5.2   The current civil law and criminal law statutes operating in Scotland and in England and Wales are comprehensively documented and commented upon in **Appendices 10 and 11** respectively. The English and Welsh system of law differs markedly from the Scottish system. The system in Northern Ireland is very similar to that found in England. New child care legislation is being introduced in all parts of the United Kingdom through the Children Act 1989, which covers England and Wales and was implemented from 1991, the Children (Scotland) Act 1995, implemented in full from 1997, and the Children (Northern Ireland) Order 1995, implemented from 1996. All jurisdictions have seen a number of recent reforms to the criminal justice system which were intended to benefit children. In Northern Ireland the Children's Evidence (Northern Ireland) Order 1995 (SI 1995 Number 757 N.I.3) brought arrangements for child witnesses in criminal proceedings into line with those for England and Wales.

Civil Law

5.3   Proceedings under the Children Act 1989 in England and Wales are better attuned to the needs of children and families than those under earlier legislation. However, while there have been improvements in the training of child care centre judges, not all judges and advocates are trained or have special expertise in this area. In reports commissioned by the Lord Chancellor into reasons for delay, Dame Margaret Booth[1] highlighted a number of problems in the operation of the Children Act. These included a lack of adequate judicial resources, and the need for constant review to try to ensure that a care judge is always available in a care centre to enable the concept of a specialist bench in family work to be maintained. She noted considerable problems arising with inexperienced advocates, ranging from delay, to cases being conducted in an unnecessarily adversarial manner; to a lack of preparation and prior consultation between lawyers, leading to cases being prolonged unnecessarily; to too many parties being involved in the proceedings; and to too many last-minute settlements which placed unreasonable pressures on participants. In practice in England and Wales, only guardians *ad litem* and the court appoint solicitors who are members of the Children Panel (not to be confused with the Children's Hearing System in Scotland, known as the Children's Panel). These are lawyers who have satisfied the Law Society that they have sufficient training and experience to represent children. However, parents, grandparents and other parties to proceedings may choose non-expert lawyers. Furthermore, no equivalent to the Children Panel exists for barristers; it is not compulsory for barristers to undertake any family law training before taking instruction in children's cases.

5.4   Dame Margaret Booth's reports raise other issues also brought to the Commission's attention. Lawyers continue to adopt an adversarial stance outside the courtroom in a way that other professionals find intimidating and unhelpful. The experience can be even worse for children and their families. Moreover, it is wholly at odds with the complex and sensitive matters to be determined. For the lawyer, the court appearance might signify the conclusion of his or her case; for the child, the family, and the professional workers concerned, it represents a very early stage in what is likely, after the case is over, to be a painstaking and difficult process of rebuilding positive family relationships. Undermining and belittling witnesses, professional or otherwise, is destructive to that process and to the concept of partnership, an underpinning principle of the Children Act upon which such work should be based. This suggests that advocates need to accept responsibility for preparing themselves, by undertaking appropriate training, for work in child protection cases. Furthermore, it strongly suggests that judges need to be sensitive to the style of advocacy they allow in such cases.

5.5   All local authorities consulted by Dame Margaret expressed concern about the lack of credibility given by courts to the evidence of social workers who, despite their training, are often accorded less credence than officers of the court. This led to local authorities feeling compelled to instruct "experts" to deal with matters which could easily be handled by their equally well-qualified social workers, who could speak with greater knowledge of the child and also had a clear duty to act in his or her interests. Courts often paid greater attention to guardians *ad litem,* who in the main have similar experiences and qualifications to local authority social workers. She concluded that, while social workers needed training to enable them to feel confident in court work, the judiciary and the legal profession equally needed to have a better understanding of the social worker's role and the extent of his or her authority.

5.6   A related issue was explored in Scotland during the course of the Fife Inquiry(2). There is a concern within the legal system that social workers are subject to management direction and restricted in their ability to act as independent assessors of the child's needs. Their recommendations are seen as influenced, and sometimes determined, by management policy. These concerns also relate to the fact that social work managers are also stewards of the resources which might be made available to the child. Given these concerns the legal system looks elsewhere for a truly independent view.

Report of the
National
Commission of
Inquiry into the
Prevention of
Child Abuse

5.7   Issues relating to **"children in need"** were raised in many submissions to the Commission. The implementation of child care legislation in England and Wales lacks investment in prevention and supportive services to children in need. The statutory requirement, being introduced in England, Wales and Northern Ireland, to assess children in need and provide services to support them and their families through social services, educational and health provision, is not fulfilled in practice in England and Wales because of a tight rationing of resources.

5.8   The requirement to assess children in need has been in place longest in England and Wales and was welcomed by practitioners, who felt that the discretionary powers of previous legislation were not sufficiently robust. There is now, however, a body of research and experience which shows that section 17 of the Children Act is largely unimplemented.(3) This section obliges local authorities, assisted by health authorities and others, to "safeguard and promote the welfare of children within their area who are in need and so far as is consistent with that duty to promote the upbringing of such children by their families by providing a range and level of services appropriate to those children's needs". Shortcomings have been highlighted in much evidence to the Commission. A recurring theme is that the Children Act has been grossly under-resourced. It is too soon to assess the impact of the new legislation in Scotland, where the concept of children in need will be implemented in April 1997, and in Northern Ireland, where it will operate from October 1996; but concerns have already been expressed to the Commission that a lack of funds is jeopardising the good intentions of the legislation.

5.9   In practice, statutory authorities tend to define "appropriate" in a manner that matches their resources rather than need. A prudent manager has little alternative other than to draw attention to serious resources deficiencies and to ensure efficient management of what is available. In Scotland the problem may seem legally less acute because the local authority will not be required specifically to identify children in need.

5.10   Many of the representations to the Commission highlighted the importance of inter-agency working in the context of family support and argued that social services departments and social work departments alone cannot provide all family support. Children Act guidance makes clear that a corporate approach to the provision of family support services should be encouraged. Unfortunately, since not all agencies are required to participate in planning and delivering these services, they can avoid contributing and co-operating in providing services to children in need.

> "Too often lawyers limit their role to simply preparing for the hearing of a dispute and there is little attempt to relate what is happening within the court process to the practicalities of family life ... Our concerns are that the system itself, rather than protecting and helping children, may increase their difficulties."
> **Association of Lawyers for Children**

Criminal Law

5.11   One issue which spans the practice of civil and criminal law is that of privilege and the disclosure of information(4). In proceedings where the welfare of the child is under

*Report of the
National
Commission of
Inquiry into the
Prevention of
Child Abuse*

consideration, the court may override legal professional privilege which would otherwise preserve or enhance the adversarial position of one of the parties. On an application for disclosure, courts must conduct a balancing exercise, weighing the importance of confidentiality, which could protect the welfare of the child, against the public interest in justice being properly served. Cases where convicted abusers have, through court documents, learned addresses and other details of their child victims, have highlighted the difficulty arising from confidentiality of statements made during investigations or care proceedings. As Professor Jenny McEwan, Professor of Law at Keele University, wrote *(Child and Family Law Quarterly Vol 7 no 4 1995):* "The area of privilege is far from straightforward mainly because there is no one consistent standard of confidentiality. The law has several kinds of privilege each having its own rationale and, therefore, its own set of rules ... Any of the various categories of privilege may be in issue in cases concerned with the welfare of children." The practical implications of this legal confusion are that children might be unprotected, those who have committed criminal assault may not be prosecuted and convicted, and social workers, guardians *ad litem* and parents can be constrained by incompatible systems. McEwan pointed out: "This unsatisfactory state of affairs ... is the depressing consequence of the rigid distinction between the civil and criminal processes in the UK and the unsuitability of such a disjointed system of justice in cases involving child abuse." The Commission recommends that the principles and law governing privilege should be reviewed.

40

Court Practice

5.12   The damaging impact of the criminal justice system on abused children who appear as witnesses was raised in many submissions from all parts of the UK. They highlighted the traumatic effect that the system can have. It is important for the prevention of child abuse that these shortcomings are addressed, since failure to do so will mean that only a minority of perpetrators will be successfully prosecuted and children will continue to be discouraged from giving evidence. The Commission received evidence that many child witnesses who have given evidence of sexual or physical abuse report that they found the experience as terrifying as the abuse itself. Research by Plotnikoff and Wolfson(5) to evaluate government policy of giving priority to child abuse prosecutions in the criminal justice system, monitored 200 cases over a two-year period and found that, far from receiving priority treatment, these cases actually took *longer* than the national average to reach disposition. New statutory procedures to expedite cases were little used and were ineffective in reducing delay. Child witnesses currently have to wait for an average of ten months before their case is heard and are often advised not to receive counselling before the trial in case this prejudices their evidence. The number of children receiving counselling before a trial varies across the country. Another survey (Kranat and Westcott, 1994)(6) found that up to half of all prosecution and defence questions were inappropriate for child witnesses. The present system is seen as so detrimental to the best interests of the child that some people suggested that it would be better if children were never to appear in court. Many children have reported that the court experience is so hostile that they felt that they, not the defendant, were on trial, and many regretted that they agreed to give evidence.

Children Giving Evidence

5.13 Previous changes in law have failed to resolve the problem of children being traumatised by the court process. Many aspects remain which jeopardise children's interests. Scottish law makes a number of provisions relating to child witnesses, including most recently changes to the rules on the admissibility of evidence in criminal proceedings, introduced in 1 April 1996 by the Criminal Procedure (Scotland) Act 1995. This may result in greater use being made of video recordings of a child's evidence, which the child would then "adopt" in court and may be questioned on. While these provisions have been welcomed, many consider that they do not go far enough and that in Scotland child witnesses need greater protection.

> "The impact of cross examination upon the child witness can be traumatic in the extreme, particularly if not held in check by the presiding judge. It is known that one child, whilst under cross examination, has been instructed by the court: to appear in person in court wearing clothing similar to that worn during the alleged assault, in order to demonstrate the level of physical maturity of the child witness; and to demonstrate with her own hands the nature of the assault upon herself."
> **Birmingham Child Witness Support Consortium**

5.14 New legislation is needed which would introduce pre-trial hearings, as recommended for England and Wales by the Pigot Inquiry in 1989(7). Evidence to the Commission revealed a wide range of support for this reform. At present, child witnesses have to be cross-examined at the trial. Legislation, through a criminal justice Bill, should be introduced to allow child witnesses to give all evidence on video at a pre-trial hearing. This substantially reduces the trauma experienced in court by abused children. It assists the child's recollection of events and, most importantly, allows the child to receive the early help necessary to reduce trauma and permanent emotional damage from the event that led to the trial.

5.15 Traditional court dress and wigs can be alarming and the courts and advocates could do more to put children at ease. The interests of formality and tradition should not take precedence over the interests of children's welfare and of justice. Language and process must, in the interests of justice, be understandable to children, and the ways in which children communicate should be understood and accepted by criminal courts. Children do not impart information in the same way as adults. There is research evidence which could be put at the disposal of courts in relation to child witnesses, how they communicate and the credibility of their evidence. This does not appear to be taken into account in the conduct of court proceedings. Those responsible for the administration and conduct of criminal cases should recognise and respond to these important issues and charge the criminal courts with responsibility for protecting the child victim's interests. Special training for criminal court judges and advocates in working with children and paying proper regard to their special requirements is essential. The Commission supports the development of projects which support child witnesses and prepare them for the court experience.

5.16 A number of submissions pointed out that the shortcomings of the criminal justice system are exacerbated when the children involved have disabilities and communication difficulties. Such children are disadvantaged at all stages, from the disclosure and

*Report of the
National
Commission of
Inquiry into the
Prevention of
Child Abuse*

investigation of allegations of abuse through to the trial. For them, the problems experienced by all children involved with courts are compounded. The ignorance and prejudice which surrounds disability can render disabled children "invisible", and allegations less likely to be pursued. However, there is increasing evidence of abuse suffered by disabled children. All those involved in the criminal justice system need to review whether they have developed the ability to investigate and prosecute in such cases and, if not, to take the necessary action to rectify this.

> "My father served three years for what he did and I am serving a life sentence without parole."
> **Letter to the Commission**

5.17   The need to protect the rights of defendants is indisputable, but the developing practice of acquiring the personal file of children involved with the local authority in an attempt to discredit them as witnesses is disturbing. This practice is abusive and discriminatory. Other child victims who are not already involved with a statutory agency will not have such a file. Intimate personal information may be placed in the public arena in a degrading manner and previous sexual experiences, whether abusive or not, may be invoked as evidence that the child cannot be believed, or provoked the assault. The argument that such practices serve the interests of justice is not convincing and the Commission believes that a child victim who happens to be involved with a statutory agency, and therefore has written personal records, should be treated like any other child victim and witness in terms of the information available to the court.

Follow-up of Offenders

5.18   Where offenders against children have been successfully prosecuted, the criminal justice system needs to have regard, in sentencing, to the need of the offenders for treatment and to the potential future risk they pose to children. Judges and magistrates should be aware of the nature of future risk and likely availability of treatment. Government departments - the Home Office, Scottish Office, Northern Ireland Office and Welsh Office - should ensure that appropriate assessment and treatment facilities are available and that there are systems to ensure that offenders who are a danger to children are identified and that the relevant information is available to responsible bodies. The same government departments also need to have regard to the management of prisons and to the danger that abusive behaviour - particularly sexual abuse - may be reinforced within prison. These issues have implications for the arrangements made for discharged prisoners.

> "Offenders need to be watched once they have been released to ensure that they have not been released back into families to reoffend. This could be what went wrong in our case; my ex father-in-law having been released as a Schedule 1 Offender on three different occasions."
> **Letter to the Commission**

Adolescent Offenders

Report of the
National
Commission of
Inquiry into the
Prevention of
Child Abuse

5.19   In order to reduce the numbers of children who are sexually abused, an effective, co-ordinated, systematic response to young abusers must be developed. Research shows that many adult abusers start abusing children while they are themselves adolescent and that the average adolescent sex offender, who does not receive treatment, will go on to commit 380 sexual crimes in his life time (Abel et al, 1984)(8). Home Office statistics for 1989 show that out of 10,729 individuals found guilty or cautioned for sexual offences, one third were aged 20 years or under. A significant proportion of young abusers have been abused as children, so they too are victims. Early intervention with young abusers is recommended. Inappropriate behaviours are easier to modify at this stage because they are less deeply ingrained than in adults and adolescents are more accustomed to learning new and acceptable skills.

5.20   Closer collaboration between child protection, criminal justice, care and welfare agencies is necessary to meet the needs of young abusers. A range of agencies have a role to play in identification, assessment, and supervision. The Faithfull Foundation urges greater clarity about the interaction of the criminal justice and child protection systems so that a consistent message is given to young persons and their families that abusive behaviour is taken seriously and that the power to intervene in their behaviour is available. Under the present legal system it is difficult to integrate child protection and criminal justice as different agencies take differing amounts of responsibility and make their own decisions in relation to their own guidelines. A change in the law may be necessary to enable young abusers to have an assessment prior to any decision being made about the legal process or care proceedings. In Scotland an assessment can be requested for a young person prior to any decision being made about welfare or criminal proceedings. This may enable more appropriate decisions to be made about the young person and the intervention needed to minimise their risk of re-offending.

43

Regulation of Offenders

5.21   The Home Office has made strenuous efforts to liaise with other government departments on the follow-up of offenders and is considering further measures, including the establishment of a national register of sex offenders. The proposals contained in the Home Office Consultation document "Sentencing and Supervision of Sex Offenders" are supported by the Commission.(9) Current procedures, including access to criminal records for employers, are not consistently applied across all areas. Other practices for recording people considered unsuitable to work with children are similarly unco-ordinated. For example, the Department of Health and the Department for Education and Employment operate different systems for listing staff unsuitable for work with children. Medical, nursing or paramedical professions have their own professional registration systems which can deregister an individual found guilty of a criminal or disciplinary offence involving children.

Report of the
National
Commission of
Inquiry into the
Prevention of
Child Abuse

5.22   The Commission proposes that there should be a statutory obligation upon applicants for employment involving contact with children to declare whether they have any previous criminal convictions or have had disciplinary action taken against them as a result of offences or misconduct in relation to children. It should also be obligatory for all people acting as referees to declare any knowledge of disciplinary action or convictions against the applicant which would render them unsuitable for employment involving children.

5.23   Employers should be required to take formal action to investigate and resolve allegations or inferences that children have been abused as a result of employee action or inaction. Government should develop guidance on the application of this proposal, including what sanctions should be applied to employers who fail to act in this way, do not provide proper references, or do not make effective checks on applicants applying to work with children.

5.24   Discharged prisoners may move around in the community and become detached from formal supervision and review. They may also be placed under the supervision of a probation officer who, under government proposals for England and Wales, may have no social work training to equip him or her to work with highly disturbed and deviant behaviour. The follow-up of violent offenders is even less co-ordinated than that for sex offenders. Much, therefore, remains to be done to co-ordinate the treatment and supervision of convicted offenders.

Regulation of the Professions

5.25   The Commission is concerned that, while professional registers in relation to offenders exist in teaching, medicine, nursing and other health disciplines, there are no equivalent registers in social work and social care. Social workers have long supported the concept of a regulatory body and the idea has recently gained much wider support in the social services field. The Commission believes that regulatory bodies should be established in those disciplines which do not have them, and that the procedures of both new and established regulatory bodies should be reviewed to ensure that they are effective in protecting the interests of children by excluding those who have been proved to be unsuitable to work with children.

5.26   Some professional activities are regulated through statutory ethical councils, for example, the British Medical Council and, in Scotland, the General Teaching Council. Such bodies have been important in setting and maintaining professional standards in a number of disciplines. Commenting on the English situation, in its evidence to the Inquiry, the Family Law Bar Association (FLBA) said that "the nature of professional responsibility is to act in accordance with the best practice and ethics of one's profession. Difficulties arise for professionals such as teachers and social workers who do not have a single governing body

*Report of the
National
Commission of
Inquiry into the
Prevention of
Child Abuse*

or code of conduct to which they all subscribe." The British Association of Social Workers has a code of ethics and the Social Care Association a code of practice to which their members subscribe, but they have no statutory backing or effective sanctions. The FLBA also cites the almost uncritical acceptance of medical opinions at case conferences, often from doctors who subsequently acknowledge their inexperience or lack of expertise. This is in part a reflection of the lower status accorded to the professional expertise of social workers, who have statutory responsibility for child protection. At case conferences involving the medical profession or the police, the balance of power is often firmly tilted away from social workers. The Commission recognises these concerns and strongly supports the establishment of a statutory General Social Services Council to set standards and regulate the activities of those working in social care.

Mandatory Reporting and Confidentiality

5.27   Unlike many American states, the UK does not have laws requiring the mandatory reporting of child abuse. Under the law, only local authority social workers, health and social service board social workers (in Northern Ireland) and police have a *duty* to report suspicions that a child is in need of care and protection. Although local child protection guidelines and professional codes of conduct may *expect* other professionals (teachers, health visitors and other medical staff) to report as part of their professional duty, they do not have to do so as a matter of law. Professionals may feel that victims' confidence in them may be adversely affected by mandatory reporting, or that children and adults may be discouraged from disclosing abuse, for fear of the consequences. There should, therefore, be encouragement to disclose information and suspicion of abuse, combined with greater flexibility of action and the exercise of professional judgement within the formal systems. The fact that social workers and others do not necessarily invoke full child-protection procedures immediately, that there are intermediate stages and that they are prepared to give advice, should be publicised more clearly, through public education and information schemes. Provision should also be made so that families and children and young people have access to confidential advice on such matters. Such advice and support should be available independently of statutory agencies.

45

> "I cannot help feeling bitter that I was let down by the system at every turn and am still being let down by the system today. The priority of the law is to protect the perpetrators rather than the victims - it is a burden in itself knowing that my stepfather knows that he owes his liberty to the fact that I could not face the ordeal of giving evidence against him in court."
> **Letter to the Commission**

Law in practice

5.28   Despite the differences between the legal jurisdictions in England and Wales, Scotland and Northern Ireland, the Commission found that the difficulties experienced in relation to the law were similar throughout the United Kingdom. In general, families see the law as threatening and as a form of policing rather than support. The problems in the

*Report of the
National
Commission of
Inquiry into the
Prevention of
Child Abuse*

relationship between the law, regulation, and child protection procedures was highlighted in many submissions.

5.29　The Commission recognises the difficulties inherent in translating legal and regulatory concepts into practice. Neither working together as agencies and individual professionals, nor working in partnership with parents is simple. In the Commission's view, however, the emphasis has been too much upon law, regulation and guidance which is prescriptive, and not enough upon principles, standards of good practice and investment in training. The more legislative and prescriptive the guidance and procedures, the more rigid and defensive practice becomes in consequence. It is not enough for the Department of Health to suggest "a lighter touch" without removing some of the barriers of its own creation. To achieve a "lighter touch" there will need to be acceptance by the government of less defensive and bureaucratic procedures and the possible risks associated with more flexibility. Similarly, true partnership with parents cannot exist if a legalistic approach is taken by either the family or professional workers. It must also be recognised by lawyers, parents and social workers that, while partnership with parents is essential, the overriding principle is the best interests of the child. It would be helpful therefore if government guidance were revised in a way which facilitates a "lighter touch". Such a revision should also take account of the need to ensure that guidance on child protection really reflects the UN Convention on the Rights of the Child(10). The promotion of a "a lighter touch" also requires the development of improved training for social workers in risk management.

5.30　There is a danger that current discussion about law and practice and a "lighter touch" could lead to under-reaction or greater tolerance of child abuse. The Commission is convinced that a "lighter touch" should refer only to the processes by which we ensure that children are protected. It should not be forgotten that many thousands of children in this country have been well protected by practitioners of all disciplines scrupulously following government regulations, guidance and local procedures. Many of those practitioners in all parts of the UK now appear confused following the publication of *Messages From Research*(11). This confusion seems to arise partly from an impression that they are being criticised for working as previously prescribed by government, and partly from the particular interpretation placed upon research commissioned by the Department of Health. Most of the research published by the Department of Health has been of a social policy or social work nature and does not include medical or other research. This research is of considerable significance but there is a need for greater clarity in its interpretation and translation into regulation and official guidance. Regulation carries the force of secondary legislation. Departmental guidance also carries considerable force and is frequently invoked by lawyers. If a "lighter touch" is not to be confused with a greater tolerance of abuse, clear guidance needs to be given by government in relation to the necessary procedures and the manner in which they are carried out.

Child Prostitution

5.31　Official responses to child prostitution are affected by the conflict between the Children Act, with its emphasis on "the best interests of the child", and the Criminal Justice System. "The Game's Up" (Children's Society, 1995)(12) supports the 1993 Council of Europe recommendation number R(91) on Sexual Exploitation, Pornography and

*Report of the
National
Commission of
Inquiry into the
Prevention of
Child Abuse*

Prostitution of, Trafficking in, Children and Young Adults which states that there should be a shift in attitudes and the legal response to child prostitution. Emphasis should be placed on treating children involved in prostitution as victims of sexual exploitation rather than as perpetrators of, or accomplices to, criminal offences. At present the law recognises the need to protect young people from sexual abuse and exploitation but also allows children as young as ten to be prosecuted for offences relating to that abuse. Criminal legislation is taking precedence over the Children Act. The emphasis of criminal proceedings should be placed, in the Commission's view, on the identification and prosecution of clients and pimps who exploit children through prostitution.

> "A clearer message with regard to parental responsibility is required, as is a clearer understanding of the needs of children, their need for love, trust, and security."
> **Northern Area Child Protection Committee, Northern Ireland**

5.32   The Commission believes that the Lord Chancellor should initiate a review of the law in so far as it relates to children involved in prostitution and their clients. Comparable arrangements should be made in other jurisdictions within the UK.

Issues to be considered include:

○ raising the age of criminal responsibility from the age of ten;

○ giving legal force to Article 34 of the UN Convention. The Article reads:

[States parties] shall undertake to protect the child from all forms of sexual exploitation and sexual abuse. For these purposes States Parties shall in particular take all appropriate national, bilateral and multilaterial measures to prevent:
a) the inducement or coercion of a child to engage in unlawful sexual activity;
b) the exploitative use of children in prostitution or other unlawful sexual practices;
c) the exploitative use of children in pornographic performance and materials.

5.33   Changing the law is one thing, implementing it effectively is another. In considering this issue in 1995, the Children's Society made a number of useful recommendations. The Commission is particularly concerned that any strategy relating to child prostitution should cause:

○ the police to implement their obligations under Children Act(s) to protect children and young people. These must take precedence over criminal legislation used to caution and convict young people involved in prostitution;

○ local authorities to recognise their obligations under the Children Act(s) to protect all children, and specifically those in their care, from all forms of sexual exploitation;

○ the Department of Health and local authorities to support the development of new interagency initiatives aimed at helping children and young people involved in prostitution;

○ police standing orders to be amended to emphasise alternatives to street and formal cautioning;

○ the practice of recording warnings and formal cautions of children to be reviewed;

○ the police to increase their investigations and, where appropriate, prosecution of adults involved in child prostitution.

47

*Report of the
National
Commission of
Inquiry into the
Prevention of
Child Abuse*

Proposed Changes in the Law

Parental Responsibilities

5.35 UK law should be harmonised and contain a specific definition of *parental responsibilities*. There are no legislative provisions in England, Wales or Northern Ireland that lay down standards of care which children can expect from their parents or, importantly, which can serve to guide or educate parents themselves. The Children (Scotland) Act 1995, however, states that as far as is practicable and in the child's best interests, a parent's parental responsibilities are: to safeguard and promote the child's health, development, and welfare; to provide, in a manner appropriate to the state of development of the child (a) direction and (b) guidance to the child; if the child is not living with the parent, to maintain personal relations and direct contact with the child on a regular basis; to act as the child's legal representative.

5.36 The Scottish Act goes some way towards defining parental responsibilities and parental rights and makes it clear that parents' rights are subsidiary to their responsibilities. This is welcome but it is too soon to say what the impact of this provision will be and this needs to be closely monitored. In England, Wales and Northern Ireland, legislation lays no duties on parents comparable to those in Scottish law. The emphasis outside Scotland is on the negative concept of "harm".

5.37 If a set of parental responsibilities were included in legislation, it would provide parents with a standard against which to measure their performance, from which both parents and children would benefit. Hoggett(13) suggests that such a list of responsibilities would refer to the "collection of tasks, activities and choices which are part and parcel of looking after and bringing up a child". The Commission therefore recommends that, in the light of the Scottish experience, consideration should be given to defining parental responsibilities in law in the rest of the UK.

Consultation with Children

5.38 The Children (Scotland) Act 1995 places an obligation on parents to consult their children on major matters and to take account of the child's views in accordance with age and maturity. Many representations to the inquiry urged that the views and wishes of children should be taken into greater account in all areas of their lives. The Commission believes that the Scottish law provision could usefully be added to the law operating in the rest of the UK.

Children's rights

5.39 A recurring theme in this chapter and in evidence to the Commission is the under-representation of children's rights in law. The Children Act 1989, the Children (Scotland) Act 1995, and the Children (Northern Ireland) Order 1995 include only certain areas of civil law, cover no aspects of criminal procedure and exclude substantial areas of children's rights. The Family Law Bar Association said that "the rights given to children and their families by the European Convention on Human Rights and the UN Convention on the Rights of the Child are in general terms and have so far not been imported with enthusiasm

*Report of the
National
Commission of
Inquiry into the
Prevention of
Child Abuse*

into individual cases under our domestic law". Legislation should be enacted which reflects the UN Convention, and brings together in statute a comprehensive set of provisions relating to children's entitlements and needs. The Commission recommends that this be done and, in their papers for the Commission, Marshall and Lyon address what such legislation might cover (**see Appendices 10 and 11**)

The Conduct of Courts

5.40   The ways in which the law, guidance, and regulation influence the prevention of abuse to children and their protection shows how the legal system and its administration have both strengths and weaknesses. Such shortcomings as there are must be addressed. The Association of Lawyers for Children voiced a view which is shared by many: "Our concerns are that the system itself, rather than protecting and helping children, may increase their difficulties." It pointed out that litigation under the present law is based on "a model in which the court after hearing both sides makes a final decision on the matter in dispute. It is a model that works well in claims for damages based on, for example, breaches of contract or tortious obligations. But not all disputes can be resolved so neatly and then the model is less helpful. This is particularly so with child care law."

5.41   Overwhelming evidence to the Inquiry supports this view. The Commission believes that there should be a thorough review conducted as a prelude to establishing a court context and process which is better equipped to deal with sensitive family matters, particularly where children are involved. Such a review should consider an investigative rather than an adversarial system in England, Wales and Northern Ireland and take into account the experiences of the Scottish and French systems and those operating in parts of Australia and New Zealand.

49

Corporal punishment

5.42   Under certain circumstances the corporal punishment of children is permitted under the law in the UK provided such punishment is "reasonable".

5.43   Section 1(7) of the Children and Young Person's Act 1993 states that the provisions of Section 1.1 of that Act, which create the offence of cruelty to children "[do] not affect the right of any parent, teacher or any other person having the lawful control or charge of a child or young person to administer punishment to him". The courts have established that such punishment must be "reasonable", but this has been accepted as a defence in cases where the child has been subjected to beatings with implements and has suffered cuts and bruising which go well beyond anything which could reasonably be described or, as some would wish, be defended as "smacking".

5.44   Recognising that there are strong differences of opinion on the issue of the law and physical punishment and having considered the issues in detail, the Commission has formed the following views:

o   As a general proposition and on the weight of evidence, physical punishment is an unsatisfactory and, ultimately, ineffective way of improving children's behaviour.

○ The general decline in the permitted use of sanctions in this form, for example in publicly maintained schools and nurseries, is to be welcomed. Alternative ways of ensuring acceptable standards of behaviour in children should be explored and promoted.

○ Whatever the legal position, occasions will arise when parents will strike a child. In these circumstance, children should be in precisely the same position as adults. It should be no defence, whether an assault be carried out by a parent or anyone else, that it was justified on the grounds of the "reasonable chastisement" of the child concerned. Section 1.7 of the Children and Young Person's Act 1933 should therefore be repealed in order to leave children subject to the same legal protection against assault as adults. This would simply require the police and prosecuting authorities to exercise their discretion, as they do already when deciding whether to charge or prosecute adults.

5.45   The Commission further believes that the ban on the use of corporal punishment of children in publicly maintained schools should be extended to all independent schools and nurseries. The use of corporal punishment by child minders or others to whom parents "control or charge of child" (see LB Sutton V Davies [1994] (1FL R 528)) should similarly be prohibited.

Recommendations

Improvement in the Operation of Current Law and Court Conduct

11. There should be regular monitoring by the Lord Chancellor's Office and by the Scottish Courts Administration of the availability of properly trained and experienced judges for civil proceedings involving children. If necessary to reduce delay, the number of such judges should be increased.

12. Within two years, all solicitors and barristers representing parties in civil proceedings affecting the care, protection, and custody of children should be trained and accredited to work in the child care field and their performance monitored to ensure that they maintain knowledge of current developments.

13. Within two years, judges and advocates acting in criminal cases involving child witnesses and/or victims should receive training in understanding and communicating with children and in how to ensure that court proceedings are conducted in ways appropriate to the age of the children involved.

14. Every case involving children should have designated judges who review cases every four weeks and give stipulated time limits for hearings.

15. Consideration should be given to allocating the same judges to civil and criminal proceedings involving the same child.

16. All courts should consider the conduct, dress and location of the court when children are active participants in cases, and make appropriate changes to facilitate the comfort and avoid intimidation of the child. Children should be brought from home to court when needed and not have to wait in court.

Report of the
National
Commission of
Inquiry into the
Prevention of
Child Abuse

17. Central government should, through changes in legislation or by regulation, ensure that other relevant services co-operate with social services and social work departments in developing a Children's Services Plan and by making explicit investment in children's services.

18. Government departments should revise guidance on child protection procedures to give a clear framework and mandate to practitioners within which they can operate with greater freedom to exercise professional judgement without leaving children at increased risk of abuse.

19. Relevant government departments should monitor the provision of services to children in need to ascertain whether the obligations set out under current legislation are being fulfilled and, if not, what is preventing them being met.

20. The principles and law governing privilege, as it is operated in civil and criminal proceedings, should be reviewed and harmonised by the Law Commission.

21. Officers of the court, the police and social workers should all receive training on communicating with and understanding disabled children and on their particular vulnerability to abuse.

22. The Crown Prosecution Service, Procurators Fiscal and other relevant parties should ensure that children and parents are kept fully informed of developments in the preparation and progress of cases including adequate notice of any requirement to give evidence.

23. The Lord Chancellor's Office, the Crown Office, and other agencies responsible for bringing child witnesses to court should consider ways of improving the arrangements for supporting and preparing children for court and for ensuring that children receive the treatment they need.

24. Judges should ensure that child witnesses are not discriminated against by virtue of any relationship they might have with a statutory agency holding a personal file. No records maintained for purposes, such as medical treatment, therapy, care, or because children have special needs, should be used in court in respect of any child.

Regulation of staff

25. Central government should establish a fully integrated and automated system, with proper safeguards, to record information about all those working in children's services found guilty of, or cautioned or subjected to formal disciplinary action for, any kind of assault against children or other serious misdemeanour which has placed children at risk. This should record findings of guilt in criminal proceedings and the outcomes of formal disciplinary action. It should be accessible to employers and voluntary organisations. In future, a UK-wide service could be linked to similar systems in other countries.

26. Applicants for work with children should be obliged to make a personal statement regarding their criminal or disciplinary record with regard to children. A false

*Report of the
National
Commission of
Inquiry into the
Prevention of
Child Abuse*

statement should be grounds for summary dismissal and this should be recorded on the relevant national register.

27. Government should establish a system requiring employers to act upon knowledge of proven misconduct on the part of any of their employees in relation to children and provide full and detailed information in any references supplied to other employers.

28. Improved co-ordination between criminal justice, child protection, and care agencies must be established to meet the overall needs of young sex offenders. The law should be reformed to enable them to receive an assessment prior to decisions about legal and care proceedings.

Proposals for New Legislation

29. Government should, in the interests of public confidence and safety, support the creation of professional regulatory bodies for all disciplines which work with children and review existing regulatory bodies to ensure their practices are specifically geared to the protection of children. In particular, the Government should support the establishment of a General Social Services Council.

30. In the light of the Scottish experience, the law in England, Wales and Northern Ireland should be amended to include the concepts in Scottish law of parental responsibilities and a general obligation to consult children on important matters affecting their future.

31. The Lord Chancellor's Office, Department of Health, the Scottish Office, the Northern Ireland Office and other relevant government departments should develop legislation which is firmly based upon the UN Convention on the Rights of the Child.

32. Legislation should be introduced to effect full implementation of the recommendations of the Report of the Advisory Group on Video Recorded Evidence, Home Office, London, 1989 (the Pigot Report).

33. The Lord Chancellor, the Crown Office, the Scottish Office and the Northern Ireland Office should review the present system of dealing with child victims, witnesses and children otherwise subject to court proceedings and consider the legislative changes that would be needed to move towards a more investigative and less adversarial method of dealing with children and young people.

34. The law, as it affects the physical punishment of children, should be amended to give children, in all circumstances, the same protection against assault as adults. Section 1 (7) of the Children and Young Person's Act 1933 should be repealed and the defence of "reasonable chastisement" should therefore be removed.

35. Government should conduct an inter-departmental review of the operation of the criminal justice system as it affects child defendants, particularly in relation to the age of criminal responsibility and the nature of the courts in which children are tried.

Child Prostitution

*Report of the
National
Commission of
Inquiry into the
Prevention of
Child Abuse*

36. In all matters affecting children involved in prostitution, precedence should be given to "the best interests of the child", as set out in the Children Act(s).

37. The emphasis of criminal proceedings should be placed on the identification and prosecution of clients and pimps who exploit children through prostitution rather than on the child.

38. The Lord Chancellor should initiate a review of the law in so far as it relates to children involved in prostitution and their clients. Such a review would include a consideration of:

    (i)   raising the age of criminal responsibility from the age of ten.

    (ii) giving legal force to Article 34 of the United Nations Convention on the Rights of the Child (see para. 5.32).

References

1. Booth M, 1996, Avoiding Delay in Children Act Cases, London: Lord Chancellor's Department

2. Kearney B, (Chairman), 1992, The Report of the Inquiry into Child Care Policies in Fife, Edinburgh: HMSO

3. Aldgate J, Tunstill J, 1994, Implementing Section 17 of the Children Act - the First 18 Months: a study for the Department of Health, Leicester: Leicester University

4. McEwan J, Privilege and the Children Act 1989 - confusion compounded? *in* Child and Family Law Quarterly, vol 7, no4, 1995

5. Plotnikoff J, Woolfson R, 1995, Prosecuting Child Abuse, Oxford: Blackstone

6. Kranat V, Westcott H, 1994, Under Fire: Lawyers Questioning Children in Criminal Courts, *in* Expert Evidence, vol 3, no 1, pps 16-24, 1994

7. Pigot T, 1989, Report of the Advisory Group on Video Evidence, London: Home Office

8. Abel G, Becker J, Cunningham-Rathner J, Rouleau J, Kaplan M, Reich J, 1984, The Treatment of Child Molesters: A Manual, New York: SBC-TM

9. Home Office (1996), Sentencing and Supervision of Sex Offenders: A Consultation Document, London: HMSO

10. United Nations, 1989, UN Convention on the Rights of the Child, New York: United Nations

11. Child Protection: Messages From Research, 1995, Department of Health, London: HMSO

12. Lee M, O'Brien R (1995), The Game's Up: Redefining Child Prostitution, The Children's Society

13. Hoggett B, 1993, Parents and Children, London: Sweet and Maxwell

53

Co-ordination of Services

*Report of the
National
Commission of
Inquiry into the
Prevention of
Child Abuse*

- That the interests of children are not the primary concern of any one Government department, leads to conflicts of approach to children' matters

- Locally, the planning and delivery of children's services reflects the lack of co-ordination at national levels

- The UN Convention on the Rights of the Child provides the best single framework within which to develop services for children

6.1   One important structural reason why the prevention of child abuse proves difficult to achieve arises from the way responsibilities of government departments are allocated. Broadly speaking, departments are organised functionally, rather than in terms of the people they are designed to serve. There are long-standing reasons for this practice but the problem, so far as children's services are concerned, is particularly acute at central government level. Responsibilities which affect children and families are distributed across the following departments:

○ Department for Education and Employment (education, the youth service; training; employment; the careers service);

○ Department of the Environment (resource allocation to local authorities; housing);

○ Department of Health (acute and community health services; social services; youth justice);

○ Home Office (criminal justice; magistrates' courts proceedings involving custody and maintenance of children; youth justice; refugees; asylum);

○ Lord Chancellor's Department (family law; court procedure);

○ Department of Social Security (social security);

○ Department of National Heritage (voluntary organisations; sport; leisure);

○ Foreign and Commonwealth Office (implementation of the UN Convention).

In Wales, Scotland and Northern Ireland, some of these functions are carried out by the Welsh, Scottish and Northern Ireland Offices. In Northern Ireland, however, health and social services are combined in one government department which is responsible for integrated regional health and social services boards.

6.2   These wide divisions of responsibility, with the exception of health and social services in Northern Ireland, are replicated at local level; for example, between the various local authority departments, health and police authorities. Lack of co-ordination locally has been criticised by a number of official reports on children's services and by successive child abuse inquiries. The under-fives and 16-19 year olds are particularly affected by split responsibility for services, but the problem is a general one. Many practitioners have, however, succeeded in working effectively across the various disciplines, despite considerable difficulties, and Department of Health guidance in *Working Together*(1) has proved a useful precedent in dealing with the problem of lack of co-ordination.

Report of the
National
Commission of
Inquiry into the
Prevention of
Child Abuse

6.3   Some of the financial consequences for children's services of divided departmental responsibilities are described in Chapter 4. Similar problems are reflected in the legislation concerning to the treatment of children. For example, the approach adopted in the Children Act 1989, with its emphasis on "the best interests of the child", is hardly consistent with that of the increasingly punitive attitude towards young offenders embodied in the Criminal Justice and Public Order Act 1994. Nor is the Department of Health's commitment to reducing teenage pregnancies altogether compatible with the parental right of withdrawing a child from sex education in school. Contrasting perspectives of this kind can determine whether, confronted by the same set of circumstances, different agencies place their emphasis on the needs of an individual child or the needs of children as a group. Such differences in approach are not always avoidable but, if not satisfactorily resolved, can impose barriers to effective collaboration between departments and authorities and the individuals working within them.

6.4   Structurally, three things are evident from this dispersal at national level of responsibility for matters affecting children. First, the interests of children are not the primary concern of any one government department. The statutes which govern their administrative processes tend to operate from cradle to grave. They are not related to specific age-groups: in particular, 0-18 year olds are not perceived as a discrete group. One obvious way of dealing with this problem would be to detach the different responsibilities for children within the different departments and place them within a newly created and distinct children's department. Such a structural change would require far-reaching alterations in the law and the prospect of any government undertaking them must be slight.

6.5   Second, considerable efforts have been made in recent years to deal with the consequences of these diverse responsibilities, local and central, for matters affecting children. The guidelines laid down in *Working Together* are perhaps the most significant example. Yet what these efforts have demonstrated is that, despite the best attempts of those concerned, there are limitations to the approach itself. In the public perception of government's approach to children, there is no clearly defined organisation, individual or group whose primary concern is to examine and report on the operation of legislation and procedures affecting children or provide objective and authoritative responses, for example to judgments on the UK's performance in meeting the requirements of the UN Convention on the Rights of the Child.

6.6   Third, whether there be a radical or an incremental approach to the improvement of children's services, any changes are likely to fail unless they are grounded in children's needs, rather than in the distinct contributions of the different professions and services designed to meet those needs. The functions of these services need not be diluted, but each must pay closer attention to the ways in which the others operate. If children who are especially vulnerable or who have special needs are to be identified and helped as early as possible, the delivery and provision of services must have the child at the centre, not the organisation. The demands that a poorly nourished child, or a child living in a highly stressful family, is likely to make upon health and social services, and the difficulty such a child will have in taking up the opportunities of the education system, must be recognised. The importance of early and correct diagnosis of physical impairment or chronic illness, both in terms of the social and educational functioning of that child and the social functioning of the rest of the family, including siblings' development and potential employment problems of parents, must also be acknowledged. Each professional must be able to recognise the implications the practices of their own discipline will have for other services and disciplines. This does not mean combining different forms of professional expertise into a single discipline but argues for "whole child" awareness to be built into the basic training of all professionals dealing with children, and for post-qualifying training to be inter-disciplinary in its emphasis.

6.7   The report commissioned by the National Children's Bureau (NCB) in 1994, *The Future Shape of Children's Services*(2), considered the problems arising from the present structure and concluded that there is no simple solution. The Commission agrees with that view and with the notion that the key to the "organisational" way forward lies in finding satisfactory answers to three questions:

○   What do children and families want and hope for from the services which are there to support them?

○   What do the hopes of children and families indicate to us about how we should organise our front-line response?

○   How is that front-line response best supported, co-ordinated and led?

The NCB report suggests that the answers to these questions should reflect "appropriate values", which it defines as "those which spring from a commitment to afford all children maximum opportunity for growth and development".

6.8   The fragmented organisation of services, competing interests between providers of services and different professional philosophies and priorities, need to find common ground. The UN Convention on the Rights of the Child, with its coherent set of principles and standards from which to develop services for children, provides what is necessary. The Commission therefore shares the view, expressed by the Children's Rights Development Office, that: "It is important to encourage and support all organisations providing services for children to make an explicit commitment to the principles and standards of the Convention and to use it as a tool for detailed analysis of all their policies and practices to ensure that they comply with its provisions. This process needs to be undertaken collaboratively between local authorities, health authorities and trusts, voluntary agencies and professional bodies to promote a shared understanding of the implications of the Convention's principles for the services that they each provide. The requirement to produce Children's Services Plans provides an ideal opportunity to begin this process."

6.9   The Department of Health recommends the use of the Convention, which it distributed to a limited number of organisations. The Commission believes more should be done to ensure that everyone working with children should be aware of the terms of the Convention, which the UK is committed to upholding.

6.10   The role of voluntary organisations and charities is valuable in bringing children's interests to public and governmental attention. In an important sense, these organisations, large and small alike, are the means by which statutory bodies and the ways in which they function can consistently be held publicly to account. The voluntary sector plays a key role in raising awareness of and meeting the needs of children.

Report of the
National
Commission of
Inquiry into the
Prevention of
Child Abuse

6.11 Nevertheless, despite these varied and, in recent years, increasingly determined efforts to develop a coherent and effectively monitored approach to children's issues, the Commission is convinced, from analysis of the evidence it received, that more needs to be done. As matters now stand, within central and local government the country has a set of co-operative arrangements between agencies whose main concerns range far more widely than the interests of children. From outside government, a number of charitable and research-based agencies produce reports on children's concerns, deal directly with those concerns, assist with inquiries into particular incidents affecting children and, in general, respond to children's needs as best they can. Valuable though these varied efforts are, they suffer from a lack of continuity and consistency. So it is that, despite these efforts, public awareness of the issues affecting children is not as well developed as it should be and pressure to improve legislation or regulatory provisions appropriately is less effectively sustained than the Commission believes is necessary.

6.12 In reaching this conclusion, the Commission was aware of the major responsibilities borne by the Department of Health and the efforts it has made to secure a degree of consistency in the regulatory arrangements of the other departments with responsibilities bearing on the needs of children and families.

6.13 It was with these considerations in mind that the Commission, though not itself established to examine complex issues of government, considered a variety of ways of dealing with the need to co-ordinate measures affecting the interests of children. It looked first at arrangements for co-ordinating children's services in New Zealand, Australia, Norway and the Republic of Ireland. In New Zealand, the Children, Young Persons and Their Families Act (1989) established a Commissioner for Children. In South Australia, an official Children's Interests Bureau was established in 1984. An Act establishing the post of Children's Ombudsman was passed in Norway in March 1981. In the Republic of Ireland, a Minister of State to co-ordinate policy and services in relation to child protection, young homeless, truancy and juvenile justice was appointed in 1994 and a Cabinet sub-committee was established to co-ordinate provision of services for the care and protection of children on a more general basis.

6.14 These examples, though not directly transferable to the UK, caused the Commission to consider how the necessary emphasis on children's needs could be achieved in this country. It concluded that the main ways of doing so would include:

o   the publication of an annual report, laid before Parliament, on the condition of children in the UK. Such a report would incorporate statistical information at present dispersed among a variety of publications. The report would also record legislative changes and, on any matter affecting children, make recommendations for improving services directed towards their needs;

o   an emphasis in such a report on consistent reporting of the incidence of child abuse, in its varied forms, and on the effectiveness or otherwise of measures to prevent it;

o   a separate analysis within and between government departments of expenditure on children's services and a consistent means, also within government, of ensuring that such expenditure was sufficient for the purposes laid down in the relevent legislation and put to best use by the different services with access to it;

*Report of the
National
Commission of
Inquiry into the
Prevention of
Child Abuse*

o   some machinery for ensuring that legislation in any way affecting children could be analysed, its impact on children assessed and, if necessary, its terms adjusted both to protect children's interests and to avoid inconsistency between different legislative measures;

o   as part of wider social policy, some means of looking specifically at issues that cut across departmental responsibilities; for example, exclusion from school, teenage pregnancy and homeless young people and, on the positive side, to consider how new opportunities, again across departmental boundaries, could be provided for the young;

o   a mechanism for ensuring that commitments under our own legislation and under international law or conventions to which the UK is a party are honoured in both the letter and the spirit;

o   a flow of accurate information to the general public on children's issues and the promotion of a "listening to children" approach which the Commission believes is an essential element in improved services to children and the prevention of harm to them.

6.15   In considering this list, the Commission recognised that considerable improvement could be made by a sustained effort to develop systems and structures that already exist and to build on work now carried out by the departments with lead responsibility for children's concerns. On the other hand, the Commission was impressed by the sharper focus to the process of government that had been achieved, in the UK and internationally, when responsibility has been firmly and publicly located in some visible form. The way the issues of disability, equal opportunity, the environment and the Charter movement have developed were instances of this approach.

6.16   The Commission went on to consider the following possibilities:

(a) a strengthened ministerial post at Cabinet level, dealing with children;

(b) a Children's unit within the Cabinet Office, or other centrally placed position;

(c) a Select Committee of the House of Commons or the House of Lords;

(d) a Children's Ombudsman, dealing principally with complaints by or on behalf of children;

(e) one or more Children's Commissioners, established by statute, with clearly defined responsibility for reporting publicly on the state of services to children, with recommendations for improving these when appropriate.

The Commission saw merit in each of these ways of concentrating attention within government or in association with it, on cross-departmental issues. It concluded that priority should be given to a Minister for Children and to one or more Children's Commissioners.

A Minister for Children

6.17   The present position is that the Secretary of State for Health, who is a member of the Cabinet, has responsibility for families and, within that remit, for children. In practice, that responsibility is carried by a ministerial colleague who is not a member of the Cabinet. The Commission suggests that the Secretary of State's title be expanded to Secretary of State for

*Report of the
National
Commission of
Inquiry into the
Prevention of
Child Abuse*

Health and Children and that the minister with specific responsibility for children, currently a parliamentary under-secretary of state, be upgraded and entitled Minister of State and Minister for Children. One function of the minister would be to report on the operation of UK legislation and developments relating to the implementation of the UN Convention on the Rights of the Child. A second function could well be to chair a ministerial committee for co-ordinating policies affecting children, on which all relevant departments should be represented. Finally, it would be important that the minister was afforded the time and support to present children's issues to the public and to promote the "listening to children approach" referred to earlier.

A relationship would have to be developed with ministerial responsibilities in Scotland, Wales and Northern Ireland and with any new ministerial arrangements, for example in relation to a Minister for Women, that might be made in the UK.

> "In the UK, in the absence of one lead government department for children's services, there needs to be clear structures for health and social services, education and the voluntary sector to share plans, examine attitudes and values, and develop practice in a co-ordinated and collaborative manner."
> **NIPPA**

Children's Commissioner(s)

6.18   The various ways of improving children's services, outlined in paragraph 6.14, are not mutually exclusive. On the other hand, with responsibilities for children already complex, additional complexity and expense of time, money and administrative effort has to be avoided. It was principally for these reasons that the Commission suggests that priority should be given to one or more Children's Commissioners, to set alongside revised ministerial responsibilities. In its consideration of the issues, the Commission appreciated the assistance it was afforded by the arguments set out in *Taking Children Seriously* (Calouste Gulbenkian Foundation, 1991)(3)

6.19   A Children's Commissioner would be appointed by the appropriate Secretary of State. He or she would not be a Civil Servant, and therefore would not be "treated as the servant or agent of the Crown". He/she would serve for five years in the first instance, with a renewable contract. The main responsibilities of a Commissioner would be to undertake a number of the functions outlined in paragraph 6.14. In particular:

○   The principal function of a Commissioner would be to promote the welfare of children throughout the geographically defined area of his/her responsibilities.

○   The principal means of doing so would be to give advice on and keep under review the working of legislation affecting children and, either independently or when required by the Secretary of State, to draw up and submit to the Secretary of State proposals for amending legislation affecting children.

○   As part of that responsibility, a Commissioner would periodically report on the degree of compliance achieved with the UN Convention.

○   As the perspective of children and young people themselves is essential to the process of promoting children's rights and welfare, a Commissioner would need to establish advisory groups of children and young people to provide input on a range of different policy areas.

○ Within budgetary limits determined by the Secretary of State, a Commissioner could conduct research or assist, financially or otherwise, any other research into children's issues which appeared necessary or expedient.

○ A Commissioner would be required to publish an annual report to Parliament which would provide regularly updated information about children. Each annual report should include a general survey of developments, during the period under review, in respect of matters falling within the scope of the Commissioner's functions. The report would contain essential statistical information and, where appropriate, be the vehicle for recommending improvements to the methodology of collection and analysis of statistics.

○ A Commissioner could issue codes of practice containing practical advice relating to the conduct of services, statutory or voluntary, for or affecting children. Such a code could simply offer advice, or it could take the form laid down in the Sex Discrimination or Race Relations Acts. Under this form of code "a failure on the part of any person to observe any provision of a Code of Practice shall not of itself render him liable to any proceedings"... but any Code of Practice issued in this way "shall be admissible in evidence"; so such a code has more force than simple advice (Race Relations Act, 1976). In relation to children, a code in either form could recommend or establish standards for delivering children's services.

○ A Commissioner would make a regular review of complaints procedures involving children and used by public authorities.

○ It should be part of a Commissioner's function to report on the extent to which recommendations of child abuse inquiries, past or present, have been or are being implemented.

6.20   An additional task for a Children's Commissioner could be to promote a Charter for Children. The Charter movement, administered by the Charter Unit in the Cabinet Office, was launched in 1991 as a ten-year programme to raise the standard of public services, make them more responsive to the wishes and needs of their users, and give better value for money to the taxpayer.

There are already Charters in existence which include elements relating to children. Although most are written with no age group in mind, the Parents' Charter (revised in 1994) covers the specific needs of children, as does the Charter for Further Education (1993). The Patients' Charter document, *Services for Children and Young People*(4), issued in March 1996, sets out how children's needs are to be met in hospital.

In noting the arrangements for children already made within the Charter movement, the Commission agreed that a Charter bringing together all issues concerned with children for which public services are responsible, could prove a valuable means of focusing attention on children's needs. The purpose of such a Charter would be to require government departments to:

○ set and raise standards of services for children;

○ provide services that meet those standards and are responsive to the wishes and needs of those using them, in particular by requiring those running the services to give good value

Report of the
National
Commission of
Inquiry into the
Prevention of
Child Abuse

for money by ensuring the co-operative planning of services and expenditure across different agencies;

o   listen and act upon the views of children.

Such a Charter should be drawn up in accordance with the principles of the UN Convention on the Rights of the Child.

The relationship between a Children's Charter and any codes of practice (6.19 above) issued by a Commissioner would need to be clear and any duplication of effort avoided.

6.21   Commissions and commissioners already established, for example, the Equal Opportunities Commission, tend to have a jurisdiction that includes several components of the United Kingdom and to operate from a central source through regional offices. This Inquiry formed the view that the different legislation affecting children, and the varied ministerial responsibilities associated with that, required separate Commissioners for England, Scotland, Wales and Northern Ireland.

6.22   The establishment of Commissioners, who would assume some functions now exercised by others, would lead to some reduction in expenditure but, with Commissioners each having a small supporting staff - some 75 in all - would cost over £3 million a year, to which any research and investigation costs would have to be added. Costs on this scale would have to be set against total expenditure on one element of children's services, dealing with child abuse and neglect, estimated to be £1 billion a year (Chapter 4).

> "Local authorities will never feel free to move from their current positions unless strong political leadership is shown which will free up professionals working in the whole child protection network into becoming more flexible and responsive towards families."
> **City of Westminster Area Child Protection Committee**

Co-ordination of services for children locally

6.23   Many of the problems in co-ordinating services for children nationally are reproduced locally. Functional departments, with responsibilities that include issues affecting children as only one part of those responsibilities, find it difficult to spare the time and resources to ensure consistently effective responses to children's needs. Nevertheless, local practitioners and managers generally have a genuine desire to work together across disciplines for the benefit of children and families. The degree of co-operation is clearly better in some places than in others and is susceptible to changes in key personnel with different priorities and motivations. However, even the most committed individuals in all disciplines feel that there are perverse incentives and mechanisms which disrupt and distort these aspirations.

6.24   The main and, in some instances, worsening problems affecting children's services locally include:

o   different and apparently unco-ordinated key indicators, objectives and priorities emanating from central government departments to different local agencies;

*Report of the
National
Commission of
Inquiry into the
Prevention of
Child Abuse*

o different boundaries of, for example, local authorities and health authorities;

o market mechanisms in education which encourage schools to find ways of transferring or excluding disruptive or low achieving pupils;

o local management of schools, which makes it difficult for local education authorities to employ a coherent approach to policy and practice;

o local politicians' and senior managers' lower interest and understanding of children's services than adult services;

o purchasing health authorities that have generalised contracts with health trusts which frequently do not separate and identify investment in children and the expected outcomes;

o the difficulty of involving general practitioners, who are responsible for an increasing proportion of the health budget, in an integrated approach to planning and investment;

o major child care voluntary organisations which tend to organise on a regional basis but, in general, with different regional boundaries; and whose integration with local services tends to be patchy and is strongly influenced by the different priorities and bias of their national organisation;

o many local voluntary organisations that have funding difficulties and are increasingly tied to local authority and health authority purchasing plans.

6.25   Despite the difficulties, in many local areas attempts are being made to develop a common approach to children's services through joint commissioning arrangements between health authorities, social services, education, and other local authority departments. Voluntary organisations and service users should also be involved in the process. Joint commissioning includes strategic planning, agreed quantification of service levels, specification of services, service procurement and provision arrangements, and joint monitoring arrangements. Initiatives that have been taken in some areas include:

o different agencies acquiring a common view of the measurement of need within a locality and ensuring services are planned in relation to the whole population;

o identifying overlaps between resources and the potential for pooling resources and joint developments;

o delivering services in relation to individual needs across agency boundaries.

One of the objectives of joint commissioning is to achieve what users would perceive as a "seamless service". Ideally, from the service users' point of view, all services which are received should be seen as an integrated package, with no need to adjust to the different cultures of the various purchasers and providers involved. Given the range of agencies involved in the prevention of child abuse and the need for collaboration, this is important.

6.26   The introduction of mandatory children's services plans will undoubtedly assist joint commissioning. It is too early to make an informed judgement of their effectiveness, even in areas where they have existed for several years. However, even at this stage, they could be strengthened by specific mandatory requirements, designed to ensure cross-agency collaboration and commitment from, among others, health, education and local authority chief executives. If this cannot be achieved through primary legislation, the Commission hopes it could be achieved through management letter, directive, or a co-ordinated

*Report of the
National
Commission of
Inquiry into the
Prevention of
Child Abuse*

approach from central government in setting key indicators, objectives and targets for different services and local management. The present legal requirements seem to suggest that while social services departments may be held to account for their clearly defined lead and co-ordinating role, other services can evade their responsibilities, because of other priorities, lack of resources or lack of conviction by senior local managers. There is also a marked contrast in the approach to community care planning and monitoring taken by central government with that taken to children's services plans. In addition to the enormous extra investment in community care, formal agreements have been required between health and social services and there has been, in the early stages, intensive and regular monitoring of local arrangements by the Department of Health and the Audit Commission. Effective monitoring must be a stronger feature of local provision of services for children.

6.27   The role and activities of child protection committees and area child protection committees (ACPCs) need to relate more closely to wider strategic planning and the delivery of children's services. Evidence received by the Commission suggests that this is not happening in all areas. The submissions received also indicate differing and conflicting views on the future direction of ACPCs with the following arguments being put forward:

○   that while ACPCs continue to exert a powerful influence on local policies and practices, child protection will continue to predominate over family support services. The scope of ACPCs should therefore be exclusively restricted to child protection concerns.

○   that the role of ACPCs should be narrower rather than wider. As joint commissioning develops that will encompass services for children in need and therefore preventive services. That would be more appropriate and less stigmatising than giving these services a child protection label through being brought within the ambit of ACPCs.

○   that the remit of ACPCs should be broadened to co-ordinate a multi-agency approach to the provision of family support services. This would help ensure that child protection is linked to wider children's services.

○   that most ACPCs have failed to develop strategies for the prevention of child abuse. This may be a reflection of their membership being restricted to child protection agencies. To extend their membership would, however, make the committees even more unwieldy than many are now.

○   that the development of the contract culture and the fragmentation of services has meant that representation on ACPCs is increasingly problematic, with increased representation from purchasers and providers and difficulties in identifying who is representing which local discipline or agency. This has undermined the effectiveness of ACPCs.

Given recent developments of children's services plans and joint commissioning since the establishment of ACPCs and these differing views of their role, the role of ACPCs needs to be considered in the light of the changing planning and commissioning context. Such a review should be conducted by the Department of Health, and the Welsh, Scottish, and Northern Ireland Offices.

6.28   Where there is difficulty in local management of children's services, the supply of suitable and skilled professionals and ancillary staff to work with children in all settings is affected. Work with children appears to have a low status in services such as health and

Report of the
National
Commission of
Inquiry into the
Prevention of
Child Abuse

social services, which cover a range of client groups. It seems remarkable that, within those services, the status and value placed upon those who spend most time with damaged, disturbed or very sick children is lowest of all. Even in a service largely devoted to children, such as education, teachers feel they are held in low regard, particularly those involved with the youngest children, where evidence suggests it is most important to get things right. Most people who work with children, many of whom have long experience and extensive training, seem to conclude that they have little or no influence over the organisational framework and organisational theory within which their service operates. In the statutory social services there is evidence that skilled and gifted staff find that the way children's services are organised is neither conducive to effective professional functioning, nor to their work's survival. As a result there is a marked drift from residential care into fieldwork services and thence into less exposed and less vilified areas of social services. This can mean that skilled staff leave children's services entirely.

6.29 These staffing issues all have major implications for the effectiveness of local organisations designed to meet children's needs. It is essential that an adequate proportion of able people are brought into children's services and that, once trained, they are retained. The work requires intelligence and maturity, good social skills, mental rigour, and compassion, as well special professional skills. To attract such people in greater number implies the need to organise a comprehensive approach to promoting more positive and accurate images of the importance of work with children. It also requires the promotion of a more realistic public appreciation of the sensitivity and risk involved in working with children, and the need to support the people who do this on behalf of all of us. Such an approach implies that society should not unfairly castigate people who work with children and use them as scapegoats for our collective responsibility when things go wrong. Such cultural and attitudinal change can only be orchestrated nationally, but can be supported through local strategy. The local organisation of children's services must be more attuned to the needs of and demands upon practitioners and be managed by senior and middle managers who are well informed and experienced in children's issues.

Recommendations

National

39. Commissioners for Children should be appointed for England, Scotland, Wales and Northern Ireland with terms of reference to include those set out in paragraph 6.19 above.

40. (i) The Secretary of State for Health's title should expanded to Secretary of State for Health and Children.

(ii) The Minister with specific responsibility for children should be upgraded and entitled Minister of State and Minister for Children.

(iii) The principal functions of the Minister should be to report on the operation of UK legislation and developments relating to the implementation of the UN Convention on the Rights of the Child; to chair a ministerial committee for co-ordinating policies affecting children, on which all relevant departments should be represented; to present children's issues to the public; and to promote the "listening to children approach".

Report of the
National
Commission of
Inquiry into the
Prevention of
Child Abuse

41.   Central government should commission an independent review of the effects on multi-agency children's services planning of local management of schools; of the purchasing and provision organisation of the health service; and of the purchaser/provider split in social services. Such a review should consider the implications of differences between the boundaries of local authorities and health authorities, and the effect of small, unitary authorities in Wales, Scotland and parts of England. The review could also compare the experience in Northern Ireland of the creation of combined health/social services trusts.

42.   Central government should initiate a review of technical obstacles to local commissioning, joint budgeting and joint management of children's services, particularly those of a legal or financial nature, and seek to remove them.

43.   The relevant central government departments should not set priorities, targets and key indicators for services affecting children without joint discussions to ensure that they are complementary and will facilitate local collaboration.

44.   Government departments should take a national view of the need to recruit able people to children's services and develop a strategy to attract and retain skilled practioners.

Local

45.   There should be additional measures to ensure all services and those responsible for them participate fully in the planning and delivery of children's services. This should be achieved by changes in primary legislation or through targets, key indicators or other formal requirements of central government departments.

46.   Local children's services planning and provision should be subject to a powerful monitoring and accountability mechanism which could operate from a regional base.

47.   Government should support and promote the development of a comprehensive approach to joint commissioning.

48.   The Department of Health, in co-operation with the Welsh, Scottish and Northern Ireland Offices, should conduct a review of the role and functions of child protection committees.

References

1. Home Office, Department of Health, Department of Education and Science and Welsh Office, 1991, Working Together Under The Children Act 1989: A Guide to Arrangements for Inter-Agency Co-operation for the Protection of Children from Abuse, London: HMSO

2. Jones A, Bilton K, 1994, The Future Shape of Children's Services, London: National Children's Bureau

3. Rosenbaum M, Newell, P, 1991, Taking Children Seriously, London: Calouste Gulbenkian Foundation

4. The Patients' Charter: Services for Children and Young People, Department of Health, 1996

Promoting a Child-Friendly Community

*Report of the
National
Commission of
Inquiry into the
Prevention of
Child Abuse*

- Few people feel willing and able to intervene if they suspect a child is being abused

- Poverty, poor housing and unemployment all make it harder for parents to care for their children properly, yet it is hard for parents to ask for help

- Community groups and neighbourhood initiatives can be effective in supporting families but their strength needs developing

- Children and young people have minimal involvement in the planning of their communities. Their needs and perceptions should be better understood

7.1   Although many children are harmed, sometimes in horrific ways, few people feel responsible for the prevention of child abuse and the protection of children outside their immediate family. While many families experience stresses in bringing up their children, they are generally left to sort out their own problems and find it hard to admit the need for help. People are reluctant to intervene if they are concerned about the wellbeing of someone else's child, often believing that intervention is the role of professionals, particularly social workers. Parents are reluctant to seek help themselves from social services, sometimes believing, wrongly, that it will lead to their children being taken away. Inquiries into deaths following child abuse have shown, in many cases, that although neighbours and other members of the family were aware that a child was being abused, they took no action to stop it. In other cases, neighbours reported their worries but their concerns were ignored. To prevent child abuse the *whole* community needs to be encouraged to take responsibility for the care and protection of children.

67

> "I suffered years of physical and mental abuse at the hands of my mother. The hitting stopped when I was 16 years old but the mental abuse carried on until I was nearly twenty. What has always bothered me more than anything else was the fact that nobody helped me."
> **Letter to the Commission**

7.2   Many influences affect children and their welfare: parents, families, peer groups and communities. Other influences include: industry and commerce; the media; statutory agencies, which regulate a healthy and safe environment, the provision of adequate income and housing and the direct personal services of health, social services and education; private sector agencies; and voluntary and community organisations. Their roles and responsibilities are described in Appendix 12.

The task is to ensure that the whole of society works towards a common purpose: that children are cared for and their needs made a priority. It means a willingness to change and compromise across a wide spectrum embracing families, communities, services and professions. It means developing a shared view of children's needs and how they may be best met, rethinking the place of children in society and persuading all those whose actions affect children to reconsider personal and professional responsibilities.

*Report of the
National
Commission of
Inquiry into the
Prevention of
Child Abuse*

> "I feel the community needs to be more vigilant. If they know child abuse is happening
> then they must report it; this also applies to families. The most important thing is that
> the child's needs are listened to. They also need to have a voice and be counted. The
> community and family need to stand by the child who is being abused."
> **Letter to the Commission**

The Needs of Children and Their Carers

7.3   While children's needs are complex and differ according to age, stage of development
and individual circumstances, there is informed consensus about what is essential to their
healthy development. This includes living conditions and physical care that ensure safety,
good nourishment, adequate shelter and attention to health needs; continuity and security
of significant relationships; love; mental stimulation and learning opportunities; exercise of
reasonable control; and appropriate scope to develop independence.

Parents and primary carers bear the main responsibility for meeting these needs but they
should be supported and assisted in their role. In circumstances where there is serious failure
to meet the child's needs, parental care may need to be formally substituted or
supplemented. However, even when children are removed from their families, most are
subsequently reunited with them. So it is important that parents and primary carers are
helped to carry out their responsibilities. Strategies designed to interrupt the "cycle of
deprivation" are necessary but need to be economically as well as personally effective.

7.4   Many needs of both children and parents should be, and normally are, met within the
family. Increasingly, however, there are many one parent family units while others become
fragmented and restructured as a result of parents separating, through divorce or death, and
the formation of new relationships. This factor alone carries many implications for the
provision of family and community support, and an improved understanding of the
complexities of modern family life is needed by the public and professionals alike.

The Impact of The Community

7.5   The role of the community in supporting families has been highlighted in many
submissions, particularly those from community-based groups. A number pointed to the
weakening of the extended family, along with its advice and support, and the resulting
isolation felt by families in many communities, urban and rural. Based on its experience in
Northern Ireland, Bryson House, a voluntary child care agency, stated in oral evidence to
the Commission: "Child abuse can often be traced to a range of factors in the community,
including financial and economic pressures, isolation and lack of support, age-related
parenting, limited ability, knowledge, mental and physical illness, poor social
circumstances, substance dependency, divorce, remarriage... If these factors are experienced
in a combination, then there is definitely a potential to place the family at risk, and parents
often feel inadequate and become caught in a vicious circle - both of poverty and of
inadequacy."

The impact of unemployment was illustrated by Bob Holman, when describing his work in
Easterhouse, Glasgow, one of the largest council estates in Western Europe: "This has had a

massive economic effect on the area. It has also had a social, almost a gender, effect. The community produced 'macho' men - tough proud men - who now find themselves unemployed for year after year. That produces even more aggression in men, which is sometimes turned inward - to drugs or crime - or externally into physical violence against their family or other men. Not a week goes by without the latest stories of who has done who in, or who is fighting whom."

*Report of the
National
Commission of
Inquiry into the
Prevention of
Child Abuse*

7.6   A number of inter-related factors affect the capacity of the community to care for its children. These include:

(i)   **Social integration or the lack of it.** The vulnerability of socially isolated and mobile families has been a characteristic of many cases that have featured in public inquiries. Such families lack support from family and neighbours, have difficulty in gaining access to supportive services and are unlikely to be known to the agencies that can networks, fewer social contacts, and less support than other parents. A review of research indicates that families in which there is maltreatment tend to suffer from social isolation and are less able to cope with stresses.

(ii)   **Social attitudes and awareness.** Society's attitudes towards children - who are accorded the status of second-class citizens - are generally unhelpful (see Chapter 3). It has been argued by Gil(1) that violence in families is "an inevitable by-product of selfish, competitive and inegalitarian values and of dehumanising, authoritarian, and exploitative social structures and dynamics which permeate many contemporary societies" and, further, that abuse cannot be overcome through "administrative, legal technical and professional measures which leave social values, structures and dynamics unchanged". Whatever the cause, society's attitudes and perceptions need to be altered through education and public awareness campaigns.

(iii)   **Imbalances of power** reflected in social attitudes. Some observers conclude that child abuse is an inevitable result of unequal power between adults and children, and between men and women. This view was expressed in many submissions to the Commission and was seen as particularly important where domestic violence and racial abuse occur. Inequality of power also exists in the wider community, between service users and professionals, as well as between different professional disciplines, and between white people and black and ethnic minority groups.

(iv)   **Ill health and disability,** which increase children's vulnerability to abuse. The Council for Disabled Children noted: "Parents of children with disabilities or other special needs are no more likely than other parents to abuse their children. *But* the additional responsibilities (and frequent lack of support) may make such families and children more at risk of abuse - and pressures of care may make families and professional carers hesitant to voice suspicions when there may be no obvious alternative source of help." The National Association for the Protection from Sexual Abuse of Adults and Children with Learning Difficulties (NAPSAC) argued that vulnerability may result from the nature of the disability, the isolation experienced by both the children and their families, the widespread prejudice against people with disabilities, and a lack of support services. The pressures faced by *all* parents are often amplified for parents of children with disability.

(v)   **Socio-economic factors.** A recurring theme in evidence to the Commission has been the effects of poverty on families' capacity to care for their children and on the ability

69

of professionals to work successfully with them, when that work is undermined by the consequences of poverty.

It is beyond the Commission's remit to examine and make proposals for changes to social structures. It wishes, however, to endorse concerns expressed in evidence about the impact of poverty, poor housing and unemployment upon children and their families. A significant number of children suffer material deprivation and, because their parents are often stressed, tired and ill, they may suffer emotional and intellectual deprivation, and sometimes abuse. The Commission urges all political parties to give high priority to stopping the waste of individual and national potential which such deprivation causes. An extension of day-care provision that allows parents to work would one be measure that would lift large numbers of children out of poverty. This is particularly important for single parents.

(vi) **Patterns of employment,** which affect how parents care for children. Alma Erlich's study for the Commission, (published in Volume 2 of this Report), shows that in the past decade there has been a 16 per cent increase in the number of working women and that 71 per cent of women of working age in the UK are now economically active. Most of this increase is in part-time work. During the 1980s, the employment of mothers of pre-school-age children almost doubled. Today, British men work the longest hours of all fathers in the European Union: for highly paid, specialised, professional and managerial workers, the job demands long hours; low-paid workers find it difficult to reduce their working hours because of financial pressures and insecurity of employment. While work undoubtedly brings additional income into the home, these patterns of employment also impose strains on family life. For example, over the past two decades there has been a sharp decline in the time parents spend with and caring for their children, and many feel guilty or frustrated about it.

On working parents and alternative care, research findings are inconclusive but suggest that an important factor affecting children is the quality and stability of the alternative care. As part of her study, Erlich reviews employers' approaches to "family-friendly" policies and practices. While there has been an increase in child-care provision in the past decade, it is still available only to a minority of employees. While "family-friendly" policies may benefit employers and parents, their effects on children have not been the focus of attention and remain unclear. The Commission supports the development of employment policies that will take account of children's needs.

> "Exhausted parents have very few resources to handle the interpersonal dynamics between themselves and their children...We must begin by thinking differently about what we consider to be of national importance and by recognising that children and their carers should be a high priority. This will require government backing and investment in education of employers across the board of industry and commerce that there is much they can do to reduce the stress on their employees who are parents."
> **Newpin**

7.7   The factors described above demonstrate the range of influences on the care and protection of children. A common theme in evidence to the Commission was expressed by the Child and Woman Abuse Studies Unit, University of North London: "Rather than simply training those who work with children to identify 'signs and symptoms' we ought to be building environments and contexts which enable help seeking." Similarly, the National Children's Bureau suggested that "professional responsibilities should be as much about nurturing community and family-based preventive strategies as about child protection procedures". These statements reflect the overall strategy proposed by the Commission: supporting families and communities, developing healthy and "resilient" children, and encouraging public knowledge and attitudes towards children which help to prevent child abuse.

Empowering Communities

7.8   A key element in submissions from families is the strength that is derived from community support, a point backed by evidence from research and professionals in the field. This implies that the most effective strategies to improve family and neighbourhood support are likely to involve partnerships in local communities. Pilot projects have shown three areas on which to focus: family support; social environment; and partnership, participation and ownership. Work in the USA also suggests that primary prevention should be centred on communities and neighbourhoods, and that establishing informal networks is one key to preventing child abuse. Evidence has also pointed to the advantages to children of approaches designed to enhance the quality of life of entire communities. In these activities voluntary groups have considerable experience and a key role to play.

7.9   A decent community infrastructure is a fundamental need of children and their families. This includes adequate housing, safe play areas, accessible schools and health care, a clean environment, transport, access to shops, reduction in fear of crime, and facilities for entertainment and meetings. Housing, public health, leisure and environmental services and the police all have an essential role in removing or reducing the environmental problems that put families under stress and which, in themselves, can be abusive. These services, therefore, must play an active role in local children's services plan. A strong theme, in evidence from parents and community organisations, was that people wanted to have more active involvement in running their communities. Sometimes direct help may be needed, such as the skills of a community worker, to facilitate their efforts. The efforts of community groups must be supported by government action to address wider structural issues. Both are needed.

7.10   The role of self help in the community is often overlooked. Many survivors of child abuse and their families who contacted the Commission referred to the benefits they derived from meeting people with similar experiences. This helped them to understand that their problems were not unique, to share information, work through possible solutions, come to terms with the abuse they suffered, and to develop strategies for gaining access to services. Many self-help groups expressed feelings of isolation, and rely on only a few active members. Some have closed through a lack of resources. Where groups are effective, they can be important not only in supporting members but also in campaigning and educating professionals about their needs. Statutory and voluntary agencies should consider how these groups can be supported and involved in the development of local strategies. There are large parts of the country without such survivor groups. The Commission therefore recommends the establishment of a national body for survivors, to act as an information

Report of the
National
Commission of
Inquiry into the
Prevention of
Child Abuse

exchange, provide support to member groups and individuals, perhaps through a 24 hour helpline, and undertake developmental work.

> "The majority of the actions of agencies that focus on child protection and prevention are carried out without the benefit of consumer feedback. If prevention is to work, children and their families must be involved in all aspects of its planning and implementation."
> **National Institute for Social Work**

7.11   In order to make full use of community resources, accessible information is necessary. This was highlighted in many submissions. People do not know what help is available and where to get it. Legislation places a duty on local authorities to publish information on services they and, where appropriate, others provide and to ensure that it reaches those who would benefit from it. The study *Implementing Services for Children in Need under the 1989 Children Act*, by Aldgate and Tunstill, indicates that so far, "publicity efforts are not very far advanced. Most of the publicity mentioned was in pamphlet form and written in English." A similar conclusion was reached by the Social Services Inspectorate (SSI) following its inspection of family support services in eight local authorities between December 1993 and March 1995. It said: "In the majority of authorities the prevailing picture was a lack of effective publicity for prospective service users and of information for the general public. It appeared to be due to a mixture of reasons: fears that it might encourage an avalanche of needs which could not be met; there not being the services to advertise; and there not being a tradition to advertise services and provide information on what was available." Encouragingly, there were exceptions: one authority, for example, had developed information promotion as part of its "customer first policy" and was distributing a wide range of well-presented and helpful material.

Greater priority should be given to the dissemination of easily understood information on services, not only to parents but also to children and young people. This is a task for both statutory and voluntary agencies that would benefit from close collaboration between agencies and service users. It is not sufficient, however, to rely on printed material: a proactive approach, involving information shops which people can easily visit as they would a citizens advice bureau, is needed.

Child-friendly Communities

> What is the thing you would most like to change about grown ups?
> "Listen to us when we have something to say and not just ignore us much of the time."
> **11 year old boy, in Commission Questionnaire**

7.12   The need to listen to and understand children and young people has been emphasised in much evidence to the Commission. This is important in preventing child abuse: children are more likely to seek help from adults if they have established a good relationship, built on respect, and if they think they will be listened to. Children's views of events and situations are different from those of adults. If their needs are to be met, it must be recognised that children are a distinct group with their own expectations and requirements. Adults must

Report of the
National
Commission of
Inquiry into the
Prevention of
Child Abuse

understand the child's world and how it operates, and develop child-friendly communities. Consulting adults about children's needs and relying on adult re-interpretation is not enough - children should have a voice or direct input into all areas of their lives and decisions affecting them. This rarely happens. (See Article 12 of the UN Convention on the Rights of the Child, Appendix 4).

> What is the thing you would most like to change about grown ups?
>
> "Should try and see things from a child's point of view more often instead of an adult's point of view."
>
> **11 year old girl, in Commission Questionnaire**

7.13   To build communities that are supportive towards children, effective ways must be found of canvassing their views and training adults to listen to what they are saying. Here, a *child-friendly index* would help. The index is a systematic examination of how children and young people define and describe aspects of their lives in any given situation. Consultation with children, and a recognition of their right to represent their views and have them taken into account, would underpin the index. The Commission proposes that a child-friendly index should be integral to local and national decision-making.

Supporting Communities to Prevent Child Abuse

73

7.14   In planning and delivering services, all relevant agencies should give greater priority to meeting the needs of children, their families and communities. The Commission recommends that central government, local authorities and health authorities should develop explicit strategies to facilitate stronger and permanent neighbourhood support and service networks. Such support should include neighbourhood "drop-in" centres and 24 hour telephone helplines, for adults and children. Health and local authorities should report to central government on community development proposals aimed at promoting and supporting a better childhood for all children.

> "Teachers, Sunday school teachers, scout leaders and other youth workers, counsellors - all should be taught to look and listen, so that they can recognise likely victims of abuse... BEFORE there's a complaint."
>
> **Letter to the Commission**

7.15   In formulating plans to support communities, consideration should be given to the training and support for community groups to help them deal with issues relating to child abuse. Cases of children being abused while taking part in community initiatives, including sports and youth activities, highlight the need for training of management-committee members, staff and others in key positions in voluntary and community groups, including religious organisations. Training should cover: awareness of the needs of children and parents; possible signs of child abuse; child protection procedures; and the dangers of failing to assess adults who work with children. Parent organisations to whom such groups may be

Report of the
National
Commission of
Inquiry into the
Prevention of
Child Abuse

affiliated, social services departments, councils of voluntary service, and local authority voluntary sector co-ordinators should promote such training. Evidence to the Commission indicates that a number of community and religious groups are responding appropriately. However, given the size of the community sector, there continues to be a need to provide training to key staff and volunteers first.

Education in the Community

> "Ways and means must be found to enable parents to take advantage of training, in whatever guise, to enable them to value their role as parents and in turn to value and respect their children."
> **Wales Pre School Play Group Association**

7.16   Education has a key role in influencing attitudes. It is not confined to the years of compulsory school attendance or to the further or higher education that may follow. The role of adult and continuing education, both statutory and voluntary, in broadening the understanding and promotion of good parenting, through parenting programmes is particularly important.

7.17   The Commission agrees with the view, expressed by Pugh, De'Ath, and Smith in *Confident parents, confident children*(4), that parent education is a life-long process, the main elements of which should be to develop parents' self-awareness and self-confidence in supporting and nurturing their children. The means by which that process takes place changes during the course of an individual's life. Programmes such as Homestart and Newpin, and some local authority services for under eight-year-olds, are aimed specifically at families where parenting problems may be arising. That approach deserves support. If a child has early experience of parenting that is at least reasonably satisfactory, he or she is less likely to develop behavioural and other problems during adolescence and is more likely to develop into a good parent.

> "Parenting is beset with difficulties and problems as well as with rewards: our belief is that society at large should be encouraged to appreciate that it is perfectly acceptable to ask for help in the resolution of all parenting problems before there is any need for crisis intervention."
> **Exploring Parenthood**

7.18   Parenting programmes emphasise the primary role of parents in children's upbringing. Most parents at some stage welcome advice but others need systematic help in carrying out their responsibilities adequately. Such help is only patchily available. As Gillian Pugh of the National Children's Bureau said: "Parent education and support is the concern of many but is often the responsibility of none."(5)

7.19   A range of people and organisations have developed parent education programmes. Most start from a view of what constitutes satisfactory parenting. "The ingredients of 'good

*Report of the
National
Commission of
Inquiry into the
Prevention of
Child Abuse*

enough parenting" were expressed by the College of Paediatrics and Child Health (CPCH), and broadly agreed by others who gave evidence to the Commission, as:

(i) Continuous loving care and commitment from parents or parent-figures;

(ii) Consistent, non-vindictive limit-setting;

(iii) The provision of opportunity for development through a range of experiences and education."

The CPCH emphasised that all three aspects of parenting were essential.

7.20   Evidence to the Commission placed emphasis on parenting at different stages. Apart from the home, school was seen by many as the place where the foundations of parenting skills should properly be laid. Encouraging by example good adult-child relationships and establishing sound behaviour policies that inhibit bullying, anti-social or racist attitudes are means by which the informal curriculum helps pupils to learn the skills that will serve them well as parents. The ethos of which these characteristics are an important part, is for each school to develop in its own way.

7.21   Schools can also teach skills directly related to parenting. The National Curriculum(6) is subject-based but has been developed in a way that enables issues such as child development and personal and social education to be covered across the curriculum, although there is no requirement that these issues be dealt with systematically, or at all.

7.22   In the Commission's view, the preamble to the Education Reform Act of 1988 should be given practical expression, so far as preparing young people for the "responsibilities and experiences of adult life" is concerned. (1) This would involve strengthening the whole approach to personal and social education, in ways set out in, for example, the report of the Elton Committee of Enquiry into discipline in schools(6).

7.23   The link between parenting styles and the subsequent development, healthy or otherwise, of children is well established and was constantly re-stated in evidence received.

7.24   A country-wide effort is now needed to establish effective, non-stigmatising parent education and, having done so, to move towards making access to such education generally available. Views differ about the age at which parenting education should start and where; for example, whether it should take place in school, in classes for parents and prospective parents, in the workplace where it could be linked to such schemes as management training, or in all of the above. The NSPCC, however, suggested that before it could be made universally available, "The Government make interim provision by enabling family life skills to be offered through nurseries and school for parents of children attending".

7.25   In the Commission's view, parent education should include:

o   **improving understanding of child development.** It is already part of the curriculum in many secondary schools but the College of Paediatrics and Child Health noted that those in clinical work were "frequently surprised by the degree to which parents were ignorant of the way normal young children behave". Misinterpretation of, for example, bedwetting and feeding problems as deliberate naughtiness can lead to punishment and children reacting in ways that further infuriate their parents.

Report of the
National
Commission of
Inquiry into the
Prevention of
Child Abuse

○ **a focus on the positive aspects of parenting, rather than emphasising what not to do.** With comparatively rare exceptions, families wish to do well by their children and are more likely to respond to constructive suggestions. Skills that have benefits outside the home might also be included, such as how to manage time and stress, and resolve conflict. It is also important for children to learn such skills.

○ **the psychological and emotional factors of parenting, particularly in classes for prospective parents.**

7.26   For parenting education to make an important contribution to preventing child abuse it must be generally available and subject to quality control:

○ general availability suggests that intervention by statutory bodies may be necessary, even though voluntary organisations have so far been largely responsible for developing parent education.

○ quality control requires some form of registration for those undertaking parent education and for the courses to be subject to approved inspection arrangements.

7.27   What emerges from the evidence is that there is a long way to go to provide education for parenthood that is systematic, universally available and of high quality. The Commission therefore recommends that voluntary agencies co-operate to put joint proposals to the Schools Curriculum and Assessment Authority and the Department of Health, inviting them to co-ordinate central and local government's response.

76

> "By far the best thing is watching my children laughing with me and even at me at times, and being able to hug them without feeling ill at ease and letting them know I love them and will always be there for them. Hopefully by having a loving and open relationship with them, I can protect them from systematic abuse like I suffered."
> **Letter to the Commission**

The media

7.28   The media has a key role to play in informing public debate. All types of media have helped raise awareness of children's issues, including abuse, through news reports, campaigns, editorial comment, features, documentaries, advice columns, helplines, chat shows and radio and television fiction. Parts of the media have helped to create a positive climate in which victims feel more able to disclose their abuse and seek help. However, children's issues, including child abuse, are not always handled in a sensitive and informed manner. Inevitably, those working in the media share the prejudices and assumptions of the wider community, including a natural tendency to disbelieve the nature and extent of child abuse. One-dimensional portrayals of children as either innocent or monstrous, often seen in news coverage, may reflect commonly held perceptions of children. Quickly moving news coverage may reflect and reinforce dominant attitudes and often over-simplify complex matters, whereas prepared and researched material is more likely to inform and to stimulate and challenge beliefs and assumptions. The coverage of child abuse is neither easy nor comfortable. Journalists and broadcasters tend in any case to believe that the public, other than in the most sensational cases, quickly loses interest in stories about abuse.

Report of the
National
Commission of
Inquiry into the
Prevention of
Child Abuse

7.29   While the media might reflect society's attitude to children, it also needs to take a more balanced and sympathetic view of children. Children's views seldom feature in news or factual reporting, even when the topic concerns them; this reinforces a popular view that children have little worthwhile to contribute. In line with its belief in promoting "listening to children", the Commission recommends that where children have an interest in a topic, the media should take their views into account. There have been some interesting developments in this area with, for example, Children's Express, a news agency set up in London in 1995 and run by children and young people, securing publication of stories in the national media from a young person's perspective.

News coverage

7.30   News coverage of child abuse has improved in the recent past and this is welcome. There are examples of responsible news coverage and comment being instrumental in identifying problems and securing action. They include the influence of newspapers in gaining a judicial review of the management of children's homes in north Wales and the exposure of unacceptable practices in children's homes in Islington, north London. However, news coverage tends to be dominated by details of extreme and/or rare cases, rather than exploring the issues involved. Less dramatic but equally damaging cases are seldom reported, which leads to inaccurate or misleading impressions of child abuse and child abusers.

7.31   The Commission supports the view of Dame Elizabeth Butler Sloss(7) in the Cleveland Report that the media generally, and editors in particular, have a responsibility "to observe moderation and have an awareness that the impact of the reporting, on television or radio or in the newspapers, can have a disproportionate influence upon those caught up in such a crisis and may create uncertainty, confusion and injustice". Many editors and journalists are aware of their responsibilities and strive to adhere to codes of good practice. There are examples of stories being withheld when the interests of children are in jeopardy but there are still too many cases when important needs of children are subordinated to those of the news agenda.

7.32   There are a number of ways in which the Commission feels that the news media, without compromising its main functions, could contribute towards the development of better informed and more sympathetic attitudes in society towards all children. This would mean acceptance by the news media that it needs to take exceptional care in reporting these issues. The Commission welcomes the new BBC producers' guidelines which include a chapter on working with, and reporting on, children. Public and professional bodies with formal responsibilities for children's services must also recognise that they should assist this process.

7.33   Many journalists have little knowledge about abuse and rely on outdated stereotypes and their own misconceptions. In wishing to encourage greater editorial responsibility and more balanced coverage, the Commission recommends that journalists' training should include issues of children and child abuse. In this the Michigan "Victims and the Media" programme might usefully be adapted for UK training. The programme is designed for both student and working journalists, and is intended to improve the skills needed to approach

Report of the
National
Commission of
Inquiry into the
Prevention of
Child Abuse

and interview victims of violence and to develop an understanding of the effects of trauma on individuals and their families.

7.34 Journalists would benefit from an independent and authoritative source of information on child abuse and children's issues. While at present a number of organisations attempt to provide this - such as the Association of Directors of Social Services, the Association of Directors of Social Work, the British Association of Social Workers, and children's charities - they do not have the necessary resources. The Commission therefore proposes that the Children's Commissioners (see Chapter 6) should have a key role in providing context to and informed comment on children's issues. There is also a need, however, for better briefing about actual cases or, where this is not possible for legal reasons, for a readily available source of background information and clarification of the issues surrounding those cases. This needs to be organised by the responsible agencies or by representative bodies on their behalf.

7.35 Media coverage of individual cases can be extremely damaging to the child concerned. In any proceedings in any court, the court can prohibit identification of minors, under section 39 of the Children and Young Persons Act 1933: this means that they can be identified unless the court prohibits it. Under section 49 of the same Act, those appearing in youth courts may not be identified. The relevant authorities - the Press Complaints Commission, Independent Television Commission, and the BBC - have, through their codes of practice, taken action to prevent "jigsaw identification", whereby it is possible to identify a child by piecing together information provided by different media sources. However, the Commission is concerned that the regulation only covers children involved in police enquiries or court proceedings concerning sexual offences. In other situations, for example where there are no enquiries or court proceedings, a child is unprotected and may be identified by the media. It recommends, therefore, that when covering news stories, the publicity of which will have a serious effect on a specific child, the media should have a responsibility to consider the best interests of the child and that failure to do so would be grounds for complaint to the relevant body.

Other coverage of abuse

7.36 Features, documentaries, agony and advice columns, and advice lines make a positive and helpful contribution to public education about children and child abuse. The tone, role, and approach of such initiatives are sensitive and relevant to families' needs. (See Appendices 14-16). There has been an impressive documentary output on child abuse in recent years, although there is a tendency to cover sensational aspects (see paragraph 7.41).

Of the thousands of letters sent each week to popular newspapers, a significant proportion concern relationship problems resulting from abusive experiences. Problem page editors and advice columnists told the Commission that they were often the first port of call for people seeking help. Similarly, helplines that are open after some programmes consistently generate a large, sometimes overwhelming, response. An inability to respond to such calls can create problems for both caller and helpline. The Commission therefore proposes that when press, radio or television deals with child abuse, telephone numbers should be given only for appropriate helplines and other support, if possible approved by the Telephone

*Report of the
National
Commission of
Inquiry into the
Prevention of
Child Abuse*

Helplines Association. It is potentially damaging to direct callers to sources that do not have the relevant experience or capacity to deal with the demand.

7.37   Advice provided through the media often directs inquirers exclusively to voluntary sector services. This may not always be appropriate, although callers often seek advice that is independent of statutory agencies. It can reinforce a view that the statutory sector deals only with extreme cases requiring legal action. It would be useful for advice columnists and bodies representing statutory services to consider together how and in which circumstances people should be referred to statutory services.

7.38   The Commission recognises the important contribution of factual broadcasting in broadening the public's understanding of issues and providing information and education about parenting, relationships, and child development. However, these programmes generally do not attract large audiences. It is inevitable that the demands of the increasingly competitive market place will restrict the supply of these types of programmes. TLC (The Learning Channel), for example, has already phased out family programming, in order to concentrate on hobby and leisure series. It is essential that such programmes continue to be available to the whole population. Those channels which carry further education programmes should be encouraged to include parenting, and the prevention of and response to child abuse, as part of their existing commitment to educational broadcasting.

7.39   Television and radio fiction often deal with children's issues and child abuse in convincing, interesting and more sustained ways than is possible with factual coverage. Such portrayals can convey the nuances, dilemmas and depths of pain and distress experienced by children and their families, and the professionals who work with them. Coverage of child abuse in television fiction is common. The Glasgow Media Group, for example, identified sexual abuse in 34 soap operas, plays and dramas in a 12-month period in 50 separate episodes on network television. This coverage can generate an identification with the characters, increase public awareness, and help correct misleading impressions. It is important that producers make every effort to provide an accurate picture of child abuse and responses to it. It is also important to portray images of good parenting.

The impact of the media on behaviour

7.40   The possible impact of the media on behaviour - both children's and adults' - was raised in a number of submissions to the Commission. Strong concerns were expressed about the negative effects of television, videos, and films on children's socialisation. Commonsense suggests that violence on film can increase tolerance of unacceptable behaviour, but the research evidence is inconclusive. The Commission therefore supports the view that, for *most* children, media images play a minor role in influencing their behaviour and attitudes. Generally, children's viewing is not of violent, anti-social or destructive programmes. Violence in the home and bullying at school provide a more plausible explanation of much of the violent behaviour in children than television - one that is rarely included in research.

Broadcasting regulatory bodies provide clear guidelines covering the portrayal of children and programme content at times when children are likely to be viewing and these are

79

Report of the
National
Commission of
Inquiry into the
Prevention of
Child Abuse

adequate. Regulatory bodies should monitor complaints relating to children and report on them separately. It is also important to provide guidance for parents and carers on how to assess appropriate children's viewing and how to help their children's gain most value from the media.

The media and professional practice

7.41   A recurring theme in evidence from professionals has been a suggestion that the media takes a hostile attitude towards their handling of children's issues, particularly social workers' involvement in child abuse cases. This mutual suspicion is long established, and while relations have improved in recent years there is still a long way to go. Social workers feel that they are singled out, more than other professionals, for critical comment. They also believe that the media portrays a misleading picture of their work and the reasons for particular courses of action. The Commission is concerned that, if coverage is biased, the public could gain an inaccurate impression of social work and child protection agencies which will undermine efforts to prevent abuse. Journalists and broadcasters, *and* social services departments and their staff, need to take responsibility for this media coverage. While there has been inaccurate reporting, social services departments have often been poor at handling media relations. The Commission recommends:

o   social services and social work departments should appoint dedicated public relations staff, to become more effective in their media relations and fulfil their duty to increase public understanding of child abuse;

o   local authorities should recognise the importance of this work, fund it appropriately, and remove bureaucratic and political barriers to a professional and specialist public relations exercise in social services;

o   all relevant professionals, including social workers, should be better trained and supported in their media relations;

o   area child protection committees and their members should become more proactive in developing and funding local public relations functions as part of strategies for protecting children and preventing child abuse;

o   national associations representing social services directors, chief education officers, health authorities and trusts, and local authorities should, with central government departments, consider how best to provide a central source of information and informed comment on children's services, to prevent an information vacuum when local authorities are unable to comment.

Advertising

7.42   Information is conveyed through all images and descriptions and it is not possible to separate messages intended to be educational from those that are not. There are concerns about the portrayal of children in both commercial and charity fundraising advertising. However, advertising is regulated according to a strict code of practice and there are few complaints about the portrayal of children. The Commission, therefore, does not advocate change but stresses the need for vigilance in enforcing the Advertising Standards Authority and the Independent Television Commission Codes of Practice. Complaints relating to

Report of the
National
Commission of
Inquiry into the
Prevention of
Child Abuse

children and advertising should be monitored and reported. Charities should reassess how they portray children and conduct research among abused child and adult victims as well as potential donors. Money raised through images of helpless victims cannot justify damage to the very people they are intended to help.

Public education

7.43   Evidence to the Commission suggests that public education campaigns could play an important role in raising awareness about and preventing the abuse of children. There have been some national campaigns on child abuse run by charities, but never over long periods. Some seem to have increased public awareness, although it is less clear whether they have changed behaviour long-term, partly because there has been no long term evaluation. Locally based "zero tolerance" campaigns have raised awareness, changed stereotypes and encouraged women to report domestic violence, mainly against women but also against children. Using positive images of women and children, Edinburgh District Council's 1992 Tolerance Campaign aimed to generate debate and focus on strategies to prevent violence against women and children, highlighting the need for adequate support services and legal protection for victims. The campaign followed local consultation and included posters displayed on billboards and indoor sites. Local and national media covered the campaign. Quantitative research indicated a high level of recognition (64 per cent) of the campaign and support for it, with eight out of ten those who were aware of it feeling positive. The campaign has since been taken up by more than 30 local authorities. Such campaigns are comparatively inexpensive to run and the involvement of local communities marks an innovative and effective approach to public education which should be encouraged.

81

7.44   As part of the national strategy, the Commission recommends an integrated public education campaign. At national level, central government should demonstrate a commitment to protecting the interests of children and set a clear agenda. Any campaign should aim to increase awareness of the general needs of children; to promote the idea that everyone is responsible for safeguarding the welfare of children; to raise awareness of the nature and extent of abuse; to improve knowledge of the signs and symptoms of abuse; and to encourage everyone to take appropriate action. Local commitment and support are essential. Any successful campaign will increase the demand for effective services for children. This will have considerable implications for social services, police, and other support services, especially if confidence in these services is to be created and maintained.

When you are concerned about a child

"To this day I am haunted by the thought of how many little girls had their childhoods ruined by this evil man ... Nobody confronted him or reported him ... Most of my nightmares are caused by the fact that nothing was done after my ordeal to prevent him from doing it again to others."
Letter to the Commission

7.45   People need to know what to do if they are concerned about a child. Evidence to the Commission indicates that many people are both unwilling to intervene and do not know

*Report of the
National
Commission of
Inquiry into the
Prevention of
Child Abuse*

what they should do. For public education to be successful, policy-makers, professionals and members of the community must agree on the key messages. Those messages should include agreement on the signs and symptoms of harm to which people should be alert.(8) The Commission recommends that central government should generate debate about what individuals should do if they are concerned about a child, and proposes a blueprint for action (see box).

What to do if you are concerned about a child

■ Get to know the signs that suggest that a child may be being harmed.

■ Make time to listen to children.

■ Take action if you think a child is being harmed - if you feel able, ask the parent or carer what is happening.

■ If a family is under stress, offer them help and support if appropriate.

■ If you are still worried or feel unable to get involved, contact someone who can give you further advice, such as: social services, the police, the NSPCC Child Protection Helpline.

■ Don't give up. Remember that it may not just be the one child who is being harmed but others as well.

82

Recommendations

49.   Central government, local authorities and health authorities should recognise and measure the benefits and costs of support for children and families and develop explicit strategies to facilitate stronger and permanent neighbourhood support and service networks. This should be achieved through:

(i)   developing and co-ordinating the statutory services (particularly, health, social service and education) to stimulate and develop community sensitivity and support, self-help and peer support.

(ii)   co-ordinated, reliable and long-term funding of voluntary and community sector activity.

(iii)   developing and co-ordinating local and national helplines and local drop-in centres for children, parents, carers and victims, to ensure comprehensive coverage and most effective use of resources. National and local government should consider the general funding and development of these services. Provision of these services should be incorporated into children's services plans.

50.   Health and local authorities should report to central government on their proposals for community development designed to promote and support a better childhood for all children.

51.   Individuals in key positions in voluntary and community groups, including religious organisations, should receive training to raise awareness of the needs of children and parents, child protection procedures, and the dangers of not vetting adults wishing to work with children.

*Report of the
National
Commission of
Inquiry into the
Prevention of
Child Abuse*

52.   A national body for survivors should be established to act as an information exchange, provide support to member groups and individuals, perhaps through a 24-hour helpline, and undertake developmental work.

Child-friendly employment policies

53.   Employers' organisations and trades unions should initiate a review of employment patterns with a view to making them compatible with parenting and family life.

Parenting education

54.   To ensure delivery of high-quality, universally available parenting education, voluntary agencies should co-operate to put joint proposals for in-school and post-school education to: (a) the Schools Curriculum and Assessment Authority and (b) the Department of Health, inviting them to co-ordinate the government's response, including that of the Department of Education and Employment, and that of Local Education Authorities.

The media

55.   Journalists' training should include child abuse issues, to improve the coverage of child abuse cases and editorial content.

56.   The Children's Commissioners should be the principal source of informed comment on children's issues so that the media can have the authoritative and independent source of information that is currently lacking.

57.   In covering news stories in which children feature, the media should have a obligation to consider the child's best interest. Failure to do so should be grounds for complaint to the relevant authority.

58.   Media regulations should separately monitor and report on coverage of, and complaints about coverage of, children's issues.

59.   Key professionals within social services and social work departments should be trained in media relations and dedicated public relations staff available to each department.

60.   A public education campaign should be developed aimed at raising awareness: of the needs of children in general, including the nature of child abuse, and of the appropriate action to take when concerned about a child. Such a campaign should be initiated by central government and the proposed Minister for Children, and supported by local communities and agencies.

83

References

1. Gil D.G, Confronting societal violence by recreating communal institution, *in* Child Abuse and Neglect, 3, 1-7, 1979.

2. Algate J, Tunstill J, 1995, Making Sense of Section 17: a study for the Department of Health, Implementing Services for Children in Need within the Children Act 1989, London: HMSO

*Report of the
National
Commission of
Inquiry into the
Prevention of
Child Abuse*

3. Social Services Inspectorate, 1996, Children in Need: Report of an SSI Inspection of Social Services Departments' Family Support Services 1993/95, London: Department of Health

4. Pugh G, De'Ath E, Smith C, 1994, Confident Parents, Confident Children: policy and practice in parent education and support, London: National Children's Bureau

5. ibid

6. Discipline in schools: Report of the Committee of Enquiry, chaired by Lord Elton, 1989, Department of Education and Science and Welsh Office, London: HMSO

7. Butler-Sloss DBE Rt Hon Lord Justice, 1988, Report of the Inquiry into Child Sexual Abuse in Cleveland 1987, London: HMSO

8. A number of checklists of the signs and symptoms of child abuse exist for professionals from different disciplines and for members of the public - see, for example: Department of Health, 1988, Protecting Children: a guide for social workers undertaking a comprehensive assessment, London: HMSO; various NSPCC leaflets for parents.

Chapter 8

Children at the Centre: Creating a Child-Centred Professional Response

- The emphasis in professional practice is on taking action *after* abuse has occured rather than on preventing it

- Some services are stigmatising, inaccessible, and only available to those considered to be at greatest risk

- The child protection system concentrates on investigations so that the social and welfare needs of children and their families are often not sufficiently considered

- The manner in which sexual offenders are dealt with leaves children at risk

- Training and support for all professionals and volunteers working with children do not give sufficient emphasis to preventive work, responding to abuse, and working in partnership with children and families

8.1   Parents have primary responsibility for the care of their children, yet many families face stress and problems at some stage and require support. Where abuse has occurred, a child may be so damaged that professional intervention is essential to protect him or her from further harm and to assist healing. A wealth of research, particularly brought together in the Department of Health's *Messages from Research*(1), demonstrates that, overwhelmingly, professionals respond to child abuse by intervening *after it* has occurred, when the prime concern becomes investigating the allegations and deciding whether the child's name should be placed on a child protection register. Research also indicates that for both children and their families, the experience of the child protection system(2) (see Appendix 17) is often negative and undermining, and they feel excluded from decisions affecting them. These findings are confirmed in many of the submissions received, including those from families with direct experience of the child protection system. There are many examples of professional practice having improved since much of this research was conducted and since the implementation of the Children Act. However, the Commission considers that insufficient priority is still given both to the prevention and the treatment of child abuse. Policy and professional practices must be more responsive to the needs of children and their families and effective in meeting them. A wide range of flexible services, responsive to and shaped by the needs of local users, is necessary. Meeting these needs should be achieved through working partnerships between professionals and the wider community, and between professionals from different disciplines.

8.2   Professional involvement with children and families is often seen in terms of contributions from health, social services and education but, as has already been argued, a wider range of professionals, agencies, and groups should have an input, including those concerned with: housing; leisure and recreation; income support; the environment; transport; employers; and voluntary organisations (See Appendix 12). All these have a significant impact on the lives of children and their families. Consideration must be given to how all professional groups can work together and place children at the centre of the services they provide.

*Report of the
National
Commission of
Inquiry into the
Prevention of
Child Abuse*

Shortcomings in Present Services

8.3 In taking a fresh look at the support and services children and families actually need and want, some familiar assumptions must be set aside. Evidence to the Commission, particularly from those who have been abused, makes a number of consistent points, all of which have implications which professionals in all disciplines need to address when planning and providing support services:

○ most abused children do not come to the attention of and never receive any help from professionals.

○ support and treatment is usually only short-term. Increased and more flexible support is needed.

○ abused children will talk to someone they trust, who may be a family member, a "lay" person or a non-specialist. Everyone must know how to respond.

○ easily accessible and confidential advice should be available to children being abused, anyone who may have been contacted by an abused person, and anyone concerned about the care and treatment of a particular child. This advice, at least in the first instance, must allow the person concerned to retain control of the situation.

○ services designed to support and assist children and families need to be non-stigmatising and easily reached. They must also be flexible to meet different needs.

○ service users sometimes feel that professionals either do not understand their problem, or focus on concerns which the user feels are less important. It is important that professionals listen to the concerns of the general public.

○ services can be limited and if the user rejects what is offered an alternative is not always provided. In some cases, users feel they have been made to accept a service they do not want.

○ self-help and peer support is often highly effective but frequently lacks adequate funds and assistance.

○ the long-term impact upon a family of investigations into child abuse, whatever their outcome, should not be underestimated.

○ children, parents and families who are the subject of case conferences are not always informed by professionals of their rights, in particular in relation to appeals and complaints procedures.

> "Where was the welfare then? Where was the counselling? ... I feel I shall never be a whole human being. My mother used to say you shouldn't live in the past. I don't, the past lives in me."
> **Letter to the Commission**

8.4 Over a 20-month period, Farmer and Owen(3) studied the experience of 44 families with one or more children on the child protection register. They concluded:

"The focus of the child protection system is firmly on investigations and surveillance to ensure the protection of children rather than on treatment and reunification. However, the research has also shown that the needs of parents and children cannot be compartmentalised in this way... Neglect of the welfare of both parent and child

*Report of the
National
Commission of
Inquiry into the
Prevention of
Child Abuse*

*contributed to the risk of further harm. Although the short-term protection of many
of the children ... was achieved during the period of investigation, it was frequently
precarious; and long-term protection could not be ensured if there were unresolved
difficulties in the aftermath of the abuse"(4)*

Another study reported(5): "Cases of neglect and emotional abuse are more likely [than other forms of abuse] to disappear from the child protection system without any services being offered." A third study(6) pointed to parents' bewilderment when the child protection system took over and they were left without any control over the situation. The impact of these interventions was shown to be most severe among parents who had no experience of social services or who had been unaware of their gathering concern. On the other hand, the researchers found a clear connection between greater parental involvement in cases and better outcomes for children. Farmer and Owen found that seven in ten parents were unhappy after the case conference and two in five still felt hurt twenty months later. Many of the children interviewed for that study felt their views were not taken into account by social workers and that they were being "quizzed". In particular, the children objected to attention being drawn to them by interviews being held on school premises and by being taken out of class.

8.5   There is concern that large numbers of children are referred to social services, and then receive no help unless they are placed on the register. Research(7) has shown that 75 per cent of children drawn into the child protection system were not at risk of significant harm. The researchers said:

87

*"Too many families struggling with child rearing problems who came to the attention
of social services departments were prematurely defined as potential child protection
cases rather than containing children in need."*

The latest report on the operation of the Children Act, from the Secretary of State for Health(8), expresses government concern that, in some areas, assessment procedures for children in need seem to be over-elaborate and unduly influenced by child protection: "Some local authorities are in danger of limiting resources to children on the child protection register."

8.6   Even if they are placed on a register, children are not always protected and their welfare improved. In the study of 44 families(9), 70 per cent of the children were protected, but 30 per cent continued to be at risk and 25 per cent were re-abused. The welfare of 68 per cent of the registered children improved, though at times only slightly. Carers' needs were met in only a third of the families.

> "We are repeatedly hearing concerns centred around the difficulties the abused and the abuser have in disclosing the abuse that is being perpetrated. A real fear is the effect of the action by police and social services - what will it do to my family?"
> **The Samaritans**

8.7   Despite these shortcomings, the system has successfully protected many children, as many of these same research studies noted. Nevertheless, there are sufficient concerns for the Commission to support a refocusing of the professional response, so that greater

Report of the
National
Commission of
Inquiry into the
Prevention of
Child Abuse

priority and resources are given to prevention and family support. This does not mean abandoning the child protection system or changing the thresholds for intervention: it is essential that children who need protection receive a professional and, where appropriate, specialist response.

A Child-centred System to Prevent Abuse

> "I cried out for help in every way I could think of. The only cry I did not make was to say something. But as young as I was, I did not know what he was doing."
> **Letter to the Commission**

8.8   To prevent abuse, children at risk must be identified early and their needs met. The Commission proposes building on existing frameworks and taking advantage of existing opportunities to observe children. It is essential that these services effectively address the issues of child protection and abuse prevention. Table 8.1 indicates the key components. Importantly:

o **child health surveillance programmes***, which form part of wider child health promotion, should include checking for signs of possible abuse and providing preventive advice. Missed appointments must be followed up.

o **day care** should be universally available. This will not only provide support to families but also opportunities to ensure that children are safe, particularly in the period between the $3\frac{1}{2}$ year health check and starting school, when children at risk of abuse may "disappear" from professional surveillance. The training of day nursery staff in identifying possible signs of abuse and how to respond is a key part of this strategy.

o **the education service**, including the school health service, should monitor children's safety and follow child protection guidelines.

o **information and advice** must be easily and freely available to parents, children and young people. Many do not know where to go for help and need to be encouraged to seek assistance at an early stage. They may wish to seek advice on a confidential basis which, as far as possible, will allow them to stay in control of what happens to them. Twenty-four-hour telephone helplines have a crucial role to play and national and local government, through children's services plans, should ensure that the need for such advice is met. In particular, a national 24 hour advice line for parents should be developed.

o **Family support services** should include domiciliary services, such as family aides and childminding - and external provision, such as drop-in and family centres. Family centres - often run on a multi-agency basis and with a substantial input from users - were praised in many submissions to the Inquiry. This has led the Commission to recommend that everyone should have access to such a centre within reasonable distance of their home.

o A strong **child protection service** is needed to respond to suspicions of abuse. It needs to be accessible, so that people can easily report their concerns; swift in taking action in response to reported concerns; and sensitive to the needs of children and their families.

o **Counselling and treatment services**, including marriage and relationship counselling, are essential in order to mitigate the possible harmful effects of abuse on victims' lives and their future relationships, including those with their own children. At present such services are under-researched and in short supply.

Report of the
National
Commission of
Inquiry into the
Prevention of
Child Abuse

Table 8.1   *A Child-Centred System to Prevent Harm*

Service	Provider	Aim	Strategy

Information and advice	• Voluntary organisations
	• Telephone helplines
	• Statutory agencies
	• Self-help groups
		• Easy access to advice and information on sources of help for:
		  i) Parents and carers under stress
		  ii) Children and young people with problems
		  iii) Members of the public with concerns about the safety of a child
			• Central and local government to identify unmet needs for information services and develop plans to meet them.
			• Statutory agencies, including social services to develop accessible and user-friendly services.
			• Telephone helplines to be effectively monitored and regulated.

Child health promotion	• General practitioners • Health visitors • Primary health care team • Hospital staff	• Specified health checks to take account of child protection concerns • Health promotion to include prevention and family support • To follow up *all* children who miss appointments	• Promotion of the core health surveillance programme recommended in *Health for All Children* • Multi-disciplinary collaboration between health, social services and education as a response to these checks • Interviews with parents and children to be held in supportive settings, for example, family centres and nurseries
Day care	• Statutory agencies • Voluntary organisations • Community groups and churches • Private sector	• To provide day nursery places to all parents who want them • Day nursery staff to identify children at risk of abuse • Training for nursery staff	• National strategy to be implemented for universal day nursery provision • Maintenance of standards of care across all sectors
Family support services	• Statutory agencies • Voluntary agencies • Community groups • Private sector	• Flexible range of domiciliary and out-of-home provisions to be available in all areas • Family centres to be available within a five-mile radius of every community	• Need for family support services to be identified and met through children's services planning mechanism

89

* The third edition of *Health for All Children*, (edited by Professor David M. B. Hall, 1996, Oxford: Oxford University Press), proposes the following checks: neonatal examination; a health visitor check when the baby is around 10-14 days old; a check by within six to eight weeks by a member of the primary health care team; immunisation within two to four months; an examination between six to nine months; a review at eighteen to twenty four months; a review at $3\frac{1}{4}$ to $3\frac{1}{2}$; and a medical examination at 54-66 months when the child enters school.

*Report of the
National
Commission of
Inquiry into the
Prevention of
Child Abuse*

Table 8.1   *A Child-Centred System to Prevent Harm- Continued*

Service	Provider	Aim	Strategy
Education service	• State schools • Independent sector	• All schools to implement child protection guidance and procedures • All schools to develop and implement whole-school behaviour policies • Personal and social education to be provided for all children	• Initial teacher training to include child protection • Headteachers and governing bodies to ensure the child protection system is operating in schools • Inspection bodies to report on operation of system
Child protection services	• Multi-agency approach: social services/ social work, police, health, education	• A swift, non-stigmatising, child- supportive response to concerns about child abuse	• To give increased emphasis to family support, while maintaining an effective child protection system • To increase user participation in decision-making
Counselling and treatment services	• Health service • Voluntary agencies • Independent sector • Self help initiatives	• To ensure that those who have been abused receive counselling and treatment when it is needed	• ACPCs/CPCs to review provision of treatment services • Central government to issue guidance on provision of treatment • Increased resource allocation.

Some of this is currently in place but at times there is a failure to provide adequate services. Fundamental to the Commission's proposals for the professional response to child abuse are: local multi-disciplinary working; accessible services; user involvement; all professionals knowing the possible signs and symptoms of abuse and what procedures to take; access to specialist services when appropriate; and partnerships between statutory, voluntary, and community agencies.

8.9   Greater use should be made of family support services in order to prevent abuse occurring. The Children Act requires local authorities to take reasonable steps, through the provision of services, to prevent children in their area being ill-treated or neglected. Government guidance and regulations[1] describe the range of possible services: day nurseries; playgroups; childminding; out-of-school clubs and holiday schemes; befriending services; supervised activities for children, including sports; parent-toddler groups; toy libraries; drop-in centres; playbuses; and family centres. The guidance identifies three types of family centre: therapeutic, which carry out intensive work with families in difficulties; community centres, which might be run by voluntary or community groups; and self-help centres which offer support services and may be run in an informal and unstructured way.

8.10   Commission field visits and evidence received indicates that family centres run in partnership between voluntary and community groups provide a supportive setting in which professionals can work with parents and children. They also provide an opportunity for parents and carers to share experiences and support each other. User involvement in running and managing a centre also enhances an individual's self worth, confidence and skills. Schemes, sometimes linked to national vocational qualifications, that train former users to work with other parents under stress can be very effective. While they may also require professional input, they may involve skills and an approach that many professionals do not possess.

Report of the
National
Commission of
Inquiry into the
Prevention of
Child Abuse

> "Health purchasers often fail to recognise the child protection element of services. Both purchasers and providers need to be more explicit about child protection."
> NHS Trust Federation

Children Living Away from Home

8.11   The special situation of children in residential units such as children's homes, schools and hospitals, is of particular concern. There are well-documented examples of extensive abuse in such settings and, while it was hoped that changes in child care legislation would stop such situations arising, the continual emergence of scandals in residential settings indicates that the abuse of children cared for away from home remains a problem. Such abusive situations are not confined to any sector and have occurred in establishments run by government, voluntary organisations, local authorities and the private sector. The Commission welcomes the setting up of a national review on residential care and believes that central government and statutory agencies must now take decisive action to ensure that high-quality care is provided and that staff are properly trained and supported in their skilled and difficult task.

91

Social services departments have an important role to play in preventing abuse both in local authority institutions and those in the voluntary and private sectors. First, they must ensure that staff selection, and monitoring and management of their own establishments is exemplary. Second, they have a regulatory function in children's homes run by other agencies, hospitals and residential schools, although in the latter case it has recently become considerably weakened.

8.12   Inspection services must have adequate resources and a sound legal framework in which to operate. It is noted with concern that small independent children's homes, with fewer than four children, and independent fostering agencies are unregulated, and that regulation within residential schools has been considerably relaxed. The Department of Health is currently conducting a review of the regulatory role and function of social services departments. The following points should be taken into account in the final determination of the future role of the social services inspection:

o   Regulation should be extended to cover all situations where children are cared for away from home.

o   There should be an integrated approach to the inspection and regulation of provisions for children away from home, whether they be predominantly education, health, or social care in emphasis.

o   The provision of care for children should not be seen in the same light as other "small businesses".

○ Regulation should not be regarded as unnecessary bureaucracy but as essential to protect children from abuse.

○ Training for residential work with children should ensure that staff are equipped to work with children and young people who have often had very damaging experiences.

Neglect of Neglect

"Neglect, although treated with some concern, is not a problem which is perceived with the same severity as physical or sexual abuse. Yet other forms of abuse are very often accompanied by neglect which many professionals do not see, in itself, as leading to significant harm. However, gross neglect can cause death or serious, long term damage and can occur where carers are systematically using it to impose their will or believe their own needs come first."

The Bridge Consultancy

8.13   Much evidence to the Commission suggested that the neglect of children has itself been neglected by the statutory services. Gibbons' research(10) found that although 21 per cent of referrals to the child protection system were for neglect, ultimately only seven per cent were registered. Many of those not registered failed subsequently to receive support. A large number of these cases of abuse through neglect could be prevented by professional intervention. Social services departments and health authorities, particularly senior managers, need to establish a consistent benchmark of neglect and to draw attention to the shortfall in provision for "children in need". As Professor Olive Stevenson, University of Nottingham, argued in her submissions to the Commission, there should be a major reappraisal of how neglect is handled, to focus on measures to assess the extent of neglect and emotional abuse, strategies for intervention, and training and support needs. The model of a working group, similar to the Department of Health-led group that produced *Protecting Children: a guide for social workers undertaking a comprehensive assessment*(11) (better known as the Orange Book), seems a good way forward.

"Health visitors are the main people who can help prevent child abuse. They see families on a regular basis and can refer families on to various organisations at the first sign of family stress. For example, social services, voluntary organisations within the community and family doctors."

Letter to the Commission

Health Services

8.14   The first five years of life are critical in a child's development and the health service has a particular role in early-years support. The Commission endorses a recommendation by the Audit Commission(12) on child health services that support should be undertaken together with other agencies dealing with children: social services, education and the voluntary sector. A similar approach is needed for school-age children. The Commission believes that this way of working is vital throughout childhood and recommends that services for children should be given higher priority within health service commissioning and be directed much more towards prevention. The Health Visitors' Association was not alone in saying that "the importance of preventive health is not recognised within the NHS where the medical illness model dominates".

Report of the
National
Commission of
Inquiry into the
Prevention of
Child Abuse

8.15   Child health services need to be accessible and supportive with greater emphasis on prevention. Primary and secondary health services need to be fully integrated. Equally important is a development of a combined child health service with community and hospital secondary care services working in close co-operation. This requires effective collaboration between health authorities, health trusts, and fund-holding general practitioners.

8.16   General practitioners have an important role to play in health promotion and child health surveillance. The Royal College of General Practitioners, in its evidence, supported this but also emphasised the implications for the education and support of GPs. Health visitors also have a vital role to play in identifying vulnerable children and the Commission is concerned that, through linking too closely with primary health care teams, the health visiting service may be losing its ability to become familiar with the problems and pressures within communities. The public health role of the health visitor must be safeguarded. There is a worrying decline in resources of staff and facilities for health visiting, which is considered by many, including the Commission, to be one of the most important of the non-stigmatising and universally available services.

> "I now know that the doctor asked my mum was there any chance I was being abused and she dismissed that from their minds. By them not asking me, that gave my stepfather a meal ticket to carry on for the five years."
> **Letter to the Commission**

8.17   The development of child health surveillance programmes within primary care and the recent emphasis on health promotion are welcome. Programmes should focus not only on the health aspects of childhood but on more general welfare of the child and family. This must be done by the health service working in partnership with local communities, education and social services.

8.18   Insufficient priority is given to medical diagnosis of abuse, which requires expert attention. All child protection case conferences should receive advice from a consultant paediatrician on the risks of further abuse. The Commission believes that such risk assessment is essential if children are to be protected and further abuse prevented. Experienced paediatricians gave evidence that severe injury to babies is becoming more common and that non-specialists may fail to recognise the importance of bruises and minor injuries in the diagnosis of abuse. In all cases involving babies, risk assessment must be carried out by an experienced consultant paediatrician.

8.19   The problem of post-natal depression is closely related to the early identification of those who may require additional help. Evidence suggested that as many as 50 per cent of mothers suffer from post-natal depression and that at least 10 per cent of mothers with babies aged under one year are clinically depressed. As a consultant psychiatrist said in evidence, "the long-term costs to the nation and its health service of neglecting this invisible epidemic are uncountable". It is clearly in the interests of parents and the well-being of young children that this serious problem is addressed as a priority. Any strategy must include a system of screening for depression.

*Report of the
National
Commission of
Inquiry into the
Prevention of
Child Abuse*

8.20   Evidence to the Commission has pointed to the value of the posts of designated nurse and designated doctor with responsibility for child protection. Such posts can take a lead in raising the profile of child protection and in providing support to staff. There is evidence that the designated posts are not working well in all districts and that they do not fit neatly into the purchaser/provider split within the NHS. Posts no longer have a district-wide remit: that needs to be addressed by health authorities.

8.21   The prevention of child abuse requires better collaboration in NHS commissioning and management. At present, a family can receive services from several different health trusts and separately contracted general practitioners. Not all health authorities commission the full range of services for children. All health authorities should commission children's services in their entirety, with specific contracts with clear outcomes. This requires the involvement of specialists in child health in the commissioning process. It also requires clear outcomes defined in contracts, with greater emphasis on prevention and collaboration with the local authority and the community.

Education Services

8.22   Schools are the only places which all young people attend for sustained periods and at which, from day to day, they can be observed by responsible adults. This places a particular obligation on schools to identify children at risk of or actually suffering abuse or neglect. Schools can exercise that responsibility in three main ways: by identifying and dealing appropriately with signs of abuse in individual pupils; by creating and sustaining conditions within school which exemplify sound inter-personal relationships, for example by the absence of bullying; and by providing, within the curriculum, the skills, knowledge and values that help pupils develop their whole approach to those relationships and to parenthood itself.

> "When I was seven I was thrown across the room and I broke my nose on the door knob. As I walked to school my nose was bleeding badly and the teacher asked me what had happened. I dared not tell her the truth so I told her I had walked into a lamp post because I knew I would get beaten if I told her who had done it."
> **Letter to the Commission**

8.23   For schools to do this, teachers and others working within the system need opportunities to improve their own understanding of the issues involved in child protection. Local education authorities (LEAs), the Schools Curriculum and Assessment Authority (SCAA), the Teacher Training Agency (TTA) and the Office for Standards in Education (Ofsted), all have responsibilities that affect the ability of schools to carry out their preventive and educational functions. These responsibilities include an LEA's role in enabling designated teachers to obtain appropriate training; Ofsted's responsibility to ensure that reports or inspections include clear statements on schools' arrangements for dealing with potential child abuse; SCAA's responsibility for encouraging the development of an appropriate curriculum; and TTA's responsibility, at initial training and in subsequent staff development programmes, for ensuring that teachers are sufficiently prepared to carry out their duties.

Report of the
National
Commission of
Inquiry into the
Prevention of
Child Abuse

8.24   In identifying and responding to signs of abuse, considerable progress has been made in recent years in setting out what schools should do. The Department of Education and Employment's circular 10/95 sets out the main requirements: all schools should be alert to signs of abuse and teachers aware of how and to whom they should report any concern or suspicion; all schools and colleges should have a designated and appropriately trained member of staff responsible for co-ordinating action and for working with other agencies with statutory responsibilities; all schools and colleges should have procedures, of which all staff should be aware, for handling suspected cases of abuse. Where abuse involving a member of staff is alleged, schools and their governing bodies should protect the rights of any individual involved by strictly adhering to the guidelines drawn up by the Council of Local Education Authorities and the teacher unions.

8.25   Schools can ensure by their own emphasis on good behaviour that abusive actions, such as bullying, name-calling and related forms of damage to children, are inhibited and effectively dealt with when they occur. Within the curriculum, as well as work on personal relationships and the development of communication and decision-making skills, there is scope for work on child development, as an initiation to parenthood; for personal and social education and for forms of sex education that encourage exploration of values and moral issues. Schools can also help children to be active in resisting and, when threatened, making known to their teachers or other responsible adults, attempts made to harm them.

8.26   Many of the right measures and procedures are in place within the school system. The task now is to ensure that they are fully and consistently implemented throughout both the system and the agencies statutorily associated with its performance. Evidence to the Commission suggests that present systems are frequently not working satisfactorily and that children are often not aware, or do not feel confident, that they can discuss personal problems at school. Head teachers and governing bodies, therefore, need to ensure that child protection systems within schools are working effectively and that children are encouraged to seek help if necessary. School Inspectorates should report systematically on how well these systems are operating.

Teacher Training

8.27   Initial teacher training is governed by the Teacher Training Agency and, ultimately, the Secretary of State. An emphasis on what are seen as the core elements of the curriculum has, in the recent past, had the effect of reducing the time spent in training teachers to identify children's welfare problems. It is sometimes unclear where responsibility for such training lies: in the training institutions or in schools where much of that training is now carried out. The Commission recommends that all institutions dealing with initial teacher-training should include in their programmes information on the UN Convention on the Rights of the Child and on ways of identifying signs of potential or actual abuse of children. Teachers must be able to recognise, for example, that disruptive behaviour, which may eventually lead to a child's exclusion from school, may be an expression of distress caused by abuse or family difficulties.

95

*Report of the
National
Commission of
Inquiry into the
Prevention of
Child Abuse*

In-service Teacher Training

8.28 It is for Local Education Authorities, the Schools Funding Agency, which is responsible for grant maintained schools, and those controlling programmes of Grants for Educational Support and Training (GEST) to ensure that all teachers with some defined responsibility for dealing with suspected or actual incidents of child abuse and neglect have received appropriate training.

Bullying

8.29 The extent of bullying is disturbing. School behaviour policies are designed to acknowledge and respond to the particular circumstances of each school. One helpful approach reported to the Commission has been the use of peer-group support for victims of bullies. In some schools, senior pupils receive training to enable them to reduce the level of bullying and are known within the school as individuals whom bullied children can trust.

Personal and Social Education

8.30 At a time of competing priorities, increased emphasis on measurable outcomes and general pressure on schools to take on new responsibilities, there is some risk that the whole area of personal and social education will receive less attention than it deserves. There are two main ways of remedying this, both supported by the Commission. The first is to increase the number of teachers trained, either initially or later, to undertake personal and social education work. This requires specifically directed and financed staff-development programmes, which could be included in the GEST budget. Precedents already exist in, for example, training programmes for key-stage curriculum co-ordinators and deputy head teachers. The second is for agencies concerned with school improvement, nationally and locally, to encourage the development of appropriate curriculum material for use in schools and colleges.

The Commission believes that the resources of time, effort and money required to establish personal and social education on a firm footing within the education system would be small in comparison with the savings, in financial and human terms, to which this would lead. A population of school leavers, better informed on issues affecting children and their responsibilities as adults, would have an important part to play in reducing the incidence of child abuse. The Commission is convinced that much of that harm arises from ignorance rather than malice.

Social Services and Social Work

8.31 Social services are not universally available to children and families. Their role is to protect and care for children in need as defined in the legislation, including those who have been abused or are at risk of abuse. Social services/social work departments have a lead responsibility to try and identify such children and give appropriate support, protection and, where necessary, special services supplied by other agencies. Direct work with children is closely related to work with their parents, who themselves may have special needs. Social services departments provide services directly, or purchase them from voluntary and private agencies. They also work with health and education colleagues to try and reach an agreed view about the needs of children, and provide a co-ordinated response. This will include some joint provision, such as health, education and social services jointly funding a residential placement for a child requiring special education, health and social care facilities.

Report of the
National
Commission of
Inquiry into the
Prevention of
Child Abuse

8.32 The Children Act takes a broad definition of children in need which can be interpreted flexibly. Social service funding dictates a much narrower interpretation of need and tight criteria for service provision. This is particularly apparent in child abuse, where highly prescriptive central government requirements have served to increase the emphasis on formal procedural responses. The Commission accepts that the response to child protection has become over-dominated by procedure. Social services and social work departments, none the less, have a duty to give the highest priority to children who have been abused or are at the most serious risk.

8.33 As social services have a lead and co-ordinating responsibility for children's services planning and the local approach to children in need, it is important that there is a shift in the balance of social service activity, placing more emphasis on preventive and supportive work. It is equally important that other services co-operate fully, even when they are not statutorily required to do so.

8.34 Within social services, children's services receive a much smaller allocation of budget than do services for adults. This carries a danger that the attention of senior managers and local politicians will be directed more towards adult services. There must be constant vigilance to ensure this does not happen. A mishandling of some cases involving children, including abuse in residential homes, has demonstrated the need for all social services/social work departments to ensure that a distinct responsibility for children's services rests at a very senior management level (second or third tier), and that line managers who carry responsibility for children's residential, field work and day care services, are appropriately qualified and substantially experienced in child care.

8.35 Competent practitioners are also required. A representative survey of more than one thousand social workers, carried out by the Commission and the journal *Community Care*, (see Appendix 18), found that 86 per cent of respondents felt that their social work training did not prepare them sufficiently for work in child abuse prevention. Evidence from the Central Council for Training and Education in Social Work (CCETSW) argued that, unlike other professions, social work and the personal social services have no tradition of post-qualifying training. Any significant level of post-qualifying training was regarded as a privilege for the fortunate few. The Commission supports the view that there is a need for improved basic social work training, supplemented by regular in-service and post-qualifying training. The social work profession has long pressed for a three-year professional training of graduate standard. The required range of competencies, maturity and professional discipline, particularly in children's services, cannot be acquired in two years of basic professional training. A minimum three-year professional training - or its equivalent - should be established, together with post-qualifying training in specialist subjects.

Report of the
National
Commission of
Inquiry into the
Prevention of
Child Abuse

There is an urgent need for more extensive training in direct work with children and families. The Commission commends the CCETSW publication "The Teaching of Child Care in the Diploma of Social Work" (1991) as a basis for this training.

The Police

8.36   In recent years, the police have take a greater role in responding to child abuse. There has been criticism in the past but evidence received by the Commission suggests that generally the standard of police work, particularly those in child protection units, has improved, partly as a result of training. In many areas there is improved collaboration between police and social services, particularly in investigations. All police officers, not just those working in child protection units, need to receive some training in children's needs, child abuse and child protection procedures, for it is not only specialist officers who respond to abuse calls. The Commission supports the recommendation of the Association of Chief Police Officers (ACPO) that patrol officers should be trained in child protection matters, to cover periods where there is no specialist child protection officer available.

8.37   The need for all police to receive basic training in child protection is underlined by the fact that police investigating other crimes may come across situations, such as domestic violence, drugs and alcohol abuse, where a child may be at risk. Children's needs are not always addressed in such cases. In dealing with all crimes, the police need to ensure that the needs of children are taken into account and that there is appropriate liaison with other professionals.

8.38   The Commission has also received evidence on the extent to which children's needs are met during investigations into allegations of abuse. Since the Home Office Memorandum of Good Practice on Interviewing Children(13) was introduced in 1992, the police have increasingly taken the lead in joint investigations. This may have inadvertently led to greater emphasis on trying to securing a prosecution, at the expense of meeting the child's needs. During investigations the best interests of the children must be paramount and should govern the pace and nature of interviews, the support the child receives and the provision of counselling or therapy where necessary. The conduct of investigations is under discussion and pilot initiatives in different parts of the country have modified the police role. It is important that these initiatives are effectively evaluated. The Commission has noted proposals made in some evidence that consideration should be given to child protection investigations being carried out by the police, the NSPCC, or specially trained cadres of investigators, thereby allowing social workers to have a primary role in supporting families. These proposals need to be considered alongside the outcome of the pilot projects already referred to.

8.39   In the first nine months of 1994, the Metropolitan Police seized 7,200 video tapes involving child pornography, a 50 per cent increase on the number seized during the whole of 1993. Evidence to the Commission shows that effective measures against pornography, including improved co-ordination at national and international levels, are being inhibited by a lack of resources. National government and police authorities should give increased priority to this important work.

Report of the
National
Commission of
Inquiry into the
Prevention of
Child Abuse

8.40   Work with known and suspected offenders must also be given greater priority by the police. Current Home Office proposals on the registration and control of offenders have implications for police practice. Multi-agency working is important, particularly with probation and social services regarding the release and rehabilitation of offenders, is important. In its submission, ACPO highlighted this issue and the dilemma posed to police over the rights of the paedophile: "Although (police) child protection officers are effectively reactive they are increasingly being drawn into situations where they are holding criminal intelligence, often emanating from social services, on convicted paedophiles who may pose a threat to children. The challenge to the police is what should be done with that intelligence. Clearly to take no action until a crime is reported may be bordering on professional neglect and yet sharing concerns, even within the professional network, is thought by some to be breaching the individual's civil liberties." The Commission is in no doubt that the safety of children must be paramount and that a multi-disciplinary plan for controlling the behaviour of known paedophiles is essential. Once Home Office proposals come into force it will be important for local agencies to agree a strategy for implementating them. ACPO suggests that structured networking between agencies, nationally and locally, is necessary to identify and target persistent offenders and that, for networking to be effective, there must be similar systems established in each ACPC area that can be linked nationally.

8.41   The more general police role in crime prevention impinges on child abuse in that police officers may undertake preventive work in the community, schools and youth groups. This is a complex area and it is important that the messages and materials used are sensitive to children's needs. This has not always been the case. The Commission proposes that the police should ensure they keep up to date with research on how children learn to avoid abuse and on associated subjects. There should be close liaison with schools, education authorities and social services/social work departments to ensure that a consistent message on child abuse is conveyed.

Better Integration of Statutory Agencies

8.42   In the interests of actively promoting children's wellbeing, preventing child abuse and giving appropriate support to children and families, the Commission urges the statutory agencies, in particular, to pay much more attention to a closer integration of all aspects of their services, specifically in planning and development, individual assessment of needs and multi-disciplinary provision of services.

8.43   It should be a basic tenet of health, education, and social services that no unilateral action is taken in changing policies, programmes or the pattern of investment, without full analysis and consultation on the impact of the proposed changes on other services and upon children and families. Those who manage children's services should also be sensitive to any inadvertent and incremental drift towards change in policy and practice.

8.44   The Commission noted comments about "cost shunting" as a result of policy changes, or a redefining of priorities and criteria by services as demand increases and resources decrease. This can have an impact on all services. An example arises in schools, where exclusion rates are now escalating and, despite efforts to prevent this, increasingly affect very young children. The consequence of these exclusions is to transfer the problem and its associated costs from schools to other agencies. In using this example, the Commission is aware that schools are themselves affected by new pressures placed upon them and that it is these circumstances that make it important for all services to coordinate their efforts to deal with this and other problems of particular significance to vulnerable children.

8.45   Operational changes could help to reduce fragmentation. There should be a more integrated approach to assessing children with special needs. Already, there are sound and well-developed systems, particularly within education and social services, that are based on different sets of legislation and regulation. Health professionals contribute to both processes and also assess children independently. The Commission suggests two things: first, practitioners and managers should be helped to overcome a natural resistance to assessing children early, for fear of not being able to provide what is needed; and, second, a multi-disciplinary system of early identification of children in need and a single integrated process should be developed.

Treatment

8.46   It follows that, having developed an integrated approach to assessing the needs of children and families, there should be an integrated approach to "treatment". In this context, treatment means a broad range of responses from practical support or the provision of stimulating environments for the child, to remedial education, health care or residential care.

8.47   Treatment, particularly therapeutic treatment, is scarce and provision for children does not appear to be based upon an objective set of criteria and priorities related to need. Resources, such as child psychiatry, are often deployed according to the demands of courts or the availability of finance. Some scarce resources are only available to those on child protection registers. Unregistered children with similar or greater need may not be able to obtain any access to specialist resources. Families investigated because of alleged abuse can be left unsupported, to pick up the pieces unaided. For fear of influencing their evidence, child witnesses in criminal proceedings are at times denied the therapy that could help them through their trauma. Children who initially receive intensive short-term help cannot gain access to services later when other events trigger the trauma. The Commission has heard how adult survivors find it extremely difficult to receive any service unless and until they experience psychiatric breakdown - and then what is provided is often inappropriate. The needs of survivors are badly neglected and seen by very few as a priority.

> "If I had got some proper counselling it's possible my father would not have got the opportunity to sexually abuse my own daughter. No one ever told me that he would carry on doing these horrendous things. I thought it was just me at that time."
> **Letter to the Commission**

8.48   Evidence indicates a general shortage of the wide range of treatment facilities for children that would help prevent abuse. There is a particularly acute shortage of specialists, such as child and adolescent psychiatrists and psychologists, and child psychotherapists.

There should be a thoroughly integrated approach both to assessing children's needs and to the provision of services and resources to meet them. This is clearly a considerable task because, as the Commission is aware, efforts have been made in many areas to secure greater integration, so far without great success. In view of this, the respective government departments should take a more active role in determining which services are required, on what scale, and to establish universally accepted channels of access to appropriate levels of therapeutic help.

8.49   Responses to adult and young offenders also need to be co-ordinated. The registering and vetting of sex offenders, (see Chapter 5) should be complemented by treatment for all offenders, particularly young offenders, so that their behaviour can be controlled before it becomes established. Adult sex offenders are receiving attention from the Home Office, which funds research and treatment programmes mainly through prison and probation services, but there is still insufficient provision. In this context, the removal of the social work element from probation training in England and Wales seems ill advised, as probation officers are expected to deal with significant numbers of offenders who are disturbed, mentally ill or have personality disorders.

A national helpline, backed by support services, is recommended so that offenders could seek advice, including when they feel they might be a risk to children. The Commission proposes investing in treatment for sex offenders as a means of preventing abuse. Priority must be given to providing treatment to young offenders, particularly since behaviour is amenable to modification before it becomes established.

8.50   In summary, the levels of treatment proposed by the Commission are:

o   confidential advice and information about available services provided by means of telephone advice lines and accessible advice points in the community;

o   a range of community-based initiatives to support children and their families, including projects providing direct support and development to vulnerable and inexperienced parents;

o   an integrated approach to the assessment of need and levels of response;

o   an integrated approach to the provision of services, including greater flexibility in the use of residential schools, children's homes and family placement, and full integration of respite-care facilities;

o   psychiatric, probation and social services with an integrated approach to the treatment needs of adult survivors and of offenders, and children's services should combine to give specific attention to their responses to young sex offenders.

o   Social Service Departments, the police, courts and probation services should develop a separate strategy for young sex offenders. This should take account of the differences in the treatment appropriate to them as opposed to that of other young offenders.

8.51   The model outlined above goes wider than the remit of the area child protection committees (ACPCs) as it embraces a range of children's services and some adult services. However ACPCs have a significant part to play and the Commission recommends that each ACPC should review the extent to which the need for treatment services is met locally and develop a multi-disciplinary plan in response. This, however, must be firmly linked to the wider children's services plan.

*Report of the
National
Commission of
Inquiry into the
Prevention of
Child Abuse*

"In relation to individual treatment of young sexual abusers, our experience is surprisingly positive... Despite high levels of emotional deprivation in these young people our experienced psychotherapists are reporting an intense engagement in this individual work, signs of early attitudinal change in some of these young people and an overwhelming sense of gratitude ... that such treatment is at last available."

Dr Eileen Vizard, Young Abusers Project

Training

8.52   The approach recommended by the Commission requires well-briefed, skilled and confident professionals and volunteers to staff children's services; and adequate information to support good practice and management. This has implications for the staff training and support referred to in 8.35 above.

8.53   The workforce providing services to children and their families is one of our greatest assets in developing strategies for preventing child abuse. Many people undertake difficult and challenging work and perform to a high standard. Others are unsuitable for the work or are inadequately trained, or both. Investment in the workforce through selection, training, and staff support is essential to improve standards and retain staff. The Commission found that many committed and skilled people in all the professions were demoralised: 62 per cent of social workers in the Commission's survey "more often found their work frustrating or stressful than satisfying" but on balance were prepared to stay with it. However, a significant minority - one in six - felt "frustrated and over stressed by child abuse work and would prefer to change their job". Some health visitors expressed discomfort at not being able to do more preventive work. Other professionals, including general practitioners and paediatricians, expressed concern at the amount of time they had to spend on bureaucracy and paperwork.

8.54   The Commission endorses a number of points emerging from the evidence that have direct implications for training key professionals. These are:

○   a wide range of professionals and volunteers working with children, including those in community groups, need to be trained in the identification of signs of abuse and local child protection procedures;

○   that training is inadequate to the demands and expectations of social workers in children's services; that a two-year qualifying training cannot satisfactorily encompass the range of skills and knowledge required; and that more rigour should be exercised at the point of entry to a profession from which disadvantaged and disturbed children and families require well-developed skills of counselling, practical support, advocacy, assessment and intellectual discipline;

○   most professional training was felt to be deficient in child development, particularly in the skills of communicating with children. Such skills are even more necessary in dealing with children with disabilities;

○   the needs of minority ethnic groups and the impact of racism on children are generally ignored by many professionals. Children from ethnic minority groups may experience particular difficulty in disclosing abuse because of fear of bringing shame in their community and suffering further stigmatisation.

*Report of the
National
Commission of
Inquiry into the
Prevention of
Child Abuse*

o   professionals do not always understand the roles and responsibilities of other disciplines and there is a need for a more comprehensive approach to developing appropriate knowledge and skills within professional disciplines to facilitate true collaboration;

o   professionals in disciplines that focus on adults, for example those with disabilities or mental health problems, have limited ability to identify situations in which children are at risk and when specialists in children's services should be involved;

o   with the developing emphasis in all services on high-priority work and with services increasingly tightening their criteria for response because of limited resource, there is a consequent loss of ability to carry out preventive and supportive work with families;

o   there is a need to establish a common methodology for assessing and managing risk. This becomes increasingly important if the emphasis is to shift to preventive and supportive work.

o   training in relation to neglect should be a priority. Staff in all disciplines need further help to ensure that seriously neglected children are identified and properly responded to at an early stage. All staff need to be alert to "neglect fatigue" among professionals who see large numbers of children whose parenting and care fall well below any objective benchmarks for the well-being of children.

"We recognise the importance of training in child development and as much emphasis is allotted to this theme as possible within the time constraints of the DipSW. However, many child care workers do not have the same opportunities as health visitors and teachers to keep their knowledge of normal development up to date once they are in employment. There is undoubtedly room for expansion of provision in this field at post qualifying levels."
Central Council for Education and Training in Social Work

103

8.55   Those with responsibility for training in each discipline need to address these training needs. While some must be met in single-discipline groups, the Commission emphasises the benefits of local multi-disciplinary training. This has the added advantage of promoting understanding of the respective roles of local professionals.

Staff Support

8.56   However well trained and experienced, individuals who are routinely exposed to children and families where there is serious neglect or abuse are subjected to high levels of stress. This can derive directly from personal involvement in the pain, distress and anger experienced by children and families. It is also a by-product of a fear of exposure to public opprobrium and managerial or political wrath. Workers in this field frequently feel that they are blamed for the harm that comes to children, whatever the facts, and that they are made scapegoats by the media, public, politicians and senior managers who for many years have ignored the messages of successive inquiries, particularly when it comes to training and resources. In some police forces, the stress and "burn out" common in such work is recognised by limiting the periods that officers specialise in child protection. In social work and other professions this is difficult. Some child-care social workers have a workload that exclusively deals with child protection or other complex and high-risk child-care situations.

*Report of the
National
Commission of
Inquiry into the
Prevention of
Child Abuse*

Health visitors' workloads are also increasingly dominated by cases involving families with severe problems. Professionals such as journalists and lawyers, who are not directly involved with abused children and families but are familiar with many of the facts, can also suffer stress for similar reasons.

8.57 Employers and senior managers in all relevant disciplines should give explicit attention to:

○ proper training for the job, regularly reinforced and updated, which at least equips individuals with the basic skills, knowledge and confidence in their own competence;

○ recognition that complex work with children and families, involving good inter-personal skills and balancing different personal perspectives and needs, is a matter for professional skill and judgement more than for prescriptive bureaucratic systems. There must, however, be well-understood frameworks and standards to ensure that collaboration is effective and consistent;

○ organisational structures and the way in which they operate are crucial to the support of key staff. They should provide acceptable ratios of supervisory staff for front-line staff to receive regular supervision and support. They must have adequate systems of workload management, so that those responsible for administration and resource allocation take responsibility for work that cannot reasonably be done by front-line staff. Senior supervisory and managerial staff in health and social services must have sound and experience-based knowledge, understanding and interest in children's services. Only managers with these insights can give real leadership, create an appropriate managerial and supervisory style and structure, and ensure that the necessary administrative systems fulfil the operational task, rather than simply meet the needs of managers and planners. Practitioners in organisations where this happens are more likely to feel, and be, properly supported in their work;

○ emphasis on creating a supportive environment for staff should be part of the mainstream organisation, supervision and management. However, there is an important place for easily accessible personal counselling services to which staff under stress can refer. This has been established in some departments and the Commission suggests that all relevant agencies should consider providing such a service, perhaps on a shared basis. As well as being staffed by appropriately skilled people, any such counselling service should be confidential and independent of the formal managerial structures. It is, however, important that it should provide suitably aggregated and anonymous general information to managers to ensure they are aware of trends and issues affecting their staff;

○ the practical demonstration that managers and supervisors in different agencies are themselves working together at every level, in an atmosphere of mutual respect and shared objectives, which is crucial to the support and confidence of staff. Inter-disciplinary defensiveness, insensitivity to wider implications, or demarcation battles about financial responsibilities severely undermine staff on the ground.

8.58 It is also important, when widening the range of people actively involved in promoting children's welfare and work with abused people, to give proper attention to their support. This is essentially a matter for the organisations and groups to which they belong and, as with professional workers, peer-group support will be extremely important. However, if the strategies suggested in paragraph 8.57 are in place, then statutory agencies

*Report of the
National
Commission of
Inquiry into the
Prevention of
Child Abuse*

are in a better position to provide adequate support and guidance to volunteer colleagues. It is important that this responsibility is drawn to the attention of agency staff and addressed in their in-service training.

The Child, The Community and The Professional Services

8.59   The strong relationship between an informed, caring and responsible community and the professional services it supports, and happy and fulfilled children and young people, needs to be emphasised. This relationship is crucial to the prevention of child abuse. Moves towards prevention will not be effective until the following building blocks are in place:

○   individuals with an understanding and a liking for children and a willingness to exercise responsibility on their behalf, whether as parents, carers, family, or members of the wider community;

○   voluntary organisations, religious groups, and other community groups willing to recognise the rights and the needs of children, even where they might conflict with those of adults; to take the trouble to equip themselves to understand and communicate with children; and to be prepared to take some collective responsibility for children;

○   professionals prepared to support community effort, to facilitate this with resources where possible, to be adaptable and open in the exercise of their professional skills and responsibilities, and to work in partnership with parents and children;

○   statutory services, national voluntary organisations, and private-sector resources that are sensitive and knowledgeable in exercising their role with children.

The community has a key role to play in preventing child abuse. Professionals and their parent organisations are part of that community. Together, they can create an environment which can do a great deal to prevent harm to children.

Recommendations

Professional Services

61.   Services should give greater emphasis to supporting children and families before abuse occurs. A clear lead should be given by government, through revised and less prescriptive guidance, and the issue should be addressed by all relevant authorities and professions. Services need to be developed that work in partnership with children and families and respect their rights to participation, consultation, and redress when errors occur. An effective child protection service must be maintained alongside improved family support provision.

62.   The components of a preventive service on which to build are: child health surveillance programmes; the education service's role in child protection; day care provision; accessible information and advice, including a national 24 hour telephone advice line for parents; family support services; and child protection services. A multi-agency response is needed to ensure that cases of abuse are identified at an early stage and support provided.

63.   All families should have access to some form of family support, such as, a family centre, advice and guidance or practical help in the home, such as that provided by Home Start.

105

Report of the
National
Commission of
Inquiry into the
Prevention of
Child Abuse

64. Through the mechanism of children's services plans, the social service, education and health authorities should aim to achieve greater integration of services for children, particularly those with special needs, through joint budgets, joint provision, a single assessment procedure for determining children's needs, and joint commissioning.

Health

65. The Health Service must give greater emphasis to preventive services. It should establish combined child health services and commission the full range of services for children, with specific contracts and clear outcomes.

66. Child health surveillance should give greater emphasis to identifying children suffering or at risk of abuse. The importance of the role of the general practitioner in identifying abuse, in child protection procedures and in providing family support should be recognised and developed. The health visiting service should be run as a universal service, and encouraged to undertake preventive work with families.

67. The training and guidance of health professionals should emphasise the particular vulnerability of babies to injury and death as a result of abuse and the need to be alert to the signs of possible maltreatment.

Education

68. To enable teachers to respond effectively to child abuse, all training institutions and schools involved in the initial training of teachers should include in their programme information on the UN Convention on the Rights of the Child, and on ways of identifying signs of potential or actual abuse of children. So far as teachers already in post are concerned, LEAs, the Schools Funding Agency and those controlling GEST programmes should ensure that all teachers with some defined responsibility for dealing with suspected or actual incidences of child abuse and neglect have received appropriate training.

69. Well-managed school behaviour policies are effective in reducing the level of bullying and every effort should be made by those responsible for implementing such policies to ensure that they are developed by all schools.

Social Services

70. All social services and social work departments should ensure that responsibility for children's services is at a senior level (second or third tier) and that line managers with responsibility for residential, fieldwork and day-care services are appropriately qualified and substantially experienced in child care.

71. Recommendations made by other inquiries, aimed at eradicating the abuse of children in residential care, must be fully implemented as a matter of high priority and backed with the necessary resources, training, and staff support.

72. Government departments and local statutory organisations should develop a clear basis for recognising and acting upon the neglect of children. The degree of neglect

*Report of the
National
Commission of
Inquiry into the
Prevention of
Child Abuse*

calling for intervention should not vary within and between geographical regions or local or health authority areas. Central government and local organisations should ensure the clear specification of when neglect requires intervention and that this is specifically identified in the planning and funding of services.

73. Doctors, nurses and social workers and other professionals who work mainly with adults, for example in the mental health services, should be trained to recognise risks to children implicit in their adult client's situation.

Police

74. All police officers must be trained in child protection, not just those working in child protection units. In investigating crimes, particularly those relating to domestic violence, drugs and alcohol abuse, police should be conscious of the needs of children and possible child protection concerns, and should liaise with other relevant professionals.

75. National government and police authorities should give increased priority and resources to the investigation of crimes involving child pornography.

Treatment

76. Each area child protection committee should review the extent to which the demand for support and treatment services is met locally for abuse victims and their families, those whose lives and relationships have been disrupted unnecessarily by child protection inquiries, and for offenders, and develop a multi-disciplinary plan for reducing any shortfall. Treatment services should be integrated with the wider children's services plan. Government departments should assist local services by developing guidance on what professional services should be provided and on what scale.

77. Greater priority must be given to the treatment of sex offenders, particularly young and adolescent sex offenders. A national 24 hour helpline, backed with support services and working with existing agencies, should be established to provide immediate help to offenders who fear they are a danger to children. Central government should consider how such a helpline might be effectively resourced.

Training

78. The basic and post-qualifying training of social workers, doctors and health visitors should give greater emphasis to: normal child development and behaviour; communication with children; recognition of the standard measure of child neglect; the needs of *all* children and those with chronic illness, disability, deprivation, and behavioural problems; mental illness in childhood; the ability to work cross culturally and to challenge discriminatory practice of any kind; the skills of working supportively in partnership with community networks and with parents; the skills and implications of multi-disciplinary working and assessment; and the signs, symptoms and treatment of post-natal depression.

79. There should be rigorous monitoring and evaluation of selection procedures for social work training to ensure that students possess the necessary maturity, sensitivity and intellectual capacity for social work.

107

Report of the
National
Commission of
Inquiry into the
Prevention of
Child Abuse

80. Social work training may encompass different educational and training routes over different timescales but the award of a social work qualification should follow the equivalent of at least three years' full-time social work education and training and be to degree standard.

81. There should greater emphasis in social work training on developing a professional culture of continuing education, and greater investment in a range of specialist post-qualifying training, including residential social work and direct work with children and families.

References

1. Child Protection: Messages From Research, 1995, Department of Health, London: HMSO

2. Farmer E, Owen M, 1995, Child Protection Practice: Private Risks and Public Remedies, London: HMSO

3. ibid

4. ibid

5. Gibbons J, Conroy S, Bell C, 1995, Operating the Child Protection System, London : HMSO

6. Thoburn J, Lewis A, and Shemmings D, 1995, Paternalism or Partnership? Family Involvement in the Child Protection Process, London: HMSO

7. Farmer E, Owen M, 1995, Child Protection Practice: Private Risks and Public Remedies, London: HMSO

8. Children Act Report 1994: A Report by the Secretaries of State for Health and for Wales, 1995, London: HMSO

9. Farmer E, Owen M, 1995, Child Protection Practice: Private Risks and Public Remedies, London: HMSO

10. Gibbons J, Conroy S, Bell C, 1995, Operating the Child Protection System, London : HMSO

11. Department of Health, 1995, Protecting children: a guide for social workers undertaking a comprehensive assessment, London: HMSO

12. Audit Commission, 1994, Seen But Not Heard, Co-ordinating Community Child Health and Social Services for Children in Need, London: HMSO

13. Home Office and Department of Health, 1992, Memorandum of good practice on video recorded interviews with children

Chapter 9
Research

Report of the
National
Commission of
Inquiry into the
Prevention of
Child Abuse

- Research into the prevention of child abuse has been given low priority

- Evaluation of good practice and effective means of preventing child abuse is urgently needed

- Research priorities include: a survey of the incidence of child abuse; research into the development of "resilient" children; an evaluation of the effectiveness of family support initiatives; and research on offenders

The need for research

9.1   The development of strategies for the prevention of child abuse has been restricted by a lack of rigorous research and evaluation. There is no lack of schemes and projects for helping to prevent abuse in its many forms. What is lacking is any consistent approach to evaluating their effectiveness. There are also important gaps in our knowledge of what is actually happening; for instance, information on child deaths following abuse is sparse. Without accurate information, there is evident difficulty in assessing what has happened and responding to it. Ways of diagnosing abuse and assessing the risk of various forms of abuse need to be improved. Government-funded research has reflected central government's policy priorities and has tended to concentrate on the operation of child protection procedures *after* abuse has happened. The Commission believes that it is essential that a research programme is developed which can authoritatively evaluate the outcome of different interventions.

9.2   There is a need to bring together research by those working within the fields of social administration, child health, education, social work and the law because if the response to child abuse should be multi-disciplinary, as is widely agreed, so too should research into the effects of those multi-disciplinary efforts. Such research as there is (see Review of Research by Gough and Murray, *Childhood Matters*: Volume Two) has mostly been conducted within a single discipline, such as social services, health or education. For example, most of the work for the *Messages From Research*(1) studies for the Department of Health was undertaken by university departments of social administration. The Economic and Social Research Council does not have child health as one of the categories which it considers for research funding. The NHS R and D initiative on children did not consider research on child abuse to be relevant to its objectives.

> "*Child protection* is currently likely to command the strongest allegiance of the majority of child care practitioners, until research can convince them more powerfully than it has done so far that *family support* provides a positive opportunity to influence the quality of life for children and their families, and that it is the essential foundation stone of any system designed to protect children in the widest sense. Family support is not an optional extra, but a fundamental requirement."
> Professor Jane Tunstill, University of Keele

*Report of the
National
Commission of
Inquiry into the
Prevention of
Child Abuse*

Obstacles to research

9.3   The difficulties inherent in research into prevention have to be recognised:

○   It is difficult to assess the effectiveness of measures to prevent abuse as, by definition, what has not occurred can only be estimated rather than measured.

○   Prevention is a long-term activity and it can be several years before results are apparent. Research in this area is therefore both complex and costly.

○   As a main source of funding, either directly or through agencies it finances, central government exerts a strong influence on research programmes. Its research priorities have been with child protection procedures after abuse has happened. The major research programme initiated by the Department of Health, following the enactment of the Children Act, focused overwhelmingly on social work interventions in England, in relation to child protection procedures. The recently established Department of Health research initiative, concentrating particularly on family support and neglect, goes a little way to redress this imbalance, although the Commission considers the scale of this investment to be too low in comparison with the research that is needed.

○   The prevention of child abuse requires a multi-disciplinary approach. This adds to the complexity of the research task and to decisions about who funds it.

○   There are ethical concerns relating to the subject of child abuse which make work in this area complex and discourage the development of research programmes. For example, it is difficult to question young children about sexual abuse. There is a need for a dialogue and educational programme with ethical committees on the issues involved.

○   The marketplace and contract culture through which services are planned and delivered has resulted in lower priority being given to research and evaluation than was previously the case and fewer resources are available locally for research. It has also led to less independent research being conducted as funders and sponsors exert an influence on both subject matter and methods to be employed. This has particularly been the case since the abolition of the Department of Health Small Grants Committee.

Improving research

9.4   In addition to the submissions and research information received, Dr David Gough and Dr Kathleen Murray were commissioned to review recent research, mainly from the United Kingdom and the United States, into the prevention of child abuse (see *Childhood Matters*, Volume Two). Their review confirms the evidence received by the Commission that on most topics there is little soundly-based research or knowledge of the effects of efforts to prevent child abuse. Many research "conclusions" are in fact based on descriptive demonstration programmes.

9.5   Knowledge of international initiatives in prevention is particularly weak. It is clear from the evidence received that UK researchers and practitioners often have only a limited understanding of what responses to child abuse are effective in other countries, particularly those which are non-English speaking.

9.6   It is important that there should be much greater liaison between complementary areas of research. For example, although there are common issues relating to the prevention

Report of the
National
Commission of
Inquiry into the
Prevention of
Child Abuse

of child abuse and the prevention of delinquency, there is little communication between the two research communities.

9.7   The Commission has received extensive evidence from people who have experienced child abuse, their families, and service consumers. This has highlighted the knowledge which such people have of child abuse and the differences between their perceptions and those of researchers and practitioners. Wattam and Woodward's analysis of letters to the Commission indicates that people who have experienced abuse often have valuable insights into how it can be prevented. The Commission therefore recommends that greater priority should be given to both participative research (which actively involves those people who are being studied) and empowering research (which helps enable those who are being studied to participate in their communities and have a greater control over their lives) than is currently the case. It is also important that research findings are shared with those who have been studied.

9.8   The dissemination of research, particularly of smaller studies, is problematic. Many policy makers, practitioners, and other researchers are not aware of the full range of research which has been conducted and have difficulties in obtaining relevant information. For practitioners and policy makers such information must be presented in a form which enables them to use it in their work. A UK-wide multi-disciplinary clearing house should be established to compile and disseminate an index of research into child abuse which has been conducted or is in progress. The Australian National Child Protection Clearing House(2), funded by the Commonwealth Department of Human Services and Health, under the auspices of the National Child Protection Council, is a useful model. It enables research, information and initiatives supporting work in the fields of child abuse and preventing neglect to be widely shared. The cost of such an initiative for the UK would initially be in the region of £40,000 a year. The Commission recommends that the Department of Health awards a grant to an independent agency to set up and run such a clearing house.

111

The way forward

9.9   The Commission proposes that in research, as in other policies affecting child abuse, greater emphasis be given to prevention. This would require major funding bodies to re-examine their present priorities. A review of current research indicates a possible research programme and is listed in Table 9.1. Although each of the proposals could usefully be researched, the financial implications of funding them all would be heavy.

Research Priorities

9.10 It is important that long-term research is conducted so that preventive interventions can be evaluated. A strategy for the prevention of harm to children would require a co-ordinated and systematic multi-disciplinary research programme such as:

i)   **A longitudinal study to assess the impact of child abuse on individuals** and its long-term effects on children and their families, including an account of the factors which assisted or impeded them in dealing with abuse.

Report of the
National
Commission of
Inquiry into the
Prevention of
Child Abuse

ii) **A survey of the incidence of the abuse of children.** To formulate effective policies and allocate resources, more detailed knowledge of the incidence of child abuse is needed.

iii) **Research into the strategies successfully used by "resilient" children.** Research into strategies used successfully by children to avoid victimisation, abuse and abusive situations.

iv) **Action research into public education to change public attitudes and behaviour towards children.** Long-term research in the UK into the effectiveness of public education to prevent child abuse is scarce. The most effective methods of public education work need to be identified.

v) **A long-term evaluation of the outcomes of family support initiatives, including health visiting.** Systematic research into different ways of supporting families is required in order to identify the most effective types of social network and support mechanisms for different types of famlily. Many schemes lack evaluation, independent or otherwise.

vi) **Research into the effectiveness of interventions with neglectful families.** Child abuse inquiries suggest that many cases of child neglect could be prevented, yet little is known about the different forms of professional involvement and how obstacles to intervention can be overcome.

vii) **Research on perpetrators.** This is important as a means of enhancing our knowledge of abuse and as a basis for preventive strategies.

viii) **A programme to improve the diagnosis of abuse.** Research into ways of ensuring early identification of abuse is needed.

112

9.10   Research should be independent of government. The prevention of child abuse and the needs of children span a range of disciplines and professions. For a co-ordinated approach to research and its funding to be established, the needs of children accorded a higher priority and multi-disciplinary research encouraged, the Commission recommends that the main research councils, particularly the Economic and Social Research Council and the Medical Research Council, establish with government an effective mechanism for the joint commissioning and funding of independent research. Commerce and industry should also consider their role in sponsoring research into prevention. Such sponsorship would demonstrate that the community as a whole should be involved in the prevention of child abuse.

Table 9.1 *Research Areas*

The following research areas have been identified arising out of the review of current research and the evidence received by the Commission. Those marked * are identified by the Commission as priorities.

Report of the
National
Commission of
Inquiry into the
Prevention of
Child Abuse

Area of research	Background/Context	Research Proposal
1. Social context of abuse	Within different socio-economic, religious and ethnic groups the social context in which abuse occurs should be addressed.	• A longitudinal study to assess the impact of child abuse on individual children and their families.* • The nature and range of "normal" family life. • The attitudes and beliefs about caring for children, discipline, appropriate punishment and "significant harm". • Public opinion on the causes of child abuse and the extent to which professional practice reflects and influences public views. • Public opinion on views of criminalisation, help and legal intervention. Consideration to be given to the impact of "moral panic" as a factor in responding to child abuse. • The influences on the status, rights and perceptions of children, and how they can be changed. This will draw on international comparisons.
2. Scale of abuse of children	There is no commonly accepted view of how much child abuse happens and how this has changed over time.	• Regular surveys of abusive behaviour and experiences.* • The pattern of prevalence and risk to different groups of children. • The extent of potentially abusive situations. • How children are abused and neglected.
3. Why does abuse happen?	There are no agreed causes of child abuse. An improved understanding is needed.	• Factors linked to abuse. • Which experiences most influence a child's relative risk and vulnerability to "good" or "bad" experiences.
4. Child development	Understanding child development is a recurring theme in evidence to the Commission. This influences both parenting and professional practice.	• Children's understanding of and behaviour in relation to violence, sexuality and resolving conflict. • The development of resilient children: strategies successfully used by children to avoid victimisation, abuse and abusive situations.* • Further research into children's understanding of secrets and "telling", to increase understanding of what actions children will take in response to abuse. • Children's socialisation into their own and others' sexuality.

113

*Report of the
National
Commission of
Inquiry into the
Prevention of
Child Abuse*

Table 9.1 *Research Areas - continued*

Area of research	Background/Context	Research Proposal
5. Parenting	Parents have prime responsibility for the care of their children. Little is known about their perceptions of abuse and appropriate responses.	• What forms of parent education are effective and how they are best delivered. • Parents' assessment of the nature and risk of abuse. • How parents protect their children and what works.
6. Role of the community	The development of a community response to child abuse is a fundamental part of any strategy for the prevention of abuse of children.	• Which types of social network and support are most effective in influencing coping and protecting children? • Which types of community prevention programme are the most effective? • Experimental trials to compare the benefits of different approaches. • Action research: public education to change attitudes and behaviour towards children.*
7. Child-friendly employment policies	Employment practices impinge upon parents' capacity to care for their children. While a number of employers are introducing such policies, the impact upon *children* is not known.	• With children's needs and experiences as a focus, to consider the effects of changing work patterns and related parenting practices and attitudes. • The effects of working and non-working parents on children.
8. Education and prevention of abuse	Education has a vital role in prevention. While the appropriate policies and procedures are broadly in place, the education system is failing to achieve its potential contribution.	• An assessment of the preventive education children currently receive at school. • Develop and test methods for combining programmes across different forms of assault and coercion - eg bullying, harassment etc. • Effective ways of providing personal and social education. • The factors and cost implications of effectively (a) reducing bullying and school exclusions; (b) working with other agencies. • Parental views on sex education: who should provide education; how do parents provide sex education.

Table 9.1 *Research Areas* - *continued*

*Report of the
National
Commission of
Inquiry into the
Prevention of
Child Abuse*

Area of research	Background/Context	Research Proposal
9. Family support services	The value of family support and home visiting schemes as a way of supporting vulnerable families is asserted in many of the submissions received by the Commission both from families and professionals. Strong claims are made about their effectiveness but there have been few conclusive evaluations. Family centres are generally viewed as being supportive towards families but a range of different models of provision exist.	• A long-term evaluation of the effectiveness of family support services. * • The effectiveness of volunteer visiting schemes. • Health visitors: activities undertaken by health visitors and their effectiveness; health visitors' relationships with parents; the potential for developing health visitors' skills and services. • Family centres: different models of provision and their effectiveness for different groups of families.
10. Race and culture	Black and minority group children are largely invisible in the professional response to child abuse. Limited research has been conducted in this area.	• A national study of the black experience of child protection and preventive services to consider how better services can be made available to such communities.
11. Victims of abuse	Work in the area of child abuse and research has concentrated on the investigation of allegations. Little consideration has been given to follow-up and support after the abuse, and the link with the prevention of further abuse.	• The efficiency of different treatment interventions for children. • The child's environment and what maximises and minimises the effects of abuse. • The support needed by parents/carers of abused children. • The experiences of survivors in carrying the suffering resulting from the abuse.
12. Perpetrators of abuse	The prevention of child abuse requires that increased priority should be given to understanding why people abuse children and what forms of treatment work.	• To enhance understanding of why perpetrators abuse children.* • Why do young people start abusing and continue to abuse? What factors are involved? • The effectiveness of different methods of treatment, involving experimental studies. • The management of offenders within the community.

Report of the
National
Commission of
Inquiry into the
Prevention of
Child Abuse

Table 9.1 *Research Areas - continued*

Area of research	Background/Context	Research Proposal
13. Child neglect	"Neglect of neglect" is highlighted in many submissions to the Commission. Cases of neglect, while being preventable, are not being identified or acted upon.	• The characteristics and causes of families who neglect their children. What forms of intervention are effective? • What are the barriers to professionals taking appropriate action in response to neglect?
14. Medical diagnosis	The diagnosis of child abuse and the identification of signs and symptoms at an early stage are currently imprecise.	• A programme to improve the diagnosis of abuse.*
15. Law and its operation	The operation of the law exerts a strong influence on reporting abuse and seeking help.	• The factors that affect the take-up of family support/children in need services under child care legislation. • Research into court practice, sentencing, compensation, and best practices in the UK. • Research into best practice in other countries in the above areas.

Recommendations

Report of the
National
Commission of
Inquiry into the
Prevention of
Child Abuse

82. The main research councils, in co-operation with government, should establish an effective mechanism for the joint commissioning and funding of independent, multi disciplinary research into children's issues.

83. Within this framework, comprehensive research should be commissioned, crossing all main disciplines, to establish evidence-based practice in the preventive field and a robust methodology for costing preventive work, which can be used for comparison with other practices within the care and penal systems.

84. The principal research financing bodies should fund the proposals outlined in paragraph 9.9 above to form the basis of a co-ordinated and systematic research programme.

85. A multi-disciplinary clearing house should be established to compile and disseminate an index of research into child abuse which has been conducted or is currently under way.

References

1. Gough D, Murray K, 1996, The Research Literature on the Prevention of Child Abuse, *in* Childhood Matters: Report of the National Commission of Inquiry into the Prevention of Child Abuse, Volume Two, London: HMSO

2. Child Protection: Messages From Research, 1995, Department of Health, London: HMSO

3. National Child Protection Clearing House, Australian Institute of Family Studies, Melbourne, Australia

Chapter 10
Summary

Report of the
National
Commission of
Inquiry into the
Prevention of
Child Abuse

The National Commission was established in 1994 to propose ways of preventing child abuse and neglect in the United Kingdom. The extent of its remit has led the Commission into taking evidence from a wide range of sources. More than ten thousand people, including a number who have themselves been abused as children, have made their views known, by letter, written submission or in person. In turn, the Commission has visited and noted the different circumstances, practices and, in some instances, the different legal position applying in England, Scotland, Wales and Northern Ireland.

During the course of the Commission's inquiry, the whole country has been shocked by a series of tragic incidents affecting children. Neither abusers nor the abused are confined to any one social class, nor is abuse confined to any one part of the UK. From Dunblane in Scotland, to Wales and Gloucester in the west of England, examples of the damage done to children by sick or depraved people, some of whom have been employed to care for them, has been exposed for all to see. In this, the media have had a vital part to play. As recent events in Belgium have shown, the problem is not the UK's alone. Those who prey upon children are not confined to any one continent. They move freely across national boundaries.

Public and media attention is understandably focused on extreme cases of abuse. The human cost of these is too high for anyone to ignore. But the Commission's task has been to consider abuse and neglect in all its forms. In doing so, it has had to conclude, on the evidence it has received, that any balanced examination of child abuse must come to terms with some uncomfortable truths. In particular, it has to be accepted that:

- despite instances of gross abuse of children by strangers or members of paedophile rings, most abuse is committed by people children have most reason to trust: by members of or individuals known to their own family, or by persons otherwise entrusted with their care;

- it is the youngest and most defenceless children that are most at risk of serious physical harm or even death;

- on the evidence of the hundreds of letters the Commission has received, at least half of the abuse that occurs, sometimes over lengthy periods of a child's life, goes undisclosed at the time it is occurring;

- despite a series of wide-ranging, well-publicised and expensive inquiries into instances of child abuse and neglect over the past twenty years, and despite a flow of recommendations deriving from those inquiries, the abuses that gave rise to those reports persist, largely unaffected by such efforts as have been made to prevent them;

- a common element in almost all instances of abuse or neglect is that much of what is happening has been known to, or at least strongly suspected by, some person or persons other than the abuser. To that extent at least, abuse and neglect are, at least in principle, preventable by some appropriate form of intervention.

*Report of the
National
Commission of
Inquiry into the
Prevention of
Child Abuse*

It is uncomfortable to have to accept that responsibility for child abuse and neglect cannot, except in a comparatively few, though often particularly brutal, instances, be placed on the perverse activities of strangers. On the other hand, it is some consolation that nearly all forms of abuse can be prevented, provided the will to do so is there.

Provided the will to do so is there. Here there are at least some hopeful signs on which to base renewed efforts to prevent child abuse. Our legislation has been moving in the right direction. In recent years, the various Children Acts applying in different parts of the UK have encouraged co-operation between the agencies charged with meeting children's needs and protecting them from harm. That legislation has been reinforced by the UK's ratification of the United Nations Convention on the Rights of the Child. The Commission believes that the wide-ranging principles set out in the UN Convention, with its emphasis on the primacy of children's needs, should be more widely known and consistently implemented than they yet are.

The effective prevention of child abuse needs more than legislation and the formal procedures that accompany it. The necessary commitment has to be shared nationwide. In the Commission's experience, to a large extent it is. The Commission has everywhere encountered a strong sense of what people want for all children, not only for their own. They want all children to develop healthily and safely into adulthood. There is a personal, community and political responsibility, widely accepted, for trying to ensure this. It is this general goodwill, allied to the principles already implicit in our legislation, that provides the solid ground on which to build a nation-wide effort to prevent child abuse and neglect. It was from that perception that the Commission adopted a wide definition of abuse in terms of which, it believes, particular aspects of abuse or neglect and policies relating to these should be considered. That definition runs as follows:

> **"Child abuse consists of anything which individuals, institutions or processes do or
> fail to do which directly or indirectly harms children or damages their prospects of a
> safe and healthy development into adulthood."**

This definition encompasses neglect and abuse in their most direct and acute forms but includes far more. Establishing the full effects on children of poor housing, health care and diet, or the indirect effects of poverty on their well-being, would have taken the Commission well beyond its remit; but the effect, both direct and indirect, of these conditions on the families in which children are brought up is certainly damaging. In some instances, it can be profoundly so.

So far as poverty is concerned, to take one example, there is no direct link between poverty and child abuse. At any level of income, parents can and do give their children a warm and supportive start to life. But when poverty is allied to other factors, such as poor family health, unemployment, bad housing, or a combination of these, the evidence is that the stresses that build up in the home make it more likely that children will suffer harm and that their secure development into adulthood will be at risk.

These indirect forms of harm are hard to quantify. That there are over four million of the country's thirteen million children living in poverty, defined as living on less than half the average national income, is a fact. That reducing that total, and thereby the stressful home conditions often associated with it, would reduce the harm those stresses do to children is indisputable; but putting a figure to that must remain a matter for speculation and further enquiry. Official statistics are little help in this respect. What estimates suggest, however, is that at least one in ten children are, at some point in their childhood, judged to be at risk of significant harm and likely to be suffering from physical, emotional, sexual or other forms of abuse or neglect. The true position is likely to be far worse than this, given the degree to which abuse is concealed by those who suffer it. Furthermore, the evidence the Commission has received from victims of abuse makes it clear that abuse is seldom one-dimensional in the way official statistics suggest. Physical or sexual abuse is nearly always accompanied by emotional suffering that may be even harder to bear and last even longer. More consistently collected and regularly published statistics, which give a full account of all aspects of child abuse and neglect, are required if policies for remedying matters are to be soundly based.

Confronted by the evidence of the scale of abuse and neglect and in the knowledge that most is preventable and that there is widespread goodwill towards efforts to reduce it, the Commission has considered why prevention is itself being prevented. The main reasons appear to be as follows:

○ Individuals, often neighbours, aware of what may be happening to children close to them are uncertain whether to intervene or whom to turn to for advice. Children themselves are often, despite the increasing use of confidential advice lines, either unaware of whom to get in touch with or afraid of doing so.

○ Busy people, such as GPs, health visitors, teachers, child care workers and others professionally concerned with children, too often, through other pressures, miss or fail to respond adequately to signs of abuse in children they meet in the course of their work.

○ Public agencies, particularly local and health authorities, wishing to make a shift towards prevention, find it difficult to do so. Prevention is hard to measure. It is always easier to focus on problems that have already arisen and can be measured. General nervousness about the consequences of failure leads to over-prescription on the one hand and over-bureaucratic responses on the other.

○ Some recent and welcome legislative initiatives are under-funded. This is notably true of children's services plans. At the same time, some £1 billion is spent each year on dealing with the varied forms of abuse and neglect, most of it on the consequences of failing to prevent them. Inquiries into the failures of protective measures can also be expensive. £3.38 million, for example, was spent on the Fife Inquiry into Child Care Policies. Reallocation of resources to preventive work, though this must be possible over time, is proving difficult.

○ The legal system itself, designed to provide justice and redress for victims of abuse, is failing to do so consistently. The way the court system operates can itself be so damaging to children that, in the children's own interests, even when the most blatant instances of abuse are involved, abusers escape prosecution. Balancing the rights of accused and accuser is notoriously difficult. On the one hand it is important that those accused of abuse should be protected against the consequences of false accusations against them. Procedures for ensuring this are in place and should be strictly adhered to. On the other hand, if the legal process causes the abused child to suffer an experience which can be as damaging as the original abuse itself, the purpose of justice is defeated.

Report of the
National
Commission of
Inquiry into the
Prevention of
Child Abuse

121

*Report of the
National
Commission of
Inquiry into the
Prevention of
Child Abuse*

o Government structures, both local and national, are not designed with children's interests in mind and too often do not serve those interests well. Children are not the principal concern of any one government department. This leads to regulations, advice, policies and even legislative measures that, at times, either conflict or lack a clear sense of direction.

o There remains uncertainty about what forms of intervention are most effective in preventing abuse and neglect and their relative cost.

The Commission's recommendations deal with ways of removing obstacles to prevention and include a number of positive suggestions. Of these, three are of particular significance:

o Close to the centre of government there needs to be a visible expression of the importance the nation places on doing the best it can for its children. Children's Commissioners would provide the necessary continuity, visibility, public reporting and consistent advocacy that is now lacking. Of equal importance would be enhanced ministerial responsibility, to ensure that children's interests were recognized, protected and promoted at all stages of the parliamentary and legislative process.

o A major emphasis on public education is now required at all levels: from education at school, to that of parents or potential parents themselves. More widely, the implications of the UK's own legislation need to be better disseminated to help create a new perception of children not as possessions but as individuals with rights and developing responsibilities of their own. So far as public awareness is concerned, it should be recognized that much abuse is committed by ordinary people under extraordinary pressures. That some abusers are evil is undeniable; that others and their families require help and a degree of support is equally true.

o There needs to be closer co-operation between education, health, social services, probation services, the police and voluntary organisations in a sustained effort to identify and respond effectively to child abuse and neglect. This response cannot simply be left to professionals. Their efforts will have to be supported by wider and better articulated public insistence that what the country wants for its children it gets. To this endeavour the media can make a valuable contribution through the way it reports, informs, and, when necessary, adds its campaigning weight.

The way children are treated in any society is a defining characteristic of that society. Despite the efforts of many individuals and agencies, both official and voluntary, too many children in the UK are abused or neglected and too little is done to prevent this. The Commission is convinced that there is widespread acceptance throughout the UK that, as the title to this Report declares, childhood matters. The recommendations that follow are designed to provide a sharper focus on the right of all children to a healthy and safe development into adulthood. Child abuse and neglect can almost always be prevented – *provided the will to do so is there*. That is the essential message of this Report.

Recommendations

*Report of the
National
Commission of
Inquiry into the
Prevention of
Child Abuse*

1. Data on the condition of children in the UK should be systematically collected, published annually and presented to Parliament either through a Children's Commissioner (see Chapter Six) or through some other agency statutorily required to carry out this function.

2. The data, reflecting a wide definition of abuse, should include information on poverty, health, and an assessment of the numbers of children "in need" as well as providing information under the statutorily defined categories of abuse.

3. The age of the victim and the relationship of the victim to the alleged offender should be recorded by the police for all crimes including sexual and violent crimes.

4. Crime statistics should separately report the extent of these crimes against children under the age of 16.

Finance

5. Government departments should co-operate to develop a "business plan for children" designed to shift investment to a preventive approach to child abuse while maintaining proper protection of those most at risk. Such plans should include the following measures:

    (a) Central government resource allocation formulae for health, education, social services and the penal system should be reviewed and factors introduced to give an emphasis to preventive services for children.

    (b) National performance indicators produced by government departments, the Audit Commission and other relevant bodies should be revised and co-ordinated to give greater emphasis to the well-being of all children, including those who have problems or who are under-achieving, and to managerial/organisational targets which demonstrate effective preventive work.

6. To accompany the children's services plan, local statutory agencies should be required to produce a financial plan. This should identify the funding invested in present services for children. In particular, there should be a requirement that the National Health Service identifies those proportions of the community health, family health services and acute services budgets that are allocated to children. Voluntary sector agencies should be encouraged to participate in this approach.

7. Government departments should stimulate joint planning and purchasing of local services through providing incentives, such as short-term funding, and removing technical and legal barriers to joint budgets and funding transfers.

8. The major child care voluntary organisations should co-ordinate their plans and funding priorities with each other and with the relevant local authorities and agencies.

Report of the
National
Commission of
Inquiry into the
Prevention of
Child Abuse

9. Government, in co-operation with the main statutory and voluntary agencies, should develop a medium to long-term funding strategy designed to achieve greater investment in preventive services while continuing to protect high-risk children and families. The strategy should include an analysis of whether there is sufficient funding in the system to achieve this and identify any shortfall.

10. Government should reassess the balance of funding between children's and adults' services in the public sector.

Improvement in the operation of current law and court conduct

11. There should be regular monitoring by the Lord Chancellor's Office and by the Scottish Courts Administration of the availability of properly trained and experienced judges for civil proceedings involving children. If necessary to reduce delay, the number of such judges should be increased.

12. Within two years, all solicitors and barristers representing parties in civil proceedings affecting the care, protection, and custody of children should be trained and accredited to work in the child care field and their performance monitored to ensure that they maintain knowledge of current developments.

13. Within two years, judges and advocates acting in criminal cases involving child witnesses and/or victims should receive training in understanding and communicating with children and in how to ensure that court proceedings are conducted in ways appropriate to the age of the children involved.

14. Every case involving children should have designated judges who review cases every four weeks and give stipulated time limits for hearings.

15. Consideration should be given to allocating the same judges to civil and criminal proceedings involving the same child.

16. All courts should consider the conduct, dress and location of the court when children are active participants in cases, and make appropriate changes to facilitate the comfort and avoid intimidation of the child. Children should be brought from home to court when needed and not have to wait in court.

17. Central government should, through changes in legislation or by regulation, ensure that other relevant services co-operate with social services and social work departments in developing a Children's Services Plan and by making explicit investment in children's services.

18. Government departments should revise guidance on child protection procedures to give a clear framework and mandate to practitioners within which they can operate with greater freedom to exercise professional judgement without leaving children at increased risk of abuse.

19. Relevant government departments should monitor the provision of services to children in need to ascertain whether the obligations set out under current legislation are being fulfilled and, if not, what is preventing them being met.

*Report of the
National
Commission of
Inquiry into the
Prevention of
Child Abuse*

20. The principles and law governing privilege, as it is operated in civil and criminal proceedings, should be reviewed and harmonised by the Law Commission.

21. Officers of the court, the police and social workers should all receive training on communicating with and understanding disabled children and on their particular vulnerability to abuse.

22. The Crown Prosecution Service, Procurators Fiscal and other relevant parties should ensure that children and parents are kept fully informed of developments in the preparation and progress of cases including adequate notice of any requirement to give evidence.

23. The Lord Chancellor's Office, the Crown Office, and other agencies responsible for bringing child witnesses to court should consider ways of improving the arrangements for supporting and preparing children for court and for ensuring that the children receive the treatment they need.

24. Judges should ensure that child witnesses are not discriminated against by virtue of any relationship they might have with a statutory agency holding a personal file. No records maintained for purposes such as medical treatment, therapy, care or because children have special needs, should be used in court in respect of any child.

Regulation of staff

25. Central government should establish a fully integrated and automated system, with proper safeguards, to record information about all those working in children's services found guilty of, or cautioned or subjected to formal disciplinary action for, any kind of assault against children or other serious misdemeanour which has placed children at risk. This should record findings of guilt in criminal proceedings and the outcomes of formal disciplinary action. It should be accessible to employers and voluntary organisations. In future, a UK-wide service could be linked to similar systems in other countries.

26. Applicants for work with children should be obliged to make a personal statement regarding their criminal or disciplinary record with regard to children. A false statement should be grounds for summary dismissal and this should be recorded on the relevant national register.

27. Government should establish a system requiring employers to act upon knowledge of proven misconduct on the part of any of their employees in relation to children and provide full and detailed information in any references supplied to other employers.

28. Improved co-ordination between criminal justice, child protection, and care agencies must be established to meet the overall needs of young sex offenders. The law should be reformed to enable them to receive an assessment prior to decisions about legal and care proceedings.

Proposals for new legislation

29. Government should, in the interests of public confidence and safety, support the

125

*Report of the
National
Commission of
Inquiry into the
Prevention of
Child Abuse*

creation of professional regulatory bodies for all disciplines which work with children and review existing regulatory bodies to ensure their practices are specifically geared to the protection of children. In particular, the Government should support the establishment of a General Social Services Council.

30. In the light of the Scottish experience, the law in England, Wales and Northern Ireland should be amended to include the concepts in Scottish law of parental responsibilities and a general obligation to consult children on important matters affecting their future.

31. The Lord Chancellor's Office, Department of Health, the Scottish Office, the Northern Ireland Office and other relevant government departments should develop legislation which is firmly based upon the UN Convention on the Rights of the Child.

32. Legislation should be introduced to effect full implementation of the recommendations of the Report of the Advisory Group on Video Recorded Evidence, Home Office, London, 1989 (the Pigot Report).

33. The Lord Chancellor, the Crown Office, the Scottish Office and the Northern Ireland Office should review the present system of dealing with child victims, witnesses and children otherwise subject to court proceedings and consider the legislative changes that would be needed to move towards a more investigative and less adversarial method of dealing with children and young people.

34. The law, as it affects the physical punishment of children, should be amended to give children, in all circumstances, the same protection against assault as adults. Section 1 (7) of the Children and Young Person's Act 1933 should be repealed and the defence of "reasonable chastisement" should therefore be removed.

35. Government should conduct an inter-departmental review of the operation of the criminal justice system as it affects child defendants, particularly in relation to the age of criminal responsibility and the nature of the courts in which children are tried.

Child Prostitution

36. In all matters affecting children involved in prostitution, precedence should be given to "the best interests of the child", as set out in the Children Act(s).

37. The emphasis of criminal proceedings should be placed on the identification and prosecution of clients and pimps who exploit children through prostitution, rather than on the child.

38. The Lord Chancellor should initiate a review of the law in so far as it relates to children involved in prostitution and their clients. Such a review would include a consideration of:

(i) raising the age of criminal responsibility from the age of ten.

(ii) giving legal force to Article 34 of the United Nations Convention on the Rights of the Child (see paragraph 5.32).

Report of the
National
Commission of
Inquiry into the
Prevention of
Child Abuse

National Arrangements

39. Commissioners for Children should be appointed for England, Scotland, Wales and Northern Ireland with terms of reference to include those set out in para. 6.19 above.

40. (i) The Secretary of State for Health's title should expanded to Secretary of State for Health and Children.

   (ii) The Minister with specific responsibility for children should be upgraded and entitled Minister of State and Minister for Children.

   (iii) The principal functions of the Minister should be to report on the operation of UK legislation and developments relating to the implementation of the UN Convention on the Rights of the Child; to chair a ministerial committee for co-ordinating policies affecting children, on which all relevant departments should be represented; and to present children's issues to the public and to promote the "listening to children approach".

41. Central government should commission an independent review of the effects on multi-agency children's services planning of local management of schools; of the purchasing and provision organisation of the health service and the purchaser/provider split in social services. Such a review should consider the implications of differences between the boundaries of local authorities and health authorities, and the effect of small, unitary authorities in Wales, Scotland and parts of England. The review could also compare the experience in Northern Ireland of the creation of combined health/social services trusts.

42. Central government should initiate a review of technical obstacles to local commissioning, joint budgeting and joint management of children's services, particularly those of a legal or financial nature, and seek to remove them.

43. The relevant central government departments should not set priorities, targets and key indicators for services affecting children without joint discussions to ensure that they are complementary and will facilitate local collaboration.

44. Government departments should take a national view of the need to recruit able people to children's services and develop a strategy to attract and retain skilled practioners.

Local Arrangements

45. There should be additional measures to ensure all services and those responsible for them participate fully in the planning and delivery of children's services. This should be achieved by changes in primary legislation or through targets, key indicators or other formal requirements of central government departments.

46. Local children's services planning and provision should be subject to a powerful monitoring and accountability mechanism which could operate from a regional base.

47. Government should support and promote the development of a comprehensive approach to joint commissioning.

127

*Report of the
National
Commission of
Inquiry into the
Prevention of
Child Abuse*

48. The Department of Health, in co-operation with the Welsh, Scottish and Northern Ireland Offices, should conduct a review of the role and functions of child protection committees.

Child-Friendly Communities

49. Central government, local authorities and health authorities should recognise and measure the benefits and costs of support for children and families and develop explicit strategies to facilitate stronger and permanent neighbourhood support and service networks. This should be achieved through:

(i)   developing and co-ordinating the statutory services (particularly, health, social service and education) to stimulate and develop community sensitivity and support, self-help and peer support.

(ii) co-ordinated, reliable and long-term funding of voluntary and community sector activity.

(iii) developing and co-ordinating local and national helplines and local drop-in centres for children, parents, carers and victims, to ensure comprehensive coverage and most effective use of resources. National and local government should consider the general funding and development of these services. Provision of these services should be incorporated into children's services plans.

50. Health and local authorities should report to central government on their proposals for community development designed to promote and support a better childhood for all children.

51. Individuals in key positions in voluntary and community groups, including religious organisations, should receive training to raise awareness of the needs of children and parents, child protection procedures, and the dangers of not vetting adults wishing to work with children.

52. A national body for survivors should be established to act as an information exchange, provide support to member groups and individuals, perhaps through a 24-hour helpline, and undertake developmental work.

Child-friendly employment policies

53. Employers' organisations and trades unions should initiate a review of employment patterns with a view to making them compatible with parenting and family life.

Parenting education

54. To ensure delivery of high-quality, universally available parenting education, voluntary agencies should co-operate to put joint proposals for in-school and post-school education to: (a) the Schools Curriculum and Assessment Authority and (b) the Department of Health, inviting them to co-ordinate government's response, including that of the Department of Education and Employment, and that of the Local Education Authorities.

The media

55. Journalists' training should include child abuse issues, to improve the coverage of child abuse cases and editorial content.

Report of the
National
Commission of
Inquiry into the
Prevention of
Child Abuse

56. The Children's Commissioners should be the principal source of informed comment on children's issues so that the media can have the authoritative and independent source of information that is currently lacking.

57. In covering news stories in which children feature, the media should have a obligation to consider the child's best interest. Failure to do so should be grounds for complaint to the relevant authority.

58. Media regulations should separately monitor and report on coverage of, and complaints about coverage of, children's issues.

59. Key professionals within social services and social work departments should be trained in media relations. Dedicated public relations staff should be available to each department.

60. A public education campaign should be developed aimed at raising awareness: of the needs of children in general, including the nature of child abuse, and of the appropriate action to take when concerned about a child. Such a campaign should be initiated by central government and the proposed Minister for Children, and supported by local communities and agencies with locally-based campaigns.

Professional Services

61. Services should give greater emphasis to supporting children and families before abuse occurs. A clear lead should be given by government, through revised guidance, and the issue should be addressed by all relevant authorities and professions. Services need to be developed that work in partnership with children and families and respect their rights to participation, consultation, and redress when errors occur. An effective child protection service must be maintained alongside improved family support provision.

62. The components of a preventive service on which to build are: child health surveillance programmes; the education service's role in child protection; day care provision; accessible information and advice, including a national 24 hour telephone advice line for parents; family support services; and child protection services. A multi-agency response is needed to ensure that cases of abuse are identified at an early stage and support provided.

63. All families should have access to some form of family support, such as, a family centre, advice and guidance or practical help in the home, such as that provided by Homestart.

64. Through the mechanism of children's services plans, the social service, education and health authorities should aim to achieve greater integration of services for children, particularly those with special needs, through joint budgets, joint provision, a single assessment procedure for determining children's needs, and joint commissioning.

Health

65. The Health Service must give greater emphasis to preventive services. It should establish combined child health services and commission the full range of services for children, with specific contracts and clear outcomes.

*Report of the
National
Commission of
Inquiry into the
Prevention of
Child Abuse*

66. Child health surveillance should give greater emphasis to identifying children suffering or at risk of abuse. The importance of the role of the general practitioner in identifying abuse, in child protection procedures and in providing family support should be recognised and developed. The health visiting service should be run as a universal service, and encouraged to undertake preventive work with families.

67. The training and guidance of health professionals should emphasise the particular vulnerability of babies to injury and death as a result of abuse and the need to be alert to the signs of possible maltreatment.

Education

68. To enable teachers to respond effectively to child abuse, all training institutions and schools involved in the initial training of teachers should include in their programme information on the UN Convention on the Rights of the Child, and on ways of identifying signs of potential or actual abuse of children. So far as teachers already in post are concerned, LEAs, the Schools Funding Agency and those controlling GEST programmes should ensure that all teachers with some defined responsibility for dealing with suspected or actual incidences of child abuse and neglect have received appropriate training.

69. Well-managed school behaviour policies are effective in reducing the level of bullying and every effort should be made by those responsible for implementing such policies to ensure that they are developed by all schools.

Social Services

70. All social services and social work departments should ensure that responsibility for children's services is at a senior level (2nd or 3rd tier) and that line managers with responsibility for residential, fieldwork and day-care services are appropriately qualified and substantially experienced in child care.

71. Recommendations made by other inquiries, aimed at eradicating the abuse of children in residential care, must be fully implemented as a matter of high priority and backed with the necessary resources, training, and staff support.

72. Government departments and local statutory organisations should develop a clear basis for recognising and acting upon the neglect of children. The degree of neglect calling for intervention should not vary within and between geographical regions or local or health authority areas. Central government and local organisations should ensure that neglect requiring action should be clearly defined and specifically identified in the planning and funding of services.

73. Doctors, nurses and social workers and other professionals who work mainly with adults, for example in the mental health services, should be trained to recognise risks to children implicit in their adult client's situation.

Police

74. All police officers must be trained in child protection, not just those working in child protection units. In investigating crimes, particularly those relating to domestic

violence, drugs and alcohol abuse, police should be conscious of the needs of children and possible child protection concerns, and should liaise with other relevant professionals.

75. National government and police authorities should give increased priority and resources to the investigation of crimes involving child pornography.

Treatment

76. Each area child protection committee should review the extent to which the demand is locally met for support and treatment services for abuse victims and their families, those whose lives and relationships have been disrupted unnecessarily by child protection inquiries, and for offenders, and develop a multi-disciplinary plan for reducing any shortfall. Treatment services should be integrated with the wider children's services plan. Government departments should assist local services by developing guidance on what professional services should be provided and on what scale.

77. Greater priority must be given to the treatment of sex offenders, particularly young and adolescent sex offenders. A national 24 hour helpline, backed with support services and working with existing agencies, should be established to provide immediate help to offenders who fear they are a danger to children. Central government should consider how such a helpline might be effectively resourced.

Training

78. The basic and post-qualifying training of social workers, doctors and health visitors should give greater emphasis to: normal child development and behaviour; communication with children; recognition of the standard measure of child neglect; the needs of *all* children and those with chronic illness, disability, deprivation, and behavioural problems; mental illness in childhood; the ability to work cross culturally and to challenge discriminatory practice of any kind; the skills of working supportively in partnership with community networks and with parents; the skills and implications of multi-disciplinary working and assessment; and the signs, symptoms and treatment of post-natal depression.

79. There should be rigorous monitoring and evaluation of selection procedures for social work training to ensure that students possess the necessary maturity, sensitivity and intellectual capacity for social work.

80. Social work training may encompass different educational and training routes over different timescales but the award of a social work qualification should follow the equivalent of at least three years' full-time social work education and training and be to degree standard.

81. There should greater emphasis in social work training on developing a professional culture of continuing education, and greater investment in a range of specialist post-qualifying training, including residential social work and direct work with children and families.

*Report of the
National
Commission of
Inquiry into the
Prevention of
Child Abuse*

Research

82. The main research councils, in co-operation with government, should establish an effective mechanism for the joint commissioning and funding of independent, multi disciplinary research into children's issues.

83. Within this framework, comprehensive research should be commissioned, crossing all main disciplines, to establish evidence-based practice in the preventive field and a robust methodology for costing preventive work, which can be used for comparison with other practices within the care and penal systems.

84. The principal research financing bodies should fund the proposals outlined in paragraph 9.9 above to form the basis of a co-ordinated and systematic research programme.

85. A multi-disciplinary clearing house should be established to compile and disseminate an index of research into child abuse which has been conducted or is currently under way.

Appendices

Report of the
National
Commission of
Inquiry into the
Prevention of
Child Abuse

Appendices

Report of the
National
Commission of
Inquiry into the
Prevention of
Child Abuse

Evidence Received

*Report of the
National
Commission of
Inquiry into the
Prevention of
Child Abuse*

The National Commission has received written and oral evidence, undertaken field visits and consulted with the following individuals and organisations.

Written Evidence

0-19 Support Team, Armley Clinic, Leeds Community Mental Health Services Trust/Leeds City Council Department of Social Services, Elizabeth Hume, Team Health Visitor

Accuracy About Abuse, Marjorie Orr, Director

Adams, Steve, Advisory Teacher (Child Protection), Derbyshire LEA

Addington School, Anne Hodgkinson, Deputy Headteacher

Addy, Mr M. G., Consultant Paediatrician, Burton Hospital

Adult Survivors of Child Sexual Abuse, Dave Simon, Director

Association For All Speech Impaired Children (AFASIC), Norma Corkish, Director

Agathonos-Georgopoulou, Helen, Director, Section of Family Relations, KaPa Centre, Institute of Child Health, Athens

Action for Governors' Information and Training, David Smith, Chair

Alridge, Jo, Young Carers Research Group, Loughborough University

Allen-Pentland, Jo, Author

Angus, Dr C.W.G., GP, Fife

Anchor,(Kite Support Group) Cath Foulds, Director

ANTIDOTE, James Park, Director

Anti-Slavery International, Lesley Roberts, Director

Appleton, Jane, Senior Lecturer, University of Hertfordshire, and Health Visitor, West Herts Community NHS Trust

Arnell, Ami, Radda Barnen (Swedish Save the Children), Stockholm, Psychologist

Association of Chief Officers of Probation, Jill Thomas, Assistant General Secretary

Association of Chief Police Officers, Tony Butler, Chief Constable, Gloucestershire Constabulary

Association of Child Psychotherapists, Eve Grainger, Chair, External Relations Sub-Committee

Association of County Councils, Dorothy Blatcher

Association of Directors of Social Services, Chris Davies

Association of Lawyers for Children, William Ackroyd, Treasurer

Association of Metropolitan Authorities, Brian Jones

Association of Radical Midwives, Ishbel Kargar, Secretary

Association of Teachers and Lecturers, Gill Sage, Solicitor

Association of Workers for Children with Emotional and Behavioural Difficulties, Sue Panter, General Secretary

Association for Family Therapy, Dave Simon

Avon ACPC, Joe Howsam, Chair

Report of the
National
Commission of
Inquiry into the
Prevention of
Child Abuse

Barber, Rosalyn, Student, Women's Studies Department, Roehampton University

Barnados Bridgeway Project, Tink Palmer, Project Leader

Barnes, Dr Jacqueline, Senior Lecturer, Leopold Muller Department of Child and Family Health, Royal Free Hospital of Medicine

BBC, Mark Helmsley, Assistant to the Secretary's Office

Bedfordshire ACPC, Wes Cuell, Chair

Begbee, Tony, Community Liaison Officer, Hailsham, Sussex

Belas, Patrick, Senior Social Work Practitioner and Family Therapist, Bromley, Kent

Bennett Britton, Steve, Consultant Paediatrician, Good Hope Hospital, West Midlands

Berridge, Dr David, Faculty of Health Care and Social Studies, Reader in Applied Social Studies, University of Luton

Birmingham Child Witness Support Consortium, Anne Mellor, Psychologist

Birmingham City Council Social Services Department, Howard Woolfenden, Head of Child Protection Services

Black Women for Wages for Housework, Cristel Amiss

Blair, Dr Mitch, Consultant Paediatrician, Nottingham Community Health Service

Blow, David, PGCE Course Leader, Edge Hill Higher Education Corporation

Booth, Wendy, Research Associate and **Booth, Dr Tim**, Reader in Social Policy, Department of Sociological Studies, University of Sheffield

Both Parents Forever, John Bell, Co-director

Boys' Brigade, Sydney Jones, Brigade Secretary

Brackenbridge, Celia, Head of Research, and **Summers, Diana**, Researcher, Department of Leisure Management, Cheltenham and Gloucester College of Higher Education.

Breakfree, Dr David Smith and Linda Pearce, Joint Directors

Bridge, The, Child Care Consultancy Service, John Fitzgerald, Director

British Agencies for Adoption and Fostering, Deborah Cullen, Secretary to the Legal Group

British Association for Community Child Health, Dr Chris Hobbs, Dr Jane Wynne, Ms H. Hanks, Ms S. Whitworth, Ms C. Parrish

British Association for Counselling, Tim Bond, Chair and Judith Baron, General Manager

British Association of Social Workers, David Colvin, Acting Deputy General Secretary

British Dental Association, Penny Whitehead, Membership Services Department

British False Memory Syndrome Society, Roger Scotford, Director

British Medical Association, M.J. Lowe, Deputy Secretary

British Organisation of Non-Parents, Root Cartwright, Chairman

British Paediatric Association, Dr Keith L. Dodd, Honorary Secretary, Marion Miles, Consultant Community Paediatrician

British Paediatric Association, Psychiatry and Psychology Group, A. N. P. Speight, Consultant Paediatrician

British Psychological Society, Ingrid Lunt, Chair, Professional Affairs Board

Bristol Crisis Service for Women, Lois Arnold and Karin Parker

Bristow, Wendy, Journalist

Broadcasting Standards Council, Andrea Millwood Hargrave, Research Director

Bro Taf Health Authority, Dr Sharon Hopkins

Brown, Hilary, Senior Lecturer in Learning Disability, Tizard Centre, University of Kent

Brown, R.J.C., Kingston, Ontario

Browne, Dr Kevin, Department of Psychology, University of Birmingham

Broxtowe Family Centre, NCH Action for Children, Trish Ross, Project Leader

Bryn Estyn Staff Support Group, John Rayfield, Secretary

Bryson House (Northern Ireland) Jo Marley, Director, Family/Caring Services

BT Forum, Joanna Foster, Director

Bull, Professor Ray, Department of Psychology, University of Portsmouth

Butler, Ian, and Dr Howard Williamson, School of Social and Administration Studies, University of Wales, Cardiff

Caldecott Community, Mrs B.A. Seymour, Assistant Director

Calderdale ACPC, Marie Denton, Chair

Camberwell Advocacy Office, Kathy West

Cambridgeshire County Council LEA, Brian Gale, Manager, Learning Support Services

Cambridgeshire ACPC, Ted Unsworth, Chair

Camden ACPC, Gerri McAndrew, Chair

Caplan, Dr Richard, Consultant Psychiatrist, Southern General Hospital, Glasgow

CARLI Project, Mairead Gormley, Project Worker

Carmarthen Women's Aid, Jane Shaw, Child Worker

Community Alternatives to Care, Harlow, Carol Young, Project Manager

Catholic Child Welfare Council, J.M. Richards, Chair Professional Issues Sub Committee

Central Council for Education and Training in Social Work (CCETSW), Tony Hall, Director

Central Region CPC, Christie Simpson, Training Co-ordinator

Centre for Family Policy and Child Welfare, University of Bristol, Elaine Farmer

Centrepoint, Radiance Strathdee, Research Manager

Cerezo, Professor Angeles, University of Valencia, Departament de Psicologia Basica, Profesora Titular de Psicologia, Directora U.I. Agresion y Familia

Child Growth Foundation, Tam Fry, Honorary Chairman

ChildLine, Valerie Howarth, Executive Director, and Hereward Harrison, Director of Counselling.

Children 1st, RSSPCC, Arthur Wood, Director

Children in Scotland, Dr Bronwen Cohen, Director

Children in Wales, Catriona Williams, Director

Children North East, Joy Higginson, Director

Children's Legal Centre, Committee on the Administration of Justice, Maureen O'Hara

Children's Rights Development Unit, Gerison Lansdown, Director

Childwatch, Diane Core, Founder/Director

Choices in Childcare, Susan McQuail, Chair of Management Committee

Christensen, Else, Danish Institute of Social Research

Church of England National Children's Officer, Ivor Hughes, Rector of Yeovil

Church of Scotland Woman's Guild, Lorna Paterson, General Secretary

Christian Survivors of Sexual Abuse, Margaret Kennedy, Coordinator

Clayden, Marion, Counsellor and Psychotherapist and John Roberts, Social Worker

Cleveland ACPC, David Behan, Chair

Cleveland Child and Family Trust, Hilary Cushman

Clossick, Jim, Prinicpal Social Worker, Northants Social Services Department

Clwydian Community Care, Dr Peter Appleton, Clinical Psychology Services Manager, Senior Lecturer in Clinical Psychology

*Report of the
National
Commission of
Inquiry into the
Prevention of
Child Abuse*

Coalition on Child Prostitution and Tourism, Anne Badger, Campaign Coordinator

Coleg Menai, Alana Gibson, School of Business

Committee on the Administration of Justice, The Northern Ireland Civil Liberties Council, Anne McKeoun, Convenor

Community Development Foundation (North), Paul Henderson, Director, North of England and Scotland

Community Education Development Centre, Anne Schonveld, Training Officer

Cook, Sue, *Sun* Counsellor and Advice Columnist

Co-operative Women's Guild, Sue Bell, General Secretary

County Durham ACPC, M.H. Sawyer, Chair

Cornwall Social Services Department, Jane Sloan, Social Work Consultant (CP)

Council for Disabled Children, Philippa Russell, Director

Council of Local Education Authorities, Ivor Widdison, Administrator

Counselling in Education, Marilyn McGowan, Chair of Working Party

Coventry Social Services Department, Malcolm Tosh, Fieldwork manager

Crown Prosecution Service, Criminal Justice Policy Division, Alison Saunders

Croydon ACPC, Joan Semeonoff, Child Protection Advisor

Dartington Social Research Unit, School of Applied Social Studies, University of Bristol, Dr Michael Little, Deputy Director

Davies, Professor David, Department of Child Health, University of Wales, College of Medicine

Day, Jackie, Practice Manager, Comberton Team, Cambridgeshire County Council

Devon Community Services, Chris Kippax, Principal Officer, Learning Disabilities

Devon Youth Council

Dingwall, Professor Robert, Professor of Social Work Studies, University of Nottingham

DMB & B, Sally Ford-Hutchinson, Executive Director of Planning

Dobash, Russell, Senior Lecturer, School of Social and Administration Studies, University of Cardiff

Doppke, Sven, Schleswig-Holstein GmbH, Germany, T.V. Producer

Dorset ACPC, Pam Rossiter, Policy Officer, Child Protection

Doyle, Celia, Lecturer in Protection Studies, Nene College

Draycott, Barry, Social Worker

Dudley Social Services Department Child Protection Team, Christine Ballinger, Child Protection Manager and Jackie Jennings, Acting Team Leader

Dudley LEA Counselling Service, Janette Newton, Teamleader

Dunfermline Incest Survivors Group, Carol M. Logan, Outreach Worker

Dunovsky, Professor Jiri, SOS Detske Vesnicky, Head of Children Centre, Prague, Czech Republic

Dyfed ACPC and Social Services Department, John Wreford, Chair ACPC, Deputy DSS

Dyfed-Powys Police, R. White, Chief Constable

Dyson, T.E., Senior Educational Psychologist, Gwent County Council

Early Childhood Development Unit, School for Policy Studies, University of Bristol, Dr Walter Barker, Director

Educational Broadcasting Services Trust (EBS), Jim Stevenson, Service Manager

Edwards, Shirley

Eekelar, John, Reader in Law, Pembroke College, Oxford

Egan-Sage, Elmarie, Counselling Psychologist, Tizard Centre, University of Kent

ENABLE, Scottish Society for the Mentally Handicapped, Norman Dunning, Director

Enfield Education Committee, Child & Family Service, Mrs E. Holmes, Principal Officer, Child Guidance

EPOCH (End Physical Punishment of Children), Peter Newell, Coordinator

Essex ACPC, Philip Thomson, Secretary

Essex County Council, Michael Leadbetter, Director of Social Services

Etherington, Kim, Counsellor/Psychotherapist

Exploring Parenthood, Carolyn Douglas, Director

Faircheck, Michael Hames, Managing Director

Faithfull Foundation, Hilary Eldridge, Clinical Director

Families Need Fathers, Stan Hayward, Research Officer

Family and Youth Concern, Valerie Riches, Director

Family Law Bar Association, Miss E.A. Lawson QC, Secretary

Family Matters, Dot Riley, Chair, and Pat McAlpin, General Manager

Family Mediation Scotland, Carol Barrett, Development Officer

Family Rights Group, Mary Ryan, Co-director

Family Service Units, Adah Kay, Director

Farmer, Nicky, Health Visitor, Oxfordshire Community Health Trust

Fartown Children and Families Team, Mike Freel, Kirklees

Fife CPC, Peter Tempest

Fife Regional Council, Regional Reporter to the Children's Panel, Alistair Kelly

Findlater, Donald, Senior Probation Officer, Surrey Probation Services

Firth-Cozens, Dr Jenny, Advice Columnist, Chartered Clinical Psychologist and Principal Research Fellow, Department of Psychology, University of Leeds

First Stop, Terri Fletcher, Student Project Worker and Cira Bracamonte, Community Development Worker

Forfar and Kirriemuir Child Care Team, Tayside Regional Council, Sue Hunt

Frankel, Jeremy, CP Co-ordinator Medway/Swale, Kent County Council, Social Services Department

Frenchay Healthcare Trust, Department of Child and Family Psychiatry, Dr D. Bazeley-White, Consultant Child and Adolescent Psychiatrist

Gadd, N. Glenys, Health Visitor

Gardiner, Alison, Counsellor

Geoghegan, Luke

Glasgow University Media Group, Paula Skidmore and Jenny Kitzinger

Gleadell, Stephanie, Community Nurse, Colchester Social Work for People with Learning Disabilities, Essex County Council

Glebe House, Friends Therapeutic Community, A. R. Hockley, Director

Gloucestershire ACPC, Georgina Robinson, Children's Services Officer for ACPC

Goulding, Jeanne, Head of The School of Science and Technology, Dewsbury College, West Yorkshire

Greenland, Cyril, Professor Emeritus, School of Social Work, McMaster University, Ontario, Canada

Report of the
National
Commission of
Inquiry into the
Prevention of
Child Abuse

Report of the
National
Commission of
Inquiry into the
Prevention of
Child Abuse

Grosser, Vicky, Trainer, Counsellor and Consultant

Gwent ACPC, John Pitman, Chair

Gwynedd ACPC, Catrin Williams, Principle Officer (Child Protection)

Gwynedd County Council Social Services Department, Gethin Evans, Assistant Director

Hackney ACPC, Anthony Douglas, Assistant Director of Social Services

Hackney Council Womens Unit, Hilary McCollum, Head

Hall, Professor D.M.B., Professor of Community Paediatrics, University of Sheffield, Sheffield Children's Hospital

Hammersmith ACPC, Sue Higginson, Chair ACPC Prevention Sub-Group

Hackney Young People's Counselling Service, Alison Rouse and Chris Cherry, Counsellors

Hyperactive Children's Support Group, Sally Bunday, Secretary

Hampshire ACPC, R.C. Hutchinson, Louise Humphries, ACPC Advisor

Happy Child Inc., San Diego, California, Ms V.A. Nash, International Field Coordinator

Hardiker, Dr Pauline, Senior Lecturer and **Mary Barker,** Senior Research Fellow, School of Social Work, University of Leicester and **Ken Exton,** Group Manager, Children's Services, York Community Services

Harrow, London Borough, Children and Family Resource Units Managers Group, J.E Montigue, Manager, Family Centre

Hartley-Brewer, Elizabeth, Author and Consultant

Health Visitors' Association, Margaret Buttigieg, Director

Heaton School, Stockport, Elizabeth Sears, Head

Henderson, Andrew, Chair of the London Lighthouse Council of Management

Hertfordshire ACPC, Jan Sayers, Head of Child Care Practice

Hewitt, Stanley E.K., Retired Policeman

Higginson, Sue, NSPCC Children's Services Manager

Hinchliffe MP, David, Labour MP for Wakefield

Holmes, Kim, Social Worker, Wiltshire Community Living Team

Howell, Edward, Mid Glamoran Social Services Department

Home-Start UK, Margaret Harrison, Founder and Organiser

Howes, Kathleen, Counsellor

Hoyal QC, Jane, Barrister, Temple

Humberside Social Services Department, Robert Lake, Director of Social Services, Humberside County Council

Hunte, Lorreene, Social Worker

Independent Care After Incestuous Relationship and Rape, Christine Latham, Director

Independent Television Commission, David Glencross, Chief Executive

Institute of Child Health and Great Ormond Street Hospital, Dr Michelle New

Institute of General Practice, University of Exeter, Professor D.J. Pereira Gray

ITV Network Centre

Itzin, Dr Catherine, Research Fellow, University of Bradford

Jackson, Professor Sonia, Head of Dept of Social Policy and Applied Social Studies, University of Wales, Swansea

Jones, Jocelyn, Course Director, Leicester University School of Social Work

Judson, Mrs Maureen, Kindercare Day Nursey and Kindergarten, Wakefield, West Yorks

Jupiter Trust, Dr Jim Phillips, Founder

Report of the
National
Commission of
Inquiry into the
Prevention of
Child Abuse

Kahan, Dr Barbara, independent consultant and Author

Kate Adams Crisis Centres and Childwatch, Kate Adams, Senior Counsellor

Keena, Georgina, Assistant Child Protection Co-ordinator, Wirral Metropolitan Borough, Department of Social Services

Kent ACPC, Peter Smallridge, Director of Social Services, Kent and Peter Thomason, County Child Protection Coordinator

Keyes, Moira, Children's Services Manager, NSPCC, West Midlands

Kidscape, Michele Elliott, Director

Kids Clubs Network, Anne Longfield, Director

Kilkerr, Anthony, Member of Pigot Committee, formerly Metropolitan Police

Kingston, Beryl, Author

Kingston College, Surrey, NNEB students on Child Protection course 1994

Kirklees Metropolitan Council Social Services Department, Tony Brealey, Unit Manager Child Protection Support

La Fontaine, Jean, Emeritus Professor, London School of Economics

Lambeth ACPC, Verley Chambers, Chair ACPC

Laungani, Dr, University of the South Bank, Senior Lecturer in Psychology

Law Society Family Law Committee, Jane Leigh, Secretary to the Committee

Lazaro, Dr C, Consultant Paediatrician, University of Newcastle

Learning Through Action, Annette Cotterill, Director

Leeds City Council, Ruth Woodhead, Chair Leeds ACPC

Leeds City Council Social Services Department, Councillor Michael Simmons, Chair

Leeds Community and Mental Health Services, Sabrina Halliday, Psychology Manager, Learning Disabilities

Leff, Dr Sonia, Consultant Community Paediatrician, South Downs NHS Trust

Leicestershire Social Services Department, Brian Waller, Director

Lincolnshire ACPC, Simon Payne, Chair, Lincolnshire ACPC

Lincolnshire Social Services Department, Malcolm Ashman, Director, Lincolnshire Social Services

Local Government Management Board, Denise Ewing, Management Advisor

London Lighthouse, Susie Parsons, Executive Director

London Weekend Television, Rowan O'Sullivan, Compliance Officer

Lothian CPC, Leslie McEwan, Senior Depute Director

Lothian Regional Council Education Department, Mrs E. Reid, Director

Lothian Regional Council Social Work Department, Glenda Watt, Principal Officer Planning Coordination (Older People)

Manchester Survivors Project, Richmond Fellowship, Morag McSween, Project Coordinator and Cath Nichols, Support Worker

Marneffe, Dr Catherine, University Hospital, Brussels, Child Psychiatrist

Mayes, Dr Gillian, Department of Psychology, University of Glasgow

McGinnity, Dr Maria, Consultant Psychiatrist, Muckamore Abbey Hospital, N&W Belfast HSS Board

McKechnie, Robert, Retired Teacher and Counsellor

Measures, Philip, Social Worker

*Report of the
National
Commission of
Inquiry into the
Prevention of
Child Abuse*

Mental Health Foundation, Elizabeth Gale, Secretary to the Learning Disabilities
  Committee

Mentors in Schools Campaign, David Harrison, Co-ordinator

Meridian Broadcasting Ltd, Patricia Powell, Editor Current Affairs

Merseyside and Region Churches, John Kennedy, Chairman

Merton Social Services Department, Unity Slade, Fieldwork Manager, Learning Disabilities

Methodist Church, Rev. David Gamble, Childrens' Work Secretary

Michael Sieff Foundation, Dr Alan Gilmour, Chairman

Mill Grove, Keith White, Director

Monck, Elizabeth, formerly Senior Research Fellow, Child Abuse Project, Institute of Child
  Health, University of London

Moore, Jean, Consultant and Trainer

MOSAIC Project, Barnardos North East, Shelagh Scott, Senior Practitioner

Mosley, Jenny, Consultant

Mothers Against Murder & Aggression (MAMAA), Celestina Schofield, Director

Mothers of Abused Children, Chris Strickland

Mothers' Union, Lydia Gladwin, Coordinator - Action and Outreach

Mothers' Union, Swansea and Brecon, Ann Williams

Moulton, Dr J.A, Senior Clinical Medical Officer

NACRO, (National Association for the Care and Resettlement of Offenders), Helen
  Edwards, Director of Communications

NAFSIYAT, Inter-Cultural Therapy Centre, Lennox Thomas, Clinical Director

National Association of Head Teachers, G. James, Senior Assistant Secretary

**National Association for the Protection from Sexual Abuse of Adults & Children with
  Learning Disabilities**, Dr Ann Craft, Director, Department of Learning Difficulties,
  University of Nottingham

National Association for Children of Alcoholics, Dr Diana Samways, Chairman

National Association for the Development of Work With Sex Offenders, The Hon Mr
  Justice David Malcolm AC, Chief Justice of Western Australia

National Centre for Mental Health and Deafness, Sharon M. Ridgeway, Research
  Psychologist and Counsellor

National Childbirth Trust, Mary Newburn, Head of Policy Research

National Children's Bureau, John Rea Price, Director

National Children's Bureau Early Childhood Unit, Liz Cowley, Senior Development Officer

National Committee to Prevent Child Abuse, Chicago, Illinois, Leslie Mitchell Bond,
  Director

National Council for Voluntary Organisations, Stuart Etherington, Director

National Deaf Children's Society, Margaret Kennedy, National Coordinator

National Early Years Network, Judith Stone, Chief Executive

National Family Trust, Professor Richard Whitfield, Chairman

National Foster Care Association, Pat Verity, Policy and Services Manager

National Institute for Social Work, Daphne Statham, Director

National Pyramid Trust, Sue Yeo, Project Manager

National Union of Teachers, Kay Thompson, Assistant Secretary, Legal and Professional
  Services

NCH Action for Children, Trish Ross, Project Leader

NCH Action for Children, Maurice Rumbold, Director of Operations

Newcastle City NHS Trust, Community Team Learning Difficulties, Janet Campbell, Manager, Community Nursing

Newcastle Social Services Department, John Brown, Co-ordinator, Community Support Team.

NEWPIN, Anne Hansen, Director

NEWSS, (North East Women's Support Service), Glasgow

Nielsen, Professor Beth Grothe, Department of Procedural and Criminal Science, Institute of Law, University of Aarhus, Denmark

NHS Trust Federation, Lorraine Paul

Northern Ireland Civil Liberties Council, Committee on Administration of Justice, Anne McKeown, Convenor

Northern Ireland Pre-School Play Groups Association (NIPPA), Siobhan Fitzpatrick, Director

Northamptonshire CPC, Jennifer Randell, NCPC Staff Officer

Northamptonshire County Council Social Services Department, Brian Atkins, Operations Manager Children's Services

Northbourne, Lord

Northern Board ACPC, Ken Wilson, Training Co-ordinator

Northern Ireland Committee Irish Congress of Trade Unions, Terry Carlin, Northern Ireland Officer

Northumberland ACPC, R.D. Jewitt, Principal Officer Child Protection

Norwood Childcare, Ruth Fasht, Director of Social Services

NOTA, (National Association for the Development of Work with Sex Offenders) Lisa Markham, Vice Chair

Nottinghamshire ACPC, Professor Olive Stevenson, Chair

Nottinghamshire Social Services, Patricia White, Service Manager Residential Child Care

NSPCC, Phillip Noyes, Director of Communications

NSPCC Black Workers Support Group, Michelle Hyams

NSPCC Cambridgeshire CPT, Christopher Durkin, Child Protection Officer

NSPCC East London Children and Family Centre, John Griffin, Area Manager, Children's Services

NSPCC East, Barry Graham, Regional Director

NSPCC, Hayle Project, Cornwall

NSPCC, Northern Region Managers, Roger Thomson, Regional Director.

NSPCC Tower Hamlets CPT, Ruma Saha

Nugent Care Society, John Kennedy, Director

Otford and Kingsdown Co-ordinated Project of Smallholders and Ecologists (Oak Copse), Mrs M. Boustred, Chair

Off the Record, Bristol, Arthur Musgrave, Director

Ogunsola, Dr Abiola, Director, Research, Development, Training and Consultation, London

O'Hara, Diane, Directorate Nurse Manager, Mid Kent Healthcare Trust

Out of Home, Preventative and Alternative Care (OHPAC), East Perth, Western Australia, Susan Diamond, Executive Officer, and Sue Ash, Chair

Report of the
National
Commission of
Inquiry into the
Prevention of
Child Abuse

145

One Plus One, Marriage and Partnership Research Charity, Penny Mansfield, Deputy Director

Orbach, Susie, Psychotherapist

Orpington Acorn Project, Sheila Birkin, Practice Manager, Orpington Child Care Team

Oxford Rape Crisis Line

Oxfordshire ACPC, Steve Bagnall, Chair, ACPC Prevention Group

Parents Against Injustice (PAIN), Sue Amphlett, Director

Parents Against Ritual Abuse (PARA), Judy Wheaton, Secretary

Parents for Children, Karen Irving, Director

Parker, Professor Roy, Dartington Social Research Unit, University of Bristol

Parton, Professor Nigel, Professor in Child Care, School of Human & Health Studies, University of Huddersfield

Philpot, Terry, Editor, Community Care

Pitcher, David, Social Worker

Plotnikoff, Joyce, and **Richard Woolfson**, Consultants/Authors

Prevention of Professional Abuse Network (PROPAN), Jenny Fasal, Steering Committee, Coordinator

Police Federation of England and Wales, G.B. Hughes, Secretary, Legislation Sub-Committee

Pound, Robyn, Health Visitor

Powys ACPC, T.L Begg, Director of Social Services

Pre-School Playgroups Association, Wales (PPA Cymru), Anne Allan, Executive Officer, Training

Pre-School Learning Alliance, Pat Dench, Assistant Chief Executive Officer, Training and Fieldwork

Pringle, Professor Michael, Acting Head of Department, Faculty of Medicine, Department of General Practice, University of Nottingham

PROMIS, Dr Robert Lefever and Margaret Lefever

Promoting Christian Care and Action, David Pearson, Director

Proops, Marjorie, Advice Columnist, *Daily Mirror*

Protective Behaviours Programme, Health Promotions Service, Milton Keynes, Diana Margetts, International Consultant Trainer

Puckering, Christine, Department of Psychological Medicine, Lecturer in Clinical Psychology, University of Glasgow

Radda Barnen (Swedish Save the Children), Stockholm, Simone Ek, Director

Ramsay, Dr Roger, GP, Wales

Rayner, Claire, Writer/Agony Aunt

Re-Solv, Society for the Prevention of Sovent and Volatile Substance Abuse, Louise Seaton

Response, Department of Education, Metropolitan Borough of Wirral Youth Service, Jeni Cockayne, Team Leader: Counselling/Support Services

Richardson, Heather, Consultant Paediatrician, Canterbury and Thanet Community Health Care

Richardson, Vanessa, Local Authority Solicitor, Devon

Rights of Women, Jill Radford

Riley, Patricia

Robertson, John, Clinical Psychologist, Learning Difficulties Centre, Highbury Hospital, Nottingham

Rotherham ACPC, J Gromwell, Chair of Policy and Practice Sub Committee

Rotherham Social Services Department, Patrick Nolan, Director

Rowland, Joan, Project Manager, NSPCC Derbyshire CPT

Royal College of General Practitioners, Dr Bill Reith, Honorary Secretary of Council

Royal College of General Practitioners, North of England Faculty, Dr James Larcombe, Secretary

Royal College of General Practitioners, Sheffield Faculty, Dr D.A. Noble, G.P., Birley Health Centre

Royal College of General Practitioners, Trent Faculty, Dr P.J. Keavney, Chair ACPC sub-committee

Royal College of Nursing, Christine Hancock, Director, Jane Naish, Advisor

Royal National Institute for the Blind, Issy Cole-Hamilton, Children's Policy Officer

Rydelius, Professor Per-Anders, Karolinska Institutet, St Goran's Children's Hospital, Stockholm

Sacks, Dr Jonathan, the Chief Rabbi

SAFE (Supporting Survivors of Ritual Abuse), Joan Coleman, Management Group

St. Bartholomew's and Royal London Hospitals Medical Colleges, Department of General Practice, Professor L. Southgate, Acting Head

St. Christopher's Fellowship, Tony Ross-Gower, Project Manager

St. John Ambulance, James Hilder, Youth Services Manager

Samaritans, Jackie Wilkinson, Director of Caller Services

Save the Children Fund, Equal Chances Project, Anna Whalen, Acting Project Co-ordinator

Save the Children Fund, United Kingdom and European Programmes Department

Save the Children Fund, Warren Centre, Hull, Annie Franklin, Assistant Divisional Director

Sexual Abuse in the Family Line (SAIFLINE), Mrs J. Wood, Co-ordinator

Sexual Abuse - Mums' Support Group, Jill Trueman, Founder/Co-ordinator

Scott, Philippa, Group Manager, Adult Services, Devon Social Services Department

Scott, Stephen, Consultant Child and Adolescent Psychiatrist, The Maudsley Hospital

Scottish Council for Spastics, M W A Martin, Quality Assurance Manager

Scottish Health Visitors' Association, David F. Forbes, General Secretary

Scottish Institute of Human Relations, J. Alan Harrow, Director

Scottish Low Pay Unit, Morag Gillespie

Scottish Women's Aid, Shirley Cusack, National Children's Rights Worker

Scout Association, Ginette Watson, Community Development Officer (Community Relations)

Scunthorpe Rape Crisis, Angie Smith

SECONDAID, Judy Fraser, Consultant

Sefton ACPC, Dennis Charlton, CP Consultant

Sex Education Forum, Anne Weyman, Chair

Shearer, Eileen, Regional Children's Services Manager, NSPCC North

Sheffield ACPC, Trevor Owen, Secretary

Sherwood Jones, D, Counsellor and Psychotherapist

Shropshire CPC, Michael Hennessy, Director of Social Services

Smith, David R, Freelance Trainer and Consultant

*Report of the
National
Commission of
Inquiry into the
Prevention of
Child Abuse*

Smith, Golda, Psychologist, Birmingham Social Services Department

Smith, G, Community Team Manager, Wakefield Metropolitan District Council

Smith, Susan, Bromley Stress Management Centre

Social Services Research and Information Unit, Carol Hayden, Research Officer

Soldiers' Sailors' and Airmen's Family Association (SSAFA), Mrs Anne Woodriff

Solihull ACPC, Vic Tuck, Convenor of ACPC Training Sub Committee

Somerset ACPC, Chris Davies, Director of Social Services, Somerset County Council

Soroptimist International of Ellesmere Port and District, Marian Livingston

Soroptimist International of Hastings and District, Sandy Lazarus, President

Soroptimist International of Northern England, Dr Moyna Clark

Soroptimist International of Southend-on-Sea, J.E. Porter FRCS, Accident and Emergency Consultant

Sound Start, Susan Stranks, Director

Southampton Rape Crisis Line, S. Grant

South Birmingham Health Authority, Children's Services Unit, Dr Geoff Debelle, Consultant Community Paediatrician

South Downs Health NHS Trust, Alan Bedford, Chief Executive

Southern Board ACPC,(Northern Ireland), R. Blair, Chair

South Essex Rape and Incest Crisis Centre, Sheila Coates, Manager

South Glamorgan Children and Families Support Services, Rosemary Mecklenburgh, Acting Principal

South Glamorgan Social Services Department, Alan Griffin, Chair, Joint Planning and Procurement Board

South Tyneside ACPC, R. Latham, Director of Social Services, South Tyneside

Southwark Diocese Social Responsibility Department, Denise Mumford, Convenor

Staffordshire Social Services Department, Sandra Shaw, Operations Director Children and Families

Stepfamily, Erica De'Ath, Chief Executive

Stepping Stones in Scotland, Isobel Lawson, Director

Stevenson, Professor Olive, Professor of Social Work Studies, University of Nottingham

Suppiah, M.C.J., Health Visitor Co-ordinator, Community Mothers' Programme, Thameside Community Healthcare

Survivors (Sexually Abused Male Survivors), Ernest Woollett, Development Worker

Survivors' Coalition, Beth Follini

Survivors' Network, Hazel Urquhart, Coordinator

Suzy Lamplugh Trust, Diana Lamplugh, Director

Symposium for Child Protection Co-ordinators, Ro Gordon

Tavistock and Portman NHS Trust, Dr Sebastian Kraemer, Consultant Psychiatrist, Child and Family Department

Taylor, Alison, Social Work Practitioner

Tayside Regional Council, Criminal Justice Services, Jim Howden, Regional Manager

Tayside Regional Council, Education Support Services, Priscilla Webster, Child Protection Co-ordinator

Tayside Regional Council, Social Work Department, Keith Redpath, Assistant Director, Professional Services

Telford Women's Resource, Rainer Foundation Project, Vera O'Shea, Project Manager

Temkin, **Professor Jennifer**, Director, Centre for Legal Studies, University of Sussex

Thoburn, Professor June, Professor of Social Work, University of East Anglia

Thomas Coram Foundation, Dr Chris Harvey, Director

TLC (The Learning Channel), Liz Barron, Commissioning Editor

Torgersen, Trond-Viggo, Commissioner for Children, Norway

Trowell, Dr Judith, Consultant Child and Adolescent Psychiatrist, Tavistock Centre

Tosh, Malcolm, Fieldwork Manager, City of Coventry Social Services Department

TTTV, Peter Moth, Director of Advertising

Tuck, Vic, Social Services Department, Solihull Metropolitan Borough Council

Tumin, Winifred

Tunstill, Jane, Professor of Social Work Studies, University of Keele

UNICEF UK, Caroline Leveaux, Liaison Officer

University of East Anglia, School of Social Work, Dr G.R. Boswell

University of Exeter, Monica Cockett, Research Fellow

University of North London, Child and Woman Abuse Studies Unit, Sheila Burton and Liz Kelly

University of Southampton, Primary Medical Care, Professor Ann-Louise Kinmouth and Dr Jenny Field

Union of Shop, Distributive and Allied Workers (USDAW), D. Garfield Davies, General Secretary

Utting, Sir William

Van Gils, Jan, Research Centre on Childhood and Society, University of Meise, Belgium

Voice for the Child in Care, Gwen Jones, Director

Voluntary Organisations Consultancy Service, Brian Donnelly

Volunteer Centre, Jean Foster, Research Officer

Ward, Angela, Health Visitor, Stour Surgery

Warren, Chris, Lecturer in Department of Social Policy and Social Work, University of Sussex

Warwick, University of, Department of Applied Social Studies, Norma Baldwin and Nick Spencer

Warwickshire ACPC, Bob Barradell, Chair, ACPC Prevention and Treatment Sub Group

Waterhouse, Professor Lorraine, Head of Department of Social Work, University of Edinburgh

Watson, Ernell, NSPCC Tottenham Child and Family Support Team, Social Worker

Watson, Richard, Author

Wattam, Corinne, Department of Applied Social Science, University of Lancaster

Way Ahead Disability Consultancy, Merry Cross, Director

Welsh Women's Aid, Sarah Williams, National Childwork Co-ordinator

Werner, Tusia and John, Teachers

West Country Television, John Prescott Thomas, Chief Executive

West Indian Standing Conference, W.I. Trant, Director

Westminster, City of, ACPC, John Dennington, Chair

Wigan ACPC, Mrs Anita Marsland, Assistant Director, (Children and Families)

Williams, Anne, Mothers' Union Social Concern

Report of the
National
Commission of
Inquiry into the
Prevention of
Child Abuse

Williams, Dr Christopher, Global Security Programme, University of Cambridge

Williams, Tony, Child Care Worker, Milford Haven Child Care Team

Willis, Audrey, Social Worker/Author

Wiltshire Social Services Department, Sonia Heywood, Assistant Director

Winnicott Research Unit, University of Cambridge Clinical School, Lynne Murray, MRC Senior Fellow

Wirral Community Healthcare Trust, Linda Buchan, Consultant Clinical Psychologist

Wolverhampton Metropolitan Borough Council ACPC, Brian O'Leary, Assistant Director Children's Services/Chair ACPC

Women Against Rape and Black Women's Rape Action Project

Worthington, Joan, Former Special Needs Teacher

Young Abusers Project, Tavistock Clinic, Dr Eileen Vizard, Clinical Director

Youth Enquiry Service (Child Advocacy Service), Plymouth, Clara Hoyland, Co-ordinator

Youth Support House, Dr Diana Birch, Director

Youth Treatment Service, Dr Kevin Browne, Research Officer, and Vincent Johnson, Leaving Care Co-ordinator

The National Commission has also received letters from over 1,000 people most of whom, have experienced child abuse. These letters have been analysed by Lancaster University. Telephone interviews were also conducted with members of the public. The Commission is grateful to all these people who have shared their experiences.

Oral Evidence

Agathonos, Dr Helen, Institute of Child Health, Athens.

Association of Directors of Social Services, Chris Davies, Jo Williams.

Association of Directors of Social Work, Romy Langeland.

British Association of Community Child Health, Helga Hanks, Dr Chris Hobbs, Dr Jane Wynne.

BBC Radio, Chris Longley, Executive Editor, Social Action.

Breakfree, Linda Pearce, Dr David Smith.

British Association of Social Workers, David Colvin, Keith Bilton.

British Paediatric Association, Dr Marion Miles, Dr Geoffrey Perham, Dr Stephen Salfield.

Bryson House Belfast, Jo Marley, Mary Connor, Dawn Thompson and Pat McCarthy.

Carmarthen Women's Aid, Jane Shaw and Mandy Baldwin.

Children 1st (Royal Scottish Society for the Prevention of Cruelty to Children), Cathy Dewar, Dr Anne Stafford and Eleanor Harbison.

Children in Wales, Pat Davies, Sarah Gittens, Jane Isaac, Eirwen Malin, Chris Perry, and Catriona Williams.

Christensen, Else, Danish Institute of Social Research.

Clarion Communications, (Zero Tolerance Campaign) Evelyn Gillan and Elaine Sanson
Council for Disabled Children, Philippa Russell.

*Report of the
National
Commission of
Inquiry into the
Prevention of
Child Abuse*

Davies, Professor David, University Hospital of Wales.
DMB&B, Sally Ford-Hutchinson

EPOCH (End Physical Punishment of Children), Peter Newell.

Glasgow Media Group, University of Glasgow, Paula Skidmore.
Greenland, Cyril, Professor Emeritus, School of Social Work, McMaster University, Ontario, Canada.

Hardiker, Pauline, School of Social Work, University of Leicester, and Ken Exton, N. Yorkshire Social Services Department.
Hartley-Brewer, Elizabeth, Author and Consultant.
Health Visitors Association, Jill Clemerson, Christine Byrne, Sue Botes.
Holman, Bob, Easterhouse Project, Glasgow.

Kahan, Dr Barbara, Independent Consultant and Author.
Kraemer, Dr Sebastian, Consultant Psychiatrist, Child and Family Department, The Tavistock Clinic.

151

Learning Through Action, Annette Cotterill, Niall Duggan and Louise Woodall.

Mayes, Gillian and Ellen Moran, Department of Psychology,University of Glasgow.
Mothers Against Murder and Aggression (MAMAA), Celestina Schofield with Ian Rush.

National Society for the Prevention of Cruelty to Children, Christopher Brown, Jim Harding, and Eileen Hayes.
Newpin, Anne Hansen.
Northern Board Area Child Protection Committee, Stephanie Irwin, Ken Wilson.
Northern Ireland Committee of the Irish Congress of Trades Unions, Ann Hope with Berni McCrea, and Miriam Titterton.
NOTA, Lisa Markham and Bobbie Print.

Parents Against Injustice, (PAIN), Sue Amphlett, Director, four families and two young people.

Rantzen, Esther, Broadcaster, Chair of ChildLine.
Royal College of Nursing, Christine Hancock, Jane Naish and Chris Middleton.

Stepfamily (National Stepfamily Association), Mike Henry and Brian Dimmock
Saatchi & Saatchi, Alex Mackie.
Stepping Stones, Isobel Lawson.
Stevenson, Professor Olive, School of Social Work, University of Nottingham.

Thomas Coram Foundation, Dr Chris Hanvey.

*Report of the
National
Commission of
Inquiry into the
Prevention of
Child Abuse*

Torgerson, Trond Viggo, Children's Commissioner, Norway.

Van Gils, Jan, Research Centre for Childhood and Society, Meise, Belgium.

Waterhouse, Professor Lorraine, Head of Department of Social Work, University of Glasgow.

Whitfield, Professor Richard, National Campaign for the Family.

Field Visits and Consultations

Aberlour Trust Child Care, Glasgow, Scotland
All Party Parliamentary Group for Children
All Party Parliamentary Group on Parenting
Anchor Project, Newcastle upon Tyne

Brent, London Borough, Urban Regeneration Programmes, Luke Geoghegan
BT Forum

Children's Resource Team, North and West Belfast Health and Social Services Trust and NSPCC, Shankhill Road, Belfast
Clermont Child Protection Unit, Brighton, East Sussex
Cleveland Area Child Protection Committee

East Birmingham Family Service Unit

Family Welfare Association

Home-Start UK, Leicester
Hackney young people
Kingston College, Surrey, NNEB Course

MOSAIC Barnardo's North East, Newcastle upon Tyne

National Council for Voluntary Child Care Organisations
Newport Advocacy Project, Gwent
NEWSS - North East Women's Support Service, Glasgow, Scotland
NSPCC Family Support Project, Hayle, Cornwall

PACSA (People Against Child Sexual Abuse) Newcastle upon Tyne
Penarth Family Centre
Promis Recovery Centre, Canterbury, Kent

Save the Children Cynon Valley Project, mid Glamorgan, Wales
South Birmingham Family Service Unit
SW Regional Child Protection Forum
Shieldfield Parents Together Working Together, Newcastle upon Tyne

Report of the
National
Commission of
Inquiry into the
Prevention of
Child Abuse

The Place to Be

Voices from Care, Cardiff

Youth Information Shop, London Borough of Brent

Conferences and Consultation Meetings/Seminars Organised by The Commission

Children in Wales Consultation
Community Care/National Commission London Conference "Towards a Strategy for the
    Prevention of Child Abuse"
Community Care/National Commission Glasgow Conference "Towards a Strategy for the
    Prevention of Child Abuse"
Newspaper Editors Consultation Meeting
NSPCC Helpline Counsellors Consultation Meeting
NSPCC Child Protection Counsellors
Prevention of Child Abuse and the Law Consultation
Prevention of Child Abuse and the Role of Education Consultation Meeting
Problem Page Editors Consultation Meeting
"Prevention of Child Abuse: A Framework for Analysing Services" Seminar
Strathclyde Practitioners Discussion Groups
University of Glasgow Social Researchers
Welsh Media: HTV and S4C Consultation

153

Conferences/Seminars Addressed or Attended by the Commission

Breakfree International Conference
Child Protection Advisers' Conference
Children 1st AGM
Children in Wales AGM
Children Rights Development Unit Seminar
Essex ACPC Conference
European Conference on Child Abuse and Neglect, Oslo
Haringey ACPC Annual Conference
Lancaster University Conference on Research and Policy
Maidstone Child Protection Committee Meeting
Michael Sieff Foundation Conference, September 1994 "Family Support in Protecting the
    Child"
Michael Sieff Foundation Conference, September 1995 "Child Protection: Research into
    Practice: Who Takes the Risk?"

*Report of the
National
Commission of
Inquiry into the
Prevention of
Child Abuse*

Michael Sieff Foundation Conference, November 1995 "Towards Three Years' Social Work
    Training: The Case for Change"
National Children's Bureau Conference, December 1995 "The Future Shape of Children's
    Services Plans"
National Children's Bureau Seminar addressed by Austin Currie TD, Minister of State at the
    Department of Health, Irish Republic
NE England ACPCs Conference
Northamptonshire ACPC Annual Conference
Northern Boards ACPC Conference
NSPCC A Voice for Midlands Children Conference
The Place to Be
University of Cardiff Centre for Journalism Studies "Victims and the Media"

Meetings

BBC, Chris Longley, Executive Editor, Social Action, BBC Radio
BBC, Roy Thompson, Deputy Head of Children's TV Programmes.
BT Forum, Joanna Foster, Director
Elliott and Shanahan, Patrick Shanahan, Social Research Consultant, Australia
Greenland, Cyril
Greenslade, Roy, Journalist
Laungani, Dr, and Joanna Dykes, South Bank University
Levine, Irene, Children's Rights Officer, London Borough of Hackney
London School of Economics, George Gaskell
Ochberg, Frank, MD (US) Trauma Psychiatrist
Princess Royal Trust for Carers, Dr Elizabeth Nelson, Stephen Wexler
SCPR/MORI, Deborah Ghate
SCPR, Julia Hall
Sussex County Council, Steve Lawless, Community Development Officer
Telephone Helplines Association, Kathy Mulville
Voice Publications

Members' Biographical Details

*Report of the
National
Commission of
Inquiry into the
Prevention of
Child Abuse*

Lord Williams of Mostyn, QC (Chairman)

Lord Williams of Mostyn graduated from Queens' College, Cambridge, and was called to the Bar in 1965. He was appointed Queen's Counsel in 1978, and was made a Deputy High Court Judge in 1986. In 1992 he became Chairman of the Bar Council. Between 1991 and 1992 he chaired the Inquiry investigating allegations of ill-treatment of boys in Ty Mawr Community Home. He was appointed House of Lords Opposition Front Bench Spokesman on Northern Ireland and Legal Affairs in 1992 and was made a Member of the Council of Justice in 1993. During 1994 he was Visiting Professor at the Institute of Sociology and Social Policy, University of Wales, Bangor, and at City University, London. Lord Williams is President of the Commonwealth and Ethnic Bar Association, President of the Welsh College of Music and Drama and Pro-Chancellor of the University of Wales.

Elaine Arnold

Elaine Arnold was educated at St Michael's Girls School, Barbados, and trained as a teacher at the Trinidad and Tobago Government Teachers' Training College. After several years of teaching, she studied Social Welfare at Swansea University, qualified as a Pstychiatric Social Worker at Manchester University and obtained MPhil in Social Studies at Sussex University. She worked as a Social Worker in Trinidad and Tobago, and in the UK where she had experience in a children's hospital and a local authority, with special responsibility for training nursery staff and inter-cultural social work. She currently teaches Social Work and Administration at Sussex University with a special interest in Child Observation. She gave evidence to the inquiry into the death of Jasmine Beckford (1985, London Borough of Brent) and served on the panel of the Public Inquiry into the death of Tyra Henry in 1987 (London Borough of Lambeth). She has written on cross cultural aspects of physical abuse of children and has served as a member of the Executive Committee of BASPCAN. She a member of the International Society for the Prevention of Child Abuse and Neglect.

Professor Stewart Asquith

Stewart Asquith graduated in Philosophy from the University of St Andrews. He is St Kentigern Professor for the Study of the Child at the University of Glasgow and was Director (1992-1995) of the Centre for the Study of the Child & Society, a centre concerned with research, teaching and training on issues relating to children's rights and welfare. He has held posts in the Scottish Office, in the Department of Criminology and Social Policy and Social Work at the University of Edinburgh. He has written widely on child related issues and, in particular, on delinquency and juvenile justice. He is currently Chair of the Children 1st Committee on Policy and Research.

*Report of the
National
Commission of
Inquiry into the
Prevention of
Child Abuse*

Michael Grade

Michael Grade was educated at Stowe and St Dunstan's College. From 1960 to 1966 he worked as Sports columnist on the Daily Mirror, before becoming joint Managing Director of London Management (Talent Agency) 1966-73. In 1973 he became Head of Entertainment and Director of Programmes at London Weekend Television and was President of Embassy Television, USA, between 1981 and 1984. He joined the BBC as Controller of BBC1 in September 1984. In addition to this post, he became Director of Programmes, Television, in June 1986 and Managing Director Designate in 1987. He took up his present appointment as Chief Executive of Channel Four in 1988.

Sir Peter Newsam

Peter Newsam studied Philosophy, Politics and Economics at Oxford before joining the Civil Service in 1952. He left to enter teaching in 1955 and, after taking a Diploma in Education, became Head of Humanities at an Oxfordshire secondary school. In 1963 he began his career in education administration and worked in the North Riding and Cumberland before becoming Deputy to Sir Alec Clegg in the West Riding in 1970. He joined the Inner London Education Authority as Deputy Education officer in 1972, becoming Education Officer in 1977. He was appointed Chairman of the Commission for Racial Equality in 1982 and was knighted in 1987. After two years as Secretary to the Association of County Councils, he became Director of the London Institute of Education in 1989, a post he held until 1994. From 1992 until 1994 he was also Deputy Vice-Chancellor of the University of London.

Deidre Sanders

Deidre Sanders graduated from Sheffield University in 1966. She has been problem page editor of *The Sun* since 1980, and was the "agony aunt" on BBC's *Good Morning*. With her team of five counselling-trained letter answerers, she sends personal replies to up to 1,000 readers and viewers each week. In 1993 she organised a national conference on the prevention of the sexual abuse of children. She is an honorary member of the NSPCC Council, is a patron of Youth Access (National Association of Young People's Counselling and Advisory Centres), a member of the British Association for Counselling, and a forum member of the Royal Society of Medicine. Her books include *Kitchen Sink or Swim?* (on the options facing women), *Women and Depression, The Woman Report on Love and Sex,* and *The Woman Report on Men.* The last two were based on one of the largest surveys of the sexual and emotional lives of UK men and women ever undertaken, and demonstrated the widespread incidence of child abuse.

Professor Jo Sibert

Jo Sibert trained at St John's College, Cambridge, and University College Hospital Medical School. He practised in London, Bristol, Oxford and Newcastle before going to Wales in

*Report of the
National
Commission of
Inquiry into the
Prevention of
Child Abuse*

1974. He worked as a Consultant Paediatrician before taking up his position as Professor of Community Child Health in the University of Wales College of Medicine in 1991. He has had practical experience of medical examination with potentially abused children for over 20 years. He is designated doctor for child protection of the Pro Taf Health Authority. His research interests include child injury prevention, child protection and children with special needs. Professor Sibert is Chair of Children in Wales, Chair of Child Safe Wales, and Treasurer of the British Association for Community Child Health. As well as this, he has experience of work locally and is a former Mayor of Penarth, where he lives. He has also been Chair of the South Glamorgan Area Child Protection Committee.

Sir Roger Sims, MP

Roger Sims was educated at City Boys' Grammar School, Leicester, and St Olave's Grammar School, London. He worked in business and served as a Justice of the Peace in Bromley, where he was Chairman of the Juvenile Court before becoming Conservative MP for Chislehurst, a seat he has held since 1974. Between 1979 and 1983 he was Parliamentary Private Secretary to the Home Secretary. He was a member of the NSPCC Central Executive Committee from 1979 to 1993 and, since 1989, has been a member of the General Medical Council. He is Joint Vice-Chairman of the Conservative Backbench Health Committee. He was a member of the Select Committees on Education (1983-87), Social Security (1987-91) and has sat on the Select Committee on Health since 1991. His special interests include child welfare, education, alcoholism, health and community care.

157

Professor Daphne Statham, CBE

Daphne Statham studied at St Anne's College, Oxford, and the London School of Economics before training at the National Institute of Social Work. She practised in both the statutory and voluntary sectors and also lectured in social work before taking up her present appointment as Director of the National Institute of Social Work in 1987. She is a past chair, and currently President, of the National Association of Councils of Voluntary Service and a trustee of the NCVO. She has been a member of the Central Council for Education and Training in Social Work and is Visiting Professor to Goldsmith's College, University of London. Her research has been concerned with social work practice and she has published extensively on the subject.

Christine Walby

Christine Walby graduated and trained as a teacher at the University College of Wales, Aberystwyth. After some time in the youth service she took a Diploma in Social Work and Social Administration at Manchester University in 1968 and worked in local authority social services in the North West, South Wales, Berkshire and the Midlands. She was awarded an MSc by the University of Wales following research into access to records by adopted people. Between 1991 and 1993 she served on the Human Fertilisation and Embryology Authority and took a particular interest in the rights and needs of children born

Report of the
National
Commission of
Inquiry into the
Prevention of
Child Abuse

as a result of the reproductive technologies. She was a Director of Social Services for ten years, first in Solihull MDC and from 1991 to 1996 in Staffordshire County Council. Throughout this time she was active in the Association of Directors of Social Services and chaired the ADSS Children and Families Commitee for several years. She is currently a Trustee of the Children's Rights Development Unit and a Senior Visiting Research Fellow of Keele University.

Appendix 3
Commission's Terms of Reference

Report of the
National
Commission of
Inquiry into the
Prevention of
Child Abuse

In inviting submissions, the Commission suggested that those giving evidence might wish to consider the following issues

○ the nature and cause of child abuse and neglect. What is child abuse and what it is not.

○ how does our culture and system of values support or prevent child abuse. What are the implications of the welfare culture for intervention and service provision?

○ how does the abuse of children differ from the abuse of adults? Should it be treated differently?

○ what is the nature of rights and the consequences of this?

○ what is the nature of professional responsibilities?

○ the effectiveness of intervention and treatment of child abuse - what works?

○ what are the characteristics of perpetrators of abuse? What are effective forms of treatment and intervention with perpetrators?

○ what are the roles and responsibilities of parents, carers, children and the community for the prevention of child abuse?

○ what are the roles and responsibilities of different sectors and disciplines?

○ how a political mandate for child abuse prevention can be achieved, how attitudes can be influenced, and how the prevention of child abuse can be effectively and efficiently resourced.

The Commission has received evidence on all of these issues.

Appendix 4

The United Nations Convention on the Rights of the Child and the Prevention of Child Abuse

1.1   The United Nations Convention of the Rights of the Child was ratified by the United Kingdom in 1991 and the government is thereby bound by the treaty's provisions. The Convention is the most comprehensive piece of international legislation setting out principles and standards for the treatment and care of children. The Convention has been ratified by 170 countries (out of a total membership of the United Nations of 174). No other convention has been accepted more quickly and comprehensively than this one. In ratifying the Convention, the UK government endorsed the majority of the provisions, entering six reservations or declarations. The government has supported those articles relating to child protection. While many, and arguably all, of the provisions of the Convention relate to the care and protection of children and therefore the Convention as a whole should be read, there are some which relate more specifically to child abuse.

1.2   The Convention begins by addressing the broader needs of children before turning to the more narrow concern of child abuse. Article 3 of the Convention has a broad approach which the Commission has reflected in its definition:

"**Article 3**
1. In all actions concerning children, whether undertaken by public or private social welfare institutions, courts of law, administrative authorities or legislative bodies, the best interests of the child shall be a primary consideration.

2. States Parties undertake to ensure the child such protection and care as is necessary for his or her well-being, taking into account the rights and duties of his or her parents, legal guardians, or other individuals legally responsible for him or her, and, to this end, shall take all appropriate legislative and administrative measures.

3. States Parties shall ensure that the institutions, services, and facilities responsible for the care or protection of children shall conform with the standards established by competent authorities, particularly in the areas of safety, health, in the number and suitability of their staff as well as competent supervision."

1.3   In Article 19, the United Nations addresses the more narrow definition of child abuse:

"**Article 19**
1. States Parties shall take all appropriate legislative, administrative, social and educational measures to protect the child from all forms of physical or mental violence, injury or abuse, neglect or negligent treatment, maltreatment or exploitation, including sexual abuse, while in the care of parent(s), legal guardian(s) or any other person who has the care of the child.

These provisions are again referred to later in the Convention

*Report of the
National
Commission of
Inquiry into the
Prevention of
Child Abuse*

"Article 24
3. State Parties shall take all effective and appropriate measure with a view to abolishing traditional practices, prejudicial to the health of children."

"Article 34
States parties undertake to protect the child from all forms of sexual exploitation and sexual abuse. For these purposes, States Parties shall in particular take all appropriate national, bilateral, and multilateral measures to prevent

(a)   The inducement or coercion of a child to engage in any unlawful sexual activity;

(b)   The exploitative use of children in prostitution or other unlawful sexual practices;

(c)   The exploitative use of children in pornographic performances and materials."

"Article 36

States Parties shall protect the child against all other forms of exploitation prejudicial to any aspects of the child's welfare."

1.4   There are also articles which relate to the child's or young person's right to express an opinion and freedom of expression. These provisions relate to the emotional wellbeing of children or to emotional abuse. Relevant articles include

161

"Article 12

1. State parties shall assure to the child who is capable of forming his or her own views the right to express these views freely in all matters affecting the child, the views of the child being given due weight in accordance with the age and maturity of the child.

2. For this purpose, the child shall in particular be provided the opportunity to be heard in any judicial and administrative proceedings affecting the child, either directly, or through a representative or an appropriate body, in a manner consistent with the procedural rules of national law."

"Article 13

1. The child shall have the right to freedom of expression; this right shall include freedom to seek, receive and impart information and ideas of all kinds, regardless of frontiers, either orally, in writing or in print, in the form of art, or through any other media of the child's choice.

2. The exercise of this right may be subject to certain restrictions, but these shall only be such as are provided by law and are necessary:

(a)   For respect of the rights or reputations of others; or

*Report of the
National
Commission of
Inquiry into the
Prevention of
Child Abuse*

(b) For the protection of national security or of public order, or of public health or morals."

1.5   The Convention specifically identifies as child abuse: physical and mental violence and injury, neglect or negligent treatment, and maltreatment and exploitation, including unlawful sexual practices into which a child is coerced, prostitution, and involvement in pornography. The Convention also, however, addresses other ways in which children are harmed or exploited and locates this within a broader context of children's needs.

1.6   A large number and range of organisations and individuals have urged the Commission to adopt such a wider approach. While it may have been anticipated that those submitting evidence to the Commission which has "child abuse" in its title might focus on a narrow definition of child abuse, this has not proved to be the case. Many of the submissions discussed the importance of promoting children's rights as a means of preventing child abuse. A number of the organisations giving evidence have adopted the *United Nations Convention on the Rights of the Child* and called for its rigorous implementation. A number of those submitting evidence also suggested that the UN Convention provides a good framework for assessing the extent to which the rights and needs of children are met. The Convention lays down a set of internationally recognised minimum standards for the treatment of children. Some argued that it constitutes an abuse of children if these rights are not respected.

Technical Definitions of Child Abuse

*Report of the
National
Commission of
Inquiry into the
Prevention of
Child Abuse*

Defining child abuse: statutory and non-statutory definitions

1.1 Technical definitions of child abuse derive from legislation and non-statutory guidance. This appendix describes the main definitions currently in use (August 1996). Legislation in Scotland (Children (Scotland) Act 1995) and in Northern Ireland (Children (Northern Ireland) Order 1995 has still to be implemented. Government guidance on child protection to accompany these pieces of legislation is being drafted.

UK child care legislation

2.1 Provisions in UK law are found in several different statutes. The Children Act 1989, which covers England and Wales and is *broadly* reflected in the Children (Northern Ireland) Order 1995, and the Children (Scotland) Act 1995 cover the care and upbringing of children and the services that should be provided for them. The legislation introduces two concepts relating to child abuse: *"significant harm"* and *"children in need"*.

163

"Significant harm"

3.1 The Children Act 1989 makes provisions for children to be protected from significant harm. Section 31 of the Act provides the following definitions:

> *"harm" means ill-treatment or the impairment of health or development;*
> *"development" means physical, intellectual, emotional, social or behavioural development;*
> *"health" means physical or mental health; and*
> *"ill-treatment" includes sexual abuse and forms of ill treatment which are not physical.*

The Children Act continues:

> *"Where the question of whether harm suffered by a child is significant turns on the child's health or development, his health or development shall be compared with that which could reasonably be expected of a similar child."*

3.2 The word "significant" is not defined in the Act. Department of Health guidance[1] states: "Minor shortcomings in health care or minor deficits in physical, psychological or social development should not require compulsory intervention unless cumulatively they are having, or are likely to have, serious and lasting effects upon the child."

Report of the
National
Commission of
Inquiry into the
Prevention of
Child Abuse

Children in need

4.1   Part III of the Children Act 1989 confers a general duty on each local authority in England and Wales to provide a range and level of services appropriate to children in their area who are "in need", to safeguard and promote the welfare of such children and promote their upbringing by their families, in so far as that is consistent with that aim. The Act also states that every local authority shall take reasonable steps, through the provision of services described in Part III of the Act, to prevent children within their area suffering ill treatment or neglect. The target of these services are "children in need" and the Act defines a child as in need if

"(a)   *he is unlikely to achieve or maintain, or have the opportunity of achieving or*
maintaining, a reasonable standard of health or development without the
provision for him of services by the local authority;
(b)   *his health or development is likely to be significantly impaired, or further*
impaired, without the provision of such services; or
(c)   *he is disabled."*

The Children (Scotland) Act includes a fourth criterion not contained in the English and Welsh legislation

"the child is affected adversely by the disability of another family member."

4.2   The definitions of children suffering from *significant harm* and *children in need* are alike to the extent that both incorporate notions of health, development, and a level of harm. Similar provisions are made in Scottish and Northern Ireland legislation.

Non-statutory guidance

5.1   The key government guidance on child protection for England and Wales, *Working Together* (1991), adopts a set of four narrowly defined categories of child abuse: physical abuse, sexual abuse, emotional abuse, and neglect. These are defined in government guidance[2] as:

"*Neglect:* The persistent or severe neglect of a child or the failure to protect a child
from exposure of any kind of danger, including cold or starvation, or extreme failure
to carry out important aspects of care, resulting in the significant impairment of the
child's health or development, including non-organic failure to thrive."

"*Physical Injury:* Actual or likely physical injury to a child, or failure to prevent
physical injury (or suffering) to a child including deliberate poisoning, suffocation,
and Munchausen's syndrome by proxy."

"*Sexual Abuse:* actual or likely sexual exploitation of a child or adolescent. The child
may be dependent and/or developmentally immature."

"*Emotional Abuse:* Actual or likely severe adverse effect on the emotional and
behavioural development of a child caused by persistent or severe emotional ill-
treatment or rejection. All abuse involves some emotional ill-treatment."

Similar definitions are provided in the guidance on child protection under the Northern Ireland (Children (Northern Ireland) Order 1995, Draft Regulations and Guidance, vol 6, *Co-operating to Protect Children*, 1996).

*Report of the
National
Commission of
Inquiry into the
Prevention of
Child Abuse*

5.2   The equivalent guidance to accompany the Children (Scotland) Act seems likely to reflect the definitions of child abuse now in operation. These derive from the 1992 Scottish Office Steering Group Report.[3] The group was set up to "recommend standard criteria for admission to and removal from local (child protection) registers". These non-statutory definitions proposed by the group are:

> "*to define an act or omission as abusive and/or presenting future risk for the purpose
> of registration, three elements must be taken into account:*
> o *whether there is demonstrable damage or harm to a child or a prediction of harm
>   to the child;*
> o *whether the injury/state of the child must have been avoidable through action by
>   parents or carers responsible for that child;*
> o *whether the potential harm or future risk is linked to the action or inaction of the
>   parent or carer. This would also apply where it was not possible to establish the
>   identity of the perpetrator.*"

To supplement this general definition, the guidance sets out five categories of child abuse: physical injury; sexual abuse; non-organic failure to thrive; emotional abuse; and physical neglect. There can be overlap and interaction among the categories and a particular case of child abuse may not always fit neatly into one category. The categories are defined as:

> "Physical injury: *actual or attempted physical injury to a child, under the age of 16,
> where there is definite knowledge, or reasonable suspicion, that the injury was
> inflicted or knowingly not prevented.*"

"Physical injury may include a serious incident or a series of minor incidents involving bruising, fractures, burns or scalds; deliberate poisoning; attempted drowning and smothering; Munchausen syndrome by proxy; serious risk of or actual injuries resulting from parental lifestyle prior to birth, for instance substance abuse; physical chastisement deemed to be unreasonable.

> "Sexual abuse: *any child below the age of 16 may be deemed to have been sexually
> abused when a person(s), by design or neglect exploits the child, directly or indirectly,
> in any activity intended to lead to the sexual arousal or other forms of gratification of
> that person or any other person(s), including organised networks. This definition
> holds whether or not there has been genital contact and whether or not the child is
> said to have initiated the behaviour.*"

"Sexual abuse may include activities such as incest, rape, sodomy or intercourse with children; lewd or libidinous practices or behaviour towards children; indecent assault of children; taking indecent photographs of children or encouraging children to become prostitutes or witness intercourse or pornographic materials.

"Activities involving sexual exploitation, particularly between young people, may be indicated by the presence of one or more of the following characteristics - lack of consent;

165

Report of the
National
Commission of
Inquiry into the
Prevention of
Child Abuse

inequalities in terms of chronological age, developmental stage or size; actual or threatened coercion.

"Non Organic Failure to Thrive: *children who significantly fail to reach normal growth and developmental milestones (ie physical growth, weight, motor, social and intellectual development) where physical and genetic reasons have been medically eliminated and a diagnosis of non organic failure to thrive has been established.*

"Factors affecting a diagnosis may include inappropriate relationships between the care giver(s) and child, especially at meal times, for instance the withholding of food as punishment and the sufficiency and/or suitability of the food for the child. In its chronic form, non organic failure to thrive can result in greater susceptibility to more serious childhood illnesses, reduction in potential stature, and with young children particularly, the results may be life threatening over a relatively short period.

"*Emotional abuse*: failure to provide for the child's basic emotional needs such as to have a severe effect on the behaviour and development of the child.

"This may include situations where as a result of persistent behaviour by the parent(s) or care giver(s) children are rejected, denigrated, or scapegoated; inappropriately punished; denied opportunities for exploration, play and socialisation appropriate to their stage of development or encouraged to engage in antisocial behaviour; put in a state of terror or extreme anxiety by the use of threats or practices designed to intimidate them; isolated from normal social experiences, preventing the child from forming friendships.

"Children who are left on their own for long periods, are understimulated or suffer sensory deprivation, especially in infancy; who do not experience adequate nurturing or who are subject to a large number of care givers(s), may also come into this category.

"Sustained or repeated abuse of this type is likely, in the long term, to result in failure or disruptions of development of personality, inability to form secure relationships and may additionally have an effect on intellectual development or educational attainment.

"*Physical Neglect*: this occurs when a child's essential needs are not met and this is likely to cause impairment to physical health and development. Such needs include food, clothing, cleanliness, shelter and warmth. A lack of appropriate care results in persistent or severe exposure, through negligence, to circumstances which endanger the child.

"Physical neglect may also include failure to secure appropriate medical treatment for the child, or when an adult carer persistently pursues or allows the child to follow a lifestyle inappropriate to the child's developmental needs or which jeopardises the child's health."

The detail of this guidance is considered helpful.

5.3   Non-statutory guidance in all parts of the UK have certain elements in common. The definitions for the purposes of registration are commonly construed as the "official" definitions. They also refer to other "types" of abuse, which are qualitatively different from those described above in that they reflect more the settings or context in which the abuse

Report of the
National
Commission of
Inquiry into the
Prevention of
Child Abuse

occurs - the abuse itself may be similar to those described for registration purposes. Thus *Working Together* refers to the abuse of children in residential settings and also to "organised abuse". It provides the following definition:

"Organised abuse is a generic term which covers abuse that may involve a number of abusers, a number of abused children and young people and often encompass different forms of abuse. It involves, to a greater or lesser extent, an element of organisation. A wide range of abusing activity is covered by this term, from small paedophile or pornographic rings, often but not always organised for profit, with most participants knowing one another, to large networks of individual groups or families which may be spread more widely and in which not all participants will be known to each other. Some organised groups may use bizarre or ritualised behaviour, sometimes associated with particular "belief" systems. This can be a powerful mechanism to frighten the abused children into not telling of their experiences."

The Northern Ireland draft guidance contains similar definitions.

References

1. Department of Health, 1991, Children Act 1989, Guidance and Regulations, London: HMSO

2. Home Office, Department of Health, Department of Education and Science and Welsh Office, 1991, Working Together Under The Children Act 1989: A Guide to Arrangements for Inter-Agency Co-operation for the Protection of Children from Abuse, London: HMSO

3. Scottish Office, 1992, Child Protection in Scotland: Management Information, Edinburgh: Scottish Office

*Report of the
National
Commission of
Inquiry into the
Prevention of
Child Abuse*

Appendix 6

Learning about prevention from people who have experienced child abuse[1]

Summary Report

by Corinne Wattam and Clare Woodward, Department of Applied Science, Lancaster University.

This report contains the findings of an analysis of letters sent to the National Commission in response to invitations in the national press, on television and in magazines. The total number of 1121 letters comprised four types: letters which told the story of people who had experienced child abuse (N=721), letters from other interested parties (relatives, friends and those with a professional interest) (N=75), letters requesting information from the Commission (N=195) and letters responding to further correspondence from the Commission (N=130). Specific recommendations for prevention are drawn from the whole sample.

The total sample represents the views primarily of women, but also of some men, who have experienced abuse as a child. For many of them the effects have been traumatic and lasting. The group is not representative of the population as a whole.

1. Nature and type of abuse

1.1 Definitions

80% of writers referred to their experience of sexual abuse, rape or molestation.

For just over a quarter (28%) the sexual abuse was cited along with other forms of abuse, most commonly physical and "mental". Physical abuse was referred to in a third of the letters, though only in 3% as a lone category. Twenty-three per cent wrote about emotional abuse and neglect in 2% with "abuse" undefined occurring for a further 5%.

Where sexual abuse occurred with emotional or "mental" abuse, writers tended to claim that the emotional abuse was more damaging. For example:

> "*Although the sexual abuse was horrific the emotional abuse was far worse and had more of a lasting effect on my life.*"

The type of sexual abuse experienced tended to be serious, involving penetration, continuing over a long period. For the minority who experienced physical abuse, the level of severity was similar, sometimes requiring hospitalisation and almost always resulting in reported injury.

---

[1] The main report of this analysis of letters to the National Commission is published separately in the accompanying volume.

Report of the
National
Commission of
Inquiry into the
Prevention of
Child Abuse

- 69% of writers were abused by one person, 20% by two people and 11% by three or more, most frequently on separate occasions.

- 67% of writers report the age of onset as being below 11, i.e. prior to the entry to secondary school, with the most frequently cited age of onset at ages 4-5.

- Only 17% report the abuse stopping before the age of 11.

- Half the writers report abuse lasting between 2 and 18 years, with a further 17% stating the duration as "all my childhood" or "years".

- Over a third (35%) of writers made reference to the fact that others were abused as well as themselves. Almost a quarter of the total sample claimed that brothers and sisters also suffered, the remainder referring to their own children, other relatives or "others" (13%). Thus in many letters writers speak not only for themselves but for their siblings, relatives and others who were abused.

- In direct answer to the question, **"What do you consider child abuse to be?"** a wide range of circumstances were given in addition to the usual categories of emotional, physical and sexual abuse and neglect. These included lack of consideration of children's rights, that it can come in many forms and that it has to do with fear, and adults having control or power.

1.2   Person believed responsible

40% of writers cited fathers or father substitutes as the alleged perpetrators. Other relatives were also given including brothers (8%), mothers and mother substitutes (7%), uncles (6%), grandfathers (4%) as well as cousins, grandmothers, aunts and sisters (5%). Alleged perpetrators outside the family included family friends and neighbours (2%), known adults (teachers, doctors, priests, lodgers) (4%), and substitute carers (3%).

- The findings show that writers suffered from abuse from their own family in 64% of cases, with the natural father being the most frequently cited single alleged perpetrator.

- 91% of the alleged perpetrators were known to their victims.

- In answer to the question **"What are its (child abuse) causes?"** the single largest cause identified by respondents involves social/cultural factors which have been grouped under the general heading of **society**. These factors comprise social attitudes and values as well as notions of taboo and stigma. Some causes were located in the family and included "inadequate parenting", relationship difficulties and unwanted children. For others, the cause was clearly located in the perpetrator and some writers suggested that the only way to get to the root cause is to ask the perpetrators themselves.

Prevention Implications

- The perceived seriousness of "mental" or "emotional" abuse needs to be highlighted in prevention campaigns.

- Stranger danger campaigns should be developed into campaigns directed at what to do if someone you know and are familiar with abuses you.

- Prevention programmes should be located and resourced in primary schools.

- Awareness programmes in secondary schools remain important, particularly in relation to the type of help on offer for victims.

*Report of the
National
Commission of
Inquiry into the
Prevention of
Child Abuse*

○ Victims themselves may be an important source of help in stopping child abuse for others known to them.

○ There appears to be a consensus among the writers about the need for a broader social change in attitudes towards children in order to prevent abuse happening to others.

2 Factors and contexts

2.1 Factors relevant to the abusive acts

66% of the writers gave details of what could broadly be termed key factors. Whilst they did not necessarily view these factors as causal, they did report them as being relevant to the perpetration of abuse. Three main key factors emerged.

a) The writer didn't know it was wrong as a child (16%). This factor was key to understanding how the abuse began.

> *"When I was about 5 I was being sexually abused by my two brothers who were about 18 years old. At the time I never knew it was wrong but I was forced not to tell anyone so I didn't."*

Lack of knowledge could be attributed to the **age of the subject** when the abuse began, or to the fact that **sex was not talked about within the family.**

> *"Why do I feel so bad, like it was my fault. I didn't even know what was happening to me at the time. I didn't even know what sex was. If I had been told by my parents at that time that if anyone fondles you by your private parts I should tell them, no matter if the other said to keep it a secret, something could have been done. But my parents never once told me anything about sex, it was never mentioned, it was a 'bad word.' "*

b) Parental factors (21%)
It was clear that in some cases relationship problems between the subject and their parents made them more vulnerable to abuse. There were examples of letters describing a craving for affection, which was often met by the abuser.

> *"I came from a one parent family with 3 children, so attention was a rare thing. This is why I went looking elsewhere. Lots of kids used to visit this old man (probably about 60). We used to ask for money for sweets and he used to oblige. I went round a few times on my own and he used to touch me up. I should have stopped going. I knew it was wrong, but it was attention. It actually made me feel wanted, so it suited me and I went back for more."*

A final parent factor had to do with the **parents mental health.** These letters only comprised a small minority, but they did point to the importance of considering the quality of life for children who live with adults with mental health difficulties.

c) Fear and blackmail.
Fear operated as a third factor, for example:

> *"I just wish that ChildLine was out at that time - it may have helped me. If I had*

Report of the
National
Commission of
Inquiry into the
Prevention of
Child Abuse

*someone to talk to that I could trust, I may have opened up but my problem was that
I was full of fear and could not bring myself to talk to someone."*

*"In my case I never told anybody because I was more afraid of the consequences if I
wasn't believed and had to go back into the family home. The beatings and abuse
would have been a lot worse. I really think I might have been killed."*

Others reported emotional blackmail.

*"He used to say to me that this was our secret and I should never tell anyone
especially mum and dad (I didn't). He never physically threatened me only using
emotional blackmail - if I loved him I would do this for him and so on."*

Other factors include alcohol use by the alleged perpetrator, substitute care and friendship.

In almost a third of the letters the factors were not clear. In terms of the way the text was
presented the key factor could only be explained as an **adult male wanting and having sexual
relations with a female or male child.**

*"All I can remember is that when I was about 3-5 years of age playing outside my
flats I was approached by a man who forcibly took hold of my hand and walked with
me as far as Westminster Bridge. There in a quiet spot he put his hands down my
trousers and felt my private parts. Realising what he was up to, I got out of his
clutches and ran all the way home. I didn't mention anything about what happened
to anyone. This is about all I can think of."*

2.2   Factors in stopping the abuse

59% of writers gave an indication as to what stopped the abuse. The findings are given in
Table 2.1.

Table 2.1   *Key factors in stopping the abuse (N = 721)*

Factor	%
Subject moved	21
Subject told	10
Someone found out	7
Person Believed Responsible (PBR) moved or died	7
Subject challenged	5
Avoidance/escape	3
One off	2
Other	4
Not clear	41
Total	100

*Report of the
National
Commission of
Inquiry into the
Prevention of
Child Abuse*

The more conventional prevention strategies of telling, avoidance and challenging did work to stop the abuse in about 18% of the cases, where they were applied. For example:

Telling

"I am a fifteen year old girl and experienced such abuse from my father about a year ago...I managed to tell my friend and she told me to phone my mum. Mum was able to tell me she understood as the same thing had happened with her foster father. She phoned the police."

Avoidance/escape

"I avoided ever being alone with him [father] and many nights I put a chair behind my bedroom door so if he visited my room it would make a noise and hopefully disturb my stepmother."

Challenged

"When I was thirteen, I suddenly connected what he was doing to me with playground dirty jokes and next time he abused me, I asked him to stop and to my surprise he did."

Someone else found out

Others finding out about the abuse worked to stop it for 7% of the sample. Generally these were situations where other children were also being abused and they told others. **There were very few accounts of children displaying symptoms and being asked.** In fact the reverse was more the case. People told about how they must have been giving off signs, but no one bothered to ask what the matter was.

"I had managed to block out all memory of the abuse...I didn't know why I behaved the way I did, nor why sex scared me so much, why it filled me with such self loathing. I had already had two overdose/suicide attempts...and I really didn't know why I felt this way. No questions ever being asked about why I always drank from my parents, as with my abuse they just ignored it all, nothing bad could, or can, filter into their lives. Does the self esteem a power of good, that does. No wonder I hated myself, they obviously hated me or else they would have stopped it, wouldn't they?"

2.3   Contexts

68% of writers gave information about the family context as relevant to the abuse.

Report of the
National
Commission of
Inquiry into the
Prevention of
Child Abuse

Table 2.2 *Family Contexts Relevant to the Abuse*

Context	%
Domestic violence and/or alcohol	11
Parental absence	9
Relationship difficulties between parents	8
Reconstituted family	7
Abuse was part of life for family members	6
Not understanding	5
Divorce or separation	4
Substitute care	4
Mother knew	3
Poverty	2
Single parent	2
Family member was paedophile	1
Parent's mental health	1
Extended family	1
Protecting siblings	1
Other	4
Not clear	32
Total	100

These contexts, like key factors, cannot be viewed as causal. However, there was something about each one which predisposed the subject to believing a link either with being abused or continuing to be abused.

Prevention Implications

o The findings suggest that **information, whilst important, is insufficient on its own as a prevention strategy.**

o **Lack of knowledge may be strongly associated with the child's relationship with the parents.** For knowledge based prevention programmes to be effective, this suggests that they also need to relate to a "distant parent" context.

o All the key factors need to be taken account of in prevention programmes. Children need to be equipped with a sufficient knowledge base and in addition need to be given skills, support or resources which address the following:

   * Relationship problems with parents and the issue of parental betrayal.
   * Parental absence and the issue of parental betrayal.
   * Fear and the very real consequences anticipated.
   * Emotional blackmail and the implication of the victim's participation.
   * How to deal with the issue of violent and substance using adults.
   * Substitute care.
   * Friendship as a source of danger.

o Contexts are difficult to tackle at a preventive level. There is much about them that is circumstantial. However, this data does support a link between domestic violence and abuse, one already indicated by other research. The implication for prevention would be

*Report of the
National
Commission of
Inquiry into the
Prevention of
Child Abuse*

to **support campaigns** aimed at stopping domestic violence or to promote joint campaigns which may act to empower women to protect their children.

○ **In direct answer to the question "How do you think community and family can help prevent child abuse?"** the following were offered as potential solutions.

* Improvements within society, including respecting children.
* Media for greater awareness.
* Education
* Talk about abuse and sex.
* See the signs of child abuse.
* Report and telling about child abuse.
* Listening.
* Social monitoring of children (including better child care and supervision and more help to be given to parents).
* Better family relationships.

The call for improvements within society could encompass many, if not all the categories listed above. Examples of views are:

"My first point is that there seems to be a difficulty in government and society's ability to absorb the evidence that the sexual abuse of children is relatively common. Almost every reputable survey shows that around 1 in 8 women (and a not insignificant number of men) experience "serious"abuse. Even if we are very cautious about these results, and (arbitrarily) halve the incidence to say 1 in 16, that would still leave one and a half million female "victims" in the UK with tens of thousands of children today who are being or will be abused."

"Maybe if it was spoken about more, accepted that this type of thing does happen in all walks of life by men and women, then this subject would not be "taboo"! I think if people were more open and stopped burying their heads in the sand we could start to prevent it."

○ Some respondents felt that it was about the community taking a **collective responsibility,** for example:

"What's it to do with me? All adults should be encouraged to take responsibility for the welfare of abused children as they would for their physical safety and also to support the efforts of all those who are trying to deal with the problem."

3. Telling and reporting

63% of writers reported that they had told someone either as child or as an adult. Less than half had told someone as a child.

Report of the
National
Commission of
Inquiry into the
Prevention of
Child Abuse

Table 3.1 *Age of Telling Someone* (N = 721)

Child	32%
Adult	31%
Never told	13%
No comment	23%

For 13% of the writers, telling the Commission was the first time they had told anyone.

Many of these writers felt it was the first time they had been asked, and therefore felt it relevant to tell.

○ Children tell those most available to them, particularly mothers (34% of those who told as children)

○ Negative or neutral responses were more likely than positive ones.

○ Those who told as children were more likely to be younger and came primarily from the under 25 age group.

○ Males are more likely than females to never tell anyone, and much less likely to tell as a child.

○ Those who were abused by natural fathers are slightly more likely to tell, and those abused by father substitutes are much more likely to tell as children.

○ Writers who told as children were in the minority. Findings from this group suggest that it is not necessarily the case that children tell either immediately or at the time of the abuse. Children are more likely to tell, if they do so at all, after their abuse has stopped.

○ Telling led to reporting to police or social services for approximately half those who told as a child. Once reported almost half were critical of the response.

Prevention Implications

○ Heightened public awareness and media campaigns coincide with an increase in reporting. The rate of telling and reporting may again subside if the subject of child abuse goes off the public agenda.

○ Prevention strategies should address **methods of responding to children and adults who tell in positive ways.** The benefits of telling need to be emphasised in that it did appear to stop the abuse in over a quarter of cases. The disadvantages, particularly in the **"child protection system" and legal processes, also need to be addressed.**

Difficulties of reporting

"This is difficult, there is obviously much more of an awareness now of abuse, but how many people would actually be willing to report suspected abuse knowing that a family could be completely split up because of it. Of course if the abuse is sexual, then a child has to be protected from that, but if dad or whoever is reported or even imprisoned, there could be such financial difficulties arising from it, making the original situation a lot worse. I would have been better off without my mother but then who would have looked after me and my sister?"

175

Report of the
National
Commission of
Inquiry into the
Prevention of
Child Abuse

Encouraging children to tell of child abuse.

"I think that mothers should be more watchful over young children, boys and girls and whether it is daddy or uncle they must tell someone what has happened and the mother must tell the children that they will not get into trouble for telling what happened."

Listen to children.

"Families can be taught to LISTEN more to the children, keeping close communications with children is one way. In regard to small children who cannot yet talk, to watch and monitor their behaviour."

and finally, to see the signs of child abuse.

"I think that clearer guidelines are needed on what to look for as "symptoms" of abuse for both professionals and the general public. In our particular case all the "symptoms" were there [but] went unnoticed for four whole years...People are completely unaware of what to look for. If only two people had got their heads together perhaps ours would have been a different story sooner."

4   Effects and help

The full report contains two chapters on the effects of child abuse in childhood and the benefits and drawbacks of seeking help. Effects are wide ranging and profound. Help is variable and often difficult to obtain.

Prevention Implications

○ Prevention should not just be viewed narrowly in terms of preventing the initial abusive experience, it should also **work on the effects to prevent further harm.**

○ **Some people who have experienced abuse need careful, sensitive and informed support** to help them to be the parents that they want to be. Many expressed the view that in some ways it helped them to be better parents.

○ There is a **cost implication to preventing child abuse** for children, rather than dealing with the consequences and effects when children become adults. Only 22% of writers felt that they had come to terms with the childhood abuse. The repercussions for parents and children were also a serious consideration.

5.   Prevention Responses

This section reviewed responses to the Commission's terms of reference.

5.1   Who else can help prevent child abuse and how?

○ Schools were viewed as having a vital role to play in helping to prevent child abuse. Within the concept of education there were three main areas:

*Report of the
National
Commission of
Inquiry into the
Prevention of
Child Abuse*

1) Education on child abuse and sex.
2) The need for parenting skills.
3) Educating children on their rights as human beings.

Education on child abuse and sex

This was in line with the finding that the majority of respondents in the "tell one's story" letters were aged under eleven when the abuse began. Many pointed to the need for education on abuse from a young age.

> *"Early use in school of appropriate information starting at nursery age. Including father/mother stories as abusers, not confining the abuser to stranger, uncle, baby sitter. Each school to have a child protection policy."*

Education on parenting skills

> *"Parents all feel that they have the right to bring up their children in the way they think fit. They receive no training for this. No guidelines have ever been given other than following the example of their own parenting. It is a sad reflection that we educate everyone to high standards of literacy, but neglect the most vital education of all - that of good parenting."*

Educate children on their rights

> *"The most difficult and important view to accept is the notion that children have the right to be regarded as equal. It would be impossible to cease to call the children one has physically given life to anything other than "mine" as we do, but the notion of one person belonging to another not only flatly contradicts the notion of human equality, but also offers a feeling of being at liberty to personally control the use of this particular possession as one does of inanimate possessions. One of the most important tasks we need to undertake if we are to halt child abuse is to educate people into an understanding that humans cannot be owned by others and that physically producing and nurturing a child confers no more rights of authority than one holds over any other human being. What it does, I think, do, is impose upon parents a duty to nurture in a manner that is respectful towards children's rights to be treated as a fellow human."*

○ The **training** of people who work with children was also expressed often by respondents.

> *"If I had a say, I would personally recommend: more information and support for children and parents: including teacher and doctor training - they are currently the least sympathetic."*

○ Also included in training is the idea that people who work with children should be **"available"**.

> *"I gave so many indications to teachers...I couldn't talk to either of them as it was too formal. I even told one teacher I was being molested. None of this did me any good. Teachers need to be aware of child abuse and need to know where the children could get help - even if there was one specialist teacher in each school. The child should be listened to carefully and then given all their options. They should be made to feel safe."*

177

*Report of the
National
Commission of
Inquiry into the
Prevention of
Child Abuse*

○ A further view is that people who work with children should **question** more, for example.

> *"The psychiatrist who saw me when I was two years old should have persisted. The schools should have probed more; my trauma was in my school work. My GP should not have accepted my nightly screaming and sleepwalking as just one of those things she'll grow out of."*

○ **Counsellors to be available** in schools, or centres, where children can receive help and support, could be set up in each town.

> *"Maybe there should be visiting counsellors going to schools, to talk to children occasionally, or maybe a teacher could take a counselling course and then see children if they wanted to talk. Better still there should be a counselling courses aimed at teachers so they can easily recognise abused children."*

5.2 How should professionals respond to child abuse?

Answers to this question highlighted the importance of a **supportive response**, which includes such things as "victim support", befriending and listening. Also mentioned was the need for professional counselling, better training of professionals and a focus on perpetrators.

5.3 Perpetrators

There were a number of comments made on what to do with **perpetrators.** This was expressed in three different ways: 1) to **monitor** perpetrators in the community; 2) to **rehabilitate** perpetrators back into the community; and 3) to **punish** perpetrators.

> *"Offenders need to be watched once they have been released to ensure that they have not been released back into families to reoffend. This could be what went wrong in our case; my ex father in law having been released as a schedule 1 offender on three different occasions."*

> *"Please! Please! the law is so unsupportive by allowing these people [abusers] to walk free."*

Linked to these was the notion of **justice.**

> *"My daughter now receives weekly counselling as do I. We are both seriously affected. My son now aged three, has 'lost' his father. Although I am in a new relationship, it is difficult because of the consequences of one man's action. My daughter's god-mother is frightened for her own daughter. In society, I am treated not as a victim, but as a perpetrator. I am outcast being a single parent; for not knowing what was happening to my daughter; or stopping it sooner. My entire family has been pulled apart, and the only freedom I could get was to move. This man walks the streets, sees other children, still has his family, and can deny the nightmare in order to continue offending. This is called Justice!"*

Report of the
National
Commission of
Inquiry into the
Prevention of
Child Abuse

5.4   If you have experience of the "child abuse system" run by professionals, what are your impressions of it? How might it be run better?

A third of respondents expressed views that were critical of the "help" given by the "child abuse system". As the "help" received by respondents varied and was not always stated, "help" was therefore coded as one broad category, which includes "help" received from, for example, counsellors, psychotherapists or doctors, as well as including police and social workers who were not actually named other than being the "child abuse system". A small group considered the system might be better now, compared to when they were a child. ChildLine was also mentioned as a "good thing".

5.5   What sort of treatments for child abuse do you think work?

Over half of the respondents who answered this question expressed the view that the provision of "support" was the most effective treatment.

Conclusion

We received many letters which commented on the profound and long lasting effects of childhood experiences. We report on writers who suffered serious mental health problems, tried to kill themselves and others, turned to alcohol and drugs and had difficulties in relationships in all spheres from the intimately sexual through to family members, friends and the wider social environment. Thus **prevention might also be aimed around addressing consequences.** Our whole child protection system is currently geared towards preventing and responding to specific types of actions (most of which are hard to prove).

The importance of social attitudes, values and organisation is most keenly displayed in the final section of the report on prevention responses. Many recommendations centre on changing societal attitudes and moving towards a collective responsibility about the welfare of children. This is less about people reporting child abuse if they have concerns and more about doing something themselves to prevent abuse from occurring. Again there is a broad range of social locations for doing something - families, neighbourhoods, institutions such as schools and health services, the media and "society".

1. **Families** - recommendations generally focused on strategies to improve relationships between parents and their children, including talking more, discussing child abuse and talking more about sex. The letters reinforce the vulnerability of children who have "absent" or "distant" parents. There was also much in the letters from people who just wanted to feel "loved, safe and secure".

2. **Neighbourhoods** - brings in the idea of "community" which in many cases is just not there.

3. **Institutions** - there were a great many comments about the role that schools could play. Summarised these had to do with:

o   Parent education

o   Parenting education for children

Report of the
National
Commission of
Inquiry into the
Prevention of
Child Abuse

○ Education about abuse as part of the school curriculum

○ Education about rights and responsibilities

○ Monitoring in schools – a "going home register", regular (annual/twice yearly) individual sessions with child

○ Teachers offering opportunities for children to talk to them

○ Counselling opportunities offered in school as a matter of routine

We received very few letters from children themselves, yet when they did write, what happens in schools was very important to them.

Issues to do with a legal system include:

○ **The prioritising of the rights of the defendant over the rights of the victim.**

○ **The difficulties of prosecutions in child abuse cases.**

○ **The system ignoring the fact that victims have to live with the crime and that they should get compensation.**

○ **The system does not treat crimes associated with child abuse seriously (particularly in terms of sentencing).**

○ **The justice system does not act as an effective deterrent.**

Inappropriate help was outlined by many of those who had experience of the child protection system. Only a minority had experiences of the system as children and their criticisms seemed to overlap considerably with criticisms of the legal system, because that was how their intervention was framed. Many felt they got no help at all. The main issue emerging from adult's experiences of help were criticisms of therapy, and the therapists and counsellors not understanding what the writer was experiencing.

4. Social change and the media

Many people felt the media had a key role to play in terms of:

○ Education for parents

○ Offering help to children

○ Education for children

○ Perpetuating or being seen to uphold values which reinforce child abuse and being able to change this

Social change focused on changing attitudes in general towards children, moving towards ensuring that children were respected as children and acknowledging their rights. Wider concerns about inadequate child care, poverty, stress from work which had repercussions in families were also expressed. In addition there was the point that society keeps abuse hidden and continues to allow it to happen by denying its real extent or consequences.

Finally, there is the view that **the victim is the expert.**

"You need more groups and a lot more cooperation with the professionals and people who have got over abuse and are now helping more abused people; because they have been in the same position and they know how the abused person is really feeling."

A Review of the Financial Implications of Programmes aimed at the Prevention of Child Abuse in the United Kingdom

*Report of the
National
Commission of
Inquiry into the
Prevention of
Child Abuse*

- **A report to the National Inquiry into the Prevention of Child Abuse,**

- **Prepared by the Institute of Public Finance Limited, May 1996.**

The time available to the researchers in preparing this report has been limited. Consequently the findings are themselves confined to a higher level of summary. Rather than frame spurious orders of sensitivity about an estimate which is approximate in nature, this review concentrates upon an assessment of the likely minimum cost. Further study would probably uncover further activities and costs. The researchers are most grateful to the Directors of Social Services, Probation and Education Services for their forbearance. In particular, we are pleased to have received the assistance of the Association of Chief Police Officers in meeting our request for information within such short deadlines, as well as many responsible officers in the service departments referred to above who responded to our survey.

Report of the
National
Commission of
Inquiry into the
Prevention of
Child Abuse

Contents

Report of the
National
Commission of
Inquiry into the
Prevention of
Child Abuse

7. **Overall Findings and Conclusions**

Appendices:

1. Survey Questionnaire used in the canvass of authorities to frame our cost assumptions.

2. Estimated and actual base data used to model the cost calculations.

*Report of the
National
Commission of
Inquiry into the
Prevention of
Child Abuse*

1. The Review in Context

1.1 Background

We were asked by the Commission to undertake a high level review to size the likely cost of child abuse in the UK. The review was to concentrate on services provided by public bodies, although we also agreed to look at expenditure by the five large voluntary child care organisations.

Although we reviewed a number of recent studies on the subject (e.g. the Department of Health publication *Child Protection: Messages From Research*), together with many of the written submissions made to the Commission, we found a surprising lack of information on the financial implications of child abuse. Given the short time available for the study we, therefore, had to make a number of assumptions and our findings must be viewed in that light. To qualify our assumptions we have often referred to responses made by a number of Chief Officers in response to a short survey we undertook in February/March 1996.

Our main focus was on public authorities and Government departments in England although, wherever possible, we attempted to obtain comparable data for Wales, Scotland and Northern Ireland. We were unable to research the availability of some data and have resorted to estimating the level of service activity.

One particular difficulty we have faced in undertaking the review has been its timing relative to the major administrative re-organisations of locally delivered services in Wales and Scotland. For this reason, we have used available data for the whole of the United Kingdom, but have necessarily restricted the appraisal of funding systems to the operations in England. Furthermore, in carrying out a survey amongst those service providers most closely involved in preventing child abuse we have confined our canvass to English authorities, where the impact of structural reorganisation has been least. However, the basis upon which most service practitioners operated is similar throughout the United Kingdom. Thus, bearing in mind the high level nature of this review, we have assumed that the level of activity, and consequent cost, could be approximated on a per capita population base in those areas for which we had no data. In this respect, we have been able to access data for all areas of Great Britain, and have assumed that the level of activity in Northern Ireland is broadly similar. A more detailed and protracted study may prove otherwise, but our approach is unlikely to overstate the global costs involved.

1.2 Terms of Reference

The detailed terms of reference to which we worked were to:

○ Review the point at which funding decisions are taken relating to the direction of resources towards the:
  * Prevention of child abuse.
  * Investigation and treatment of the consequences of child abuse.

○ Comment on the legislative, administrative and other limitations relating to this funding.

○ Explore the formulaic principles upon which agreed resources are distributed, highlighting inconsistencies of practice and appropriateness of the systems.

○ Map the expenditure targeted at catering for children at risk, covering:

*Report of the
National
Commission of
Inquiry into the
Prevention of
Child Abuse*

* Central Government direct programmes e.g. DSS benefits, redistributed taxes etc.
* Central Government departmental programmes e.g. DfEE, Home Office etc.
* Locally determined programmes e.g. NHS, local authorities.
* Voluntary agency programmes e.g. within the five major child care voluntary organisations.
* Any other indirect expenditure.

o Make international comparisons on the level of funding for social and educational programmes.

o Assess the level and extent of duplication which might occur between different level and programme areas and comment on the areas of savings or additional resources which could be freed if co-ordination was introduced.

o Extend the comment to observations on the possible differences relating to practices adopted in England, Wales, Scotland and Northern Ireland.

o Examine the lack of definitions and forms of account relating to this area which give rise to the facility of accurate information to monitor policy issues in the prevention of child abuse. In this respect, it would add context to the review if comments could be made on the lack of knowledge which might occur about the opportunities for inter-programme co-operation arising from the lack of such data.

o Summarise the above review by suggesting a set of recommendations for the Commission of Inquiry to consider.

185

1.3   Scope of Services

Any attempt to assess the resources available and expended in the area of child abuse has to contend with the complexity of the area under review, in particular:

o The numerous organisations and individuals involved, from both the public and the independent sectors.

o The wide range of services, many of which involve professionals from a number of different disciplines.

o The fact that the services may be targeted at the families of the children involved or at offenders, not only or necessarily at the children themselves.

The nature of the services provided cover:

o Regulation.
o Prevention.
o Investigation.
o Intervention.
o Treatment and therapeutic services.
o Financial and Other Support.

The range of authorities and agencies involved is similarly wide:

o Local Authorities - in particular, Social Services, Education, and Housing, but also including Legal Services.

o The NHS - Health Authorities, GP Fundholders, NHS Trusts, and GPs.

*Report of the
National
Commission of
Inquiry into the
Prevention of
Child Abuse*

○ Police Authorities.

○ The Probation Service.

○ Prison Services.

○ The Courts.

○ Crown Prosecution Service.

○ Other Central Government Departments - DOE, DOH, DSS, the Home Office, DfEE, OFSTED, SSI, Police Inspectorate.

○ The Voluntary Child Care Sector - including the NSPCC, Save the Children, NCH Action for Children, the Children's Society, and Barnardo's.

○ Private Sector - e.g. private nurseries, child care providers, etc. - a very small sector.

Table 1.1 summarises the key agencies involved by reference to the nature of the services provided. ["VCC" refers to the Voluntary Child Care Sector.]

Table 1.1   *Key Public Agencies Involved*

Service Areas	Key Public Agencies Involved
Regulation	Central Government.
Investigation	Police, Social Services, NSPCC.
Assessment	NHS Trusts, GPs, Social Services, Police, VCC.
Intervention	Police, Social Services, Courts, Probation Service, VCC.
Treatment and Therapy	Social Services, NHS Trusts (e.g. medical, psychiatric, psychological and counseling services), VCC.
Prevention	Social Services, Education, Police, Health Authorities, NHS Trusts, GPs, Health Visitors, Probation, VCC.
Financial/Other Support	Local Authorities, VCC.

2   Key Authorities in England

Resources are allocated to, and expenditure incurred by, individual authorities, not by reference to inter-agency programmes/services. We have, therefore, used the different authorities involved as the most appropriate framework for examining resource allocation, activity and expenditure data.

2.1 Local Authorities

Structure

At the time when we were undertaking our review, there were 410 principal local authorities in England:

○ 32 London Boroughs.

○ The City of London.

○ 36 Metropolitan Districts.

○ 2 Unitary Authorities.

Report of the
National
Commission of
Inquiry into the
Prevention of
Child Abuse

○ 38 County Councils.

○ 294 Non-Metropolitan District Councils.

○ 7 Fire and Civil Defence Authorities serving London and the Metropolitan Areas.

The above structure is not fixed. As a result of the proposed reorganisation of local government in the shire areas (ie county councils and non-metropolitan districts), a number of additional unitary authorities will come into operation on 1 April, 1996, 1997 and 1998.

Services

The key service departments of interest in relation to child abuse in its widest sense are:

○ Social Services and Education, which are provided by county councils, metropolitan districts and unitary authorities.

○ Housing which is provided by district councils, metropolitan districts and unitary authorities.

Social Services are the lead agency in relation to child protection. The Children Act 1989 requires local authorities to provide a range of services for children, e.g. accommodation for children and their parents/guardians, facilities in Family Centres, advice, guidance, cultural or recreational activities, home helps, travel subsidies to access other support services and assistance with holidays. They may also apply for Education Support Orders to ensure that children receive appropriate education.

Social Services are responsible for co-ordinating:

○ The work of Area Child Protection Committees (ACPCs).

○ The preparation of child protection plans for children.

○ Multi disciplinary case conferences for children.

○ Children's Services Plans.

There are, therefore, a wide range of local authority staff who may be involved in child abuse work, including:

○ Social workers.

○ Teachers.

○ Educational psychologists.

○ Education welfare officers.

○ Nursery and playgroup staff.

○ Housing officers.

○ Legal and other "Support" staff.

○ Leisure staff.

2.2   The NHS

In considering healthcare services, it is necessary to differentiate between the purchasers and providers of care. The main purchasers and providers in England as at 1 April, 1995 were:

*Report of the
National
Commission of
Inquiry into the
Prevention of
Child Abuse*

Purchasers

○ 8 Regional Health Authorities (RHAs).

○ 112 District Health Authorities (DHAs).

○ 90 Family Health Services Authorities (FHSAs)

○ 8,500 GP Fundholders (GPFHs).

Providers

○ 419 NHS Trusts.

○ 2 Special Health Authorities.

○ 22 Directly Managed Units.

○ 27,000 GPs.

Once again the structure is subject to reorganisation. With effect from 1 April 1996, the 8 RHAs will be abolished and the DHAs and FHSAs will be merged to form 100 new Health Authorities. A review of the boundaries of the new authorities suggests that, as far as possible, they have been drawn-up to be coterminous with one or more local authorities. This position is likely to change with the establishment of unitary local authorities.

188

Health authorities and trusts have a duty under the Children Act 1989 to assist any investigation by a local authority under Section 47 of the Act, by providing relevant information and advice.

Healthcare professionals' involvement in relation to child protection ranges over the areas of identification, assessment, prevention and treatment. The services may be provided in relation to children, their families and/or offenders. Those involved can include:

○ Paediatricians

○ GPs

○ Health visitors

○ Midwives

○ Psychiatrists

○ Clinical psychologists and counsellors

○ Accident and emergency staff

○ Community psychiatric nurses

2.3   Police Authorities

From 1 April 1995, responsibility for policing in England transferred to 38 newly constituted Police Authorities, plus the Metropolitan Police Authority which is responsible for police and other services in around the capital.

Police have an investigative duty in relation to child abuse. By the nature of their work, they may be involved with children, their families and/or offenders. In addition, police surgeons may be called upon to provide medical assessments of children. The police may also be involved in preparing children or their families to appear in court.

2.4   Probation Services

The Probation Service in England is divided into 48 probation areas and consists of probation officers and various supporting staff who are employed by Probation Committees.

While the Probation Committees are corporate bodies independent of central and local government, the Home Secretary is responsible to Parliament for the work of the Probation Service and is assisted in this by the Probation Service Division of the Home Office and HM Probation Inspectorate. Furthermore, four fifths of expenditure incurred by Probation Committees is provided by the Home Office by way of cash limited specific grants to local authorities who provide the remainder. Grants are based on budgeted expenditure for the year.

The Probation Service's involvement may be with children, their families and/or offenders.

2.5   The Courts

The hierarchy of the court system is described below:

○ House of Lords.

○ Court of Appeal (Civil Division).

○ High Court Level - Family Division.

○ County Court Level - Family Hearing Centres, Care Centres, Other County Courts(e.g. Divorce Courts), District Judges.

○ Magistrates Level - Family Proceedings Court, Youth Court.

Most public law cases will start and be dealt with at the Family Proceedings Courts, although transfer to other courts is possible e.g. if the case is particularly complex or urgent.

2.6   Central Government

A number of Central Government departments have an involvement in the child protection process in its widest sense, the main ones being:

○ The Department of Health promotes programmes through local points of service, where SSDs, Health Authorities and Local Education Authorities actually implement the Child Protection policies.

○ The Department for Education and Employment promotes programmes in a similar way.

○ Home Office, Prisons, Probation Service, Police Service

○ Crown Prosecution Service, which is responsible for the independent review and conduct of criminal proceedings instituted by the police forces in England and Wales. There is a head office and 33 area offices, 31 in England and 2 in Wales.

○ Lord Chancellor's Department, which is responsible for promoting general reforms in civil law, for the procedure of the civil courts and for the administration of the Supreme Court and county courts in England and Wales.

○ Department of Social Security, Benefits Section.

*Report of the
National
Commission of
Inquiry into the
Prevention of
Child Abuse*

*Report of the
National
Commission of
Inquiry into the
Prevention of
Child Abuse*

○ Department of Environment - inner cities, rural areas, housing, etc.

3. Resource Allocation Systems in England

We undertook to examine how funds are allocated to the main authorities involved in child abuse, given the importance of resource availability in determining how much can be spent on a particular service.

In looking at resource allocation systems, we have focused on the three main bodies involved - local, police and health authorities. We would emphasise, at the outset, that the formulae used to allocate resources do not imply any ring-fencing of monies, such that they must be spent on particular services or client groups. For example:

○ Although Revenue Support Grant to Local Authorities is built-up on a service-by-service basis from a number Standard Spending Assessments (SSAs), one of which is Personal Social Services (PSS), each authority is free to make its own decisions on the allocation of its total resources between services.

○ Similarly, although Health Authorities receive a block allocation for all Hospital and Community Health Services (HCHS), they are free to decide how the funds are allocated, both across services and among service providers.

In examining the resource allocation systems, we concentrated on two main aspects:

○ Do the systems differentiate between types of authority or authorities in different parts of the country.

○ Do the methodologies for allocating funds take specific account of child abuse or of the factors which might be a feature in child abuse cases.

With regard to the latter point, it is difficult to state definitively which factors can be said to cause or lead to abuse. Current thinking, however, accepts that a combination of social, economic and environmental factors play a part. In this respect, *Messages From Research* refers to a number of studies which point to some relationship between the children dealt with under the child protection process and the following factors. In one study undertaken by Jane Gibbons:-

○ 36% of cases were headed by a lone parent.

○ 57% lacked a wage earner.

○ 54% were dependent on Income Support.

○ Domestic violence in the family featured in 27% of cases.

○ Mental illness in the family featured in 13% of cases.

In a second study by Thoburn and colleagues:-

○ In 23% of cases a member of the family had suffered an accident or serious ill health during the previous year.

It is clear that there is a circumstantial association between the backgrounds of such cases and the stress arising in socio-economically deprived areas. We have not, however, had the opportunity to test the "causal" relationship between such factors and the incidence of child abuse.

Report of the
National
Commission of
Inquiry into the
Prevention of
Child Abuse

3.1   Local Authorities

Local authority Standard Spending Assessments (SSAs) are defined as *the amount the Government considers appropriate for each local authority to calculate as its budget requirement for a given year consistent with the amount the Government considers it would be appropriate for all authorities to spend.*

The SSAs are, therefore, a measure of relative spending need rather than the absolute spending need for individual local authorities. As stated above, although they are built-up on a service-by-service basis, monies are not ring-fenced and the SSA for a particular service is not meant to be used as a spending target for that service.

The SSAs of particular relevance to this review are:

o   Personal Social Services (PSS).

o   Education.

o   Police.

3.2   Social Services

The Social Services SSA for 1996/97 totals £6.9 billion, broken down as follows:

o   Children's Services   £1,754.7M.

o   Services for the Elderly   £3,737.4M.

o   Other Social Services   £1,416.5M.

Children's Social Services

The SSA for Children's Social Services includes all services provided for children and their families, including residential, foster and day-care, social work support and the associated administration costs.

The basis for this SSA is the number of children in each local authority expected to need social services help, multiplied by the estimated cost of caring for them. The proportion of children expected to need social services help is estimated by reference to:

o   The proportion of children living in lone parent families.

o   The proportion of children living in families in receipt of Income Support.

o   The proportion of children under 16 years of age living in rented accommodation.

o   The average number of homeless households including dependent children or pregnant women accepted as having a high priority for housing expressed as a proportion of the number of children.

The SSA calculations do not use data on the actual number of children at individual authority level in receipt of social services help. There is, however, research evidence to show a link between the first three factors above and the proportion of children needing social services help.

*Report of the
National
Commission of
Inquiry into the
Prevention of
Child Abuse*

The SSA assumes that the proportion of children needing social services help varies significantly from one part of the country to another, and this is borne out to some extent (but not to the same scale) by the proportion of children on Child Protection Registers (CPR).

Table 3.1   *Proportion of Children Expected to Need Social Services Help*

Type of Authority	Proportion of Children for SSA Purposes %	Proportion of Under 18s on CPR %
County Councils	0.8	0.27
Metropolitan Districts	1.2	0.38
Outer London Boroughs	1.1	
		0.39
Inner London Boroughs	2.0	
All England Average	1.0	0.31

In the same way that the calculations do not use actual data for children receiving social services help, the unit cost figures are not based on the actual costs of caring for children. Nor are they based on any research evidence of the factors which influence the costs of care. The SSAs assume that the costs of care will be influenced by:

o   The proportion of the population living in accommodation which is not self-contained.

o   The proportion of children in non-white ethnic groups.

The SSA calculations imply that in 1996/97 each child expected to need social services help will cost a varying amount according to which part of the country he or she lives:

Table 3.2   *1996/97 Average Unit Costs Per Child*

Type of Authority	1996/97 SSA £ Per Child	Unit cost of Child in Care 1995/96 Estimates		
		Residential	Foster	Day Care
County Councils	£13,240	£46,100	£7,000	£6,200
Metropolitan Districts	£13,970	£40,000	£7,200	£6,800
Outer London Boroughs	£21,064			
		£43,100	£10,600	£6,200
Inner London Boroughs	£27,284			
All England Average	£15,564	£43,000	£7,600	£6,300

At individual authority level, the range of expected (SSA) costs extends from £11,480 per child in North Lincolnshire to £31,336 in Kensington and Chelsea. However, and in general, the costs actually incurred by local authorities do not appear to differ so much between areas.

The methodology used in the Children's PSS calculations, in particular the unit cost element, has been subject to considerable criticism since it was introduced in 1994-95. Statistically, the costs produced by the SSA calculations do not match the costs reported by local

Report of the
National
Commission of
Inquiry into the
Prevention of
Child Abuse

authorities. The factors used in the SSA calculations appear to *explain* only 46% of the actual cost differences between authorities in relation to children's social services. The Department of Health plans to review the methodology when further research evidence is available, and we understand that the University of York are undertaking a study at the present time.

It is not surprising, given the differences in both the proportions of children expected to need social services help and the expected costs of caring for them, that the SSA for Children's personal social services should differ dramatically from one authority to another.

For example, the SSAs imply that:

	The equivalent 1995/96 CIPFA Estimates for Children & Families were:
○ County Councils need to spend only £111 for every child aged 0-17 years in order to provide a full range of children's personal social services; but	£135
○ Metropolitan districts need to spend £168 per child.	£183
○ Outer London boroughs need to spend £243 per child.	
	£314
○ Inner London boroughs need to spend £557 per child.	

193

There is no specific reference to child abuse in the Department of Environment guide to SSAs. However, the SSA for children's personal social services must, by definition, include most areas of cost which local authorities face in connection with child abuse even though, in practice, the actual costs impact on both children *and their families*.

The inference from the SSA allocations for children's personal social services is clear:

Either:

○ The incidence of child abuse is lower in rural areas (i.e. progressively so, outside London and the Metropolitan areas): or

○ The costs of dealing with child abuse are lower in rural areas: or

○ Both the incidence of child abuse and the costs of dealing with it are lower in rural areas.

We are not aware of any detailed research evidence which would support these alternatives, but we have noted that there appears to be a higher proportion of children on the CPR in the urban areas. [see Table 4.1].

Other Social Services

The PSS Other Services element has some relevance to the care of children and their families. This includes the services for those in the 18-64 years age group who are mentally ill,

Report of the
National
Commission of
Inquiry into the
Prevention of
Child Abuse

physically or mentally disabled, suffering from HIV/Aids and those who abuse alcohol and/or drugs.

The factors used to calculate entitlement under this SSA include;

o The extent to which the population in the 18-64 years age group in each local authority area is more or less likely than the average to have a limiting long-term illness.

o The proportion of people living in accommodation which is not self-contained or which is not permanent.

o The proportion of the population living in overcrowded conditions.

o The proportion of households living in rented purpose-built flats.

o The proportion of people who were born outside the UK, Ireland, the European Community, the Old Commonwealth and the USA.

Again, there are considerable differences in the 1996/97 allocations per head across the country, which mirror the pattern of costs which local authorities anticipated incurring in 1995/96, but which considerably underestimate the actual amounts.

Table 3.3   *1996/97 Other Social Services SSA Allocations*

Type of Authority	1996/97 SSA £ per Head	1995/96 budget spend £ per Head
County Councils	40	115
Metropolitan Districts	50	150
Outer London Boroughs	59	213
Inner London Boroughs	97	
All England Average	47	137

The methodology used to calculate this SSA element has also been subject to criticism since it was introduced in 1994/95, as there is no evidence of any causal link between the incidence of a number of the factors used and the incidence of mental illness, mental or physical disability or the other problems which come within the ambit of the *Other* Social Services element.

3.3   Education

The Education SSA for 1996/97 totals £17.8 billion, broken down as follows:

o Primary   £7,302.9M

o Secondary   £7,531.9M

o Post 16   £1,067.0M

o Under 5s   £1,076.8M

o Other Education   £853.6M

*Report of the
National
Commission of
Inquiry into the
Prevention of
Child Abuse*

The SSA calculations assume that the costs of providing education will be higher in and around the capital, in sparsely populated areas and in areas with high proportions of:

o Children living in lone parent families.

o Children living in families which are in receipt of income support.

o Children who were born outside the UK, Ireland, the European Community and the USA, or whose head of household was born outside these areas.

The above three factors are combined into a single indicator called the Additional Education Needs (AEN) indicator. This is used as a proxy for an authority's need to provide the following services, most of which are relevant when one is considering child protection:

o Special education.

o Remedial teaching for pupils.

o Support services such as education welfare and school psychology services.

o Home to school transport.

o Financial assistance for pupils.

Local authorities in urban areas tend to have higher scores on the AEN indicator than other authorities. The combined effect of the AEN indicator and the adjustment for higher costs, which local authorities in and around the capital are said to face, produces materially higher SSAs for local authorities in London than in other parts of the country. For example, the provision for the cost of educating pupils in each local education authority's schools (pupil-led element) and the provision for the costs of special education, which includes psychology and welfare services, (the resident pupil-led element) vary as follows for 1996/97:

Table 3.4   *1996/97 Education SSA Allocations*

Type of Authority	Primary Education		Secondary Education	
	Pupil-led £/Head	Resient Pupil-Led £/Head	Pupil-Led £/Head	Resident Pupil-Led £/Head
County Councils	1,710	269	2,278	362
Metropolitan Districts	1,735	295	2,311	398
Outer London Boroughs	1,959	341	2,605	459
Inner London Boroughs	2,361	501	3,148	680
All England Average	1,766	292	2,346	392

At the extremes, the differences in the level of provision are substantial, for example:

o £567 per primary school pupil for special education in Tower Hamlets, compared with £231 per pupil in South Gloucestershire.

o £771 per secondary school pupil for special education in Tower Hamlets, compared with £312 per pupil in South Gloucestershire.

There is no specific reference to child abuse, or the costs associated with it, in any commentaries on the Education SSAs. However, if there is a link between child abuse and,

Report of the
National
Commission of
Inquiry into the
Prevention of
Child Abuse

say, the need for "teacher vigilance", education psychology and welfare services, then the SSAs appear to imply that:

○ Either the level of abuse is lower in rural areas than in urban ones; or

○ The costs of dealing with abuse are lower in rural areas than elsewhere.

We have noted a higher incidence in urban areas of the proportion of children registered on the CPR , but have no firm evidence to assess whether the real costs of Education Welfare are lower in non metropolitan areas.

3.4   Police Forces

Like Personal Social Services and Education Services, there is an element of funding within the Police SSA which depends upon factors of "deprivation". The proportion of lone parent families is such a measure which is employed in the Police SSA but its purpose is to provide a proxy, amongst other measures, of the pressure on Police Forces for resources to fight crime. It is, therefore, impossible for us to comment on whether or not the funding flows reflect the needs for Child Protection, simply because there are no elements within Police SSA which are designed to cover specific services to Children and Families.

There is, however, a significant role played by Police Forces in both investigating cases and protecting children. In England and Wales, the Association of Chief Police Officers estimated that cost consequences of implementing those parts of the Criminal Justice Act, 1991, for the video recording of child witness evidence was £2.47 millions. Furthermore, Police Forces' Child Protection Units and the Criminal Investigation Department will be organised on diverse bases across the country. Some units limit their involvement to incidents involving the family or persons "in loco parentis" (e.g. teachers, youth leaders). Others extend their work to include stranger abuse. Even so, there appears to be some considerable demand on Police Forces to investigate all aspects of alleged Child Abuse, which can often extend to dealing with victims and their families. The role is, therefore, not simply one of investigating and processing offenders. Given this significant (if varied) activity, it is worth noting that the Association of Chief Police Officers estimate that approximately 1,300 police officers are engaged on child protection work in England and Wales.

3.5   The NHS

There are two main health programmes, both of which are relevant in considering services for children and their families:

○ Hospital and Community Health Services (HCHS), which covers all hospital care and a wide range of community health services and is estimated to be around £21 billions in 1996/97.

○ Family Health Services (FHS), which covers expenditure on GP services (including health visitors) and the *drugs* budget.

*Report of the
National
Commission of
Inquiry into the
Prevention of
Child Abuse*

3.6   Hospital and Community Health Services

Target allocations for health authorities, to which they are being moved over time, are based on weighted resident population. Allocations are based on the resident population of each area, adjusted to reflect:

○   The age structure of the population - the Age/Cost Adjustment.

○   Local needs - the Needs Adjustment.

○   Differences in input costs - the Market Forces Factor.

Age/Cost Adjustment

It is accepted that the very young and the elderly make greater demands on health services than the rest of the population. The Age/Cost Adjustment seeks to take account of this by weighting different age groups as shown in Table 3.5 overleaf. This shows that children aged 5-14 have the lowest of all weights, which suggests that the cost per head of providing for children in this age group is less than for those in every other age group. Indeed, the next lowest cost per head is for that age group representing the parents of these children, and it is therefore clear that the age/cost adjustment re-distributes allocations away from areas of higher "children and family" concentration.

Table 3.5   *1996/97 Age/Cost Weightings*

Age/Bands	Weights NB These are 95/96 weights
Births	10.54
0 - 4	2.23
5 - 14	1.00
15 - 44	1.39
45 - 64	2.06
65 - 74	3.93
75 - 84	7.33
85 +	13.24

Needs Adjustment

A considerable amount of recent work has been done on factors which affect the need for inpatient services. As a result, two new indicators of need were adopted in 1995/96:

○   A general and acute index which is applied to approximately 64% of the HCHS budget.

○   A psychiatric index which is applied to approximately 12 % of the HCHS budget.

However, this leaves around 24% of the budget with no weighting for need. This 24% includes community mental health as well as the majority of general community health services.

The variables used in establishing the other two indices were the:

○   Proportion of pensionable age living alone.

Report of the
National
Commission of
Inquiry into the
Prevention of
Child Abuse

○ Proportion of dependents in single carer households.

○ Proportion of economically active who unemployed.

○ Standardised mortality ratio (SMR) under 75.

○ Standardised limiting long-standing illness ratio under 75.

○ Proportion of persons in lone parent households.

○ Proportion born in the New Commonwealth.

○ Proportion of dependents with no carer.

○ Proportion of adult population permanently sick.

A number of criticisms have been levelled at the new formula, mainly in relation to the lack of any weighting for 24% of the budget. The overall effect of this adjustment is to move resources into the inner cities at the expense of other parts of the country.

Market Forces Factor

This adjustment seeks to take account of the higher costs of providing services in London and the South. There have, however, been criticisms of the scale of the adjustment.

Health Authority (HA) Target Allocations

The end result of the above adjustments is to produce HA Target Allocations which vary significantly across the country, as can be seen from Table 3.6. The range is from £352 to £555 per head of population, with an all England average of £425.

Table 3.6   *1996/97 Initial Health Authority Target Allocations*

District Health Authorities	£/Head	District Health Authorities	£/Head
Camden & Islington	555	Cambridge & Huntingdon	352
Kensington/Chelsea/Westminster	541	North & Mid-Hampshire	367
East London & The City	538	South Staffordshire	370
Lambeth/Southwark/Lewisham	532	Buckinghamshire	370

As discussed above, the formula used to allocate HCHS resources makes no specific mention of the likely cost to health authorities of child protection. Indeed, as the Age/Cost adjustment demonstrates, services for children aged 5-14 are assumed to cost less per head than those for all other age groups. This may, however, be because children in this age group make proportionately greater demands on primary as opposed to secondary healthcare services.

We have insufficient evidence to comment on whether or not the children and families in the child protection process make significant demands on the health service, or demands which are much heavier than other families. Activity data would suggest that total demand is not significant e.g. only 0.42% of all children under 18 are referred for social services help, and only 0.31% are registered on Child Protection Registers (CPRs). However, the number of children on CPRs is not necessarily a good indication of the total demand on health services by the children, their families and offenders.

Although we cannot comment definitely on health need in this area, we can make some observations on the distribution of total resources to health authorities. What is clear from the above, is that HCHS allocations assume that the overall cost of providing equal opportunity of access to healthcare differs significantly from one part of the country to another. The position has many similarities with that described in relation to funding for local authorities. Thus, both local and health authorities in outside London will have less resources to call upon per child than authorities in other parts of the Country.

3.7   Family Health Services (FHS)

We stated above that children and their families in the child protection process may make greater demands on primary care than on secondary care. [ie they may make a greater number of visits to their GPs and may make heavier demands on the time of health visitors.] Again, we have no evidence to enable us to comment on this definitively.

As far as resources for such services are concerned, allocations to cover the majority of GP expenditure are made through the FHS health programme. In general, the system is intended to reimburse GPs for all expenditure incurred. It does not, therefore, give rise to the type of analysis described above for other health services and for local authority services.

If, however, it is considered that families experiencing or at risk of child abuse make significantly higher demands on GP services, it might be worthwhile considering whether or not a higher capitation fee should be paid for such people. Capitation fees are annual fees payable for each patient registered on a GP's list and represent a little over half the gross income a GP derives from fees and allowances. At present, different amounts are paid for the following categories of patient:

o   Under 65 years

o   65 to 74 years

o   75 years and over

o   Children being provided with child health surveillance

o   Patients for whom a deprivation payment is due [ie Patients residing in areas identified as deprived.]

o   Patients for whom a rural practice payment is due.

4.   Activity Data

The primary source of data on children at risk of abuse is the Child Protection Registers (CPRs) maintained by local authority Social Services Departments. These list all children in the area who are considered to be at risk of abuse and are, therefore, the subject of an inter-agency plan to protect them. Registration takes place as a result of a child protection conference.

The following Table shows some key statistics for the year to 31 March 1995.

*Report of the
National
Commission of
Inquiry into the
Prevention of
Child Abuse*

Report of the
National
Commission of
Inquiry into the
Prevention of
Child Abuse

Table 4.1 *CPR Statistics 1994/95*

	County Councils	Met. Dists.	London	All England	Wales	Scotland	Great Britain
Total Children Under 18 (000's)	6.943	2.665	1.544	11.152	0.672	1.159	12.983
Initial Case Conferences Total	28,029	12,254	7,093	47,376	2,400	2,995	52,771
Children on CPR: Number	18,762	10,190	6,002	34,954	1,668	2,666	39,288
Per 10,000 Pop. Under 18	27	38	38	32	25	23	30
Legal Status Looked after by LAs	3,841	2,739	1,220	7,800	380	745	8,925
Per 10,000 Pop. Under 18 *Of whom:*	5.5	10.3	7.9	7.0	5.7	6.4	6.9
Foster parents and other placements	3,490	2,372	987	6,849	338	648	7,835
Accom. in homes	351	367	233	951	42	97	1,090
% on CPR who are LA responsibility	20%	27%	21%	22%	23%	28%	23%

Sources

(i)   DoH Key Indicator Statistics

(ii)   CIPFA, PSS Statistics

The main points to note in relation to the data are:

o   They refer to what has been counted, rather than the latency of "Children at Risk".

o   Not all cases will represent equal caseload or resource requirements.

It can be seen from the above that the number of children on child preotection registers ranges from:

o   23 per 10,000 aged under 18 years in Scotland to 38 in the urban areas of London and Metropolitan Districts. Excepting London, these areas are also those where the local authorities take higher proportions into their direct care.

These figures contrast with those used in the local authority SSA calculations, which concentrate solely on the notional number of children upon which funding is calculated, rather than the cost arising from caring for them.

5. Expenditure by Local Authorities (including Health and Police)

*Report of the
National
Commission of
Inquiry into the
Prevention of
Child Abuse*

5.1 Overview

The approach we took to estimating expenditure is discussed below in relation to each key service. Due to the high level nature of the exercise, a large number of assumptions have had to be made. The estimates, therefore, need to be viewed in that light.

We have estimated total minimum costs incurred by the local public authorities in England to be in the region of £735M as shown in Table 5.1. We estimate that about 40% of this expenditure arises from preventive action or policies in the services administered by local public services [i.e. £290 millions]. The remainder (60%, or £445 millions) arises from the relevant services having to intervene as cases arise. We have erred on the side of caution and believe this to be a conservative estimate of the likely total cost. The methods we used to calculate these costs are set out at paragraph 5.2 and onwards.

The costs shown in Table 5.1 include:

Dealing with the consequences; investigating; and, preventing the circumstances in which it occurs. Given the general way in which we have estimated the costs, we have taken a reasonably wide perspective of the definition. The areas, under which the costs occur, are managed by different agencies and arise broadly as follows:

201

o Personal Social Services:
  * including other related local authority activities in Education and Housing;

o Health:
  * including GP and Hospital based services;

o Public Protection:
  * including the Home Office responsibilities for:
  * Police;
  * Courts;
  * Prison service;
  * Probation service.

o The Voluntary Child Care Sector.
  (The costs of which are assessed separately in section 6).

There are various data available describing the extent and scope of expenditure in most of these areas. However, there are very few indicators which allow us to attribute how the proportion of these costs are distributed. Consequently, we have made various assumptions, which are framed within broad bands of sensitivities to arrive at global estimates. In different services there are varying levels of specificity of information for different countries. Therefore, in many instances, the financial mapping has depended upon using observed values in one country and assuming that the same rate applies to another, where the data are lacking.

*Report of the
National
Commission of
Inquiry into the
Prevention of
Child Abuse*

202

Table 5.1   *Child Abuse - Costs to local public authorities*

Estimated Costs for United Kingdom	Estimated Cost £M			Proportion of total costs	Method of estimating this cost described at paragraph:
	Preventive Services	Intervention Services	Total		
Personal Social Services:					
Care for Children in homes/ foster placement	12	107	119	16%	5.2 (a)
Initial case conferences (All services)	8	25	33	5%	(b)
Reviewing cases (All services)	-	25	25	3%	(c)
Intermediate treatment	101	116	217	30%	(d)
Direct preventative action	116	-	116	16%	(e)
Management overheads (SSR)	4	5	9	1%	(f)
	241	278	519	71%	
Other Welfare Services:					
Homelessness	3	5	8	1%	5.3
Education	4	6	10	1%	5.4
	7	11	18	2%	
Health Services:					
General Practice	2	3	5	1%	5.5(g)
Paediatrics	3	5	8	1%	(h)
Child & Adolescent Psychiatry	13	20	33	4%	(i)
	18	28	46	6%	
Home Office Services:					
Probation	-	19	19	3%	5.6(k)
Magistrates & Crown Courts	-	22	22	3%	(m) & (n)
Police	24	49	73	10%	(l)
Prisons	-	38	38	5%	(j)
	24	128	152	21%	
Total Local Public Services					
	290	445	735	100%	

Note: The cost of attending case conferences for all services is shown under the Personal Social Services heading.

Report of the
National
Commission of
Inquiry into the
Prevention of
Child Abuse

To substantiate our assumptions we canvassed all Directors of Social Services, Chief Probation Officers, Chief Education Officers, and Chief Constables in England using the questionnaire attached at Appendix 1.

The costing assumptions are described below.

5.2   Personal Social Services

We (IPF) collate financial information, on a consistent basis, for all Social Services (Social Work in Scotland) Departments in Great Britain. The main heading under which relevant expenditure arises is "Children and Families". Within this heading, we have made estimates under some sub-heads using other data sources as follows:

(a) **Consequent costs of care for Children (and Families) when included on C.P.R.**

    (i)   Children's homes   As reported to CIPFA for G.B.

    (ii)   Foster and other placements   As reported to CIPFA for G.B.

We have estimated a proportion of such costs arising as a result of "child abuse" by dividing the number of children on the CPR, and categorised as being looked after by the local authority, by the total number of client children reported by the local authority.

The cost in Northern Ireland has been estimated using the G.B. costs per head of population aged under 18.

(b) **Cost of initial case conferences.**

In the Department of Health *publication "Child Protection: Messages from Research",* reference is made to the incidence of professionals attending child protection conferences, as described by Hallett and Birchall. We have applied estimated costs of these professionals incorporating associated overheads without which these staff would not be able to effectively operate. [For this reason, the daily costs vary considerably according to the type of professional output and our calculations are exemplified in Appendix 2.] This leads us to conclude that the average case conference costs about £620. Several of the respondents to our survey reported unit costs at this level or slightly lower (£500).

Based upon this average cost per case conference, we have derived an aggregate G.B. cost using the total number of initial case conferences reported to the Department of Health. Again, the cost in Northern Ireland, is assumed to mirror the same per capita rate for Great Britain.

(c) **Cost of reviewing cases**

The cost of placing a child on the CPR is assumed to be included in the estimates at (a). However, the cost of reviewing a case on the CPR is assumed to equate to the investment needed for an initial case conference although, in practice, fewer professionals will usually be involved. Therefore, we have multiplied the available data for Children on the CPR for Great Britain by the average case conference costs assessed at (b). The cost in Northern Ireland was estimated by using the same capitation rate described above.

203

Report of the
National
Commission of
Inquiry into the
Prevention of
Child Abuse

(d) **Intermediate and preventive support expenditure**

These costs are monitored directly by CIPFA and hence global estimates exist for the whole of Great Britain. The cost in Northern Ireland was estimated by using the same capitation rate described above.

(e) **Direct preventive action costs**

There are other activities focused on the specific prevention of "child abuse" which entail education programmes and also include policy research initiatives. We have assumed that 5% of the budget devoted to Children and Families is consumed by such programmes. We have no other objective base in arriving at this assessment, other than an awareness of the fact that such activity does take place.

(f) **Service Strategy and Regulation costs**

These are the costs arising from a central management which is needed to direct the statutory requirements of the Social Services/Work authority. The data for Great Britain are collected by CIPFA, and a proportion of these are set against Child Abuse (pro-rated according to the share that (a) to (e) above represent of total Social Services/Work expenditure).

5.3   Homelessness

Expenditure incurred by local authorities on the short term solutions to homelessness (hostels, bed & breakfast, refuge centres) is monitored by CIPFA. The proportion of this total cost arising as a result of "child abuse" has been assumed to equate to the "child abuse" share of total Personal Social Services Expenditure. [i.e. 6.4%]

5.4   Education

The focus of expenditure arising under this heading is on the education welfare function. (The cost of education psychologists, and other special education staff time has been included at (b) and (c)). CIPFA identify the global cost of the education welfare service, the staff of which will be dealing with problems arising from Child Abuse. The proportion of their time devoted to child abuse cases has been assumed to be 12.5% on the basis of averages reported by Education Officers in our survey.

5.5   Health

The Department of Health, in the section devoted to "Performance and Use of Resources" of their latest annual report show the real terms cost of each GP consultation at £12.77 and the inferred number of consultations per GP at 5.1 per person on the GP's list. [Table 21 FHS: Key Statistics on GMS]. Furthermore, an analysis by IPF of the Annual Accounts returned by NHS Trusts provides key cost figures per outpatient attendance for:

Paediatrics	£71.26
Child & Adolescent Psychiatry	£134.11

Using these benchmarks, the costs arising in the Health Service have been estimated as follows:

Report of the
National
Commission of
Inquiry into the
Prevention of
Child Abuse

(g) Cost of GP Consultations

The costs have been estimated as the product of 10 visits for every child on the CPR, (to include the child and other family members), and the average cost per consultation.

(h) Cost of Paediatric Consultations

The cost per attendance has been applied to an average of 3 visits per child on the CPR.

(i) Cost of Child and Adolescent Psychiatry

The cost per consultation has been applied to an average of 6 visits per child on the CPR. This higher level of consultation is intended to cover the cost of counselling requirements over a longer and sustained period.

5.6   Home Office Services

This area of activity, which broadly includes the various public protection functions, is mainly described in the financial data returned to CIPFA. The exceptions are the Prison and Crown Prosecution Services. CIPFA surveys cover Police, Magistrates Courts and the Probation Services. The assumptions employed in all of these services has focused on the proportion of "offenders" connected with "child abuse". The approach we have adopted has been to review the available statistics for the Prison service in Scotland, and England and Wales so as to estimate the proportion of convictions of a sexual/violent nature where children are the victims. The proportion of such overall prison sentences has been used to estimate what share of overall public protection services costs are attributable to child abuse. We are aware, that this is a broad brush approach given the fact that there could be a difference between the general distribution of crimes occurring, and the distribution of prisoners by convictions. The various costings were undertaken as follows:-

(j) Prison Services

The prison populations, and the costs per prisoner place are quoted in the Annual Reports published by HM Prison Services in England and the Scottish Office. The report for England and Wales differentiates the reasons for the "immediate custodial sentence". Furthermore, a Home Office Statistical Bulletin (issue 42/89), published 5th December, 1989, shows those "Criminal proceedings for offences involving violence against children". Using the data and findings set out in these sources, the costings shown in Appendix 2 are derived, providing a global estimate (4.1%) or the Prison Service's expenditure arising from offenders who have (or were) abused children.

(k) The Cost of the Probation Services

The expenditure, as measured in returns made to CIPFA have been apportioned to child abuse, in the same proportion as observed for the Prison Service, [4.1%]. The reasoning employed in this calculation reflects the assumption that the case mix will be similar.

(l) The Cost of the Police Services

The expenditure for Police Services are collected by CIPFA. Based upon the evidence submitted by the Association of Chief Police Officers, we have compared the number of staff dedicated to "children protection" units with the full establishment of Police Forces. This equates to a little more than 1%. We have, therefore, simply assumed that this same proportion of the budget relates to child abuse. It is known that the Police Service has a

205

*Report of the
National
Commission of
Inquiry into the
Prevention of
Child Abuse*

leading role in investigating cases of child abuse, and this method of estimating costs is unlikely to over state the consequent expenditure implications.

(m) The Cost of Magistrates Courts

Similar assumptions *[as employed at (m) and (n)]* have been used to estimate the cost of pursuing cases in such courts, (4.1%).

(n) The Cost arising from referrals to the Crown Court

The Home Office Bulletin, Issue 42/89 *[see paragraph (l) above],* provides information from which it can be inferred that for every 425 cases pursued in the Magistrates Court, a further 190 defendants will be committed for trial at the Crown Court. Such cases refer specifically to violence against children. On this basis it has been assumed that the Crown Prosecution Service Costs are 45% the value of the Magistrates Court Costs. In reality the costs will be considerably higher because the severity of the cases will undoubtedly involve more lengthy procedures for each case processed.

The above assumptions (a) to (n) describe the method of estimating the global cost of the local services for the prevention/treatment of child abuse. Underlying these costs is a latent additional expense arising from the various investigations and prosecutions which fail. Therefore, our estimates represent a sum which can be considered as a minimum quantifiable amount. We have also attempted to map these costs geographically by weighting the calculations on observations at local level. Such observations, when based on CIPFA statistics, refer to the financial inputs directly. In other instances the calculated costs are apportioned to the local area according to such data as the distribution of children on the CPR. These geographic disaggregations will, therefore, be very coarse approximations and further research would be necessary to verify their implied distributions.

Table 5.4 *Estimated Costs to local public authorities - £Millions (Rounded to nearest Million).*

	Personal Social Services	Other Welfare Services	Health Services	Home Office Services	Total
London	106	6	7	32	151
Metropolitan Areas	120	3	12	31	166
English Shires	204	7	21	64	296
England	430	16	40	127	613
Wales	17	1	2	6	26
Scotland	57	1	3	15	76
Northern Ireland	15	(<1)	1	4	20
United Kingdom	519	18	46	152	735

6. The Voluntary Child Care Sector

6.1 Overview

Although there are a large number of charitable organisations which provide services to children and their families in the U.K., the principal bodies are:

○ NSPCC.

○ NCH Action for Children

○ Barnardo's.

○ Save The Children.

○ The Children's Society

Evaluating the costs relating to child protection is complicated as:

○ Many of the charities receive funds from the public sector and care needs to be taken to avoid double counting.

○ The costs of responding to child abuse are not necessarily separately identified.

For this reason, the agents involved have not been able to be specific about the proportions of their spending which relates to either prevention or dealing with the consequences of child abuse. Therefore, we have made some assumptions ourselves, in many instances.

6.2 The NSPCC

The NSPCC is the only national organisation in this country devoted exclusively to the problem of child abuse. It is also the only agency from the voluntary sector authorised under the Children Act, 1989 for investigation of allegations of child abuse.

A review of the NSPCC accounts revealed the following income and expenditure for the year-ended 31 March, 1995:

Table 6.1 *NSPCC Income and Expenditure 1994/95*

	£M
Income:	
Donors	36.1
Local Authorities	4.3
Department of Health	0.2
Other	1.3
Total	42.0
Expenditure:	
Services to Children	32.1
Administration etc.	9.8
Balance	0.1
Total	42.0

The associated activity data for the year is given in Table 6.2.

Report of the
National
Commission of
Inquiry into the
Prevention of
Child Abuse

Table 6.2   *NSPCC Activity Data 1994/95*

	Nos.
Requests for Service	14,480
Other Calls of Concern	49,256
Child Protection Teams:	
Requests for Service	6,859
Open Cases at any one time	2,411
Analysis of Open Cases:	**%**
Investigation	6
Treatment	54
Consultation	5
Assessment	25
Prevention	10

On the basis of the above figures, we estimate that the additional costs, which should be added to the £735M total public cost of child protection are as follows:

	£M
Services to Children	32.1
Less Contributions from Public Authorities	4.3
	27.8

6.3   NCH Action For Children

NCH provides 250 innovative projects aimed at supporting children and families in the community:

o   Family and community centres.

o   Community projects for young offenders.

o   Services for children with disabilities.

o   Homeless projects.

o   Counselling.

o   Residential homes and schools.

o   Specialist treatment centres for children who have been sexually abused.

A review of NCH's accounts for the year-ended 31 March, 1995 showed the following income and expenditure:

Report of the
National
Commission of
Inquiry into the
Prevention of
Child Abuse

Table 6.3 *The NCH Action for Children Income And Expenditure 1994/95*

	£M
Income:	
Donations	14.6
Fees	12.6
Grants	19.8
Other	1.1
Total	48.1
Expenditure:	
Social Work	42.8
Administration etc.	9.0
Balance	(3.7)
Total	48.1

On the basis of the above figures, we estimate that the additional costs, which should be added to the £735M total public cost of child protection are as follows:

	£M
Services to Children	48.1
Less grants	19.8
	28.3

6.4 Save The Children

Save The Children works on an international basis, not only in the U.K..

Its income and expenditure for the year-ended 31 March, 1994 is given in Table 6.4.

The main problems in extrapolating from the data lie in the difficulty in identifying:

o The expenditure which relates to child protection in the U.K..

o Whether or not grants have been included in the costs taken into account in our analyses of public sector costs.

Table 6.4 *Save The Children Income and Expenditure 1994/95*

	£M
Income:	
Voluntary Income	41.35
Gifts In Kind	2.78
Grants	46.37
Investment Income	1.48
Total	91.98

On the basis of the above figures, we estimate that the additional costs, which should be added to the £735M total public cost of child protection are as follows:

*Report of the
National
Commission of
Inquiry into the
Prevention of
Child Abuse*

	£M
Services to Children	92.0
Less grants	46.4
	45.6

Say 10% = 4.6

However, the actual cost could vary between the total net sum availale (£45.6M) and nil.

6.5   Barnardo's

Barnardo's is the largest children's charity in the U.K. and is dedicated to improving the lives of the most disadvantaged young people and their families. It aims to provide social welfare services for the benefit of children and young people most in need of them. Services include:

○   Counselling for children who have been sexually abused.

○   Support for disabled children.

○   Family centres.

○   Temporary accommodation for homeless teenagers.

○   Foster and adoption schemes.

○   Residential schools for expelled teenagers.

○   Shared houses for teenagers leaving care.

In 1991 Barnardo's launched an Agenda for Action to develop new work in three priority areas - sexual abuse, homelessness, and HIV/AIDS. By March 1995 a total of 103 proposals had been approved, the majority of which are extensions to existing projects, rather than entirely new ventures. During 1994/5 expenditure amounted to £2.0 million.

It is difficult to estimate exactly the amount spent on child protection services because these are often part of a broader service and because the extent of contribution from public bodies to each project varies.

It is estimated, however, that 25% of the service, or parts of services, funded by Barnardo's voluntary funds are related to child protection. On that basis, the following calculation provides a sum to identify money spent by them on that process:

	£M
Services to Children	72.8
Less Contributions from public bodies	40.5
	32.3
25% of this amount relating to Child Protection	8.1

6.6   The Children's Society

The Children's Society is a voluntary society of the Church of England and the Church in Wales. It exists to work for children and young people, irrespective of race or religion. The main thrust of its work continues to be local communities through 54 family and neighbourhood centres in areas where there is severe hardship. Its Streetwork Projects include support services, residential and foster care refuge, drop-in services and outreach work.

Its income and expenditure for the year-ended 31 March, 1995 is given in Table 6.6.

The main problems in extrapolating from the data lie in the difficulty in identifying:

o   The expenditure which relates to child protection in the U.K.

o   Whether or not grants have been included in the costs taken into account in our analyses of public sector costs.

Table 6.6   *The Children's Society Income And Expenditure 1994/95*

	£M
Income:	
Donations	14.49
Fees, Grants, Local Authorities, Central Government	6.56
Miscellaneous	0.56
Investment Income	1.63
Total	**23.24**
Expenditure:	
Child Care	16.75
Education, Information, Publications	1.21
Administration etc.	4.37
Total	**22.33**

211

The Society's work is carried out in six programmes.

1. A Good Start.	Work aimed at the under eights.
2. Protection.	Work to protect children in the widest sense including safety.
3. Just and Fair Treatment.	This programme is concerned with children and young people in the child care systems and youth justice systems.
4. Sufficient Income.	Work concerned with issue of poverty and its implications.
5. Somewhere to Live.	Work concerned with homelessness and independent living.
6. Listening to Children.	Work concerned with rights and advocacy.

Taken together the costs of the Child Protection element of these programmes amount to £4 Millions.

*Report of the
National
Commission of
Inquiry into the
Prevention of
Child Abuse*

6.7   Voluntary Child Care Sector Summary

The overall estimated expenditure incurred by the major voluntary child care organisations is, therefore, likely to approximate as follows:

	£M
NSPCC	27.8
NCH Action for Children	28.3
Save the Children	4.6
Barnado's	8.1
Children's Society	4.0
	£72.8
	[Say £75M]

It will be noted that there are many other voluntary organisations working in this area (e.g. Childline, Homestart, Newpin, FSU, FWA). Therefore, there is considerable additional expenditure devoted to the prevention of child abuse and after care services which are provided by these other organisations.

7.   Overall Findings and Conclusions

7.1   During the course of undertaking this review we have observed that there is a paucity of firm data both describing the extent of child abuse cases and the costs to all those organisations called upon to investigate, treat the consequences, and prevent such cases. Therefore, our review is general in scope and approximate in its findings.

7.2   The overall expenditure incurred by the public services is likely to exceed £735 Millions at current cost. This is equivalent to £12.60 per head of population in the United Kingdom, which is more than is spent on Refuse Collection or the Public Library Service, for instance.

7.3   Despite this cost we have not been able to trace any funding mechanism which specifically directs resources towards the prevention of child abuse. There are some indicators, most notably employed in Personal Social Services and Education Services, which indirectly aim resources towards "children requiring help". However, the pattern of resources distribution does not appear to reflect the cost of care for children and families.

○   In *Social Services* we note that the proportion of persons aged under 18 years included on the Child Protection Registers is highest in London and the Metropolitan Districts. However, there appears to be no evidence to suggest that the cost of care is much greater in these areas, although Standard Spending Assessments direct higher levels of resources towards London. Indeed, in London there appears to be a much lower proportion of the children registered on the CPR actually placed within local authority residential or foster care.

○   In *Education Services* we have noted a higher incidence in urban areas of the proportion of children registered on the CPR. There is no firm evidence to assess whether or not the real costs of Education Welfare are lower in non-metropolitan areas. However, the "Additional Education Needs" (AEN) indicator is the main proxy for calculating resources needs for such support services as Education Welfare, and this directs more resources towards London.

○ In the *Police Services* there are no specific indicators employed in the SSA to resource the activities of Forces in investigating cases of child abuse, and protecting children at risk.

○ The make-up of the resourcing formulae for the *Health Services* puts a lower proportion of emphasis on the 5 - 14 years age group within the "Age/Cost Adjustment" to the Hospital and Community Health Services allocations. The separate Family Health Services allocations to General Practitioners make no differentiation for the relative weightings on consultation times which arise from Child Abuse cases.

Report of the
National
Commission of
Inquiry into the
Prevention of
Child Abuse

7.4   According to figures collated by the Department of Health (Key Statistics), there are more than 50,000 initial case conferences each year leading to approximately 40,000 children being placed on the Child Protection Registers at any one time. However, no systems of information for the collation of data on the resources devoted towards the prevention of child abuse exist. It is doubtful whether the main agents of prevention and investigation of child abuse know the respective levels of funding each make at either the national or local level. Consequently, despite the considerable cost each devotes to such co-ordinated approaches as case conferences, none of the parties know the full extent of expenditure brought to bear, nor the value of the "pay-off" for their efforts. There appears to be an urgent need to address this lack of information both at National Department level, and at Local Authority level. The formulation of a "programme area" approach at National level would be an effective way of ensuring that the appropriate information is collated.

213

7.5   A further difficulty encountered by various agencies is the different approaches each takes for accounting for the provision of services. Therefore, a constraint arises on their potential co-operation in adopting policies which might share the costs, or even reduce them, simply because the appropriate financial implications cannot be assessed on a common basis. For this reason, the importance of properly defining a programme area approach at the National level becomes more urgent.

7.6   The cost to the Voluntary Sector of responding to the abuse of children is likely to be about £75 Millions which we have estimated to fall on the major organisations. There will also be further costs borne by a large number of other voluntary organisations working in this area (e.g. Childline, Homestart, Newpin, FSU,FWA). However, based upon our consistently conservative estimates of public sector costs, this Voluntary Sector expenditure represents nearly 10% of the total programme area input. For this reason we would suggest that consideration is given to involving these organisations within the framework of data exchange, (recommended at 7.4).

7.7   The difficulty we have encountered in making a high level estimate of the resources being applied to the investigation, prevention and consequences of child abuse suggests that there is a need for a more thorough investigation. A co-ordinated programme of action to properly focus resources on the prevention of child abuse in its widest sense, could lead to substantial improvements in the value all agents derive from their efforts.

*Report of the
National
Commission of
Inquiry into the
Prevention of
Child Abuse*

Appendix 1 (to Appendix 7)
Survey Questionnaire used in the canvass of authorities to frame our cost assumptions

IPF LIMITED

Consultancy and Research
Placements
Property Management
Training and Training Products
Systems and Software

**Institute of Public
Finance Limited**

Suffolk House
College Road
Croydon CR0 1PF
Telephone 0181 667 1144
Facsimile 0181 681 8058

21st February 1996

Dear

The National Commission of Inquiry into the Prevention of Child Abuse has asked us to investigate the costs associated with the programmes being implemented by all authorities / agencies who are active or responsible for dealing with "Child Abuse".

We acknowledge that the cost of such programmes can only be estimated in very approximate terms, and we intend to apply various assumptions to national statistics. However, I am writing to seek your assistance in providing some information to assist us in framing these assumptions.

The Commission's reporting deadline (end March), means that I am forced to ask for this help urgently. Therefore, I hope that you would be prepared to provide your considered estimates rather than spuriously precise answers to the questions set out overleaf, by **14th March, 1996**.

We are anxious to take into account both the cost consequences of cases that are identified, and the resources which are applied to activities specifically undertaken to prevent Child Abuse. Therefore, I would be grateful for any further anecdotal information that you could attach to the completed questionnaire.

I am aware of the highly subjective nature of this canvass, but hope that you will hazard your judgement so as to better inform our otherwise detached assumptions.

I shall, of course, be available to answer any enquiries should you wish to telephone me.

Thank you for your forbearance.

Yours sincerely,

Phillip Ramsdale
Managing Director

This letter is being circulated to Chief Constables, Directors of Social Services, Chief Probation Officers and Chief Education Officers.

IPF: Incorporated in England and Wales under registration number 2376684
IPF: Employment business registered with the Department of Employment under number SE17801
IPF: VAT registration number 429 7738 06
IPF: Registered address – 3 Robert Street, London WC2N 6BH
n:\letters\phillip\poch *IPF Ltd is a wholly owned company of the Chartered Institute of Public Finance and Accountancy*

Report of the
National
Commission of
Inquiry into the
Prevention of
Child Abuse

National Commission of Inquiry into the Prevention of Child Abuse

For IPF use only:

Name of Authority & Department / Service   :

Name of person completing this form   :

Tel. No. and ext. (including STD code)   :

If possible, please include the resources of your entire authority / organisation when providing your best estimates in response to the following questions.

1 Does the information provided below refer to the whole authority or just your department ?

WHOLE AUTHORITY / SINGLE DEPARTMENT
Delete as appropriate

2 Staff devoted to preventing, investigating or treating consequences of Child Abuse:-

	Full Time Equivalent No. of Staff:	Proportion of their time:
Professional Staff* No:		%
Admin/Support Staff No:		%

* Include: *Social Workers / Doctors / Teachers / Education Welfare Officers / Ed. Psychologists / Policemen / Health Visitors / Family Care Staff / Domiciliary Staff / Probation Officers / Solicitors.*

3 Has your authority / organisation purchased insurance cover to underwrite the cost consequences of Child Abuse claims?

YES / NO   If yes, at what premium? £
Delete as appropriate

4 What do you estimate to be the cost to your authority / organisation of a single typical case of Child Abuse when you:

(a) Conduct an investigation   £

(b) Place the child on the Child Protection Register   £

(c) Provide post registration counselling & support to child / family   £

[Include the cost of staff time in preparing for and undertaking case conferences, investigations, liaison with other organisations and the cost of providing care].

5 Please estimate the cost of "family support" services, aimed at families at risk of abusing their children which:

(a) your authority provides   £

(b) your authority finances others to provide   £

6 What other costs related to Child Abuse arise?   £
[e.g. Publicity campaigns and literature]

Please return this form by Friday 14th March to:

Martin Jennings, IPF, Suffolk House, College Road, Croydon. CR0 1PF.

Tel : 0181 667 1144   Fax : 0181 681 6741

215

Report of the
National
Commission of
Inquiry into the
Prevention of
Child Abuse

Appendix 2 (to Appendix 7)
Estimated and Actual base data used to model the cost calculations

216

APPENDIX 2

POPULATION (a) / CHILD PROTECTION REGISTER (b)

	Total Population Mid 1995	Population Aged Under 18 Mid 1995	All Children Initial Stage Conference 1995	All Children Initial Stage Conference as a % of Population Under 18	Children on Child Protection Register	Children on CPR as a % of Population Under 18	Numbers at 31 March 1995 looked after by LA		
							Total	Children's Home	Foster or Other Placement
LONDON	6,944,483	1,543,547	7,093	0.4595	6,002	0.3888	1,220	233	987
METROPOLITAN AREAS	11,208,737	2,665,324	12,254	0.4598	10,190	0.3823	2,739	367	2,372
ENGLISH SHIRE AREAS	30,650,805	6,942,651	27,129	0.3908	18,762	0.2702	3,841	351	3,490
ENGLAND	48,804,025	11,151,522	46,476	0.4168	34,954	0.3134	7,800	951	6,849
WALES	2,916,600	672,201	2,400	0.3570	1,668	0.2481	380	42	338
SCOTLAND	5,126,255	1,159,434	2,995	0.2583	2,666	0.2299	745	97	648
GREAT BRITAIN	56,846,880	12,983,157	51,871	0.3995	39,288	0.3026	8,925	1,090	7,835
UNITED KINGDOM	58,488,580	13,358,102	53,371	0.3995	40,423	0.3026	9,183	1,121	8,061

SOME DATA HAVE BEEN ESTIMATED AND THE UNITED KINGDOM TOTAL HAS BEEN CALCULATED BY INTERPOLATION

SOURCES:
(a) OPCS
(b) Dept of Health
(c) CIPFA

PROBATION 1995/96 (c) / MAGISTRATES' COURTS (c) / POLICE (c) / HOMELESS (c) / EDUCATION (c)

	Total Expenditure £'000	Family Assistance and Care and Supervision Orders Per 1,000,000 Population Aged Under 18 — Number	1995/96 Total Expenditure £'000	1995/96 Total Expenditure £'000	1995/96 Total Expenditure £'000	1995/96 Education Welfare Officers £'000
LONDON	78,836	38	55,697	1,678,009	73,297	11,348
METROPOLITAN AREAS	112,954	235	81,456	1,386,742	10,144	21,400
ENGLISH SHIRE AREAS	221,144	603	172,829	2,962,830	42,526	31,639
ENGLAND	412,934	876	309,982	6,027,581	125,967	64,387
WALES	21,751	30	21,615	308,905	3,534	2,587
SCOTLAND	36,079	89	32,865	592,651	4,927	6,638
GREAT BRITAIN	470,764	995	364,462	6,929,137	134,428	73,612
UNITED KINGDOM	484,359	1,024	374,987	7,129,246	138,310	75,738

PERSONAL SOCIAL SERVICES 1995/96 (c)

	Total Net Expenditure £'000	Children Net Expenditure £'000	Gross Expenditure Residential Care £'000	Gross Expenditure Foster Placements £'000	Gross Expenditure Intermediate Treatment, Preventative & Support Services £'000	Net Expenditure SSR £'000	Children in Residential Care	Children in Foster Placements	Children on CPR looked after by LA as a % of all Children in Care — Children's Home %	Foster or Other Placement %
LONDON	1,440,224	484,192	121,653	73,015	49,314	36,528	2,739	6,806	8.5	14.5
METROPOLITAN AREAS	1,633,566	488,216	150,742	73,209	46,217	22,984	3,652	10,049	10.0	23.6
ENGLISH SHIRE AREAS	3,426,644	938,588	267,760	150,019	77,443	47,874	5,437	20,455	6.5	17.1
ENGLAND	6,500,434	1,910,996	540,155	296,243	172,974	107,386	11,828	37,310	8.0	18.4
WALES	414,894	80,043	16,394	14,936	6,636	3,711	422	2,285	10.0	14.8
SCOTLAND	958,734	253,330	89,600	26,476	28,621	18,318	1,861	3,181	5.2	20.4
GREAT BRITAIN	7,874,062	2,244,369	646,149	337,655	208,231	129,415	14,111	42,776	7.7	18.3
UNITED KINGDOM	8,101,460	2,309,185	664,809	347,406	214,245	133,152	14,519	44,011	7.7	18.3

Report of the
National
Commission of
Inquiry into the
Prevention of
Child Abuse

Appendix 2 - Continued - Prison Service Costs

1 H.O. Stats Bulletin 5.12.89 para 4 shows that 7% of violent offences were against children.

2 The same Bulletin showed that the distribution of offences against children led to convictions for :

Violent offences	195	=	51%
Rape	9	=	2%
Other Sexual offences	179	=	47%
			100%

3 On this basis, the distribution of expected convictions can be applied to the known prison populations under sentence at 30 June 1993, as follows:

Males under sentence for:

Violent offences	7273 x 7% (Note 1)
and, Rape	509/51% x 2% (Note 2)
and, Other Sexual Offences	509/51% x 47% (Note 2)

4 The actual distribution compared with the expected distribution of prison populations provides a basis for further estimating the proportions under sentence for Child Abuse related convictions:

Males under sentence for:	Total	Child Abuse (see Note 3)		
Violent offences	7,273	509	=	7%
Rape	1,593	20	=	1%
Other Sexual offences	1,572	469	=	30%

These data derive from the Prison Services Annual Reports

5 It is thus possible to carry forward the proportions calculated, at note 4, to provide an approximation of the prison population under sentence for Child Abuse related offences:

	England and Wales 1993	Scotland 1994
Total population under sentence:	33,136	5,630
Offence:		
Violent Offences (Note 4 × 7%)	7,489= 524	1,273= 89
Rape (Note 4 x 1%)	1,594= 16	271= 3
Other Sexual Offences (Note 4 x 30%)	1,586= 476	270= 81
Total Child Abuse related	1,016	173
Unit cost per prison place p.a.	£22,712	£26,479
Total cost (£M) for Child Abuse related offences where Prison services are housing offenders:	£23.075 M	£4.581 M
Total cost in G.B.	£27.656 M	

6 Furthermore, it will be seen that the proportion of prison service costs (and prison population) relating to Child Abuse is:

1,189 ÷ 38,766 = 3.1%

We have assumed that it would be reasonable to add a further 1% to this proportion to cover the hidden costs where offenders may have been the victims of abuse during their youth. ➔ 4.1%

217

Report of the
National
Commission of
Inquiry into the
Prevention of
Child Abuse

Appendix 2 - Continued - Cost of Case Conferences

	Weighted % of Cases	Standard Cost =£168	Survey Product	Source
Paediatric junior doctor	5.0	£8	£11	TFRs @ 31/03/95
GP	7.5	£13	£33	FHS Key Statistics 93/94
Class teacher	10.0	£17	£23	CIPFA Education Ests 95/96 Col 203 / Cols 12+13+14
Consultant paediatrician	12.5	£21	£82	1.5*GP
Area manager	12.5	£21	£21	IPF Staffing Survey Jan 95
Child protection co-ordinator	15.0	£25	£14	IPF Staffing Survey Jan 95
NSPCC	15.0	£25	£25	As per Area Manager
Solicitor/ court	17.5	£29	£31	IPF Staffing Survey Jan 95
Education welfare	20.0	£34	£9	CIPFA Education Ests 95/96 Cols 352 / Col 206
Nurse manager	25.0	£42	£42	IPF Staffing Survey Jan 95
Headteacher / deputy	25.0	£42	£87	1.5*Class teacher
Minute taker	25.0	£42	£14	IPF Staffing Survey
Principal / team leader	30.0	£50	£50	IPF Staffing Survey
Health visitor / school nurse	37.5	£63	£17	As per E.W.O.
Police	45.0	£76	£100	CIPFA Police Ests 95/96 col 367
Social worker	67.5	£112	£61	IPF Staffing Survey Jan 95
		£620	£620	

TOTAL COST PER CASE CONFERENCE: £620

Number of Initial Case Conferences:

			Millions
England	47,376	=	£32.240
Wales	2,400	=	£0.862
Scotland	2,995	=	£33.102
	52,771		

+ Northern Ireland

U.K.

Appendix 8

Financing the Prevention of Child Abuse: The ICL Decision-Conferencing Workshop

*Report of the
National
Commission of
Inquiry into the
Prevention of
Child Abuse*

As part of its analysis of expenditure on responses to child abuse, the National Commission asked ICL (International Computers Limited) to organise a workshop on the allocation of resources on services for children. This paper describes the techniques used at the workshop and some of the broad conclusions that were reached. The National Commission is grateful to ICL for running the workshop and for donating the use of its methodology.

1 Decision Conferencing Process

1.1   Decision conferencing is a process used during a workshop for group decision making. The purpose of decision conferencing is to help decision makers to explore and come to understand and share their preferences, beliefs and professional judgements in the context of particular choices and problems facing them. Decision makers are helped by a facilitator and an analyst.

1.2   For budgeting, in particular, a modelling tool is used to represent the effects of different resource allocations. This enables the group to explore the implications of their judgements and preferences and reach conclusions and decisions about how resources could be best allocated between various investment areas.

1.3   The facilitator's role is to lead the decision makers in an impartial way, to question, challenge and occasionally, referee.

1.4   The analyst assists decision makers by building and interpreting computer models to help them appreciate various facets of the problem faced, and also provides the facilitator with support.

1.5 Through the facilitator and analyst team, the decision conferencing process brings together knowledge, skills and techniques arising from research in:

○   **decision theory**: providing a structure and language in which decision makers can think and talk about their problem.

○   **information technology**: providing the means whereby decision analyses can be undertaken with the decision makers at the time, and whereby the results of such analyses can be presented to them in a simple form.

○   **group processes**: to ensure that the group of decision makers interact constructively.

1.6   The decision workshop itself is a structured meeting, usually taking place over two days, at which all of the "owners" of a problem, (the participants), gather together to agree upon a solution.

Report of the
National
Commission of
Inquiry into the
Prevention of
Child Abuse

1.7   The main stages involved in a resource allocation workshop are as follows:

(a)   **Preparation** - before the workshop the group prepares by considering what strategies or options would be adopted in each investment area involved if more or less resources were available. Other relevant background information is also prepared.

(b)   **Introduction, Key Issues and Assumptions** - a short introduction by the facilitator is followed by group discussion of key background issues and sets the context within which the decisions are to be made.

(c)   **Review Options** - the group discusses and reaches a shared understanding of the strategies within each of the investment areas.

(d)   **Agree Criteria** - the group determines what benefit criteria are to be used to measure gain or loss of benefit if an option is implemented.

(e)   **Preference Scales** - the group considers the options against the agreed criteria and measures the relative gains or losses against each of the criteria. This is expressed as a preference scale.

(f)   **Weighting** - the group reviews the size or importance of the benefits shifts from the least beneficial option to the most beneficial one in each investment area and allocates a weighting factor to each area.

(g)   **Presentation of the Model** - when the model is complete it can be reviewed. The group is given a "guided tour" of the model, which is projected from the computer onto a screen. This is normally available in the afternoon half of the second day of a two day workshop.

(h)   **Revision and Sensitivity Checks** - sometimes the group will have been unable to agree on a preference score or weighting. The model is revised to accommodate the differing views and the group decides whether revision is necessary before proceeding.

(i)   **Analysis** - the group then explores the model in a number of different ways. Generally, the first is to look at the current status quo spend or commitment of resources, and see whether a different allocation of resources would result in more benefits. The group then builds on this to explore how it could accommodate a cut or increase in the total resources whilst still maintaining the maximum benefit available at that level of resources. The key outcome of such a process is a "value for money curve". Essentially, this can show that with the same total amount of resources under consideration, the group could achieve a mixture of more benefits. Alternatively, an equivalent level of benefits or value can be shown to be obtained with less resources.

(j)   **Conclusions** - the group finally agrees on one or more possible sets of budget or resource allocation patterns.

(k)   After the workshop a report is produced and circulated to all participants.

1.8   Experience shows that the success, or otherwise, of such workshops is directly related to the amount of preparation and time commitment that can be afforded by the participants in advance of the workshop. Discussions during the workshop can be extremely challenging and there are very tight time pressures.

1.9   Again, in general terms, if the preparation is good, participants should leave the workshop with a clear impression that they have all learnt something new about other services and problems, that they have gone through a structured approach leaving little to chance, and have left "no stone unturned".

2   Experiences in Staffordshire

2.1   In response to a request from the National Commission, an ICL decision conferencing revenue budget workshop was held in Staffordshire on the 28 and 29 February 1996. The objectives set for the event were as follows:

o   to identify the key issues impacting upon the prevention of child abuse in Staffordshire.

o   to reach a shared understanding of the options available within and between the relevant social services, education and health services for children.

o   to evaluate these options against agreed criteria.

o   to generate a set of alternatives leading to a pattern of investment with a more preventive emphasis.

o   to agree methods of implementation and recommendations for a workshop report.

2.2   In addition to a facilitator and analyst from ICL, the participants were drawn from the National Commission itself, and representatives of the two health authorities, education and social services departments of the county council, and a professor of social work studies at a local university.

221

2.3   By way of preparation, all participants were asked to think through ideas on the following key issues:

o   how to determine the preferred way to achieve a reduction in services to children:

(i)   in their own organisation.
(ii)   in related organisations.

o   how to determine the absolute minimum level of any service to children provided by their organisation.

o   how to decide where to invest an increase in resources.

o   what criteria to use to measure gain or loss of benefit from reductions and increases in resources applied to services, given that the prevention of child abuse, in its widest sense, is a major objective.

2.4   In advance of the Workshop, each participant was asked to prepare nine proposals to achieve 20% savings and nine proposals to achieve 20% growth in resource allocation. Reduction proposals would be from their own organisation but the growth proposals could be in any children and family services. As far as the health service was concerned, "organisation" was interpreted to mean any relevant part of the health service within the health authority area rather than a particular trust or commission.

2.5   At the outset, in considering background issues, assumptions and obstacles to progress with regard to the prevention of child abuse, matters raised included:

o   demographic, eg parenting styles, environment, unemployment, increasing poverty (very low disposal incomes in Staffordshire), high pupil-teacher ratios.

Report of the
National
Commission of
Inquiry into the
Prevention of
Child Abuse

○ lack of available research in relation to outcomes from various inputs.

○ outcomes tend to be driven more by specific targets and statistics, eg carrying out visits is more important than what they actually achieve; only two *Health of the Nation* children's issues (smoking and sexual health).

○ lack of resources in all agencies, getting worse, with increasing focus on reaction (fire-fighting) rather than prevention.

○ difficulties in **measuring** prevention.

○ limited, small pockets of good practice of inter-agency working exist. But different agencies are working with different models and understanding of what is "need", who makes the decisions, who holds the money.

○ no equivalent drive/support nationally seems to be on hand for children to be supported at home, compared to adults (care in the community).

○ impact of Department of Social Security and other external changes not thought through. This leads to "cost-shunting" concerns. Other examples of this or simple recycling of existing resources include: the local authority standard spending assessment (SSA) mechanism (eg although Education had a 5% increase for 1996/97, this was committed on pay awards and pupil increases, but Social Services only a 1% increase - still leads to budget cuts); concern over nursery vouchers; similar problems for Health.

2.6   Lengthy debate and discussion took place in order to agree five criteria, and possible ways of measuring these, against which agencies' resource growth and reduction options could be measured and compared. Those agreed were:

i)   maximise *support* to children and families at an early stage in an acceptable way, for example, levels of immunisation, adequate vocabulary.

ii) optimise *early identification* of children in need, for example, levels of awareness, children attending/arriving at school, health checks.

iii) optimise adequate *protection* of children at high risk, for example, levels of injury, death).

iv) effects on *other* services in *Staffordshire*, for example, an increase/decrease in expenditure for other services - police, probation, prisons, voluntary sector, as well as services represented at workshop.

v)   ability to *implement* the option, for example, in the light of statutory requirements, practical and professional concerns.

There was particular difficulty in agreeing the fourth criterion, with wide-ranging debate about how to grapple with the potential resource "knock-on" effects changes might have on other agencies and organisations. There was also uncertainty about what might constitute a realistic timescale for changes, growth or reduction, and projects to be implemented – for example, there may be a need to provide "bridging finance" and capital set-up costs.

2.7   During the course of the workshop, some interesting themes were observed. These give an insight into the difficulties currently faced in trying to take the prevention of child abuse forward in a multi-agency context

○ it is not easy to grasp what other services do and or understand their terminology - if senior managers have difficulty understanding this, it may be even more difficult for those working at the "sharp-end." This suggests a need to invest more time and effort in explaining the purpose and aims of services and projects.

o   this goes some way to explain why such questions were raised as "... who is best placed to provide that service", "... what precisely is that service", and "... idea sounds good, but would those sort of children be there in the first place".

o   interesting perspectives on the "achievability" of changes, for example, the importance of the political dimension and public concerns. Even with growth options, potential problems were identified: the purchaser/provider split in the health service and the extent to which a growth option would have a knock-on effect on another service; apparent "automatic" assumption that more volunteers, foster carers, etc may be readily available for expanded or developing provision.

o   concerns about the current primacy of service and professional-led models of provision and the lack of reliable cause/effect research data.

o   it is easier for social services and, to a lesser extent education, to identify what is spent on children and families. There are problems for the health services, with added difficulties due to the purchaser/provider split and the identification of who holds the money and makes the key decisions.

o   the process was felt to be very successful by all participants, in terms of leading to a better grasp of respective priorities, concerns and what could be achieved by a more radical agenda. If all agencies were able to focus on a specific programme area, (prevention of child abuse), then better value for money could be achieved.

2.8   In part, these observations illustrate widely-acknowledged difficulties experienced elsewhere in relation to joint planning, working, and commissioning:

(a)   **Structures**

Change and re-organisation is a constant problem. Authorities have different area boundaries and populations. London and metropolitan areas have unitary authorities. Changes are underway in the shire counties. Police authorities are separate. The purchaser/provider splits in health and social services create tensions and competition. Devolution of activity has occurred in key areas, for example schools, NHS trusts. Voluntary organisations are expected to be more business-like. In addition there are some developments which are pulling in the opposite direction, for example, health purchasing (District Health Authority/Family Health Service Authority) merging and getting bigger, GPs getting stronger, and social services and education getting smaller.

(b)   **Behaviour and Cultures**

There are different concepts of accountability, probity, and democracy between agencies. Bureaucracy and paperwork varies - perceived as well as actual. Committee and board structures differ. The extent of Government influence varies. The importance of individual leadership varies between agencies.

(c)   **Professional Conflict and Trust**

Corporate, as opposed to departmental tensions, exist in statutory agencies. Financial and needs pressures challenge professional specialisms, for example, leading to lower

223

*Report of the
National
Commission of
Inquiry into the
Prevention of
Child Abuse*

levels of skills/experience but more of a "mix" within a team. Management rivalries can be pervasive. There can be a failure or unwillingness to understand respective problems and priorities.

(d) Budget and Planning Cycles, and Timescales

Political timescales and priorities exert an influence. Purchaser/provider perspectives of priorities and emphases vary. Complicated sets of planning and purchasing documents and processes, some general, some targeted at specific clients, have different focus. Financial planning and resource allocation systems vary also. Revenue and capital arrangements are different: onset of "bidding cultures", some multi-agency (including private sector), some specific, but an increasing emphasis on central government directives and ring-fencing; some are specific as opposed to unhypothecated funding; financial planning horizons differ and budget cycles do not match. Everyone has financial constraints but vary in extent and timescale, for example, "payback" requirements and value for money objectives may be different. There are concerns that joint working may be more costly. There is an unwillingness to let others commit your money.

(e) Powers and Duties

Mandatory requirements, areas of discretion and the concept of "ultra vires" in the public sector exert an influence. There are limitations of legal and financial constraints to spend money – for example, Section 28a agreements, grant-giving powers, and associated requirements. There are pressures to establish contracts with detailed specifications (costs, as well as benefits). The mixed economy of care and provision can lead to frustrations about having to follow processes, for example, joint consultative committee meetings. Political and financial objectives are not always congruent.

3. Next Steps

3.1   The exercise demonstrated that resources for prevention could be found by recycling money from other services, not from child protection, and not necessarily from extra taxes.

3.2   The three agencies are all spending resources on the same client group - for example, the children causing problems in schools or not attending school are also social services clients and are, or were, those who did not get health checks, or call on their general practitioners regularly.

3.3   What needs to be done now? A key problem is that much is in central government's domain or may require political consideration. On a more practical level, certain matters could be progressed without the need for such intervention: more efficient local machinery and bureaucracy; "education" about respective roles and services; commitment to transparent and ring-fenced resources led from the top; investment in cause/effect research; finding ways to foster more team-work at the "sharp end" through, for example, bids for multi-agency projects; highlighting pockets of good practice now and building on them; agreeing both short and longer-term action plans; greater clarity over what is currently spent on children and families by all agencies.

The Cost of Child Abuse: Some Case Histories

*Report of the
National
Commission of
Inquiry into the
Prevention of
Child Abuse*

1 Introduction

The National Commission of Inquiry into the Prevention of Child Abuse wished to investigate the costs of child abuse, as part of their broader work. To this end we were commissioned to:

o develop a small number of case studies which attempted to cost both the direct and indirect financial implications of abuse.

Direct costs were taken to include such items as:

o child protection investigations

o case conferences

o fostering

o individual treatment

Indirect costs were taken to include such as items as:

o truancy

o delinquency

o imprisonment

o mental health services responding to depression

o costs of medication

o GP consultations

o time out of employment

o marriage guidance counselling

This exercise was to complement work being carried out by IPF (CIPFA) who were developing an estimate of the total cost of child abuse by analysing national data.

2 Sources of the Cases

The cases presented in this report have been drawn from two main sources. When the Commission was first established, invitations were placed in a number of newspapers and magazines asking readers to tell their own stories about child abuse. In total over 1,000 responses were received. These are the subject of a separate report by the University of Lancaster[1]. A proportion of these responses were followed up by detailed telephone interviews. It is the transcripts of these interviews which have formed the basis of the case studies presented here. In addition, Parents Against Injustice (PAIN) have supplied some cases. In order to protect the confidentiality of respondents, the cases have been anonymised.

Report of the
National
Commission of
Inquiry into the
Prevention of
Child Abuse

3   Methodological Issues

When respondents were asked to write to the Commission they were simply asked to tell their story not to identify in detail the agencies who were involved or the time taken by their case. Mostly the respondents focused on the circumstances of the abuse rather than the detail of its aftermath.

The cases selected have been chosen because they gave a level of detail about the consequences of their abuse and because they offered a range of stories. They do not therefore comprise a random sample.

To some extent, the case histories reflect the way cases were managed in the past. The case of DH is a good example. She is a woman who was abused in the late 1940s and early 1950s. However, she did not come into contact with the child abuse system until she suffered a nervous breakdown and hospitalisation in the 1990s. We would hope that a child suffering similar abuse today would receive support at an earlier stage. Nevertheless, DH is a real case and there will be other similar cases in the 'pipeline' where the social costs are incurred many years after the actual abuse.

However, the cases presented here have been deliberately drawn from incidents in the 1990s in order to give a picture of the financial impacts of the contemporary management of abuse and its aftermath.

In working with these case histories, we have operated with two key assumptions. First, that the abuse described did take place and second, the consequences ascribed by respondents to the abuse were indeed caused by that abuse. For example, a number of the cases we reviewed involved periods of unemployment which the respondents attributed to the stress they had been under. It is conceivable that they would have lost their jobs anyway. In any exercise of this kind it is always extremely problematic to separate out the precise causal relations between events. This caveat needs to be borne in mind throughout.

IPF in their report to the Commission[2] identify the lack of information on the financial implications of child abuse. We would concur with this. The estimates we have given are no more than estimates based on assumptions and the best information we have been able to find in the time available. We have made explicit our assumptions and show our sources throughout. We have erred on the side of caution throughout. The costs we show can only be indicative of the costs incurred. Unless otherwise stated the costs shown are from current data.

Finally, we would note that the financial costs we estimate can in no way measure the emotional, physical and psychological damage done to children by abuse.

4   Sources of Information and Assumptions

4.1   Social Work Costs

There has been no detailed research, nor does there appear to be any being conducted at the moment, into either the financial costs or time implications for social work departments of managing child protection and the delivery of palliative services. The estimates used in the case histories have been developed from figures kindly supplied by Staffordshire Social Service Department. Staffordshire's costs are in line with what one would expect based on the estimates produced by IPF and the Social Services Research Unit at the University of Kent. It seems reasonable, therefore, to use them as accurate indicators of the costs involved.

Staffordshire identify four sets of costs associated with four types of case ranging from a simple investigation lasting a few days to a major intervention lasting for a year and involving continuing social work support, the provision of foster care and the issuing of a Care Order.

Specifically, they estimate the costs of:

o Case 1 - A simple investigation of minor bruising including the normal checks, interview of the child and the acceptance of the explanation provided. c£250

o Case 2 - An investigation where the case proceeds to a case conference, where a decision is taken not to register the child and there is no further involvement from social services. c£650

o Case 3 - The case proceeds to conference and the child is registered and a service plan developed. The family receives a total of 52 hours of social work support over six months and the child has 2 days a week nursery provision. After six months the case is reviewed, the child deregistered and the case closed. c£3,650

o Case 4 - The case proceeds to conference where it is decided that the matter is sufficiently serious for the child to be placed in a foster home and a Care Order is required. Contact is maintained between the family and the child twice a week. Social work support is offered to the family and a considerable amount of time is spent coordinating other services. The Care Order requires 4 interim hearings and a 2 day final hearing. The case is reviewed according to statutory requirements. For 12 months: social work time c£6,100, for the care order c£5,950, accomodation of child c£20,850.

4.2   Average Cost of Criminal Prosecutions

To deduce the average cost of criminal prosecutions the total cost of prosecutions needs to be divided by the total number of prosecutions. Costs were taken from the IPF report which identifies the estimated cost of Police Services and Magistrates and Crown Courts for the UK. This was built on figures for the individual countries. In England and Wales the cost of Police Services dedicated to child protection is estimated to be £65m, for Magistrates and Crown Courts £15m. This then gives a estimated total cost in England and Wales of prosecutions related to child protection of £80m (IPF based on Home Office figures). It should be noted that this figure excludes the cost to the Legal Aid budget of defending these cases.

In 1994 there were 4,003 prosecutions (Home Office[3]) for a range of violent and sexual offences against children. This includes infanticide, cruelty and neglect, buggery, indecent assault, gross indecency and encouraging or causing prostitution. It should be noted that this figure excludes prosecutions for actual or grievous bodily harm and murder. It also excludes cases taken under civil action. Therefore, the estimated average cost of a child protection prosecution in England and Wales is £19,998.

Report of the
National
Commission of
Inquiry into the
Prevention of
Child Abuse

It is assumed that the effect of excluding prosecutions for actual or grievous bodily harm and murder together with cases taken under civil action and the absence of Legal Aid costs in the total costs is neutral overall. However, it is probable that there are only a relatively small number of prosecutions excluded, while the additional cost of Legal Aid is likely to be substantial. On balance, the estimated cost of a child protection prosecution of c£20,000 probably understates the position.

4.3   Average Cost of Police Investigations

To deduce the average cost the total cost of investigations needs to be divided by the total cost of investigations. Costs were taken from the IPF report which identifies the estimated cost of Police Services for the UK. This was built on figures for the individual countries. The cost of Police Services dedicated to child protection in England and Wales is estimated to be £65m (IPF based on Home Office figures).

The Home Office figures for recorded offences are incomplete. It is therefore necessary to estimate the number of investigations. The position is further complicated by the fact that recorded offences in one year may lead to cautions and prosecutions in following years. Likewise cautions and prosecutions in one year may have originated from an offence recorded in a previous year. In the table below which shows statistics from 1994, it is assumed that these effects will balance each other out and that it is possible to estimate the proportion of recorded offences which result in either a prosecution.

Offence	Recorded Offences	Prosecutions	Recorded Offences leading to prosecutions
Child Abduction	343	82	24%
Unlawful sex w. girl <13	275	88	32%
Unlawful sex w. girl <16	1,446	202	14%
Gross indecency w. children	1,518	216	14%
Total	3,582	588	16%

Source: Home Office.

Obviously not every recorded offence is investigated. If the total number of prosecutions equates to 16% of recorded offences and there were 4,003 prosecutions then the total number of recordable offences would be 25,018 in England and Wales. This gives an average cost of £2,518.

In 1994-5 there were 36,622 children on the child protection registers in England and Wales. As with recorded offences not every child who is placed on the Child Protection Register will be the subject of a police investigation, although the overwhelming majority will. If, say, 75% of cases on the register are investigated by the Police this will be c27,500 cases. This would give an average cost of £2,363

If there were twenty thousand police investigations in England and Wales related to child protection would give an average cost of a child protection of £3,250. Even if the number of

*Report of the
National
Commission of
Inquiry into the
Prevention of
Child Abuse*

investigations is dramatically higher, say 40,000, the average cost only falls to £1,625. Likewise if the number of investigations is lower, say only 10,000, then the average rises to £6,250. Overall, therefore, while precision is difficult, it seems not unreasonable to estimate the average cost of a child protection investigation in England and Wales to be in the order of a few thousand pounds. And a notional average of £2,500 seems appropriate.

4.4 Runaways

Estimating the financial cost of managing children running away from home as a result of abuse is extremely difficult. The child may end up on the streets, in a police station or staying with a friend. What can be calculated is the cost of crisis intervention.

The Centrepoint Glaxo Refuge in the west end of London is registered under section 51 of the Children Act and specifically caters for run away children aged under 16. It has ten bedspaces and annual budget of £358,000. It would seek to charge the run away child's home local authority £98 per night of occupancy. This figure is based on 100% occupancy. Because of the particularly transient nature of its potential occupants, occupancy levels vary widely and a typical average is 65%. Taking this as the actual occupancy level. The actual cost per occupied bed space night is £150.89.

While this figure marks the highest level of intervention, it does not take account of the longer term and second order financial costs to the child, the child's family and to the wider society. While acknowledging its limited base, it seem to us reasonable to take this figure as a reasonable proxy in calculating the cost of running away from home.

4.5 NHS Costs

The costs of all NHS staff and General Practitioners has been taken from *Unit Costs of Community Care 1996* published by the Social Services Research Unit at the University of Kent. These reflect the costs of these services in 1995-6.

While it has been possible using these figures to estimate the costs of NHS staff time, it has not been possible to make any estimates of the medication involved in the management of any of these cases.

Several of the cases involve suicide attempts. A literature search was conducted to find any published data on these costs. No such data was found. Given the short time scale, the lack of good quality information and the complexity of the task, it was deemed inappropriate to make an estimate for the specific costs associated with suicide attempts.

4.6 Prison and Probation

This estimates are taken from figures produced by National Association for the Care and Rehabilitation of Offenders (NACRO)[4]. They were in turn based on Parliamentary Answers and Home Office statistics.

229

Report of the
National
Commission of
Inquiry into the
Prevention of
Child Abuse

4.7   Cost of Unemployment

The psychological and physical damage caused by abuse is often a contributor to difficulties in finding and retaining employment. The current level of unemployment benefit is £48-25 per week. Once a claimant has been unemployed for more than six months they move onto Income Support, if they are eligible. Income Support is calculated on an individual basis and the levels to be paid will vary from person to person. In addition to the receipt of state benefits, the other cost of unemployment is in the tax and national insurance lost on the wage the unemployed person was receiving. Again levels of tax and National Insurance will vary from person to person. This makes the development of a proxy number extremely problematic. In the end, we have used the simple unemployment benefit payment as the simplest figure to work with. Taking this headline figure certainly understates the cost of unemployment.

5   The Costs of Child Abuse

In the case histories which follow we identify as best we can the costs involved. In none of the cases, have we offered a total cost. This is because we are only too well aware of the gaps in our knowledge and the difficulty of correctly attributing effects to causes in this type of case.

However, a review of the nine case histories we offer in this report, together with the larger number of cases we considered, quickly demonstrates that child abuse costs several hundred pounds as soon as it comes within the public domain and investigation is undertaken. This rises to £600 - £700 with the calling of a case conference. The registration of a child and any further activity quickly pushes the costs into small thousands. In cases where abuse is substantiated, an abuser is prosecuted and imprisoned, and the victim receives therapeutic support, the cost can easily amount to more than £50,000.

The other striking feature of the costs is the expense of institutional responses after the event. In patient psychiatric care and prison both cost on average £20 - £40,000 per person per year. And we know that the victims of child abuse are over represented in the populations of both prisons and psychiatric hospitals[5]. It is clear then that the economic benefits of preventive work could be considerable.

The Case Histories

Outline	Estimated Cost	Notes and Sources
NL is a 41 year old female. A 'friend' abused her daughter while childminding in 1990.		
NL went to Social Services and a case conference was held. This was a "very difficult meeting".	Child Protection Conference £650	See S4.1
NL contacted the Child Protection Team 2 days later. CPT sent officer to home. An investigation was begun.	Police investigation £2,500	See S4.3
The CPT stayed in touch with the family.	Continuing contact £3,650	See S4.1
The abuser was arrested twice in '91 but not charged because of age of children involved.		
The alleged abuser was arrested again in '92. The CPS made error on the charge sheet and the case dismissed.	Case coming to court £20,000	See S4.2
NL and her daughter and 13 year old son all received counselling for 1 year from consultant psychiatrist.	Counselling cost c£8,250	3 x 50 sessions at £55 per session (SSRU)
NL has had support from her GP for last 3 years.	GP support £576	1 consultation per month for three years at £16 per visit (SSRU)
RM was a teacher who had an allegation made against him by a child in his class. He was suspended for six months before being reinstated. The case affected his health and after six months sick leave he took early retirement five years ago. Even with an enhanced pension and two part time jobs his annual income is approximately £10,000 per year less than he would be earning if he had remained a teacher.	Costs to Educ'n Dept of disciplinary: say four hours pw for 26 wks at £25 per hour = £2,600	Estimated average based on case being handled by senior management
	£10,000 pa x 5 years = £50,000	
His case was handled by his trade union. They were in contact two or three times a week for the six months of his suspension.	Say 4 hours per week for 26 weeks at £15 per hour = £1,560	

231

Outline	Estimated Cost	Notes and Sources
DG was accused of sexually abusing his teenage daughter over a period of years. A case conference as called. DG paid his solicitor to be present.	Case Conference £650 Solicitor Fee: £450	
The case went to court and after 9 hearings over the course of 18 months it was dropped. DG's legal costs were then paid for out of Legal Aid. He and his wife were separately represented. The local authority apologised and paid DG an undisclosed amount of compensation.	Court Case: Local Authority costs: £9,000 Legal Aid costs: £18,000 Compensation: £Unknown	Assume 9 hearings take a total of 6 days in court. There is an additional 6 days preparation time. Solicitors time for all sides: £57 per hour. Barristers time for all sides £400 per day. Add 20% for other costs (travel and waiting, handling paperwork, etc). The cost for each party is then c£9,000
DG made a complaint through the local authority complaints procedure which found largely in his favour. The Director of the Department failed to act upon the complaint, so DG appealed to the Local Government Ombudsman. This appeal is still being considered. The daughter is now receiving counselling paid for by the local authority. There is an understanding that this will continue until 1998 if necessary	To date £4,800 Potential additional costs to 1998: c£14,000	£120 per week x 40 weeks
GB was about to begin access proceedings against his ex wife to let him see their 4 year old daughter when his wife made an allegation of abuse against GB. The case was then delayed. Social Services and the Police investigated and found that there was no reason to proceed. No conference was called.	Social Services Investigation: £250 Police Investigation: £2,500 GB time off work: 1 day	I/view with GB
The Court case resumed and the Investigating Officer was subpoenaed to appear. Social Services then re-opened the investigation and called a case conference. This conference registered the child and a care plan was put in place. After 6 months on the Register, the Review Conference decided to de-register the child. The Court case was suspended again.	Social Services Investigation, Registration, Support and Review: £3,650 GB time off work: 7 days	
The Court case then resumed and after a total of 11 days in court, GB was exonerated by the judge, won access to his child. The Court was extremely critical of the way Social Services had handled the case. The costs to GB were so great that by the end of the case he became eligible for Legal Aid.	GB time off work: 13 days Total solicitors bill for GB: £21,000 Legal Aid for GB: £3,000	Total time spent by GB in attending court, meetings with solicitor and barrister, Divorce Court Welfare Officer, etc: 18 days. Normally solicitors' estimate such cases take: c5 days. Therefore additional time = 13 days
GB had made a complaint against Social Services after the Case Conference. GB is handling this complaint himself because he can't afford to pay his solicitor to do it on his behalf. This has now passed through the review panel to the Local Government Ombudsman and is still being processed.	GB time off work: 4 days Additional work to date by GB preparing letters, reports etc: 190 hours	

Outline	Estimated Cost	Notes and Sources
KL is a 22 year old female. She was abused from the age of 8 until she was 12. She didn't disclosed her abuse until she was 19. She reported it to the Police who are now investigating. She spent the ages of 16–21 in out and and out of psychiatric hospital for depression. She had three separate spells as an in-patient totalling 15 months before attempting suicide at 18 and spending the next three years as an in-patient.	Police investigation £2,500 Hospitalisation cost £162,180	See S4.2 51 months in hospital at £106 per inpatient day (SSRU) Assumes not in London
Now discharged she is receiving regular support each month from a social worker, community psychiatric nurse and doctor	Community support per month £194 For 12 months: £2,328	Social worker 4 x 1 hour session per month at £21 per hour (SSRU) CPN 2 x 1 hour session per month at £47 per hour (SSRU) GP 1 consultation per month at £16 per session (SSRU)
CM is a 26 year old female. She was abused for 2 years. She was put on the Child Protection Register and given continuing social work support for 12 months but the abuse continued.	Social work support for 1 year £7,850	See S4.1
Suffering from low self esteem and confidence led to a suicide attempt.	Suicide Attempt £Unknown	
She spent eight months in a psychiatric unit followed by eighteen months of private counselling.	Hospitalisation costs £58,085 Counselling £3,900	18 months as psychiatric in-patient at £106 per night (SSRU) 18 months of counselling of 1 session per week at £50 (IoS)
As a result of the suicide attempt the police investigated the abuse allegations which led to a court case. Her abuser got 2 years probation for indecent assault.	Police investigation £2,500 Court case £20,000 Probation £2,520	See S4.3 See S4.2 Annual cost of supervising offender on probation order £1,260 (NACRO)
"Despite lots of counselling the abuse still affects my feelings and daily life."		
EN is a 24 year old male. He was abused as an 11 year old. The Police investigated but EN only told part of the story. The case came to court and resulted in a conditional discharge. There was no support for EN. He says he now felt "worthless". He began missing school and breaking into houses. At 16, EN was convicted and sentenced to 2.5 years in prison.	Police investigation £2,500 Court case £20,000 Court case £20,000 Imprisonment £56,800	See S4.3 See S4.2 See S4.2 Average cost of imprisonment is £437 pw (NACRO)
Since his release he has periods of employment and unemployment (roughly 50:50). "I can't seem to stick jobs because I still feel worthless".	Unemployment £6,273	Two and a half years unemployment at £48.45 per week. See S4.7
He has been caught and charged for driving without insurance three times. EN claims panic attacks on buses and in crowded places. On his last court appearance a psychiatric report said suffering anxiety and tension was probably caused by abuse.		

Outline	Estimated Cost	Notes and Sources
CE is a female. She was abused from the age of two. At 12 she attempted suicide. At 13 she ran away with her sister. After a week they went to the Police.	Running away £1,050	Seven nights 'on the run' at £150 per night, see S4.3
A case conference was held and a social worker appointed. A Care Order was made and CE stayed with foster parents for 6 months. Then she went home.	Social Work Support: £6,100 Care Order £5,940 Fostering costs £10,608	See S4.1 See S4.1 Foster care £408 per child per week (SSRU)
At 14 she became pregnant and was taken into residential care where she stayed for two years. She missed exams.	Residential care £127,712	104 weeks of care package for child in community home at £1,228 per week (SSRU)
At 16 she began to receive a lot of support and help from a voluntary organisation in a group home	Support from Vol. Org. £14,664	2 years at £141 per week (SSRU)
She is now married, buying own home, catching up on education.		
SD is a female. As a young teenager she was suffering problems at home. She was offered support by an adult who then abused her. When she subsequently got into trouble at school she told the head teacher. The Police became involved. Her parents said SD was attention seeking and the Police dropped their investigation. She was subsequently abused by her sister's landlord at 14. Further major problems at home which led to a suicide attempt.	Initial investigation £2,500	See S4.3
	Suicide attempt £Unknown	
After the birth of her second son SD suffered post natal depression which led to 6 months in a psychiatric hospital. More depression and suicide attempts.	Hospitalisation £19,292	Six months hospitaliation at £106 per night (SSRU) Assumes outside London
She has been offered counselling and psycho drama and she attended for three months but she was too scared to complete therapy.	Counselling and Therapy £1,066	Counselling for one session per weeks at £50 per session (IoS) One x two hour drama therapy session per week at £16 per hours (SSRU)

Report of the
National
Commission of
Inquiry into the
Prevention of
Child Abuse

Footnotes

1 *And Do I Abuse My Children? No!*, Corinne Wattam and Clare Woodward, Commission Report, Volume 2.

2 *A Review of the Financial Implications of Programmes Aimed at the Prevention of Child Abuse in the United Kingdom*, Institute of Public Finance, Commission Report, Appendix 7

3 Home Office Sundry Statistical Tables

4 NACRO Briefing 23

5 For example, the 1991 National Prison Survey found that more than a quarter of all prisoners had been in local authority care compared with a figure for the population at large of 2%. Clearly, not everyone in local authority care has suffered abuse, but a good proportion of them will have done.

Published Sources:

IPF — *A Review of the Financial Implications of Programmes Aimed at the Prevention of Child Abuse in the United Kingdom*, Institute of Public Finance Ltd, National Commission Report, Volume 1

Home Office — *Statistical Bulletin Issue 42/89*, Home Office, December 1989
Number of Persons Prosecuted at Magistrates' Courts for Sexual Offences Involving Children Under 16 1984-94, Home Office 1996
Number of Persons Convicted at All Courts for Sexual Offences Involving Children Under 16 1984-95, Home Office 1996
Notifiable Offences Recorded by the Police for Sexual Offences Involving Children under 16 1981, 1986, 1993, 1994, Home Office, 1996
Number of Persons Prosecuted at Magistrates Courts for Sexual Offences Involving Children Under 16 by Type of Disposal 1981, 1986, 1993 and 1994, Home Office, 1996
Number of Persons Tried at Crown Court for Sexual Offences Involving Children Under 16 by Type of Disposal, 1981, 1986, 1993 and 1994, Home Office 1996
Number of Persons Sentenced for Sexual Offences Involving Children Under 16 by Offence, Type of Disposal and Court, Home Office 1996
Notifiable Offences Recorded by the Police; Cautions and Defendants Prosecuted at the Magistrates' Court and Found Guilty at All Courts for Specific Offences Involving Children Under 16 and by Gender 1994, Home Office 1996
National Prison Survey 1991, Home Office 1992

IoS — *The Happiness Directory*, The Independent on Sunday, 17 March 1996

NACRO — *The Costs of Penal Measures*, NACRO Briefing 23, April 1995

SSRU — *Unit Costs of Community Care 1995*, PSSRU, University of Kent, 1995

Other Material Provided Direct to Authors

Centrepoint Glaxo Refuge
Charges to Local Authorities and Occupancy

Staffordshire Social Services Department
Estimated Costings of a Range of Child Protection Cases

235

*Report of the
National
Commission of
Inquiry into the
Prevention of
Child Abuse*

6 Acknowledgements

Many people contributed to the development of this report. We would like to thank in particular:

Anna Capaldi, Management Perspectives

Philip Ramsdale, IPF

Ian Brady, Centrepoint

Sue Millman, ARP

Lorraine Watson, Home Office

Sally McCormick, Home Office

Information Department, NACRO

Information Department, NISW

Kings Fund Library

Ann Netton, Personal Social Services Research Unit, University of Kent

Corinne Wattam, Lancaster University

Clare Woodward, Lancaster University

Institute of Psychiatry Library

Sue Amphlett, Parents Against Injustice

Margaret Sutherland and colleagues, Staffordshire Social Services Department

The officers of the National Commission

The National Commission of Inquiry into the Prevention of Child Abuse: Legal Provisions, Scotland

by Kathleen Marshall, Solicitor and Fellow in Children's Rights, University of Glasgow

Report of the
National
Commission of
Inquiry into the
Prevention of
Child Abuse

Contents

1.   Introduction

Report of the
National
Commission of
Inquiry into the
Prevention of
Child Abuse

The aim of this paper is to explore the question: To what extent does the law contribute to or impede the prevention of child abuse and neglect?

The law can set standards for the treatment of children. It can enforce those standards through child care and criminal measures. In order to **prevent** child abuse and neglect, the standards must be adequate, clear, understood by all those involved and respected. Respect involves elements of attitude and compulsion. Primarily, those in a position to abuse or neglect children must be educated to expect and accept high standards of care. This must also be backed up by enforcement mechanisms, even though one might wish to limit their use. There are some whose attitudes seem to be beyond change; fear of the consequences may be the only restraining factor.

2.   The Scottish Legal System

The main piece of Scottish legislation relevant to child abuse and neglect is the Social Work (Scotland) Act 1968, as amended, (referred to in this document as "the 1968 Act"). This contains provisions relating to social work support and to compulsory measures of care. The greatest innovation of the 1968 Act was the establishment of the children's hearing system. This was based on proposals by the Kilbrandon Commission[1] which was set up largely to look at mechanisms for dealing with young offenders. The Commission proceeded on the basis that offending behaviour by a child was only one of a number of indicators of a need for care. The children's hearing system which was set up as a result, makes no distinction between offenders and others. At a hearing, three trained members of the public, appointed to a local "children's panel", meet with the child, the parents and other professionals. The system operates on the basis of a division of powers between the hearing and the sheriff court. If there are disputed matters of fact or law, they must be determined by the court, meeting in private. The hearing's task is to decide whether a child needs compulsory measures of care, and what measures are required. Procedure is informal, with encouragement for all to contribute to the discussion.

Other relevant legislation is referred to in the body of the document.

In July 1995, Royal Assent was given to the Children (Scotland) Act 1995 (referred to in this document as "the 1995 Act"). This was the product of a review process started in 1988 with the appointment of the Scottish Child Care Law Review. Some of the recommendations contained in their 1990 report[2] were overtaken by the events leading to the Orkney Inquiry, and the subsequent report by Lord Clyde.[3] Many other documents also affected the content of the Act, including the Review of Adoption Law in Scotland[4].

The contributing reports are listed in the 1993 White Paper "Scotland's Children - Proposals for Child Care Policy and Law" which preceded the Act.

The Act also contains provisions on private law, relating to children and parents generally. This reflects the recommendations of the Scottish Law Commission.[5] Whilst most of the relevant recommendations were accepted, the Commission's carefully considered limitation and clarification of the parental right of physical chastisement was omitted.

Whilst a very few provisions came into force on 1 November 1995, it is expected that the private law provisions will be brought into force on 1 November 1996, and the remainder of the Act on 1 April 1997.

239

Report of the
National
Commission of
Inquiry into the
Prevention of
Child Abuse

3. Basic Principles

Current Scottish law with regard to children is founded upon a welfare principle. A variety of formulations of this principle is found within the legislation:

○ In proceedings relating to parental rights, the welfare of the child is "the paramount consideration".[6]

○ In children's hearings cases the hearing must "consider ...what course they should decide in the best interests of the child".[7]

○ In adoption cases, the court must give "first consideration ...to the need to safeguard and promote the welfare of the child throughout his childhood".[8]

The UK's ratification in 1991 of the UN Convention on the Rights of the Child provided a new set of minimum standards for the rights of children. Article 3 says that in all actions concerning children, the best interests of the child shall be "a primary consideration". This formulation of the welfare principle is weaker than that of current Scottish law in some areas. Article 42 of the Convention anticipated this possibility and provided that, in cases where current standards were higher, the Convention was not to be used as a justification for lowering them.

In the wider sphere of children's involvement in society, the UK currently fails to meet the standards of Article 3. The UN Committee has made it clear that this Article obliges legislative and administrative bodies to take the interests of children as "a primary consideration" in all actions concerning them. This has implications which may be relevant to the prevention of child abuse and neglect.

The UN Convention is based on the principle that the family is the fundamental unit of society and that children are best brought up by their own families. In Scotland, the White Paper which preceded the 1995 Act claimed to have framed its proposals on the basis of the following principles derived from the Convention:

○ Every child should be treated as an individual.

○ Children have the right to express their views about any issues or decisions affecting or worrying them.

○ Every effort should be made to preserve the child's family home and contacts.

○ Parents should normally be responsible for the upbringing and care of their children.

○ Children, whoever they are and wherever they live, have the right to be protected from all forms of abuse, neglect and exploitation.

○ Every child has the right to a positive sense of identity.

○ Any intervention in the life of a child or family should be on formally stated grounds, properly justified, in close consultation with all the relevant parties.

○ Any intervention in the life of a child, including the provision of supportive services, should be based on collaboration between all the relevant agencies.

There may be a tension between the child's right to protection and the strong emphasis on the position of parents which is supported by a high level of formality in the processes of compulsory intervention. In principle, this approach is consistent with the presumption of the Convention that children are best brought up by their families. In practice, there are some fears in Scotland that the new provisions of the 1995 Act, in their eagerness to respect formal and legal rights, may work to the disadvantage of children - and possibly of some parents.

The rest of this paper addresses issues under a number of headings following a more or less chronological order. This is preceded by a synopsis and critique of relevant aspects of the current law and the 1995 Act, and followed by a paper looking towards the establishment of a more comprehensive legal system for children.

241

4. Current Law on Intervention

Current Law on Intervention	Critique	Children (Sc) Act 1995	Critique	Recommendations
S15 of the 1968 Act. Although known as "voluntary care", conditions for reception into care are restricted to ○ abandonment of child ○ inability to look after the child or ○ child being lost.	Not enough scope for true "voluntary" care. No requirement to consider child's views about coming into care.	S25 introduces concept of "accommodation" for children when: ○ no-one has parental responsibility ○ lost or abandoned ○ carer cannot provide suitable accommodation or care. Additional power to provide accommodation to safeguard and promote child's welfare.	Does make provision for a wider "voluntary" arrangement. Specifically requires the local authority to have regard to child's views before providing with accommodation.	
S16 of the 1968 Act. **Assumption of parental rights** by the local authority of child in care if: ○ parents dead and no guardian ○ in care for 3 years ○ child abandoned ○ parents incapable due to permanent disability ○ mental disorder renders parent unfit ○ habits or mode of life render parent unfit ○ parent persistently failed to meet obligations, with no reasonable cause.	○ No provision for assumption on basis of parental agreement. ○ Unjust procedure; administrative resolution creates a situation which a parent then has to challenge. ○ 3 year rule difficult to justify. ○ No mechanism for child to object if no objection made by parents.	S86 introduces new **Parental Responsibilities Order**, available on application to court if: ○ parents agree ○ parents not known, can't be found, or incapable of giving agreement ○ parents withholding agreement unreasonably ○ persistent failure to meet certain parental responsibilities ○ serious ill-treatment of child, and reintegration unlikely. Note: same as grounds for dispensing with agreement to adoption.	Meets objections to previous law. Move to court-based procedure incorporates procedures to ascertain views of child; details will be in Rules of Court. (Also implied by S17(3)).	

Current Law on Intervention	Critique	Children (Sc) Act 1995	Critique	Recommendations
S37 of 1968 Act. Place of Safety Order available if: o Schedule 1 Offence believed to have been committed against child, or child in same household. o Child is or likely to become member of same household as a suspected or proven Schedule 1 Offender. o Child of vagrant is prevented from receiving education. o Lack of parental care likely to cause unnecessary suffering or serious impairment of health. o Child can also **"take refuge in a place of safety"** and thus initiate proceedings.	o Grounds too specific. Not targeted sufficiently on the likelihood of significant harm. Could encompass some not in need of emergency protection. o Order authorises only detention of the child. No specific authority to regulate access or authorise medical examination or treatment or investigative interviewing. o Some concern about whether the procedures satisfied the standards of the European Convention on Human Rights. o Some of these issues identified by the Scottish Child Care Law Review in its 1990 Report. Higher profile and more detailed consideration through the Report of the Orkney Inquiry, 1992. o "Taking refuge" possibility not well known or widely used.	**S57 Child Protection Order** available if o reasonable grounds to believe child is or will suffer significant harm, and order necessary to protect the child. o Provision for court directions re contact, medical examination and treatment, interviews, etc. o More numerous and complex procedures for review and appeal. o "Taking refuge" provision omitted, but S38 makes provision for **short term refuges.**	o Some concern about interpretation of "significant harm", although most welcome the change. o Concern that proliferation of review and appeal procedures might confuse and distress children, and some parents. o Concern at adequacy of the refuge provisions, both re the permitted length of stay and because it lacks the element of choice of refuge open to children under the current law.	

243

Current Law on Intervention	Critique	Children (Sc) Act 1995	Critique	Recommendations
S32 of the 1968 Act. **Grounds of referral** to a Children's Hearing which determines the need and form of compulsory measures of care: o Beyond control of parent. o Falling into bad associations or exposed to moral danger. o Lack of parental care likely to cause unnecessary suffering or seriously impair health or development. o Child concerned or another child in same household has been victim of a Schedule 1 Offence. o Child is or likely to become a member of same household as a Schedule 1 Offender. o Female child is member of same household as female victim of incest perpetrated by a member of the household. o Truancy. o Child has committed an offence. o Child has inhaled volatile substance (glue-sniffing). o Child transferred from another part of the UK under similar provisions. o Child in care requires special measures of care and control.	o Debate re whether should move to a single ground of referral based on welfare of child. Decided that retention of specific grounds more consistent with the principle of justified intervention on formally stated grounds. o Debate re truancy - whether it was truly a symptom of a family problem or should be removed to the educational arena. Decided to retain the truancy ground. o Debate re whether grounds adequately addressed the issue of emotional abuse. New ground suggested but not included in new legislation. o Identified necessity of extending the incest ground to boys. o Debate re definition of Schedule 1 Offence - particularly the issue of physical chastisement by parents. How clear is the trigger for intervention? (See Para. 6 below.)	S52 grounds of referral - some minor amendments. o Incest ground extended to boys. o misuse of drugs or alcohol is included.	Emotional abuse was not specifically included. The ground of referral suggested by the Child Care Law Review was dropped.	Consultation with Reporters to ascertain whether they consider any further amendments need to be made to the legal framework to address cases of emotional abuse. Clarification of the actions designated as "Schedule 1 Offences." (See Para. 6 below).

Current Law on Intervention	Critique	Children (Sc) Act 1995	Critique	Recommendations
o S24 and 26 - regarding **aftercare** - limit assistance to those who were in care on or after school leaving age. The local authority duty to advise and guide applies only up to the age of 18. There is an additional power to contribute to costs of accommodation and maintenance of those aged up to 21 (longer in restricted circumstances), linked with education, training, employment or the search for employment.	o The Child Care Law Review recommended removal of the restriction about school leaving age. Assistance should be available to those who were in care for a significant part of their lives over the age of 12. The duty should last until age 21. o Concern about care-leavers is justified by research showing the damaging effects of being in care. Care leavers are 70 times more likely than other young people to be homeless. This could be seen as institutional abuse.	o S29 extends duty to advise and guide by one year - up to 19th birthday, with power to do so up until 21. o S30 power to contribute towards accommodation and maintenance up to 21 (longer in restricted circumstances), linked with education, training, employment or the search for employment. o To qualify for either section, must have been "looked after" on or after reaching school leaving age.	Amendments do not substantially address the criticisms of the 1968 Act.	Duty under S29 should extend up to 21. Threshold re school leaving age should be abolished or revised downwards - possibly to 12.
Matrimonial Proceedings (Children) Act 1958 - allows court to put child in care if, in the course of matrimonial proceedings, it considers that "there are exceptional circumstances making it impracticable or undesirable for the child to be entrusted to either of the parties to the marriage." Court may also place child under local authority supervision if "there are exceptional circumstances making it desirable that the child should be under the supervision of an independent person."	o Concern that this was an "untidy" entry into care. Lack of clear grounds. No regular review of child's situation outwith the local authority. Conclusion that better to channel these cases through the Children's Hearing System.	S54 - court may refer cases to **Principal Reporter** if it appears any of the grounds of referral set out in S52 are established (apart from commission of offence by child). If Reporter considers compulsory measures of supervision are necessary, he shall arrange a children's hearing. The **grounds will be regarded as having been established** - so no further proof is necessary.	Some concern about how the matter will be dealt with by the sheriff. Will child and parents know that the goalposts have been changed? This may be dealt with in Rules of Court.	
Guardianship Act 1973 - similar provisions to the Matrimonial Proceedings Act, but applies where applications for custody are heard outwith matrimonial proceedings.	o Similar concerns as re the Matrimonial Proceedings Act.	Same as re **Matrimonial Proceedings Act.**	Same as re Matrimonial Proceedings Act.	

Current Law on Intervention	Critique	Children (Sc) Act 1995	Critique	Recommendations
o Matrimonial Homes (Family Protection) (Scotland) Act 1981 - contains provisions for **exclusion orders** to be made if necessary to protect physical or mental health of applicant or child. **Matrimonial interdict, with power of arrest**, also available to prohibit conduct towards a child.	o Application must be by spouse or cohabitee with occupation rights. Puts heavy onus on spouse who may already be under pressure. Difficulties with enforcement. Matrimonial interdicts not available after divorce, although ordinary interdicts, with no power of arrest attached, may be. Matrimonial interdicts limited to activity in the vicinity of the matrimonial home. Does not apply to house rented or bought by spouse after separation or to the child's school, although ordinary interdicts would be available. The Scottish law Commission has recommended amendments to address some of these issues, but parliamentary time has not been found to enact them.	To supplement the availability of this private law exclusion order, S76 introduces a **public law exclusion order**. A local authority may apply to the sheriff for an order excluding a named person from the home. The grounds are similar to those for a Child Protection Order. The threat of harm must be related to the "named person". The sheriff must be satisfied that removal of that person would better safeguard the child's welfare than removal of the child from the family home. An interim exclusion order can be made without hearing the "named person."	The principle is very much welcomed. There is some wariness about how it will work in practice. Training will be essential. It will not be appropriate for all cases. There is a fear that if, through a lack of training and discernment, it gets off to a bad start, it will lose credibility.	Training in the new 1995 Act exclusion order as a top priority for all relevant parties. Enactment of the Scottish Law Commission's proposals for exclusion orders and interdicts in private law.
o Foster Children (Scotland) Act 1984 o Allows the local authority to inquire into the circumstances of **privately fostered children** and to regulate or prohibit the keeping of foster children by certain persons. Children may be removed from unsuitable placements.	o Not much debate re these provisions.	Consequential amendments only.		

Current Law on Intervention	Critique	Children (Sc) Act 1995	Critique	Recommendations
o **Adoption**(Scotland) Act 1978: o Regulates the placing of children for adoption and the freeing of children for adoption. Consent of parent and child required, if child is 12 years of age or more. Consent of parent may be dispensed with if parent: o cannot be found or is incapable of giving agreement. o is withholding agreement unreasonably. o has persistently failed to discharge parental duties. o has abandoned or neglected the child. o has persistently ill-treated the child and rehabilitation is unlikely. o has seriously ill-treated the child. There are, in addition, ongoing issues about inter-country adoption.	o There was debate about the possibility of replacing the grounds for dispensing with consent with a single, composite ground regarding the child's welfare. The Scottish Adoption Law Review decided against this for the same reasons as above re grounds of referral to a children's hearing. (Para 6.25). It did recommend minor changes to the grounds which have been enacted by Schedule 2 of the 1995 Act.	**Minor changes to grounds for dispensing with parental consent.** Now the same as re Parental Rights orders (see above).		

247

5. Current Law on Promotion of Welfare

5. Current Law on Promotion of Welfare	Critique	Children (Sc) Act 1995	Critique	Recommendations
S12 of the 1968 Act - Duty of local authority to **promote social welfare.** Regarding children under 18, the duty is focused on the need to prevent reception into care, or retention in care, or referral to a children's hearing.	The Child Care Law Review thought this was too negative a formulation and recommended that the duty be framed more positively.	S22 restricts the duty to a category of "**children in need**", defined in S93(4)(a).	Restriction to category of "in need" is largely regarded as unhelpful and stigmatising. The definition is similar to that in the Children Act 1989, but includes children affected adversely by the disability of another member of the family.	Monitoring of this provision, and a commitment to change if it disadvantages children. Could local authorities notify a central point if they are having difficulty maintaining or providing supportive services within the limits of the law? This is where a Children's Commissioner would be useful.

6.   Current Criminal Law

6. Current Criminal Law (Largely unaffected by the 1995 Act)	Critique	Recommendations
Child protection measures frequently refer to Schedule 1 Offences. This is a reference to Schedule 1 of the Criminal Procedure (Scotland) Act 1995. It includes offences under Part I of the Criminal Law (Consolidation) (Scotland) Act 1995, Sections 12, 15, 22 or 23 of the Children and Young Persons (Scotland) Act 1937, any other offence involving bodily injury to a child under 17, and lewd, indecent or libidinous practice or behaviour towards a child under 17.	Whilst the phrase "Schedule 1 Offence" is well known, the content of the category is complex. A proposal to provide an index of offences has not been proceeded with.	Make Schedule 1 more accessible and comprehensible.
General law on assault etc. – with specific exception re physical punishment	Whilst an assault on a child would generally fall into the category of a Schedule 1 Offence, there is a specific exception in the case of actions by a parent deemed to fall into the category of "reasonable chastisement". This is contained in S12(7) of the Children and Young Persons (Scotland) Act 1937. Case law has indicated that the boundaries of this category are unclear. The Scottish Law Commission recommended that the limits of reasonable chastisement be narrowed and clarified. Their proposal to achieve this, contained in their 1992 Report on family law, was the result of much consultation with professionals and the public. Nevertheless, the government chose to drop this proposal from the Children (Scotland) Act 1995. This leaves the situation as unclear as before.	First option should be to make physical punishment illegal; second option would be to support enactment of the Scottish Law Commission's more limited proposals.
Plagium is a common law crime of **theft of a child**, based on the ancient Roman concept of the child as property of the parent. It applies only to children under the age of puberty, which is held to be at 12 for girls and 14 for boys. Below puberty, a child can be "stolen". The wishes of the child are said to be "as irrelevant as the wishes of a stolen sheep or dog."	The fact that a criminal offence is involved is authority for the police to be involved in recovery of the child as if a piece of stolen property. Whilst this is sometimes welcomed in the case of young children abducted by a parent with no right to custody, it can be a disadvantage in cases where the child has sought an alternative place of residence and some space is required to discover what is going on. The child might at this stage be unwilling to disclose his or her real concerns.	Rationalisation of the law to facilitate police intervention in appropriate cases and exclude it in others.

249

Report of the
National
Commission of
Inquiry into the
Prevention of
Child Abuse

7.   Non-Statutory Definitions of Abuse and Neglect

In 1992, a report was published of a Scottish Office Steering Group set up "to recommend standard criteria for admission to and removal from local [child protection] registers."[9]

These non-statutory definitions support action related to inclusion of a child's name on a Child Protection Register. Such Registers form an administrative system for identifying children at risk and co-ordinating inter-agency plans to minimise that risk. In the event of formal child protection measures being required, the case would have to fit into the legal definitions set out above. The definitions proposed by the Steering Group are as follows:

> *"To define an act or omission as abusive and/or presenting future risk for the purpose of registration, 3 elements must be taken into account:*
>
> o   *whether there is demonstrable damage or harm to a child or a prediction of harm to the child;*
>
> o   *whether the injury/state of the child must have been avoidable through action by parents or carers responsible for that child;*
>
> o   **whether the potential harm or future risk is linked to the action or inaction of the parent or other carer.** *This would also apply *where it was not possible to establish the identity of the perpetrator."*

To supplement this general definition, the guidance sets out 5 categories of child abuse, but exhorts readers to bear in mind that there can be overlap and interaction amongst the categories. A particular case of child abuse may not always fit neatly into one category. The categories are:

Physical Injury

Actual or attempted physical injury to a child, under the age of 16[10], where there is definite knowledge, or reasonable suspicion, that the injury was inflicted or knowingly not prevented.

Physical injury may include a serious incident or a series of minor incidents involving bruising, fractures, scratches, burns or scalds; deliberate poisoning; attempted drowning or smothering; Munchausen Syndrome by Proxy[11]; serious risk of or actual injuries resulting from parental lifestyle prior to birth, for instance substance abuse; physical chastisement, deemed to be unreasonable.

Sexual Abuse

Any child below the age of 16 may be deemed to have been sexually abused when any person(s), by design or neglect, exploits the child, directly or indirectly, in any activity intended to lead to the sexual arousal or other forms of gratification of that person or any other person(s) including organised networks. This definition holds whether or not there has been genital contact and whether or not the child is said to have initiated the behaviour.

Sexual abuse may include activities such as incest, rape, sodomy or intercourse with children; lewd or libidinous practices or behaviour towards children; indecent assault of children; taking indecent photographs of children or encouraging children to become prostitutes or witness intercourse or pornographic materials.

Activities involving sexual exploitation, particularly between young people, may be indicated by the presence of one or more of the following characteristics - lack of consent; inequalities in terms of chronological age, developmental stage or size; actual or threatened coercion.

Non-organic Failure to Thrive

Children who significantly fail to reach normal growth and developmental milestones, (i.e. physical growth, weight, motor, social and intellectual development) where physical and genetic reasons have been medically eliminated and a diagnosis of non-organic failure to thrive has been established.

Factors affecting a diagnosis may include inappropriate relationships between the care-giver(s) and the child, especially at meal times, for instance the persistent withholding of food as a punishment and the sufficiency and/or suitability of the food for the child. In its chronic form, non-organic failure to thrive can result in greater susceptibility to more serious childhood illnesses, reduction in potential stature, and with young children particularly, the results may be life threatening over a relatively short period.

Emotional Abuse

Failure to provide for the child's basic emotional needs such as to have a severe effect on the behaviour and development of the child.

This may include situations where as a result of persistent behaviour by the parent(s) or care-giver(s) children are rejected, denigrated or scape-goated; inappropriately punished; denied opportunities for exploration, play and socialisation appropriate to their stage of development or encouraged to engage in anti-social behaviour; put in a state of terror or extreme anxiety by the use of threats or practices designed to intimidate them; isolated from normal social experiences, preventing the child from forming friendships.

Children who are left on their own for long periods, are understimulated or suffer sensory deprivation, especially in infancy; who do not experience adequate nurturing or who are subject to a large number of care-givers, may also come into this category.

Sustained or repeated abuse of this type is likely, in the longer term, to result in failure or disruptions of development of personality, inability to form secure relationships and may additionally have an effect on intellectual development and educational attainment.

Physical Neglect

This occurs when a child's essential needs are not met and this is likely to cause impairment to physical health and development. Such needs include food, clothing, cleanliness, shelter and warmth. A lack of appropriate care results in persistent or severe exposure, through negligence, to circumstances which endanger the child.

Physical neglect may also include a failure to secure appropriate medical treatment for the child, or when an adult carer persistently pursues or allows the child to follow a lifestyle inappropriate to the child's developmental needs or which jeopardises the child's health.

8.   Defining Child Abuse and Neglect

Current Scottish law tells parents what they must not do rather than what they should do. There is no definition of the responsibilities of parents. This is unsurprising as the law still uses the terminology of parental rights. This concept is a legacy of the historic debt owed by Scotland to the law of ancient Rome. Within the Roman system, the father of the family had extensive powers over his descendants. They equated to a right of property. Whilst the law has been softened over the years so that now it is accepted that parental rights are validly exercised only in pursuit of the child's interests, this is not yet reflected in the basic concepts of Scottish law.

In contrast, the 1995 Act defines parental responsibilities and parental rights, and makes it clear that the rights are subsidiary to the responsibilities.[12]

The limits on parental rights are to be found in those laws, set out above, justifying state intervention, whether on a civil basis, to protect the child, or a criminal basis, when the parent's actions constitute a criminal offence. There needs to be greater clarity about what those limits are.

Conclusions on Defining Child Abuse and Neglect

Professional awareness of the needs and rights of children is running well ahead of public awareness. As well as doing children a disservice, this is unfair to parents as they do not know the standards against which they will be judged if an issues arises.

There needs to be greater public education about the rights of children under the UN Convention and about the application of current standards. There should also be a clarification of some standards, such as "reasonable chastisement" which remain unclear and demonstrably inconsistent. This will require legal reform backed up by an education programme.

9.   Identifying Child Abuse and Neglect

The identification of abuse is clearly related to the clarity of definition. Whilst some types of physical abuse may result in easily identifiable symptoms, sexual abuse was for long misunderstood. Emotional abuse is hard to define, open to interpretation and susceptible to cultural variation.

Opportunity is also a key factor in the identification of abuse and neglect. Compulsory education has provided an opportunity for the care of many young people to be open to the scrutiny of adults outwith the family. Education legislation also contains some provisions for compulsory examinations.[13]

Concern is sometimes expressed at the lack of opportunity with regard to pre-school children. Development checks are voluntary. Whilst hesitating to make them compulsory, a report of an independent working group in 1993 recommended that:

> "Throughout the UK, health legislation should ensure that there is a clear obligation to make available specified appropriate developmental checks for all children in their area between notification of birth and age of starting school, and (subject to the child's right to consent) at appropriate intervals during the period of compulsory schooling."[14]

Report of the
National
Commission of
Inquiry into the
Prevention of
Child Abuse

There may be concerns about a child which are difficult to substantiate without access, and access may be denied. The Orkney Inquiry Report stated that Place of Safety Orders should not be used as a means of gathering evidence.[15] Instead it recommended an Interim Protection Order. The 1995 Act has built on this concept to introduce a Child Assessment Order.

There needs to be general public awareness and closer co-operation between professionals to share their knowledge of abuse and the interpretation of symptoms. Problems in Cleveland arose because of what was later seen as over-reliance on a particular diagnostic technique. Problems in Ayrshire arose partly through differing interpretations of dental evidence, which was a crucial factor in corroborating the statements of the children. In the field of HIV and AIDS, medical knowledge is still developing. The World Health Organisation recommends that women in developed countries do not breastfeed if they are infected with the virus because of the risk of transmission to the baby. In developing countries, the risk from bottle feeding is still greater than the risk of transmission through breast milk. Given that what is at stake is the survival of the child, should child protection agencies regard breast feeding by HIV mothers as an objective lack of parental care opening the doors to state intervention? A late amendment to the Children (Scotland) Act (Section 85) allows a case to be reopened if new evidence becomes available. This may involve a new interpretation of evidence previously submitted. This amendment arose directly out of the Ayrshire case referred to above. Whilst initially wary of it being manipulated to the disadvantage of children, most practitioners appear reconciled to its appropriateness.

253

Conclusion on identification

To a certain extent, as the above examples indicate, those faced with the task of identifying child abuse and neglect must come to terms with living with uncertainty. Humility is appropriate, but it should not keep us from acting on the basis of the best available knowledge where the welfare, or even the life, of a child is at stake.

The law is often seen as dealing in absolutes; right and wrong; guilty or not guilty. There must be greater public awareness of the nature of legal decisions in matters concerning children. They are often provisional and dependent on the state of knowledge in other professions and the degree of confidence with which those professionals feel able to express their opinions.

The law can help provide parameters. Public confidence in living with the uncertainty in between could be increased by a greater professionalisation of social work, backed up by a

Report of the
National
Commission of
Inquiry into the
Prevention of
Child Abuse

commitment to more extended training. Lord Clyde made several recommendations to this effect in the Orkney Inquiry Report. The recommendation regarding an extended period of training was rejected by the Government.[16]

10.   Reporting Child Abuse and Neglect

Under current Scottish law, only the local authority has a duty to report suspicions that a child is in need of care and protection.[17]

Although local child protection guidelines expect other professionals such as teachers, health visitors and other medical staff to report as part of their professional duty, they do not have to do so as a matter of law. The 1995 Act extends the mandatory duty to police constables. In the course of the parliamentary process, an MP raised the question of a possible duty on staff of residential schools. This arose out of a case involving a constituent. Whilst having some sympathy with the proposal, child welfare agencies were wary of it. Other countries do have mandatory reporting procedures; some extend it not just to professionals but to all adult citizens, sometimes with one or two exceptions. It was felt that more needed to be known about the experience of these countries before considering the introduction of mandatory reporting on a wider scale in Scotland.

A basic concern was the effect this would have in curtailing children's access to confidential advice. The experience of ChildLine has shown the value children place on confidentiality. Often they will not tell their story if they believe they will lose control of what will happen. The approach of ChildLine and other children's advice agencies is to support the child towards disclosure as the most appropriate option in most cases.

Conclusions on reporting

There should be greater public awareness of current reporting procedures and practices on confidentiality. There should be an investigation into the outcomes for children in countries with wider mandatory reporting duties.

11.   Responding to Child Abuse and Neglect

Children and adults will draw back from reporting suspicions if they fear an inappropriate or unhelpful response. This can be fear of an over-reaction or an under-reaction, or a reaction by an agency whose approach is disliked.

Although the social work department do not have a legal obligation to report suspicions of child abuse and neglect to the police, local child protection guidelines, backed up by national guidelines and the Orkney Report, expect early reporting and co-operation with the police. The Orkney Report emphasised that investigation was a matter for the police rather than social work. This, combined with the criticisms emanating from the Orkney and Ayrshire cases, has caused some social work feeling that they should indeed be withdrawing and leaving the police to it. The problem is that very few cases are successfully prosecuted, therefore some would argue that this is a case of "the tail wagging the dog." The expectation of police intervention makes some people reluctant to report. Is there a better way?

Report of the
National
Commission of
Inquiry into the
Prevention of
Child Abuse

Fear of under-reaction can also be a problem. For example, teachers have on occasion indicated that, when they have raised concerns, the headteacher has swept them aside on the basis that the child concerned is bound to be lying. Some feel that it is fear for the reputation of the school, or of the antipathy of powerful parents that makes headteachers reluctant to respond.

Other professionals, aware of the criticisms aimed at recent high profile cases of alleged abuse, have also expressed themselves more reluctant to get involved. There seems to be a feeling surrounding the question - Who really knows what child abuse is, how to identify it and how to deal with it? Lack of confidence in the system's ability to come up with an appropriate response can stop people from reporting.

High profile cases such as Cleveland, Orkney and Ayrshire have led to calls for an approach based on "partnership with parents." This is often understood as meaning that voluntary measures should be preferred to compulsory ones. There can be problems with this. Firstly, because it might hold agencies back from intervening forcefully at an early stage in some appropriate cases. Secondly, because there can be a fine line between persuasion towards voluntary measures and professional blackmail. This issue arises sometimes in relation to cases on the child protection register. A social worker who tells parents that if the father does not leave they will have to take a Place of Safety Order, might see herself as just being straight and helping the parents to face the realities of the situation in the least damaging way. Sometimes this can be experienced by parents as a threat which leaves them in a legal limbo, with no procedural mechanisms short of refusal to comply. A recent Department of Health Document - "The Challenge of Partnership in Child Protection: Practice Guide" - explores these issues in a helpful way.[18]

Conclusions on Responding

Wider dissemination and training on the Department of Health's guidance. Greater openness concerning fears about responding and reporting.

Confidence in the system is partly about knowledge and partly about substance. Whilst knowledge of law and practice might lead to an "informed fear", it is still likely to be less paralysing than an "uninformed fear".

12.   Investigating Child Abuse and Neglect

Police and social work have different aims and different agendas. Whilst much effort is being put into establishing joint working procedures and joint training, professionals from both agencies often express dissatisfaction in private.

Conclusions on investigation

Problems can be linked to the existence of a clash of professional cultures. It might be better to have a cadre of trained child protection investigators aware of the evidential needs of both the police and child protection agencies, and skilled in communication with children.

255

Report of the
National
Commission of
Inquiry into the
Prevention of
Child Abuse

13. Legal Processes

Some issues about the divergent interests of the child protection and criminal investigation agencies have already been referred to. Much has been written about the position of child witnesses, particularly in criminal proceedings where they can be subject to prolonged, hostile questioning. In Scotland, legal measures to alleviate the situation were introduced by the Law Reform (Miscellaneous Provisions) (Scotland) Act 1990 and the Prisoners and Criminal Proceedings (Scotland) Act 1993. These provisions are now contained in Section 271 of the Criminal Procedure (Scotland) Act 1995. The 1990 Act made provision for the evidence of children to be taken by live television link. Research by Kathleen Murray of Glasgow University's Centre for the Study of the Child & Society was recently published concerning implementation of this provision.

The 1993 Act introduced a possibility of the evidence of children being taken "on commission", to avoid the child having to appear in court. This evidence can take the place of examination and cross examination. This appears to have been little used so far.

In addition, changes to the rules of admissibility of evidence in criminal proceedings, which were introduced from 1 April, 1996 by the Criminal Procedure (Scotland) Act 1995, may result in greater use being made of video recordings of a child's evidence, which the child would then "adopt" in court and may be questioned on.

Whilst these measures indicate some willingness to take account of the needs of child witnesses, many would consider that more needs to be done. Some feel that the Scottish requirement for evidence in criminal trials to be corroborated, disadvantages the prosecution and the child victim in cases of child abuse. Defence lawyers are however already concerned at what many see as a dangerous erosion of the rights of the accused and the standards of evidence and procedure, and would resist further protective measures.

It is understood that some countries appoint counsel or representatives for the complainant. A reference to this is made for example in Sweden's Initial Report to the UN Committee on the Rights of the Child.[19] It may be worth considering whether someone should be appointed in criminal cases to look after the interests of the allegedly abused child.

The Swedish report goes on to state that, "A person under 15...cannot testify on oath, nor can he incur any sanctions... for refusing to testify....On the other hand, a child can be forcibly conveyed to court." This raises the interesting question of whether children should be exempt from the sanctions attached to the obligation to testify in criminal case. Should the choice about testifying be left to the child or persons appointed to protect the child's interests?

In the area of child protection, the children's hearing system operates on the principle that the interests of the parent and child are the same, and that parents are the best people to protect the interests of the child. This may be a legacy of its roots in juvenile justice. Since its inception, the proportion of child protection cases has increased dramatically.

As a result of the English Maria Colwell case, the Children Act 1975 introduced a new person into the children's hearing system to address situations in which the interests of the child and parent appeared to be in conflict. The "Safeguarder", as this person is known, has been very little used since the legislation was brought into force in 1985. There has however been an increased interest in recent years. The Orkney Report made some recommendations about extending the role. The White Paper endorsed this.

The 1995 Act accordingly removes the restriction on the criterion for appointment, so that a conflict of interest is no longer necessary. It is sufficient to show that the appointment itself is considered necessary to safeguard the interests of the child. There has been concern about the lack of training and consistent expectation of the role of safeguarders. The Scottish Office has a working party dealing with the issue.

There is some concern about delays in the criminal justice system. This can mean that therapeutic work with children can be limited until the process is complete. There was also disappointment that the 1995 Act did not include a principle about avoidance of delay in proceedings affecting children, although there may be a reference to this in the Rules of Court that are currently being drafted.

Conclusions on legal processes

Further consideration should be given to the rules of evidence and procedure in cases involving children. In particular, consideration should be given to the appointment of a complainant's counsel in cases of alleged abuse or neglect. Consideration should be given to exempting children from sanctions for refusal to testify.

In the course of debate about the Children (Scotland) Bill, questions were raised about reversing the present procedure about Safeguarders, so that they should be appointed unless reason is given for not doing so. As this did not win the day, it would probably be unrealistic to suggest legal amendment at this stage. However, it may still be possible to influence draft rules of court and practice in the direction of recognition of the valuable contribution to be made by trained and confident safeguarders.

Vigilance should also ensure that the new Rules of Court address the question of delay. However, it will be instructive for Scotland to take note of the English and Welsh experience. Despite the prominence of the principle in the Children Act 1989, the Children Act Advisory Committee Reports show that delay is an increasing problem.[20]

14. Outcomes for Children

The desired outcome in child protection proceedings is clearly defined in terms of the interest of the child. In criminal proceedings it is defined in terms of the interest of society. It is undoubtedly true that conviction of a child abuser can be protective of other children by triggering vetting processes which reduce his potential for access to commit further offences. There must be an ethical dilemma in some cases in deciding whether to prosecute. The child victim may now be safe, and it may be considered that involvement in criminal proceedings will not serve that child's interest and may even be damaging. Is it legitimate to force a child to participate for the sake of others?

Report of the
National
Commission of
Inquiry into the
Prevention of
Child Abuse

257

*Report of the
National
Commission of
Inquiry into the
Prevention of
Child Abuse*

Conclusions on outcomes

Policy on decisions regarding prosecution should be formulated with reference to the rights of the child under the UN Convention.

15.   Specific Issues

Children who abuse others

Some attention has been given to this matter recently by, eg. NCH Action for Children and the Centre for Residential Child Care in Glasgow. In general, the Scottish approach is to direct offending children to the children's hearing rather than the court. In serious cases, the jurisdiction of the court can be involved. If we are to be true to Article 3 of the UN Convention, decisions about such children must still take their best interests as a primary consideration. It is questionable whether this is the case.

Commission on Children & Violence

The Gulbenkian appointed Commission on Children & Violence reported in November 1995. Amongst its recommendations were:

○ removal of the defence of "reasonable chastisement" which justifies the practice of physical punishment of children;

○ enactment of a legal definition of parental responsibility and parental rights based on the UN Convention (Scotland has one in the 1995 Act); and

○ revision of the criminal justice system to ensure full compliance with the UN Convention on the Rights of the Child.

Conclusions on specific issues

Children who abuse other children should still come within the ambit of the children's hearing system. Either the age of criminal responsibility should be raised to at least 12, preferably 14 or 16, or the Lord Advocate's Guidelines on cases to be reserved for prosecution should be amended to this end.

Specific effort should be expended to pursue implementation of the recommendations of the Commission on Children & Violence.

16.   A Legal System for Children

This section looks at some of the issues that need to be addressed in order to establish a legal system tailored to the needs and rights of children.

Enacting the UN Convention on the Rights of the Child

The UN Convention is not, as a whole, easily translatable into Scottish law. Some articles are short and present clear principles which the courts could apply, although I expect that the Government would want to hedge them with exceptions. Thus Article 6 says:

1. States parties recognise that every child has the inherent right to life.

2. States parties shall ensure to the maximum extent possible the survival and development of the child.

Paragraph 1 has already been made subject to some exceptions by the UK's reservations to the Convention. Paragraph 2 might cause some anxiety because of its effect on, eg. rights to expensive medical treatments. Nevertheless, the principles themselves are reasonably clear.

Article 17 is concerned with access to appropriate information. It talks about "recognising" the important functions of the mass media and "encouraging" dissemination of material, international co-operation and development of guidelines. It is not language that would fit easily into a British statute. This means that it would not be appropriate for the UN Convention to be incorporated into law in the way that, eg. the Hague and European Conventions on international child abduction were, through inclusion in a schedule to an Act of Parliament.

Specific provisions can be translated into law. Thus section 6 of the Children (Scotland) Act 1995 seeks to implement Article 12 of the convention, concerning the child's right to be consulted about major decisions within the family.

It may be possible to look for other ways of encouraging recourse to the convention in the application of law by the courts. Some judges are already referring to the convention in their judgments. This might be strengthened by taking the following alternative measures, in decreasing order of comprehensiveness:

1. a short Interpretation Act creating a presumption that all UK law is to be interpreted in a way that accords so far as possible with the UN Convention;

2. insertion of interpretation sections into specific Acts creating this presumption; or

3. encouraging a practice of deliberate Ministerial statements in Parliament that the legislation is designed to comply with the UN Convention.

It might be argued that option 1 replicates an existing rule of statutory interpretation. There is indeed such a principle in operation, which has undergone some development over recent years. Its boundaries are not very clear. The Act would put the matter beyond dispute so far as the UN Convention was concerned, would raise the profile of the convention, would ensure that the principles were applied to all law, not just that enacted after the international obligation was entered into, and should be extensive enough to cover the exercise of statutory powers including the exercise of discretion. This would bring the convention into the arena of judicial review of administrative action.

Even if a Bill introduced on this basis did not complete the parliamentary process, any ministerial statements about the current status of the convention as an aid to interpretation could be used to further this cause. Any statements to the effect that the convention could not be so used would create a reaction which might show the need for legislation to make sure that we comply with this and other international obligations. So it would not be a wasted effort.

Report of the
National
Commission of
Inquiry into the
Prevention of
Child Abuse

*Report of the
National
Commission of
Inquiry into the
Prevention of
Child Abuse*

A Proper Children's Act

It is not just a question of what such an Act would cover, but how it is written and the systems and procedures which support it. It would have to:

○ be based on a clear set of principles rooted in the UN Convention on the Rights of the Child.

○ Be a clearly written Act which sets out what is expected of children and parents and what their rights are.

○ establish a unified system for resolving matters and making decisions, based on these principles.

○ establish procedures which are inquisitorial rather than adversarial.

○ be principled and consistent in its approach to representation of the views and interests of children.

○ ensure access to appropriate information is presented in a way the child can understand.

○ establish procedures for withholding or delaying access to information which protect the rights of the child.

○ establish clear rules on confidentiality which ensure children have ready access to confidential advice.

○ clarify the first step a child can make to have a problem addressed and make sure children and adults know about this.

Example

Part 1

Overarching principles.

Part 2

Rights of children.

Responsibilities of parents.

Access to information and advice.

Mediation.

Resolution of disputes.

Part 3

Support for children and families - local authority responsibilities.

Part 4

Compulsory intervention (including provision for child offenders).

Child protection.

Systems and procedures.

Part 5

Long term planning for children who cannot remain at home.

References

Report of the
National
Commission of
Inquiry into the
Prevention of
Child Abuse

1   *Children and Young Persons: Scotland* (1964) Cmnd 2306 (Report of the Kilbrandon Commission).

2   *Review of Child Care Law in Scotland* (1990) Edinburgh: HMSO.

3   *The Report of the Inquiry into the Removal of Children from Orkney in February 1991* (1992) Edinburgh: HMSO.

4   *Review of Adoption Law in Scotland* (1993) Edinburgh: Scottish Office.

5   *Report on Family Law* (1992) Edinburgh: HMSO.

6   Law Reform (Parent and Child) (Scotland) Act 1986, section 3(2).

7   Social Work (Scotland) Act 1968, section 43(1). The Children (Scotland) Act 1995, section 16 makes it "the paramount consideration" except in cases members of the public need protection from serious harm.

8   Adoption (Scotland) Act 1978, section6. The Children (Scotland) Act 1995, section 95 upgrades this to "the paramount consideration".

9   Child Protection in Scotland - Management Information, Scottish Office, 1992.

10   **All categories of abuse** - in certain circumstances, such as children with special needs (mental or physical disability) or children subject to supervision requirements, the upper age limit may be extended to 18.

11   An adult suffering from Munchausen's Syndrome characteristically presents themselves at hospitals with symptoms of physical disease and may have undergone many operations. They appear to seek the security and support of a medical environment. In Munchausen's Syndrome by Proxy, the adult uses the child to obtain medical attention by creating medical symptoms in the child, often induced by highly dangerous procedures (e.g., asphyxiation, poisoning) or ensuring that a series of invasive tests and/or operations are carried out on the child.

12   Section 1 of the 1995 Act defines parental responsibilities: "(a) to safeguard and promote the child's health, development and welfare; (b) to provide, in a manner appropriate to the stage of development of the child (I) direction; (ii) guidance, to the child; (c) if the child is not living with the parent, to maintain personal relations and direct contact with the child on a regular basis; and (d) to act as the child's legal representative.." Section 6 requires those making major decisions in the exercise of parental responsibility to have regard to the views of the child in accordance with age and maturity.

13   Education (Scotland) Act 1980, sections 57 and 58.

14   *One Scandal Too Many...the case for comprehensive protection for children in all settings;* Calouste Gulbenkian Foundation, London: 1993, Section 2.4, Rec. 1.

15   *The Report of the Inquiry into the Removal of Children form Orkney in February 1991,* (The Clyde Report), HMSO, Edinburgh: 1992, Para, 16.4.

16   *Ibid.,* Recommendations 168 to 178.

17   Social Work (Scotland) Act 1968, Section 37(1A).

18   *The Challenge of Partnership in Child Protection: Practice Guide,* Department of Health Social Services Inspectorate, HMSO, London, 1995.

19   UN Committee on the Rights of the Child, Ref. CRC/C/3/Add.1, para.40.

20   *The Children Act Advisory Committee Annual Report 1993/94,* The Lord Chancellor's Department, London, 1994.

261

*Report of the
National
Commission of
Inquiry into the
Prevention of
Child Abuse*

Appendix 11

The Impact of Legal Provisions, England and Wales (with Occasional Notes on Northern Ireland)

by Professor Christina M. Lyon, University of Liverpool

Contents

Report of the
National
Commission of
Inquiry into the
Prevention of
Child Abuse

*Report of the
National
Commission of
Inquiry into the
Prevention of
Child Abuse*

Introduction - Highlighting Some Issues

The aim of this paper is to consider the extent to which the law and the legal system in England and Wales contributes to, or impedes, the prevention of child abuse and neglect. It is intended first to highlight a number of issues which demonstrate perceived ambiguities, tensions and conflicts within both current and proposed legislation and within and between the civil and criminal justice systems in England and Wales. It is difficult to assess the situation in Northern Ireland since the Children (Northern Ireland) Order 1995 only comes into force in October 1996 but some notes are offered on the new Northern Ireland provisions.

Whilst the law can seek to set standards for the treatment of children and to enforce those standards through child care and criminal measures it is clear that if child abuse and neglect are to be prevented, as Marshall suggests, the standards set by such laws should be such as to achieve the desired level of protection of children, to be clear and comprehensible to everyone involved and to be respected by the whole of society. She then goes on to state that "in order to prevent child abuse and neglect, the standards must be adequate, clearly understood by all those involved, and respected".

One of the problems with the legal provisions which may be seen by parents, and more importantly by children, as relevant to the issue of the prevention of child abuse and neglect in England and Wales, is that no clear standards are actually laid down in primary or secondary legislation and the legal system itself conveys very mixed messages to parents and children.

a.   Physical Punishment of Children

A classic example of such a mixed message is to be found in the provisions relevant to the punishment of children, which may involve abusive techniques. As is noted later the Children and Young Persons Act 1933 states that the provision of the offence of cruelty committed by persons over 16 having the care of children if they wilfully cause or procure that child to suffer assault, ill treatment, neglect, abandonment or exposure in a manner to cause the child unnecessary suffering or injury to health in s1(1) *does not affect the right of any parent, teacher, or any other* person having the lawful control or charge of a child or young person *to administer punishment* to him (s1(7)CYPA 1933). The issue of the physical punishment of children is not addressed either expressly or implicitly in the Children Act 1989, although, it should be noted that guidance issued by the Department of Health following on the Children Act 1989 prohibited the use of corporal punishment in the form of smacking, both in nurseries and by childminders. This guidance has, however, been revised since the decision of the High Court, Family Division, in the London Borough of Sutton v Davies [1994] (1 FLR 737). In this case, the right of a parent to delegate the parental facility (as described by the court) to physical chastisement of a child was recognised as being capable of delegation to a childminder, and the court took the step of emphasising that the guidance issued by the Department of Health was merely "guidance" as to the factors to be borne in mind when determining the fitness of a childminder to act as such, and not binding as against the parental right to delegate their facility of punishment of a child. In this case it was implicitly acknowledged that the smacking of a two year old child constituted appropriate punishment . In recognition of the fact that the use of corporal punishment in schools sent out the wrong message to children and, in addition, that it was difficult to regulate and control, the Government outlawed the use of corporal punishment in relation to state funded schools or state funded pupils in private schools in 1986. (S47 Education [No.2] 1986). Nevertheless, the Government in seeking to respect parental choice in selecting private education which did allow corporal punishment was, as a result of cases taken before the European Court of Human Rights, forced into enacting a provision in S293 Education Act 1993 that any such corporal punishment, inflicted on privately funded pupils, could not be "inhuman or degrading". It is clear that the Government thinking on the issue of corporal punishment is muddled and confused. This also represents the feeling of many in society who find it difficult to reconcile the notion that hitting children in schools is wrong whilst hitting children in the home is right.

It should not be surprising if children and young people find it very difficult to reconcile the notion that acts which would be regarded as criminal assaults if committed on adults even within a family setting, are recognised by government and by the law as being an aspect of parental rights deserving of special protection.

b.   The Exercise of Parental Responsibility - Promoting Children's Welfare?

There are no legislative provisions in England and Wales or in Northern Ireland which lay down the standards of care which children in these jurisdictions might expect from their parents, nor importantly do they exist to guide or to educate parents themselves. This has to be contrasted with the guidance, albeit limited, issued to Scottish parents and children in the Children (Scotland) Act 1995. Thus, S 1 of the Children (Scotland) Act 1995 defines parental responsibilities as follows -

"(a) to safeguard and promote the child's health, development and welfare; (b) to provide, in a manner appropriate to the state of development of the child (i) direction; (ii) guidance to the child; (c) if the child is not living with the parent, to maintain personal relations and direct contact with the child on a regular basis; and (d) to act as the child's legal representative."

This provision gives a limited but nevertheless welcome positive direction with regard to the exercise of parents' responsibilities towards their children and, it should be noted, imposes upon them a duty to safeguard and promote the child's health, development and welfare. There is no such direction contained within the Children Act 1989 which applies to England and Wales, and which has been in operation since October 14 1991, nor in the Children (Northern Ireland) Order 1995, which comes into force in October 1996.

The critical question to be asked, however, is whether the right to assault one's child can seriously be included within the responsibility to safeguard and promote the child's health, development and welfare. The criminal law in England and Wales, as in Scotland, exempts punishment of children from the offence of cruelty to children provided, according to case law that the particular punishment is in some way commensurate with the child's alleged transgression and can in some sense therefore be deemed to be reasonable (see S1(7) CYPA 1933)but such a notion takes no account of the difficulty of assessing the harm caused by

265

Report of the
National
Commission of
Inquiry into the
Prevention of
Child Abuse

abusive punishment techniques. This problem is not limited to England and Wales and the failure of the various U.K. jurisdictions to ban physical punishment of children by their parents was the subject of serious criticism in the UN Monitoring Committee Report. Indeed, during one of the evidence sessions in January 1995 one member of the Monitoring Committee apparently observed that

> *"the U.K. position represented a vestige of the outdated view that children were in a sense their parent's chattel."*

(See Lansdowne G. Representing Children in Representing Children Vol.1 No.2 pp41-48 at page 46 [1995]).

Although it most assuredly was not their intention, the Law Commission's attempt to define parental responsibility as "including all the rights, duties, powers and responsibilities which by law the parent of a child has in relation to the child and his property" (see s3 [1] Children Act 1989) [implementation date October 14th 1991] has inevitably reinforced the notion of parental rights and powers over children casting them once again, therefore, as objects in terms of the exercise of parental rights and powers (this came especially to the fore in London Borough of Sutton v Davies - see above).

c.   The Problem of System Abuse of Abused Children

Since no positive duty is laid upon parents nor do any statutory guidelines exist in the legislation of the other United Kingdom jurisdictions comparable to those laid down in the Scottish legislation, it is, therefore, the case that a negative issue takes precedence, and that emphasis is laid on the fact that civil child protection proceedings will be instituted if the child is suspected of suffering , or is actually suffering from, significant harm . Criminal proceedings may also be instituted arising out of the same facts if, for example, chastisement has gone beyond what may be deemed to be "reasonable" or an offence has been committed generally under various provisions of Offences Against the Persons Act 1861 (usually under the terms of s47, s39, s20 or s18 and where sexual abuse is suspected under the provisions of the Sexual Offences Act 1956 as amended) but only if the Police and the Crown Prosecution Service are satisfied that there is admissible, substantial and reliable evidence that a criminal offence known to the law has been committed by an identifiable person. As is made plain by the Code for Crown Prosecutors (Crown Prosecution Service, January 1992) a bare prima face case is not enough, the Service must apply the test of whether there is a realistic prospect of a conviction. Thus, in relation to children, the inevitable question has to be asked as to whether a child witness is going to be both a credible and reliable witness?. Will the child stand up to rigorous cross-examination by barristers for the defence? Despite much increased police involvement in child abuse investigations, research studies, as well as anecdotal evidence, suggest that successful prosecutions are rare. For example, Moran Ellis et al "Investigation of Child Sexual Abuse : An Executive Summary", (University of Surrey 1991), revealed prosecution rates of 12% and 7% in sexual abuse cases at two respective research sites, and Creighton's study in 1992 reported that criminal proceedings occurred in 17% of the registered sexual abuse cases of a sample of 1732 and significantly perhaps, in 9% of the sample of 2,786 physical abuse cases in the period 1988 to 1990, (see Creighton, S (1992) "Child Abuse Trends in England and Wales 1988 to 1990". London: NSPCC. Research by Plotnikoff and Wolfson (1995) entitled "Prosecuting Child Abuse, An

Report of the
National
Commission of
Inquiry into the
Prevention of
Child Abuse

Evaluation of the Government's Speedy Progress Policy", following Government statements in 1988 that child abuse prosecutions would be speeded up, has sadly shown that they take much longer than the national average to reach disposition, which in turn means there is greater scope for the criminal justice system itself in England and Wales being laid open to the charge of being iatrogenic.

Once the case is within the criminal justice system the dynamics of adversarial criminal trials demand that the defence lawyers seek to undermine the credibility of child witnesses, label them as liars and constantly belittle them.

The low conviction rates achieved send out further mixed messages to children who have plucked up the courage to speak out and the links between the civil child protection and criminal adult prosecution processes may ultimately result, in some cases, in the child being returned to the abusive household.

d. The Issue of Emotional Abuse

Thus far, this introduction has tended to concentrate on concerns about potential physical and sexual abuse although in the context of domestic violence, emotional abuse of the children may well be a cause for extreme concern amongst child welfare professionals. The issue of emotional abuse defined by the Department of Health guidance document "Working Together" (DOH 1991 P49) as "actual or likely severe adverse effects on the emotional and behavioural development of a child caused by persistent or severe emotional ill treatment or rejection", is much more difficult to assess and discuss in terms of the impact of the law and the legal system. The fact that in England and Wales children are not perceived by law as having a voice or any kind of say within their families or within the educational system in which they spend the bulk of their childhood means that there is considerable scope for emotional abuse within families and schools, such that many children may potentially suffer from emotional abuse and see no way in which they can sensibly complain given the lack of outward manifestation of such abuse. We remain within the legal system, unconvinced that children are not objects but are people. As children themselves have put it

267

> "How can I complain when there are no marks which can be seen. The hurt is inside. I feel like I am nothing - when you say that out loud to someone it is almost like admitting you're nothing. After all if your mum and dad think you're nothing, you are nothing."

> "You just can't imagine how I feel when he (the young person's teacher) keeps shouting at me all day that I am useless, stupid and good for nothing. I can't help it if I have missed so much school that there are huge gaps in what I know and I feel really stupid having to ask all the time, but he doesn't realise he makes me feel so stupid that now I think I am. I can't bear to be in school, I just want to be out away from him but where is that going to leave me when I leave school - out there on the scrap heap that's where."

e. The Issue of "Neglect"

The concept of neglect is also extremely difficult although it does span both civil and

Report of the
National
Commission of
Inquiry into the
Prevention of
Child Abuse

criminal law provision in England and Wales either implicitly as is the case with s31 Children Act 1989 or expressly under criminal law provision such as s1 Children and Young Persons Act 1933. Section 31 Children Act 1989 does not expressly mention neglect in its definition of harm and whilst s1 (1) of the Child and Young Persons Act 1933 does expressly use the term 'neglect', this is nowhere defined.

Neglect is clearly a very emotive term but from both anecdotal evidence and documentary evidence from the Department of Health Children Act Reports in successive years, it would appear that neglect is being positively identified as a steadily growing category by reference to which children are entered on local authority Child Protection Registers (see Children Act Reports 1992, 1993 and 1994 - Department of Health HMSO).

f.   The Problem of Domestic Violence

Another area where both civil and criminal systems should unite to the benefit of victims is that of domestic violence. Such is not always or even in the main, however, the case. Perceived primarily even today as a problem for mothers or women to solve by accessing relevant procedures in the civil law, the legal system in England and Wales helps to privatise the situation and to hide what may be real problems for children in violent households behind the mask of so-called "protective" orders such as non-molestation injunctions and ouster orders. Under current legislation only the adult partners can apply for the orders or injunctions, which provide short term relief with, in the majority of cases, perpetrators returning fairly swiftly into their households. Whilst provisions, in the Children Act 1989 (s37) enable courts in England and Wales to direct enquiries to be conducted by local authorities where concerns about children arise in domestic violence applications, there is little or no evidence of judges making use of this power. Part of the problem may be that its availability for use in such situations is not expressly described in the legislation. Thus the s37 power is utilised infrequently and generally in those circumstances involving concerns over disputed private arrangements concerning the residence and contact with children of the parties to the proceedings.

g.   The Impact of the New Divorce Law Reforms

The Family Law Bill as it was originally presented to Parliament contained few provisions focusing on the needs of children caught up in the divorce process and yet most would argue that children are the main casualties of their parents' divorces. The reason for this omission was stated to be due to the fact that the 1989 Act deals with the problems of children and the Bill was supposed to be concentrated on the process of divorce. Such an approach, however, ignored the gaps which have been revealed in the process since the enactment of the 1989 Act.

Amendments providing that the cooling off period is extended from 12 months to 18 months where the parties have children, took no account of those situations in which children may be at risk of further emotional, physical and even sexual abuse if in some way their parents are forced to stay together ostensibly for the children's benefit. Divorce is anyway described by all children as upsetting and traumatic and to prolong the agony is no answer to their problems arising from divorce. The Lord Chancellor suggested when such amendments were being moved by Baroness Young and Lady Olga Maitland that twelve months is a very

*Report of the
National
Commission of
Inquiry into the
Prevention of
Child Abuse*

long time in a child's perception of time and eighteen months is far too long, but such statements were ignored and for children and their parents the period is 18 months (Family Law Act 1996, s7).What is needed to protect children again from abuse by the system, as well as to protect them from potential abuse by their parents, is to extend to them opportunities for information, consultation and representation. All parties in care proceedings in England and Wales, including children, are represented because it is recognised that children are the main party affected. Children affected by parental divorce or relationship breakdown are also principally the parties affected.

To prolong a cooling off period, where a parent and possibly also the children have been physically or emotionally abused or perhaps even sexually abused, is to prolong the torture for the children without giving them any voice or ability to complain. In other more straightforward situations, it is true that for many agreements between parents amicably reached may be the best solution and one can acknowledge the system's reluctance to admit interference within the realm of private family arrangements. But English Law does not provide for the child to be informed or consulted unlike Scottish Law (see Children [Scotland] Act 1995 s6) and the child will only be represented if they initiate proceedings themselves or the level of concern for them is so great that the court invites the Official Solicitor to represent them.

Children telephoning children's charities such as IRCHIN and Childline and young people at Seminars in the Centre for the Study of the Child, the Family and the Law have repeatedly protested against the damage being done to their lives by the contact and residence arrangements reached by their parents with such obvious disregard for the social welfare and social development of their children. This, in itself, arguably constitutes another form of abuse in that it comes within the terms of impairment of development as laid down in s31 of the 1989 Act. (see s31 [9] [10]).

There are so many problems with the provisions of English Law and the English Legal System that it is probably appropriate at this stage to set out the relevant legal provisions which impact upon attempts to prevent child abuse and neglect within this jurisdiction.

2.   The Legal System in England and Wales (with notes on Northern Ireland)

The principal piece of civil legislation in England and Wales relevant to child abuse and neglect is the Children Act 1989, as amended, (referred to hereafter as the 1989 Act). This piece of legislation contains provisions relating to the important issues of parental responsibility, the duties of others having the care of children, the duties of local authorities in relation to the support of children and their families, and to compulsory measures of child protection. (This legislation has now been mirrored in Northern Ireland by the enactment of The Children (Northern Ireland) Order 1995 S.I.1995 No 755 (N.I.2)).

The 1989 Act, its consequent court rules and innumerable sets of regulations achieved a number of crucially important objectives. The Act was based on proposals made by the Law Commission in its Report - Law Commission No.172: Family Law, Review of Child Law, Guardianship and Custody, which are largely contained in Part I and Part II of the Act

Report of the
National
Commission of
Inquiry into the
Prevention of
Child Abuse

published in 1988, and upon the DHSS review of Child Care Law published in 1985 and followed by a Government White Paper entitled "The Law on Child Care and Family Services" published in January 1987 which together formed the basis for Parts III to XII of the 1989 Act.

The 1989 Act was intended to be, and has been, a radical overhaul of much of the civil law relating to children in their families and the only sphere of law relating to this area omitted was that of adoption. Reform of the English Law of Adoption is, in some people's minds, long overdue and again there have been extremely detailed reports relating to the reform of the law in the form of the inter-departmental review of Adoption Law 1990/1991 and a Government White Paper on the Reform of Adoption Law published in November 1993. A further Consultation Paper was issued in April 1995 and the Department of Health released an Adoption Bill for consultation and response by July 1996.

A major effect of the Children Act 1989 has not only been to go a long way towards achieving a unified system of the substantive civil law relating to children in their families in England and Wales, but also to establish the system within a unified courts structure. (CA 1989's 92 and Sch.11). Pursuant to the establishment of this unified jurisdiction, cases whether of a public law or private law nature, can be heard by the magistrates family proceedings courts at magistrates court level, by designated family hearing or care centre county courts, at county court level, and by Family Division Judges at High Court level. (Children [Allocation of Proceedings]) Order 1991) as amended). The unification of much of the civil law within this statute, therefore, means that provisions on parental responsibility, local authority support for children in families and compulsory intervention in families in order to protect children, as well as compulsory intervention in other institutional settings, are all brought together under the umbrella of one statute.

The 1989 Act contains no provisions relating to criminal law other than the abolition of what was known as the criminal care order (a care order made in criminal proceedings where a juvenile was found guilty of a criminal offence and committed to the care of the local authority and whose practical consequences were, therefore, the same for the juvenile offender as they were for the child victim of physical or sexual abuse). Thus, under the 1989 Act, the criminal care order was abolished and the provisions with regard to the making of supervision orders in criminal proceedings were also abolished. (see CA 1989 s90 (I and II).

In addition to the preparatory work of the Law Commission, the DHSS review of Child Care Law and the DHSS White Paper, the other major events which had an influence on shaping the provisions of the Children Act 1989 included the Cleveland Inquiry (see Report of the Inquiry into Child Abuse in Cleveland 1987 [1988 HMSO], (the "Cleveland Report") and the events surrounding Pindown. (See The Pindown Experience and the Protection of Children: The Report of the Staffordshire Child Care Inquiry (1991, Staffordshire Social Services)).

Whilst the 1989 Act thus contains a mixture of private law and public law provisions relating to children and parents generally and their relationships with the State in the form of local authorities, it does not achieve either what many parents had desired out of such a piece of legislation nor what many children expected when hearing about the Act for the first time. Thus, where parents were told that the Act contained provisions on parental responsibility, many expected a list of such responsibilities and where children thought to find a piece of legislation setting out clear rules and principles mirroring those contained in the UN Convention on the Rights of the Child, they found almost nothing which could be compared with that document.

The 1989 Act has now been in force for nearly five years in England and Wales and has had the type of "life experience" not matched by any other modern piece of legislation. Implementation of the Act was postponed until after the enactment of a great many court rules and regulations governing the conduct of local authorities and also until after comprehensive training had been provided to all professionals, including the judiciary up to the level of the Court of Appeal, which was totally unprecedented and had never before happened. All professionals from across the board, whether involved in private law, or public law provisions, submitted themselves for training and the Government announced a series of research initiatives which would monitor the implementation of the Act and its effects in its first few years. (see Department of Health Children Act Report 1992 Chapter 10 [DOH 1993 HMSO]).

Also unprecedented was the series of guidance issued by the Department of Health to all professionals involved with children in the different areas covered by the 1989 Act. These volumes of guidance were issued under Section 7 of the Local Authority Social Services Act 1970 which requires local authorities in the exercise of their social services functions to act under the general guidance of the Secretary of State. This guidance to the Act and the attendant regulations ran in all to some twelve volumes including the two introductory volumes entitled "The Care of Children - Principles and Practice in Regulations and Guidance", and "An Introduction to the Children Act 1989".

Volume 1 covered Court Orders, Volume 2 - Family Support, Day Care and Education Provision for Young Children, Volume 3 - Family Placements, Volume 4 - Residential Care, Volume 5 - Children in Independent Schools, Volume 6 - Children with Disabilities, Volume 7 - Guardians ad Litem and other court related issues, Volume 8 - Private Fostering and Miscellaneous, Volume 9 - Adoption Issues and Volume 10 - General Issues and Index. In total the volumes stretched to five and a half inches on concerned professionals' book shelves and, in addition, in the crucial area of child protection a special document entitled "Working Together - a guide to arrangements for inter-agency co-operation for the protection of children from abuse" was also issued. (Home Office, DOH, DES and Welsh Office 1991 HMSO). Specialist guidance was also produced by the Department of Health for senior nurses, health visitors and mid-wives entitled "Child Protection" (DOH [1992] HMSO)and a guide for all National Health Service personnel entitled An Introductory Guide to the Children Act 1989 (DOH [1991] HMSO) was also published.

Many professionals felt subject to information overload and the anxieties caused by such a huge amount of guidance taken together with intensive periods of training meant that by the date of the coming into force of the Act on the 14th October 1991, everyone was almost literally holding their breath. Professionals were so uncertain about how to interpret the new provisions that there was indeed at least a six months lull with very few cases being brought to court and with the judges worrying constantly that the new principles laid down

Report of the
National
Commission of
Inquiry into the
Prevention of
Child Abuse

*Report of the
National
Commission of
Inquiry into the
Prevention of
Child Abuse*

in the statute, principally the emphasis on working in partnership with parents and trying to ensure that children stayed with their families as much as possible, had meant that social workers were reluctant to intervene to protect children from potential abuse and neglect.

3.   The Basic Principles

In the period between November 1989 when the 1989 Act was originally passed and the date of implementation in October 1991, the author, in common with many others, did a massive amount of training on the 1989 Act. In devising training on the 1989 Act I came up with what I referred to as the "six P's" in relation to the basic principles in the Children Act. These "six P's" were as follows -

Paramountcy of the child's welfare - at least in relation to proceedings involving any questions concerning the custody and upbringing of the child, s1 of the 1989 Act provides that the child's welfare shall be the court's paramount consideration when reaching any decision. This principle applies both to decisions made in disputes between parents or between parents and the state (viz.Child protection proceedings where the local authority intervenes to protect children at risk from their own families). (See also Article 3 The Children (Northern Ireland) Order 1995).

272

Parental responsibility - s2 of the Act provides that married parents share equally parental responsibility for their children. (See Article 5 The children (Northern Ireland) Order 1995). In the case of unmarried parents the mother automatically has parental responsibility but the unmarried father must either reach a formal witnessed agreement registered with the Principal Registry of the Family Division in London and referred to as a parental responsibility agreement or may apply for a Court Order for parental responsibility under s4 1989 Act. (See article The Children (Northern Ireland) Order 1995).

The 1989 Act puts a great deal of emphasis on the notion of parental responsibility but fails to define it properly, providing only in s3 (i) that parental responsibility includes all the rights, duties, powers and responsibilities which by law the parents of a child have in relation to the child and his property. (Article 6 of The Children (Northern Ireland) Order 1995 provides a comparable provision in 6(1) but goes on to delineate in greater detail rights and duties in relation to the child's property (see 6(2) and (3)).

Partnership between Parents - the Act is predicated on the basis that parents will not only possess parental responsibility but will exercise that responsibility responsibly.(See J. Eekelaar, Parental Responsibility: State of Nature or Nature of the State [1991] J.S.W.F.L. 37-50) It presumes that on divorce or relationship breakdown, parents would continue to act responsibly and would not seek to subject their children to court proceedings except in the most extreme circumstances.

It, therefore, works on the basis that parents should reach agreements about what happens to their children on divorce or relationship breakdown, who they are to live with and with whom they are to have contact.It assumes that parents will work together even though they no longer live together to ensure that arrangements made for their children will work out to the best effect but imposes no obligation upon parents to inform, consult with, and take into

*Report of the
National
Commission of
Inquiry into the
Prevention of
Child Abuse*

account the views of, their children when making such arrangements (unlike the Children [Scotland] Act 1995 s6) The notion of partnership and parents, however, is not only linked to partnership between each of two parents but also links in with the notion of partnership between parents and the State where necessary to support the continued placement of the child within its own natural family.

Provision of support to families by local authorities - s17 of the 1989 Act provides that it shall be the general duty of every local authority to safeguard and promote the welfare of children within their area who are in need and so far as is consistent with that duty to promote the upbringing of such children by their families, by providing a range and level of services appropriate to those children's needs. As will be seen later this provision can be widely interpreted and is more specifically enhanced by provisions set out in Part 1 of Schedule 2 of the Act. Specifically, of course, these provisions in the Act can be linked to the issue of prevention of child abuse and neglect and this will be further examined later. (See Pt.4). (Compare with Article 18 and Schedule 2 The Children (Northern Ireland) Order 1995 which makes broadly similar provision).

Protection - Pts IV to XII of the Act are then concerned with the important principle of protecting children in whatever environment they are being looked after, whether this be by their parents or relatives in their families, in local authority community homes, in homes provided by voluntary organisations or private individuals, in private fostering arrangements, in child minding and day care provision, and in accommodation provided by health authorities residential care homes or independent schools. This is by far the greater body of the Act and contains a great deal with regard to the protection of children which is further expanded upon in the detailed volumes of guidance on the Act referred to earlier. (See Parts V and XI and Part XIII of the Children (Northern Ireland) Order 1995 for similar provision hereafter cited as the N.I. Order 1995).

273

Procedures - the last important principle upon which the Act is predicated is that procedures will all work towards the recognition of the paramountcy of children's interests. Thus, under s1 (2), delay is presumed to be prejudicial to children (see Art 3(2) N.I. Order) 1995) and special procedures are introduced in s11 (see Art 11 N.I Order 1995) and s32 (see Art 51 N.I. Order 1995) whereby the court can set its own timetables for proceedings involving children. Despite these provisions, however, it has become apparent that after an early lull in proceedings being taken under the Children Act, the volume of activity in the court is such that delay is almost back to pre-1989 Act levels and is now the subject of a research project funded by the Lord Chancellor's Department and led by Visiting Professor Dame Margaret Booth of the Centre for the Study of the Child, the Family and the Law at the University of Liverpool - Faculty of Law. For Dame Margaret Booth's preliminary findings on delay in children's cases see Delay in Public Law Children Act Cases in Representing Children Volume 1 No.4 pp 41 - 48.

In the U.K.'s First Report to the UN Committee on the Rights of the Child, the United Kingdom Government claimed that

> *"So far as the law on the care and upbringing of children in England and Wales was concerned we have in the Children Act 1989, legislation which clearly reflects the principle of the Convention. It brings together in one statute both the public and the*

Report of the
National
Commission of
Inquiry into the
Prevention of
Child Abuse

private law. It makes clear that, except on adoption, parents never lose responsibility
for their children. It seeks to ensure that the welfare of the child is the paramount

consideration when arrangements are being made for the care of children following
divorce or separation of the parents and that the child's wishes are taken into
account. This is an important safeguard for an increasing number of children where
the divorce rate has been rising in the U.K.

The Act recognises that whenever possible children are best brought up by their
parents in their own home. It places a duty on local authorities to provide services for
children in need to held parents bring up their children. When it is necessary for
courts and local authorities to intervene in children's lives they are required to have
the child's welfare as their first consideration. A local authority looking after a child
has a duty to plan effectively for the child and to keep the plan under review to ensure
the child's best interests are served.The Act provides for the regulation of foster
placements and for the registration and inspection of children's homes and day care
provision so that when children are away from their parents their welfare can be
safeguarded." (p2)

It is apparent from this report that the United Kingdom Government was clearly of the view
that the set of minimum standards for the rights of children as contained in the UN
Convention of the Rights of the Child, was being met in full by the provisions of the
Children Act 1989. One can immediately highlight the fact, however, that children's wishes
in divorce arrangements only have to be taken into account in cases which are disputed.
Now that the vast majority of cases are dealt with on paper, it is unlikely that the welfare
checklist can really be applied and consideration given to the wishes and feelings of children
who are never seen and whose parents may report them as being happy with arrangements
when this is far from being the case.

Marshall notes on page 4 of her paper that the Children (Scotland) Act 1995 is said to be
based on a number of principles derived from the Convention and she there sets them out.
She notes in relation to the 1995 Act in Scotland, which is also the case with the 1989 Act in
England and Wales, that there may be a tension between the child's right to protection and
the strong emphasis on the position of parents which is supported by a high level of
formality in the processes of compulsory intervention. Nevertheless, as she notes these
approaches are consistent with the presumptions of the UN Convention that children are
best brought up by their families.Marshall states that in practice, that there are some fears in
Scotland that new provisions of the 1995 Act, in their eagerness to respect formal and legal
family rights, may work to the disadvantage of children - and possibly of some
parents.Many professionals working in England and Wales including a large number of the
judiciary have voiced the concern that this is precisely what has happened in the years since
the implementation of the Children Act 1989. There is still considerable concern about cases
of child abuse and neglect in which social services may be unable to act or unaware of the
necessity to act due to a starvation of resources and to a concentration on other avenues of
activity with regard to family support. Despite proclamations by several of the tabloid
newspapers, the Department of Health publication "Child Protection - Messages from
Research" (DOH 1995 HMSO) does not actually convey the message that social workers
are intervening unnecessarily to protect children but rather in several places highlights the

fact that there are many serious cases of child abuse where intervention is both urgently needed and which, for a variety of reasons, may not be practised.

Whilst this initial position paper concentrates primarily on the legislative provisions and system applicable in the jurisdiction of England and Wales it has been noted - in passing - that in Northern Ireland the civil law relating to children has been revised to bring it broadly into line with the position in England and Wales under the Children Act 1989. This has been achieved as indicated by The Children (Northern Ireland) Order 1995 SI 1995 No.755 (N.I. 2). Thus far commencement orders have brought a number of provisions into force in Northern Ireland with the remainder being implemented in October 1996, and in order to ease the position of child witnesses in criminal proceedings in Northern Ireland provisions have now been made comparable to those contained within the Criminal Justice Act 1988 and 1991 of England and Wales. (See later Pt.13) This has been done through the Children's Evidence (Northern Ireland) Order 1995 (SI 1995 No.757 (N.I.3).

The remainder of this Paper will consider a number of the relevant civil and criminal law provisions in England and Wales. It will go on to consider issues relating to the identification, reporting, investigation, and legal process in relation to child abuse and neglect, and will finally return to focus on the specific areas of concern highlighted in the Introduction.

275

4. Current Law on Prevention

Current Law on Prevention	Critique	Recommendations
S17 of the Children Act 1989. Under this provision local authorities, effectively through their social services department, are placed under a very wide duty "to safeguard and promote the welfare of children within their area who are in need and so far as is consistent with that duty, to promote the upbringing of such children by their families by providing a range and level of services appropriate to those children's needs".	Very general and very widely drawn. See for more detail on this Pt 11 of this document. The use of the word appropriate leaves it to local authorities to determine the range and level of services which are appropriate to children's needs. The problem with this is that no entitlement to services is identified and all the evidence has shown (see Children Act Reports 1992 onwards [DOH]) that most local authorities have been forced, in consequence of a shortage of resources, to focus on safeguarding children's welfare. Thus most effort has gone into dealing with families who are already causing concern to social services and where some abuse or neglect has already taken place.	Local authorities have now been required to produce their Children's Services Plans and, as a result of the messages emerging from Child Protection – Messages from Research (DOH 1995) it would appear that local authorities will be focusing more attention on providing support services generally into families of children in need rather than allegedly focusing on crisis management, highly expensive, complex and fraught child abuse investigations and unnecessary court proceedings.

The questions that need to be considered here are both whether the right message has been taken from Child Protection – Messages from Research and whether this is an attempt to divert attention from the most pressing issue and that is the question of the proper resourcing of all family support and child protection work undertaken by local authority social services. |
| S17 (2) of the 1989 Act goes on to provide that for the purpose of facilitating the discharge of their general duties under S17 , local authorities must have specific regard to their duties and powers set out in Sch.2 , Pt.I 1989 Act. | The powers and duties set out in Sch 2 Pt1 are very extensive but are frequently drawn by reference to words of discretion such as what is reasonable or appropriate . e.g Sch 2 Part 1 paragraphs 1(1); 1(2)(a)(ii); 4(1); 7; 8; 9(1); 10. | |

Current Law on Prevention	Critique	Recommendations
Sch.2 Pt.1 para 1 Under this provision, local authorities are required "to take reasonable steps to identify the extent to which there are children in need within their area", and it is further provided that local authorities must publish information about services provided by them and by voluntary organisations", and must "take such steps as are reasonably practicable to ensure that those who might benefit from the services receive the information relevant to them".	Each of the successive Children Act Reports produced by the Department of Health have identified a varying degree of compliance with this requirement by local authority social services departments. Some publish extremely useful information leaflets setting out details of those children who may be regarded as being in need and what services are available to support their families. Others have not produced such leaflets. Even where they have been produced, there has been a failure to distribute them widely to those people who might have the need of, or might benefit from, the services being provided and thus there is considerable criticism about the whole process. (See Part 11) It is hoped that the requirement to produce children's services plans imposed now upon all local authorities will result in greater information being made available. Thus far, however, children's services plans have tended to be deposited in public offices such as libraries and Town Halls and most people in need of such services do not necessarily have the time to visit such offices.	Again, subject to proper resourcing, local authorities should make the information on services to children more widely available. This begs the question, however, as to whether there are the relevant services to be made available to such children in need and of such a type and quality as to prevent the risk of child abuse and neglect. There is also an important question as to the difference between what exists on paper and what can be offered when the pressure to gate keep available resources is so strong. Field workers often report that managers concerned with budgets prevent their being able to offer the necessary support.

277

Current Law on Prevention	Critique	Recommendations
Sch.2 Pt.1 para 4 . This provision is a rather more positive requirement that every local authority shall take reasonable steps through the provision of services under Pt.III of this Act, to prevent children within their area suffering ill treatment or neglect".	The difficulty here lies in interpreting what are reasonable steps and what services should be provided as part of such steps.	Specific guidelines should be provided as to what might constitute the reasonable steps to be satisfied and what services might be provided as a reasonable response".
(Para.4 [2]) The provision goes on to place on local authorities a duty to inform another local authority if it is understood that the child's family will be moving to the area of the other authority. It further requires the notifying local authority to specify to the receiving local authority the harm they believe the child is likely to suffer and, if they are able, where the child lives or proposes to live.	This type of requirement was felt to be a necessary insertion into the Act in order to try to deal with the sorts of problems raised by the Kimberly Carlile Inquiry. Evidence available from the Department of Health Reports on the Children Act would tend to suggest that local authorities find this provision to be working well and to be useful. The difficulty is the demand on scarce resources which results from attempted compliance with this requirement. Inevitably personnel have to be used to process and transfer delicate information which means less time for other work.	As the demand for more transfer of information increases, and the possibility that more information will be stored on registers in respect of certain individuals, it is self evident that centrally provided resources are necessary. Local authority social services budgets are being reduced all the time, not expanded and these services simply cannot be provided by L.A.s without removing other critical and essential services.
Sch.2 para 7 Provides further reinforcement of local authority's duty to safeguard by requiring them to take reasonable steps designed to reduce the need to bring care or supervision order proceedings with respect to children in a local authority's area .	Methods by which L.A.s establish which children require safeguarding services depend upon the measures for inter-agency collaboration in the identification process laid down by local Area Child Protection Committees pursuant to the guidance provided in Working Together (1991, DOH).	"Working Together" points out that "co-operation at the individual case level needs to be supported by joint agency and management policies for child protection, consistent with their policies and plans for related service provision". (at Ch.2.4) Coherent prevention policies and plans are, therefore, necessary if L.A's are to take seriously their duty to safeguard children within their area.

278

Current Law on Prevention	Critique	Recommendations
To emphasise the point that children who abuse are, potentially, equally to be viewed as "children in need" as are those children who are abused, the L.A is also required to take "reasonable steps designed to reduce the need to bring criminal proceedings against children within its area and to take reasonable steps to encourage children within its area *not* to commit criminal offences". (Para.7 [a] (ii) and 7 [b]).	This is an area where if one talks to anyone in Social Services one will be told that this is the first target for cuts because, politically, "helping troublesome kids is not popular", it is "not a vote catcher".	Again the major difficulty here is with regard to the available resources to achieve the goal of prevention. L.A.s need to devote not only more attention to prioritising resources in the direction of preventive services but also require the necessary resources from central government to do so.
It is important to recognise that the duties of **safeguarding, supporting** and **prevention** are linked to the definition of a "child in need". S.17 (10) – Under this section a child is taken to be in need if: • "the child is unlikely to achieve or maintain, or to have the opportunity of achieving or maintaining a reasonable standard of health or development without the provision for him/her of services by the local authority; • the child's health or development is likely to be significantly impaired or further impaired without the provision for him of such services; the child is disabled" S17 (11) further expands the definition of the child in need by reference to the concept of health, development and disability. • " 'development' means physical, intellectual, emotional, social or behavioural development; 'health' means physical or mental health; and, • a child is described as "disabled" where he is blind, deaf or dumb or suffers from a mental disorder of any kind or is substantially and permanently handicapped by illness, injury or congenital deformity or such other disability as may be prescribed".	In many parts of England and Wales, L.A.s have expanded upon the definition of "child in need" and have produced their own "children in need" documents which contain information about services available. It should be noted that preventive work has now been elevated by the 1989 Act to the top of local authorities' child protection agendas. This should, therefore, mean that the provision of day nursery places, playgroup places, childminding facilities, family aids, family centres, respite care, short holidays and access to various educational and health facilities (all of which services are envisaged by Pt.III of the 1989 Act and Sch.2 Pt.2) will all have been considered, and some will have been used, before resort is made to legal action through such means as care proceedings. Yet again, however, managers within local authorities, who are essentially seen as the gatekeepers of local authority social services resources, constantly have to emphasise to field social workers that budgets are severely cash limited, services must be carefully rationed,	Greater consideration needs to be given to the proper and adequate resourcing of local authorities by Central Government if the goal of prevention of child abuse and neglect is to be realised. Examples of good practice occurring where pressure on local authority resources meant that developments could not take place which required actual funding have prompted some social workers to devise micro-level services plans in collaboration with voluntary organisations, parents, schools and other organisations working within the local community. These micro-level services plans which require the drawing of a "map" of services in the area could be replicated more generally but require a considerable input of resources in human terms from the local authority social workers in a particular area. In many areas this is not possible within LA budgets because of the pressure to provide "firefighting support".

279

Current Law on Prevention	Critique	Recommendations
	and thus priority tends to be given to what is generally known as firefighting support . In some areas, it is undoubtedly the case, that practical support meets the theoretical requirements of the statute but in many areas the shortage of resources and the constant requirement every year to cut back in annual social services budgets means that the aims of the Act cannot be achieved.	Central government, therefore, has to face the important question of the proper resourcing of the legislative duties imposed by the Children Act 1989. There is a vital question to be answered by the public as a whole in England and Wales as to the type of society in which they, as a body of people, wish to live. "Services" for children in need are not and should not be just about prevention work for children in need in families with obvious difficulties, but a truly supportive children and young people in their families and in the community policy. The lack of such a policy can be witnessed in all areas of society in 1996, and a strong line backed up by proper resources now needs to be taken, if we are to meet the challenges of a new century as a united society.

Current Law on Prevention	Critique	Recommendations
S20 1989 Act provides, that as part of the services which can be offered to children in need and their families, local authorities should provide accommodation for a child in need where— • there is no person with parental responsibility for him • he is lost or has been abandoned • or the person who has been caring for him is prevented (whether or not permanently, and for whatever reason) from providing him with suitable accommodation or care. S20 (4) states that a "local authority may provide accommodation for any child within their area, even though a person who has parental responsibility for him is able to provide him with accommodation, if they consider that to do so would safeguard or promote the child's welfare". S20 (6) requires that "before providing accommodation a local authority must, so far as reasonably practicable and consistent with the child's welfare— • ascertain the child's wishes regarding the provision of accommodation and give due consideration (having regard to his age and understanding) to such wishes of the child as they have been able to ascertain and the local authority may not provide accommodation if any person who— • has parental responsibility for him and is willing and able to provide accommodation for him or arrange accommodation to be produced for him • objects".	These provisions were intended to underline the general principles implicit in the Act that LAs would work together with parents in partnership in order to ensure the best outcomes for their children. All the guidance produced for social workers and other professionals in the context of child abuse stressed that, wherever it is possible to promote and protect the welfare of the child by leaving him in his family, this approach is to be preferred to damaging and possibly unnecessary removal (see Protecting Children : A Guide for Social Workers Undertaking a Comprehensive Assessment [1988, DOH]; The Care of Children – Principles and Practice in Regulations and Guidance [1989 HMSO at Ch.2 paras 5,6,7,8;] It should be noted, however, that if a local authority cannot persuade the parents to allow the children to come into accommodation provided by the local authority in a child protection situation, then if the local authority feels there is no other way of protecting the child or children it will be forced to consider compulsory child protection proceedings under Pt. V of the 1989 Act.	These provisions appear to be working well when one looks at the steady fall of the numbers of children being looked after since implementation of the 1989 Act but the DOH has recognised (see Children Act 1989 Report [1993 DOH] that those children who are now in the residential care of the local authority, include a higher concentration of the most difficult cases. A large proportion of children who are provided with accommodation by the local authority are looked after by the local authority for short episodes and many of these are placed with foster parents. It has been recognised by local authorities that where they have children who are being provided with accommodation by them in the long term, then consideration should be given to what special needs such children will have. Whilst the DOH has recognised that these may be the more difficult children there has been little recognition that **more financial support** must be given to local authorities in order to support the increasing expenditure by them on providing for difficult children in residential care. In reality, local authority provision for children's residential care has repeatedly been subject to cuts in resources with the consequent disasters in terms of child abuse controversies centred on children's residential care in England and Wales.

281

Current Law on Prevention	Critique	Recommendations
S22 of the 1989 Act provides for the general duties of local authorities in relation to any children being looked after by them. In particular it requires the local authority, "before making any decision with respect to a child whom they are looking after, or proposing to look after, it shall so far as it is reasonably practicable ascertain the wishes and feelings of– • his parent's any person who is not a parent of his but who has parental responsibility for him; and • any other person whose wishes and feelings the authority considers to be relevant, regarding these matter to be decided" (**S22 [4]**).	The clear intention of these requirements is to ensure that children and their families and other people, who might be relevant in terms of possibly being able to offer accommodation to the child, will be widely consulted **before** a child is provided with accommodation by the local authority, **and,** that where a child is being looked after subsequent to agreement reached with such other relevant people or as a result of a care order, then appropriate consultation takes place in respect of decisions taken by the local authority.	Consideration should be given to the extent to which research studies could be undertaken, concentrating on children's experience of the admission to the accommodation process and the treatment they are given in accordance with the requirements of S22 and the relevant Review Regulations. There is already research evidence indicating that children feel they do not have a voice in the reviews of their cases. Their perspective on the admissions process and their view of the protection offered by the provision of accommodation would be extremely informative.

Current Law on Prevention	Critique	Recommendations
It is further provided in **S22 (5)** that in making any such decision the local authority must give due consideration– • having regard to his age and understanding, to such wishes and feelings of the child as they have been able to ascertain; • to such wishes and feelings of any parents, person with parental responsibility or any other relevant person as they have been able to ascertain; and to the child's religious persuasion, racial origin and cultural and linguistic background.	In addition, the provisions in S22 (5) were intended to ensure due account was taken by local authorities of the child's religious persuasion, racial original, cultural and linguistic background but there are variable views as to the extent to which such factors are properly taken into consideration and a widespread concern that children who are provided with accommodation in the context of fears for possible abuse and neglect feel that they become further victims of the system.	It is suggested that clearer guidance should be given to local authority's social workers with regard to the consideration to be given to family placement within the extended family but there must be a recognition that the steps required to check such an extended family placement constitute an extra drain on resources which are in such short supply within local authorities.
S23 (1) provides that it shall be the duty of any local authority looking after a child to provide accommodation for him and **S23 (3)** includes placing the child with a relative of the child or any other suitable person.	This imposed a clear duty upon local authorities, before offering accommodation with local authority foster parents or in a local authority children's home, to consider very carefully the possibility of placing the child within his or her own extended family and thus, with a relative or where relevant and possible, placing the child with some other person whom the local authority considered to be suitable. Social workers in a number of authorities have voiced the concern that if they are fearful, about the risk of potential abuse to a child, they are understandably reluctant to place the child within the extended family when the potential abuser might have easier access to the child. This can, therefore, prompt social workers to "safe" and "speedy" placements in children's homes or with foster parents, especially where a great deal more work would be required to check out the potential homes on offer within the family.	

283

5. The Law on Child Protection

The Law on Child Protection

S47 of the 1989 Act requires local authorities to make such enquiries, as they consider necessary, to enable them to decide whether they should take any action to safeguard or promote the welfare of any child in respect of whom they have been informed that the child is the subject of an emergency protection order, is in police protection or where they have reasonable course to suspect that a child who lives, or is found, in their area is suffering, or is likely to suffer significant harm. (For much greater detail on this, see Part 12 of this document).

Dealing first with the provisions laid down in Pt.V of the Act concerning emergency measures and those steps which may be taken where there are suspicions of child abuse or neglect, it is important to note that the 1989 Act introduced a new Child Assessment Order available under s34 thus:

A local authority or NSPCC worker may apply to the Magistrates Court which can make a child assessment order, but only if, it is satisfied that

a. the applicant has reasonable cause to suspect the child is suffering or is likely to suffer significant harm;

b. an assessment of the state of the child's health or development, or of the way in which he has been treated, is required to enable the applicant to determine whether or not the child is suffering, or is likely to suffer, significant harm; and

c. it is unlikely that such an assessment will be made, or be satisfactory, in the absence of an order under this section.

S44 of the Act provides for the issuing of what is known as an emergency protection order which can be issued by the family proceeding courts to any person provided the court is satisfied that –

a. there is reasonable cause to believe that the child is likely to suffer significant harm if –

i) he is not removed to accommodation provided by or on behalf of the applicant;

ii) he does not remain in the place in which he is then being accommodated.

Critique

For a detailed critique of the provisions on investigation and the steps which should be taken by local authority social services department and other agencies see Part 12 of this document.

It is apparent from the Children Act Advisory Committee Reports (Lord Chancellor's Department 1992 – 1995) that applications for child assessment orders over the whole of England and Wales have run at a very low rate, scarcely 200 a year. The reason for this is felt to be that when social workers can say to parents that they will be able to obtain an order in order to confirm their suspicions that parents are more inclined to work together with the social worker to avoid the need to resort to court.

Early problems with this provision where parents sought to use it where they were unable to gain an ex-parte residence order under s8 of the Act has now been dealt with by allowing such ex-parte applications under s8.

There is considerable evidence that as compared with the old "place of safety order" under the 1969 Act, significantly fewer applications are being made for this type of emergency order. (Children Act Advisory Committee Report 1991 – 1994 – in 1994 Report see Table 2b.)

Recommendations

It would be useful if the statistics which were made available indicated by whom applications for emergency protection orders are being made under the provision of s44.

The Law on Child Protection	Critique	Recommendations
S44 [1] (b) provides that in the case of an application for an emergency protection order by a local authority the court may grant the order only if it is satisfied that –	These **inquiries** will be being made under s47, which requires a local authority to investigate where they have cause to suspect a child may be suffering or likely to suffer significant harm or is the subject of police protection.	
i) inquiries are being made with respect of the child whom the local authority had reasonable cause to suspect is suffering or is likely to suffer significant harm.		
ii) those inquiries are being frustrated by access to the child being unreasonably refused to a person authorised to seek access and that the applicant had reasonable cause to believe that access to the child is required as a matter of urgency.		
S44 [1](c) provides that in the case of an application made by an authorised person (which only includes the NSPCC) the courts may only make an emergency protection order if satisfied that	There is no evidence available from the statistics with regard to the numbers of applications being made by the NSPCC. The statistics do not provide a break-down by way of applicants.	It would be interesting if the statistics could provide more detail on the type of applicants for EPOs.
a) the applicant has reasonable cause to suspect the child is suffering or is likely to suffer significant harm;		
b) the applicant is making inquiries with respect to the child's welfare and		
c) those inquiries are being frustrated by access to the child being unreasonably refused to a person authorised to seek access and the applicant has reasonable cause to believe that access to the child is required as a matter of urgency.		
S44(6) provides that the court when making an emergency protection order may direct that the child be made the subject of a medical or psychiatric examination or **other assessment** of the child [author's emphasis added].	It is felt that the words **"or other assessment"** are extremely widely drawn and have generally been interpreted to include social work assessment in accordance with the terms of the Orange Book .	Clearer guidelines need to exist with regard to who should be passing information on to children and at what stage. There should also be clearer guidelines as to how one determines in this context whether a young person is of sufficient understanding.

285

The Law on Child Protection	Critique	Recommendations
S44 (7) however, goes on to provide that where a direction is given with regard to such medical psychiatric examination or other assessment the child **may**, if he is of sufficient understanding to make an informed decision, **refuse** to submit to the examination or other assessment. [author's emphasis added].	There are a number of problems here with regard to who determines whether the child is of sufficient understanding and the nature of an informed decision. In order to determine whether even the right to say no is passed on to the child seems to be dependent upon somebody making the determination that the child is of sufficient understanding. Given that information is power and that further examination may lead to an exacerbation of the trauma already experienced by the child, there is room for considerable confusion as to who should do what here. Talking to children over the age of 11 about this particular issue in child abuse investigations has tended to reveal that they have not generally been informed of their right to say no .	Young people should however be warned about the effects of the decision in South Glamorgan County Council W and B [1993] 1FLR 574, in which Douglas Brown J. ruled that the High Court could rely on powers derived from its inherent jurisdiction to overrule the child's statutory right to refuse such assessment or examination.

Parliament should consider whether it intended that the statutory rights which were given to children in the Act could be overruled by High Court judges using their inherent powers. If it did not so intend then it must be made clear that the s44(7), s43(6) and s38(6) rights to refuse given to children under the Act, cannot be avoided by High Court judges relying on inherent powers. Such rights must be put beyond the reach of paternalistic High Court judges however well meaning. |
| **The 1989 Act s46** preserved the ability of police constables to remove children from conditions in which they find them if the police constable has reasonable cause to believe that the child would otherwise be likely to suffer significant harm. This is not dependent on any court order and gives police officers a considerable amount of discretion in what may be potentially very dangerous situations. | It does, however, demand that police officers are aware of difficult issues which may arise in potential child abuse cases especially where such child abuse may arise in the context of domestic disputes. Police officers arriving on the scene will have difficult questions to determine with regard to family dynamics and whether victim partners may be able to do sufficient to protect their children. | Greater training needs to be provided to police officers to understand the possibility of child abuse of one form or another as defined in s31 (9 & 10), being present in a situation involving domestic violence or repeated acts of domestic violence against one parent. In those cases where there are ongoing domestic problems but where the victim partner is refusing to leave and may potentially, therefore, be unable to protect the children, there needs to be much closer investigation and monitoring of the children. |

The Law on Child Protection	Critique	Recommendations
Where the local authority investigation under **s47** has been frustrated by an unreasonable refusal of access to the child, it should be noted that such refusal may constitute grounds for the local authority to seek an emergency protection order under s44 [1](b) (see above)	These provisions taken together, have clarified the procedure to be followed by social workers when access to the child is being denied and addresses the problems raised by A Child in Mind; Protection of Children in a Responsible Society (1987, London Borough of Greenwich, The Kimberly Carlile Report)", which criticised the social workers for failing to be aware of, and to use, powers under the old laws to gain access to Kimberly Carlile, which, had they been invoked might have prevented her death. (Note, however, this old provision is further retained in the **1989 Act** by virtue of **s48 (9)**.	
In any event, under the provisions of **s47**, where the Local Authority or person authorised by it has been refused access or denied information as to the child's whereabouts in the course of an investigation, the Local Authority is bound to apply for an emergency protection order, child assessment order, care order or supervision order, unless they are satisfied that the child's welfare can be satisfactorily safeguarded without their doing so. (s47 [6]). **For a much more detailed consideration of s47 see Part 12.**		
In order to conduct proper investigations, even in an emergency, local authorities may, as well as checking the Child Protection Register and checking with all other potential agencies involved, decide that it is necessary to hold, what is known as, a child protection conference. This may have to be postponed until after the taking of emergency action or in a non-emergency situation where there is felt to be a risk of abuse which has not yet materialised, it may be possible to convene the conference with all the relevant personnel and an opportunity is thus provided for giving measured consideration to taking further legal steps such as obtaining a child assessment order (see **s43** below) or the institution of proceedings for a care or supervision order (see **s31** below, **part 8** below, and see figure 3 in Appendix to this Report).	It must be remembered that, even in an emergency, it is essential to adhere to the principles underpinning the **1989 Act** and, in particular, that of partnership with parents. This is the focus of particular attention in Child Protection – The Messages from Research and it was interesting that the findings of the study Paternalism or Partnership? Family Involvement in the Child Protection Process (University of East Anglia (1995)) demonstrated that more positive partnership with parents tended to follow from involving the parents in the process. One of the parents in the University of East Anglia said of a social worker who claimed to be working with the family – she didn t care about us all – she was interested in was doing a good job, doing it by the book! . It is clear from the University of East Anglia's study that much remains to be done in terms of encouraging parental participation.	Clearly much more training is still needed on the notion of working in partnership with parents and whilst much has been done a great deal remains to be done.

The Law on Child Protection	Critique	Recommendations
Pt.IV of the 1989 Act concentrates on the provisions relating to the making of care and supervision orders s31-35, including the making of education supervision orders (S36) Whilst intervention in the family on emergency grounds or on grounds concerned to allay suspicion may have been initiated, not all of these actions will then be converted into long term moves by the local authority as represented by Pt.IV of the Act. Only local authorities or authorised persons can take proceedings for care and supervision orders and thus, although any member of the public, a member of the police or a member of the NSPCC, in addition to local authorities social workers, can initiate protection action under Pt.V of the Act as described above, in practice it is only local authorities which actually apply for care or supervision orders. S31 (1) provides that a Local Authority or authorised person may apply to the court for an order placing the child in the care of the designated local authority or putting him under the supervision of a designated local authority or probation officer. It is provided in S31 (2) that the court may only make a care order or a supervision order if - a. the child is suffering or is likely to suffer significant harm; *and* b. the harm, or likelihood of harm is attributable to i) the care given to the child or likely to be given to him if the order were not made, not being what it would be reasonable to expect a parent to give to him or ii) the child being parental control	The evidence has suggested in successive reports of the **Children Act Advisory Committee**, and the **Department of Health Children Act Reports** that considerably less use is being made of care and supervision orders under the **1989 Act** than was the case with the old **1969 Act**. This was particularly the case in the early days after implementation of the statute in October 1991 but the number of orders made in proceedings is dramatically lower than those under the **1989 Act** (see Children Act Report 1993 [published May 1994 para 3.10]) Nevertheless the Department of Health's own **Children's Act Reports** have tended to reveal that a large number of cases in which there are concerns for children suffering or at risk of suffering from significant harm are being unallocated to social workers as a result of a shortage of resources. Thus concerns are expressed in such forums as Child Protection Conferences, a move is then made to place the child on the Child Protection Register but the case then remains unallocated.	Clearly, in some cases, there will be little tendency to move on to intervention in the form of taking care or supervision order proceedings if there is no one in place monitoring the child's progress and there is certainly judicial concern at the dramatic reduction in the number of proceedings coming before the courts. Given the concerns noted by the Department of Health and the judiciary generally, further consideration should be given to focusing attention on those authorities which remain unable to allocate social workers to children in families where a clearly identified need has been established. Simply looking at the numbers of care and supervision order proceedings which may result in any one year is no "real" guide to what is going on out there in the families of children who have been identified as being at risk but for whom no social worker has been allocated.

The Law on Child Protection	Critique	Recommendations
The provisions in **s31** have been subjected in a number of cases to close judicial scrutiny with regard to such issues as the meaning of **"significant"** harm, the meaning of the words **"is suffering"** and the notion of the comparison to be made with regard to other children (**s31 [10]** the **"similar child"**).	Careful attention needs to be focused on the interpretations which courts are giving in relevant cases. See for example RE O [1992] 2FLR 7] for an interpretation of harm; Re M [1994] 2FLR 577H L, for the interpretation to be given to the words is suffering; and Re H and R [1996] 1FLR 80 HL, for the standard of proof required in sexual abuse cases involving children.	There should be greater and more immediate dissemination of important reported cases to all professionals working in the field in order that they can be properly guided in the execution of their work. The actual official law report copy should be distributed so that the professionals can read and understand the case, rather than relying on others interpretations of what the case decides.

289

6. The Criminal Law

Current Criminal Law	Critique	Recommendations
S1(1) of the Children and Young Persons Act 1933 (as amended by the 1989 Act) provides that any person who is at least 16 years old, and has responsibility for any child or young person under that age, and who **wilfully** causes or procures that child to suffer assault, ill treatment, neglect, abandonment, or exposure in a manner to cause the child unnecessary suffering or injury to health, will be liable to criminal prosecution . [author's emphasis added]	It should be noted that the word **wilfully** qualifies all five actions or omissions and makes it clear that any offence under **S1** requires a state of mind on the part of the offender directed towards the particular act or failure to act which constitutes the actus reus and warrants the description wilful seen in the leading House of Lords case **R v Sheppard** [1981] A.C.394 H.L. this is the leading authority on the interpretation of wilful in criminal statutes.	
	It appears from **R v Hayles** [1969] 1 QB 364, where the Court of Appeal indicated that the defendant's conduct could fall within more than one statutory category, e.g. neglect, that this may in certain circumstances also be described as ill treatment.	
CYPA 1933 s1(1) lists five types of cruel conduct which may overlap with each other. The types of ill treatment referred to are - 1. assault	Physical assault involves "any unlawful interference with a person's body which causes the apprehension of harm, whether or not there is physical violence". Note – merely causing the child astonishment and disgust is not assault within the meaning of the section. As far as assault under **s1(1)** is concerned, it is clear from the case of **R v Hatton** (1925 2KB 322 Cr.APP.R29, CCA] that in order for an assault to fall within this section there must be something more than a mere common assault. The section provides that not only must there be "wilful assault" but it must also be committed "in a manner likely to cause the child unnecessary suffering or injury to his health".	

Current Criminal Law	Critique	Recommendations
2. ill treatment	As far as **ill treatment** is concerned there is no definition of this word in the Act but it may be assumed that it is intended to cover wilful ill treatment, and that **bullying** or **frightening** will suffice, or any course of conduct calculated to cause unnecessary suffering or injury to health. There is no need to prove an assault or battery but clearly a series of assaults, even though not coming within the scope of the assaults envisaged by the section, might amount to wilful ill treatment. It is, however, to be noted again that it is a defence that the alleged ill treatment consisted in reasonable correction by a parent, teacher or other person having lawful control of the child (see **S1 (7)** below).	
3. neglect	As far as the term **"neglect"** is concerned Lord Diplock said, in giving the leading judgement in **R v Sheppard** that, "the actus reus of the offence with which the accused were charged in the instant case, does not involve construing the verb 'neglect' for the offence fell within the deeming provision (**s1 [2a]**) and the only question as respects the actus reus was did the parents fail to provide medical aid that was in fact adequate in view of his actual state of health at the relevant time? This is a pure question of objective fact to be determined in the light of what had become known by the date of the trial to be child's actual state of health at the relevant time."	
	If the answer was "yes" then by virtue of the deeming provision the actus reus, namely neglect in the manner likely to cause injury to health was established but it still has to be proved that the neglect was wilful (see earlier).	

Current Criminal Law

Critique

Recommendations

It was held in **R v Ryland** (1867 **LR.1CCR.99**) that the word **neglect** sufficiently alleged the ability of the parents to provide for the child and that it was not necessary for the indictment to allege specifically that the parents had means. The old cases on "means", however, are of less importance in the welfare state. A failure to resort to the assistance authorities for the means of maintaining a child where a parent cannot do so out of his own pocket would presumably amount to neglect (see **S2[1]**).

Refusal to permit an operation may be, but not necessarily, such a failure to provide medical aid as to amount to **wilful neglect causing injury to health.** The question is one of fact to be decided in each case upon the evidence (see **Oakey v Jackson [1914] 1 K.B 216, DC,** as to a deliberate omission to supply medical or surgical aid on conscientious grounds, the case of **R v Senior [1899] 1 K.B 283** should be referred to.

In this case the parents were members of the "Peculiar People" a religious sect which did not believe in medical interventions, but on a charge of neglect under the statute, the child's father was liable because he knew that the child's physical suffering would be alleviated by the treatment but had deliberately refrained from having recourse to it because he thought to do so would be sinful as showing an unwillingness to accept God's will in relation to the child.

Where a father who earned a sufficient wage did not pay over to his wife enough to clothe and feed the children properly, it has been held to be no defence for the father, when charged with neglect, to say that by resort to the assistance authorities the mother might have obviated the affects of the father's neglect: see **Cole v Pendleton (1896) 60 J.P 359.** Evidence of the possession by the accused of such means at a date before the neglect as would presumably not be exhausted at the date of neglect, is some evidence of the possession of means at the date of neglect. See **R v Jones (1901) 19 Cox 678.**

4. abandonment

R v Boulden ((1957) 41 Cr App R 105), after the children had been abandoned by first their mother and then their father, the court held that the criterion to be employed was: did the parent take all reasonable steps to ensure that the child had been received into care? The fact that the father had left them alone and unattended with only a small quantity of food, in this case, was sufficient to constitute abandonment of his children.

5. exposure

It would appear to constitute an offence under this category of offence, the exposure need not necessarily consist of the physical placing of the child somewhere with intent to injure it. (**R v Williams** (1910) 4 Cr App R 89).

In **R v Whibley** [1938] 3 All ER 777, five children had been left at a juvenile court. It was held that this action was unlikely to cause them unnecessary suffering or injury to health, since this was not a place which would expose them to injury.

293

Current Criminal Law	Critique	Recommendations
	It has been held that wilful exposure under s1(1) does not extend to exposure to risk (**R v Gibbins** [1977] Crim LR 741), where a father took his eight year old son and five other boys onto a piece of timber on a disused section of the London docks and entered them into deep water; in fact, none suffered harm. This, it is submitted, that if injury had, in fact, been suffered the father would have been libel. It has to surely depend on whether the risk actually materialised.	
Where there is a perceived apprehension of harm by the child then a possible alternative to **S1 CYPA 1933** may be used for alternative charges such as that of common assault under **S42** of the Offences Against the Person Act 1861 or under **S39** (common assault and battery) of the Criminal Justice Act 1988.		
S1(2) describes the kind of persons who may be held liable for committing the prohibited types of conduct stipulated in the section. Under S1 CYPA 1933 [as amended by the 1989 Act] it is provided that i) any person who has parental responsibility for the child or young person; or is otherwise legally liable to maintain him; and any person who has care of him shall be presumed to have responsibility for that child or young person; ii) a person who is presumed to be responsible for a child or young person by virtue of this shall not be taken to have ceased to be responsible for him by reason only that he does not have the care of him.		
The provisions of **S1(7) of the CYPA 1933** are referred to in detail in the main text. (see **Pt.13** of this report) **S1(7)** refers back to **S1(1)** and states that the provisions of **S1** do not affect the right of any parent, teacher or any other person having the lawful control or charge of a child or young person, to administer punishment to him.	This situation is dealt with as indicated in more detail in the Introduction where account is given of the questions which are now being raised with regard to the administration of corporal punishment by parents.	Abolition of the parental right to impose punishment including physical punishment on any child or young person.

Current Criminal Law	Critique	Recommendations
In addition to the particular offences against children, provided for by the **Children and Young Persons Act**, there are, of course, all the offences which can equally be applicable to children under the **Offences Against the Person Act 1861** and the **Sexual Offences Acts 1956-92/3**. Under the **Offences Against the Person Act 1861, S.27** there is an offence of abandoning or exposing children under 2 whereby the child's life would be endangered or the health of such a child shall have been or shall be likely to be permanently injured then, any person convicted of the offence shall be liable to imprisonment for any term not exceeding five years. Cases of common assault are now covered by **S39 Criminal Justice Act 1988** under which they are classified as summary offences and ...... in the Magistrates Courts. This offence would cover the cases of assault which are not serious enough to produce the **"unnecessary suffering"** or **"injury"** that **S2 CYPA 1933** requires. More serious cases of assault would come under **s.18, 20** and **47** of the **1861 Act**, in cases of unlawfully and maliciously wounding, or causing grievous bodily harm to the child with the intention of doing him some harm. It should be noted that in every case an additional charge under **S.1 CYPA 1933** may be brought even when any of these offences are charged. The current law on sexual offences is contained in the **Sexual Offences Act 1956-92** and of particular relevance will be: the provisions on assault generally already described; offences concerning sexual intercourse with a girl under 16 under **S6 of the Sexual Offences Act 1956**, although in the case of a man aged under 24 the presence of reasonable cause to believe that the girl was over the age of 16 years is a valid defence provided the defendant has not been previously charged with a similar offence. There are various provisions under **S10 of the Sexual Offences Act** with regard to the commission of incest with a girl by a man and under **S11** with a boy by a woman, all of which are relevant with regard to children, especially where there may be allegations of sexual abuse.	Thus the relevant provisions are in place for charges to be made with regard to any act of physical abuse, sexual abuse, emotional abuse and neglect. The real problems surround the question of whether the police pass charges forward to the Crown Prosecution Service and then whether the Crown Prosecution Service decides to prosecute (see **Pt.13** generally).	Far more extensive training should be given to the Crown Prosecution Service on the reliability of children as witnesses as compared with adults, and on techniques of examining and cross examining children. Many more Child Witness Support schemes should be implemented across all courts and in all jurisdictions; and guardians ad litem should be made available to support children in very serious cases. There should be much greater liaison across the civil and criminal law jurisdictions as is already practised by judges in the Liverpool courts.

295

Current Criminal Law	Critique	Recommendations
There are a number of provisions concerning the admissibility of evidence in criminal proceedings which are dealt with in detail below and also in **Pt.13.** These include many important amendments effected by recent Criminal Justice Acts.	All of these provisions are considered in greater detail below and in **Pt.13** dealing with legal processes and also in **Pt.14 Outcomes for Children.**	Full implementation of **all** the recommendations of the Pigot Report on Video Evidence (1989, Home Office).
Amongst the most important are the new provisions allowing unworn evidence from children in criminal proceedings (**S.52 CJA 1991** inserting a new **S.33 [A]** into the CJA 1988)		
Under the new **S.32 (A)** inserted into CJA **1988** it is now possible to substitute a pre-recorded interview with a child witness to replace the child's evidence in chief in cases involving certain sexual offences and offences of violence and cruelty. The child must, however, still be available for live cross-examination at the trial using the live link i.e. communicating through television, where appropriate. A further valuable amendment effected by **S.55 (6) CJA 1991** was that the category of persons eligible to use the live link have been enlarged by raising the age limit in sexual cases to 17 and by providing for cross-examination to be by live television link if pre-recorded evidence is used instead of evidence in chief.	These provisions must be read in conjunction with the associated **Memorandum of Good Practice on Video Recorded Interviews** with child witnesses for criminal proceedings (Home Office with DOH (HMSO) 1992) See also The Child, the Court and the Video – A study of the implementation of the Memorandum of Good Practice (Social Services Inspectorate (1994)).	
Again, if a particular court does not possess live link facilities, CJA 1991 provides for the hearing to be moved to a court area which does.		
See also **s32 Criminal Justice and Public Order Act 1994** which abolished the compulsory giving of warnings about the possible unreliability of the uncorroborated evidence of complainants in cases of sexual assault.	In May 1995, in **R v Makanjula** and **R v Easton** the Court of Appeal issued guidelines about the use of the warning, leaving the trial judges a fairly wide discretion. It had been argued in this case on behalf of a man convicted of an offence of indecency against a young child that the trial judges decision **not** to warn about the dangerousness of convicting on the uncorroborated evidence of a person, who is the complainant, in a case of sexual assault was grounds for an appeal. The CA held that it was not and that the Trial Judge properly used his discretion in deciding not to give a warning in this case.	

Current Criminal Law	Critique	Recommendations
s32 Criminal Justice and Public Order Act 1994 *continued*	The CA emphasised that the warning was discretionary and that to continue to give the old warning in cases in which there were no specific indicators for so doing would be contrary to the spirit and intentions of s32 Criminal Justice and Public Order Act 1994. Judges, the CA said, should consider the manner in which a witness's evidence was given as well as its content and make an evaluation on that basis. Cases in which a warning was appropriate would be ones in which these factors were judged to be unreliable. There would be instances in which the judge saw fit to warn the jury to exercise caution before acting on the unsupported evidence of a witness, and the fact that a witness was a complainant in a case of sexual assault would not of itself be grounds for the warning to be issued. In consequence of these recent changes children are in some important respects able to give evidence on a similar basis to their adult counterparts.	

7. Law on Domestic Violence

Law on Domestic Violence (current)	Critique	Family Law Act 1996	Critique
The Domestic Violence and Matrimonial Proceedings Act 1976. **Note** – this is an extremely short statute which was enacted to provide specifically for the problems of partners suffering from domestic violence and to give them a short term remedy to protect them from molestation and to enable them to occupy property pending resolution of property interests.	These provisions were only intended to provide a short term remedy and a number of problems of interpretation had to be resolved by the courts.	The aim of the provisions in Pt.IV of the Family Law Act 1996 is to bring into much closer alignment the jurisdictions of the magistrates courts, county court and high court to grant both molestation orders and occupation orders . The basic terms of the new orders in the Family Law Act correspond quite closely with those contained in the Domestic Violence and Matrimonial Proceedings Act 1976.	**Note** – the provisions of the new Act are unlikely to be implemented before January 1998 at the earliest and it is being suggested possibly as late as the year 2000. New Court Rules and Regulations will have to be drawn up and training provided to all levels of the judiciary to deal with the provisions of the new Act which, of course, also for extensive reforms of the law on divorce.
S1 provides that County Courts (and now the High Court as well) has jurisdiction to grant an injunction restraining the other party to the marriage from molesting the applicant, and a child living with the applicant, and excluding the other party from the matrimonial home or a part of the matrimonial home or from a specified area in which the matrimonial home is included; and/or requiring the other party to permit the applicant to enter and remain in the matrimonial home, whether or not relief is sought in any other proceedings.	Molestation has been determined by the courts to include a wide range of behaviour and to effectively include such things as pestering or making a nuisance of oneself to the detriment of the other party generally.	The Family Law Act 1996 allows non molestation orders to be obtained by spouses and co- habitants equally before the courts and also by a range of other people who come within a list as laid down in **s62(3)**. Thus an associated person can apply for and obtain a non-molestation order if they are married or formerly married; if they are co-habitant or former co-habitant; if they live or have lived in the same household otherwise merely than by reason of one of them being the other's employee, tenant, lodger or boarder; or they are relatives.	
S1.(2) Ensures that the provisions apply equally to a man and a women who are living with each other in the same household as husband and wife as it applies to parties to a marriage and that any reference to the matrimonial home is to be construed accordingly.			

Law on Domestic Violence (current)	Critique	Family Law Act 1996	Critique
	This provision, therefore, allowed for exactly the same protection to be given to male and female partners where they are not married. It does not, however, extend to allowing members of homosexual couples or members of the wider family generally to obtain orders protecting them from domestic violence.	Under this Act, members of same sex couples will be able to obtain non-molestation orders provided they can bring themselves within the definition of an associated person . (See s62(3)).	
S2 of the Act provides that where a Judge grants an injunction restraining the other party to the marriage (or partners to a co-habitating relationship) from using violence against the applicant or **against a child living with the applicant** or excluding the other party from the matrimonial home or from an area in which the matrimonial home was included, the Judge has the power, if satisfied that the other party has caused *actual bodily harm* to the applicant **or to the child,** to attach a power of arrest to the injunction.	The use of the power of arrest in enabling a criminal sanction to be attached to a civil law remedy is recognised as somewhat anomalous but the whole problem of domestic violence poses innumerable difficulties for the law. One of the major problems in this area is a tendency, even in 1996, to perceive domestic violence as a domestic problem . Despite enormous strides forward made by the police as exemplified by **Home Office Circular No.6,1990** and the provision of many police Domestic Violence Units throughout England and Wales, victims argue, and commentators have observed, that the offences which might be committed under the criminal law in a domestic situation are not treated in the same way as they would be if they were offences involving strangers.		

Law on Domestic Violence (current)	Critique	Family Law Act 1996	Critique
The Domestic Proceedings and Magistrates Courts Act 1978 S16 provides Magistrates Courts with the powers to issue a **personal protection order or an exclusion order** where an application is made to the court by a spouse. The court can only grant an order for **personal protection** where satisfied that the respondent has used or threatened to use violence against the person, the applicant or **a child of the family** and that it is necessary for the protection of the applicant that an order restraining him from using or threatening to use violence against the person of the applicant or against the person of a child of the family is necessary. [author's emphasis added].	It should be noted here that these provisions are confined to **married parties** only; the granting of an order is conditional upon the use or threat to use "**violence**" which is much narrower than the term **molestation** under the 1976 Act described above. It should also be noted that orders can only be issued to protect a child of the family rather than any child living with the applicant. This has been felt to be highly unsatisfactory and positively dangerous for children in such circumstances.	The provisions for protecting children in the Family Law Act 1996 be much wider – see below.	

Law on Domestic Violence (current)	Critique	Family Law Act 1996	Critique
S16 (3) further provides that where the court is satisfied that the respondent has used violence against the person of the applicant or child of the family, or that **he has threatened to do so and has used violence** against some other person, or he is in contravention of an existing personal protection order, and that the applicant **or child of the family** is in danger of being physical injured by the respondent (or would be in such danger if the applicant or child were to enter the matrimonial home), then the court may make one of the following orders that is to say - i) an order requiring the respondent to leave the matrimonial home; ii) an order prohibiting the respondent from entering the matrimonial home.	Problems with these provisions are the necessity to prove **violence** or the use of violence against some other person if one is alleging that the respondent has threatened the applicant or a child of the family with violence. This can be very difficult to prove and the Act is seen as unduly restrictive thus prompting most parties to a marriage to use the 1976 Act at a consequent greater cost to the Legal Aid Board.	There is much more protection offered to family members generally and as far as children are concerned, the provisions allow for orders to be granted in respect of a person termed a "relevant child", who is defined in **s62(2)** as "any child who is living with or might reasonably be expected to live with either party to the proceedings; any child in respect of whom an order may be being considered in the proceedings; and any other child whose interests the court considers relevant". Under **sections 33, 35, 36, 37 or 38,** which allow for occupation orders to be made in respect of married or formerly married or co-habiting or formerly co-habiting partners, a range of provisions exist which allow the court to regulate the occupation of the parties, home and such clauses providing for regulation, must be included by the court unless it appears to the court that	It is, therefore, the case that greater protection is now extended to all children and this is to be welcomed. It would also appear, in line with current case law concerning ouster injunctions, that the Family Law Act 1996 gives greater attention to the needs of children and also to the respective harm which may be suffered if the relevant court orders are not made. There is thus in every provision dealing with both occupation orders and non- molestation orders what is termed a balance of harm test . The burden of the court to make such orders as set out is now quite considerable.

7. Law on Domestic Violence (current)	Critique	Family Law Act 1996	Critique
		a. the respondent or any relevant child is likely to suffer significant harm if the provision is included in the order, and	The provisions of the Family Law Act 1996 in so far as they concern children living in violent relationships are to be welcomed. Nevertheless it has to be realised that such provisions are of a "private" nature and particularly where the children are young, and depend on one of the parties to the violent relationship initiating action.
		b. the harm likely to be suffered by the respondent in that event is as great or greater than the harm likely to be suffered by the applicant or child if the provision is not included. With regard to non-molestation orders, the court is directed in deciding whether to exercise its powers under **s42(5)** to have regard to all the circumstances including the need to secure the health, safety and well being of the applicant and of any relevant child.	
		Nevertheless the Family Law Act 1996 does provide **s43** that a child under the age of 16 can apply for an occupation order or a non-molestation order **provided the child has the leave of the court.** The leave of the court will be given if the court is satisfied that the child has **sufficient understanding** to make the proposed application.	This provides a "Gillick" type test for allowing the court to consider whether they should allow children to apply for occupation orders or non molestation orders. The Act does not however provide any information as to how children should seek help to obtain such orders.
		Provision is further made in the Family Law Act 1996 for ex-parte orders to be made in emergencies for both occupation and non- molestation orders in s45 .	

Law on Domestic Violence (current)	Critique	Family Law Act 1996	Critique
S18 of the 1978 Act provides that magistrates court can attach a power of arrest to either of the orders where it is satisfied that the respondent has **"physically injured"** the applicant or a child of the family and considers that he is **likely to do so again.**	The problem with this area is that it requires that the applicant should have suffered physical injury whereas the requirement under the 1976 Act was that the applicant or a child has only suffered actual bodily harm. This can, of course, be constituted by something less than physical injury and again it was found that the 1978 Act was unduly restrictive.	By s47 provision is also made for attaching a power of arrest to an occupation or non-molestation order where the court has made such an order and it appears to the court that the respondent has used or threatened violence against the applicant or a relevant child unless satisfied that in all the circumstances of the case the applicant or child will be adequately protected without such a power of arrest being attached. A power of arrest may be attached to ex-parte orders if it appears to the court again that the respondent has used or threatened violence against the applicant or a relevant child and that there is a risk of significant harm to the applicant or child if the power of arrest is not attached to such orders immediately. This again will guarantee far greater protection using power of arrest provisions than previously existed under the current law.	This again will guarantee far greater protection using the power of arrest provisions than previously existed under the current law. The provisions with regard to attaching a power of arrest in the Family Law Act 1996 are more extensive than those in current legislation. Thus where it was stated to be extremely rare for an ex-parte ouster or exclusion order to be made, the new Act will make it slightly easier and demands that attention be given to the risk of significant harm to the applicant or relevant child if the order is not made immediately. These provisions are again more extensive than those in existing legislation since there is now no longer a requirement to prove either actual bodily harm or physical injury but that the respondent has either used or "threatened to use" violence against the applicant or a relevant child. Again it is further provided that in urgent cases a power of arrest can be attached to an ex-parte occupation order.

Law on Domestic Violence (current)	Critique	Family Law Act 1996	Critique
			It is suggested that circumstances in which this might arise would be very rare but there will be such situations. It is suggested that publicity is given to this provision as widely as possible so that children are aware that, if necessary, they themselves might seek to support a non-violent partner in trying to get a violent partner away from the family home and family setting.
			Clearly the provisions of the Family Law Act 1996 can do little to address the problems arising from the fact that victims do not perceive the police as either their first or best port of call in trying to deal with domestic violence. The only way in which this can be addressed is through a tightening up of criminal law and procedures (see earlier and Parts 10 and 11).

8. Non-statutory Definitions of Abuse and Neglect

*Report of the
National
Commission of
Inquiry into the
Prevention of
Child Abuse*

As has been pointed out earlier (see **Introduction** and **Part I**), the Department of Health issued a number of Volumes of Guidance with regard to the implementation of the 1989 Act. It was further noted that this guidance included a volume entitled *"Working Together under the Children Act 1989 – A Guide to Arrangements for Inter-agency Co-operation for the Protection of Children from Abuse"*. (DOH, HMSO 1991) Since a number of child abuse inquiries had established that good child protection work required good inter-agency co-operation, it was recognised that all professionals should combine an open-minded attitude to alleged concerns about child abuse with decisive action where that was clearly indicated.It was also recognised as a result of the various inquiries that intervention in a family, particularly if court action is necessary, has major implications for the family even if the assessment eventually leads to a decision that no further action is required.It was acknowledged that public confidence in the child protection system could only be maintained where a proper balance is struck avoiding unnecessary intrusion into families whilst at the same time protecting children at risk of significant harm. (See for further detailed analysis Lyon C.M. and de Cruz S.P. **Child Abuse** (2nd ed) Family Law 1993) **"Working Together"** is thus a significant document in that it consolidates previous guidance procedures for the protection of children and recommends developments aimed at making these more effective. The document was prepared jointly by the Department of Health, the Home Office, the Department of Education and Science and the Welsh Office. **"Working Together"** takes into account the requirements of the Children Act 1989 and lessons learned from individual cases which had caused public concern, such as Cleveland and Orkney, as well as examples of good practice provided by a number of agencies . **"Working Together"** does not attempt to provide guidelines on the practice of individual professions in the recognition of child abuse or subsequent care or treatment but is concerned with inter-professional and inter-agency co-operation. Indeed, the document opens with a cautionary note that it should be read in the light of all relevant guidance issued to individual agencies and professions. In the same way as the volumes of guidance issued by the Department on the 1989 Act itself, **"Working Together"** is issued pursuant to s7 of the Local Authority Social Services Act 1970, which requires local authorities in their social services functions to act under the general guidance of the Secretary of State. A further cautionary note is sounded in the introduction to the document with the statement that it thus *does not have the full force of statute*, but, as guidance issued under that section, it should be complied with unless local circumstances indicate **exceptional** reasons which justify a variation.

"Working Together" has, in effect, become a working bible on inter-agency co-operation. It grew out of a number of circulars and earlier documents of guidance issued with regard to this subject. Whilst the document recognises that the grounds for initiating care proceedings under the 1989 Act relate to the notion of significant harm as developed and expanded in s31 of the Children Act 1989, (See **Working Together** 1991 HMSO at p.49) the document sets out clear criteria which are intended to guide the admission to, and removal from, local child protection registers. At p48 there are accordingly four categories which are laid down which relate to the issue of registration. Placing a name on a local child protection register provides an easy and quick reference system for professionals concerned with identifying children at risk and it also promotes co-ordination of inter-agency plans to minimise that risk. If, however, formal proceedings need to be taken, then the professionals involved

Report of the
National
Commission of
Inquiry into the
Prevention of
Child Abuse

would have to fit the case into the definitions set out in s31 of the 1989 Act. (For more detailed analysis, see Lyon C.M. and de Cruz S.P. sup.cit)

It should be noted that the inclusion of a child's name on the child protection register will only occur following a child protection conference (see figure 3 in the Appendix for a tabular representation of the steps leading to such conferences and the recommendations which can be made), the exception being when a child on another local authority's register moves into the area. Such children will be registered immediately pending the first child protection conference in the new area.

Both the requirements for registration and the actual categories of abuse for registration produced at paragraphs 6.39 and 6.40 of Working Together are now set out below.

Requirements for Registration

6.39   Before a child is registered the conference must decide that there is, or is a likelihood of, significant harm leading to the need for a child protection plan. One of the following requirements needs to be satisfied:

(i)   There must be one or more identifiable incidents which can be described as having adversely affected the child. They may be acts of commission or omission. They can be either physical, sexual, emotional or neglectful. It is important to identify a specific occasion or occasions when the incident has occurred. Professional judgement is that further incidents are likely; or

(ii)   Significant harm is expected on the basis of professional judgement of findings of the investigation in this individual case or on research evidence. The conference will need to establish so far as they can a cause of the harm or likelihood of harm. This cause could also be applied to siblings or other children living in the same household so as to justify registration of them. Such children should be categorised according to the area of concern.

Categories of Abuse for Registration

6.40   The following categories should be used for the register and for statistical purposes. They are intended to provide definitions as a guide for those using the register. In some instances, more than one category of registration may be appropriate. This needs to be dealt with in the protection plan. The statistical returns will allow for this. Multiple abuse registration should not be used just to cover all eventualities.

Neglect: *The persistent or severe neglect of a child, or the failure to protect a child from exposure to any kind of danger, including cold or starvation, or extreme failure to carry out important aspects of care, resulting in the significant impairment of the child's health or development, including non-organic failure to thrive.*

Physical Injury: *Actual or likely physical injury to a child, or failure to prevent physical injury (or suffering) to a child including deliberate poisoning, suffocation and Munchausen's syndrome by proxy. See explanation of this syndrome in Marshall's paper pp16-17.*

Sexual Abuse: *Actual or likely sexual exploitation of a child or adolescent. The child may be dependent and/or developmentally immature.*

*Report of the
National
Commission of
Inquiry into the
Prevention of
Child Abuse*

Emotional Abuse: Actual or likely severe adverse effect on the emotional and behavioural development of a child cause by persistent or severe emotional ill-treatment or rejection.

The guidance which is issued in **"Working Together"** can be contrasted with that issued in Scotland in the document **Child Protection in Scotland – Management Information,** (Scottish Office 1992). (See Marshall's paper). Many professionals have found the guidance set out in the Scottish document to be extremely useful and make reference to it as well as to **"Working Together".**

"Working Together" does, however, helpfully define the notion of organised abuse. This is described in **"Working Together"** as *"a generic term which covers abuse which may involve a number of abusers, a number of abused children and young people, and often encompasses different forms of abuse. It involves, to a greater or lesser extent, an element of organisation" (at para 5.26.1). Paragraph 5.26.2 goes on to state that a "wide range of activity is covered by this term, from small paedophile or pornographic rings, often but not always, organised for profit, with most participants knowing each other, to large networks of individual groups of families which may be spread widely and in which not all participants will be known to each other".* It then explains that *"some organised groups may use bizarre or ritualised behaviour, sometimes associated with particular belief systems generally".* Thus, forms of organised abuse may or may not involve the use of satanic rituals and it is incorrect to simply classify ritualistic and organised abuse as one and the same form of child abuse (see further on this Lyon and De Cruz Child Abuse (supcit at Ch.2 and 3)). Paragraph 5.26.2 of the document stresses that *research suggests some caution in sharp distinctions between types of abuser.* **Working Together** points out that knowledge is growing in this area of abuse and the Department of Health has commissioned research into its frequency and characteristics. (see further **The Extent and Nature of Organised and Ritual Sexual Abuse: Research Findings** Jean La Fontaine [London School of Economics] HMSO 1994). It should be noted that a number of authorities in England and Wales, such as Nottinghamshire, Lancashire, Rochdale, Manchester and Cheshire have had experience in this complex area of work and have lessons to share with those who have yet to experience the phenomenon of organised abuse.

307

It is worth repeating at this stage that, as is the case with Scottish Law, English Law and the new Northern Ireland legislation concentrate on a negative issue, highlighting behaviour or conditions which would suggest, or be indicative of, neglect and abuse. There is no definition of the responsibilities of parents and the Law Commission in explaining this omission from the draft Bill which it prepared as part of its Report on Family and Child Law, felt that to provide a list of responsibilities would be too difficult and would constantly change. It is submitted that this is nonsensical since many family law and child law textbook writers have had little problem in coming up with a list of parental responsibilities. The Law Commission itself managed to come up with a fairly comprehensive list of such responsibilities and it is to be noted that these have not radically changed over time. Since this is the case, there is little reason why a list, including examples, could not be provided in statutory form and it is suggested that serious attention should be focused on reform of the law in this way as parents would then be given a standard against which to measure their performance.

*Report of the
National
Commission of
Inquiry into the
Prevention of
Child Abuse*

The deficiency of the definition provided in section 3 (1) of the 1989 Act is troublesome. The intention, apparently, was to make parental rights subsidiary to responsibilities in that the concept of parental **responsibility** is the one that is stressed as comprising all the other rights, duties, powers and responsibilities. Nevertheless, as indicated above, the decision not to include a list of parental responsibilities seems disingenuous in the extreme and does nothing to help the vast majority of parents who seek some guidance from somewhere in a society which thus far has done little through its educational system to promote the concept of either family or children's responsibilities. People often ask what are the limitations placed upon the rights of parents but in a sense this seems only capable of discovery when the parents have gone beyond the bounds of what is acceptable without knowing what is acceptable. Where a parent steps outside the bounds of what is acceptable then his or her conduct will be visited by reactions from both civil and criminal authorities in the form of local authority social services officers and police officers. Both parents and children would benefit from there being clearer sets of guidelines laid down as to what parents should and should not be doing.

In sharp contrast where there is a dearth of guidance for parents and children, a great deal of guidance exists for professionals working in the areas of family child relationships. The problem is that the sharpened awareness of what children do and do not need, and the levels of care which they might be able to expect, is concentrated in the hands of the professionals and is not passed on to parents. This again is not in line with the policy or indeed the principles of the United Nations Convention on the Rights of the Child since this demands that support be given to parents in bringing up their children (Article 18 [2] U.N. Convention on the Rights of the Child). As has been pointed out by the author in other documents (see Lyon CM **Legal Issues Arising from the Care and Control of Children with Learning Disabilities Who Also Present Severely Challenging Behaviour** Mental Health Foundation 1994), there should be far greater clarity surrounding issues such as what constitutes **"appropriate punishment"** if the parental right of punishment is set to remain a parental right in England and Wales. Given the censure of this position by the United Nations Convention Monitoring Committee, the question remains as to whether parents should be left with this so-called "right". The current social and legal acceptance of hitting children is perhaps the most symbolic indication of their low status in our society. A number of European countries have now prohibited all physical punishment of children (Sweden in 1979; Finland in 1984; Denmark in 1986; Norway in 1987; and Austria in 1989).

A recommendation of the Council of Europe Committee of Ministers in 1985 urged member states, including the U.K., to review their legislation on the power to punish children in order to limited or indeed prohibit corporal punishment, even if violation of such prohibition does not necessarily entail a criminal penalty . (see Violence in the Family: Recommendation No.R [85] 4, adopted by the Committee of Ministers on 26th March 1985. Strasbourg: Council of Europe: 1996)

What is clearly missing, therefore, is some authoritative statement or guidance contained in the law about what parents ought to be doing. The problem with the current vacuum left by section 3 (1) of the 1989 Act is that it leaves parents at large.Is it seriously to be expected they will be able to run to law books to consult what are all the rights, duties, powers and responsibilities which by law a parent of a child have in relation to the child and his property? Urgent legal reform is needed in this area.

Report of the
National
Commission of
Inquiry into the
Prevention of
Child Abuse

In addition, there is a woeful amount of ignorance with regard to even the existence of the U.N. Convention on the Rights of the Child and arguably, if this had been more widely publicised, it might have constituted the type of guidance which most parents feel they need as to what they should be doing for their children. The Department of Health went to the trouble and expense of producing a comprehensible leaflet of guidance for children on the subject of the UN Convention although most children have never seen nor received copies of this leaflet. (See **The Rights of the Child – A Guide to the UN Convention**, DOH CAG 9 (1993) Perhaps it might more usefully have been directed at all parents and distributed to them.

The Department has also produced a number of leaflets with regard to the Children Act 1989 (See CAG 1-8 Guidance leaflets on the Children Act 1989 available free from the Health Publication Stores, Manchester Road, Heywood Lancashire OL10 2PZ). Most of these leaflets have never reached the people for whom they were originally intended and whilst a similar explanatory leaflet on parental rights, duties, powers and responsibilities would no doubt be found extremely useful, this begs the question as to how it might be disseminated given the poor record thus far on dissemination of such information leaflets by relevant Government departments.

9.   Identifying Child Abuse and Neglect

As can be seen from the preceding section, the early identification of child abuse and neglect is closely bound up with the definitions contained in statutory and non-statutory guidelines. Physical abuse and physical neglect may be easier to detect and this may also now be the case with sexual abuse following much greater publicity and much greater professional awareness (The Cleveland Report), but concerns remain over the problem of emotional abuse.

Article 19 of the United Nations Convention on the Rights of the Child which imposes, in clause 1, an obligation on States Parties to take measures to protect children from abuse, continues in clause 2, to state that;

> *"such protective measures should, as appropriate, include effective procedures for the establishment of social programmes to provide necessary support for the child and for those who have the care of the child, as well as for other forms of prevention and for* **identification, reporting, referral, investigation, treatment and follow up** *of instances of child maltreatment described heretofore, and, as appropriate, for judicial involvement"*

It has been pointed out in Pt.4, that as a result of a chronic lack of resources few would assert that the Children Act 1989 could be said to have included effective procedures for the establishment of social programmes to provide necessary support for the child and for those who have care of the child. Nevertheless, it has been argued that the combination of the 1989 Act and various Volume of Department of Health guidance (including, most importantly, Working Together), have contributed towards the construction of a more effective **framework** for the identification, reporting, referral, investigation, treatment and follow up of child abuse cases. Arguments may continue to rage about whether the new grounds for care proceedings have raised or lowered the threshold of state intervention in

Report of the
National
Commission of
Inquiry into the
Prevention of
Child Abuse

the lives of children and their families, but most would acknowledge that the 1989 Act provisions represent **potentially** a very responsive and effective framework when such intervention is determined necessary.

As **Working Together** indicates, (at chapter 4), a very wide range of agencies or individual professionals may be called upon at different stages in situations where child abuse is suspected and individual professionals or members of the community may also be involved by reason of their initial voicing of concern about a child. Those often described as being in the front line in cases of child abuse include those who are most likely to come into contact with children in the course of their daily work. This would, therefore, tend to include, for the under five's: those professionals working in day care or child minding situations, all types of health workers, such as health visitors, community nurses, general practitioners, paediatricians and staff in accident and emergency units and, for 5-16 or 18 year olds teachers, youth workers, and those involved with the sporting activities of children such as swimming instructors and sports instructors generally. As Marshall notes, *opportunity may be a key factor in the identification of abuse and neglect particularly for the under five's where as a group as a whole they may not be in constant daily contact with such professionals.* This is a major resource issue which needs still to be addressed.

As far as 5 – 16 or 18 year olds are concerned, those who feel themselves particularly in the forefront either of identifying child abuse and neglect or of having it communicated to them, are teachers. Yet, of all the professionals dealing with children, this is probably the group which have had least training on matters concerning the identification of child abuse and neglect, and of the approach which should be adopted when disclosures are made to them.

Unlike the guidance produced for nurses, health visitors and midwives and for those working in the health service generally,(See **What every Nurse, Health Visitor and Midwife Needs to know about the Children Act 1989** [DOH 1992] and **Child Protection – Guidance for Senior Nurses, Health Visitors and Midwives** [DOH, HMSO, 1992] no documents of guidance similar have been produced for teachers or indeed for those working in day nurseries and nursery schools or for registered child minders, although DfEE Circulars 10/95 and 11/95 were issued in October 1995 to give some direction, respectively for those concerned with the role of the Education Service in protecting children from abuse, and for those caught up in allegations of abuse in schools. Large numbers of teachers and schools with whom the author has been involved report never having seen these circulars and not having been made aware of their existence.

There is thus clearly a need for both further training and the production of more detailed guidance for relevant professional groups who might consider themselves to be in the front line in the process of identifying child abuse and neglect, or having it communicated to them. It should be stressed, however, that in whichever way agencies or individuals are involved, they are unlikely to view the law as any sort of universal panacea for dealing with the problem of child abuse but rather as "one **possible** resource for dealing with social troubles". (see Dingwall et al **Protecting Children, Controlling Parents: State Intervention in Family Law** [1983, Blackwells] emphasis added).

When identifying the fact that abuse or neglect **may** have taken place, the 1989 Act now usefully provides that a **child assessment order** maybe sought from the family proceedings court in order to allay or confirm such suspicions. It should be pointed out, however, that this procedure, available under section 43 of the 1989 Act (see **Pt.5**), should only be used where it is not possible to persuade parents to take their child to a doctor and to obtain a report from that doctor in order to allay the concerns of professionals. The 1989 Act, as was noted earlier, is predicated upon the principle of partnership between parents and local authorities, thus it is important that voluntary partnership and voluntary action should be tried first when seeking to assess whether or not a child has been abused. Indeed, since one of the most difficult tensions inherent in the Act is that of the balance to be struck between children's needs and families' rights, which is a tension at the heart of all child protection work, it is not surprising that official guidance recognises the risks of law based intervention.

Thus, in **"The Care of Children – Principles and Practice in Regulations and Guidance"** it is stated that *"measures which antagonise, alienate, undermine or marginalise parents are counter productive, for example taking compulsory* powers over *children can **all too easily** have this effect though such action may be necessary in order to provide protection".* (at para 2.7, emphasis added).

The building of a partnership relationship between the child's family and various concerned agencies may have been a continuing one, involving a prolonged period of contact with, and service provision into, the child's family. Regrettably, however, most cases of child abuse triggering intervention through the court will come from those families with whom the relevant agencies have an existing contact (see Dale et al **Dangerous Families** [1986 Tavistock] at Ch.2, generally), rather than from families with which there has been little or no pre-existing contact. As Morrison points out, whatever efforts and measures are directed towards voluntary partnership with parents, there will always be a significant proportion of abused children for whom a level of intervention involving Court Orders will be necessary. (see T.Morrison **Change and Control of the Legal Framework** in Adcock in White, Hollows eds **Significant Harm** [1991, Significant Publication]).

What, perhaps is also different about the 1989 Act is that the positive advantage principle contained in section 1 (5) of the 1989 Act requires local authority social services to demonstrate that the rights given them by court orders will assist in the process of actually **improving** the child's situation and possibly changing the child's family conditions.

It is always difficult to tell whether the processes which might lead to earlier identification are actually working. As has already been noted there are many problems simply in coming up with a definition of what constitutes child abuse and neglect, but as pointed out in **Child Protection – Messages from Research** (DOH 1995) policy makers, researchers and practitioners are likely to consider the context in which such incidents occur before they will define them as abusive.

To assist in identification the Department of Health has also published guidance known in the social work profession as the **"Orange Book"**. This publication – **Protecting Children: A Guide for Social Workers Undertaking Comprehensive Assessment** (HMSO 1988) has been helpful for practitioners trying to identify instances of child abuse and neglect in highlighting the circumstances surrounding maltreatment. One of the problems in such an

Report of the
National
Commission of
Inquiry into the
Prevention of
Child Abuse

approach to identification, however, is that it can become a self-fulfilling prophecy – thus behaviour can be seen to be abusive as soon as it is described as such.In order to be able to identify abuse and thus to be able to identify what is abnormal there must be sufficient evidence for professionals to look to in defining what is normal . Much of the research which is highlighted in **Child Protection – Messages from Research** actually helps by providing evidence as to what normally happens in families and what are the long term outcomes of different parenting styles. As is pointed out in **Child Protection – Messages from Research** (DOH 1995), "such information, in combination with data on other harmful experiences, leads to **a perspective** on child abuse (as opposed to **a definition** of child abuse) which emphasises the *needs* of children and the *context* in which *maltreatment* occurs (own emphasis added).

This in itself may pose more problems for professionals at the daily cutting edge of exposure to potential child abuse than answers but provided such professionals are always open to questions, conduct themselves with due care and consideration for the child and the family's position, then it can only be hoped that we will emerge with an approach to child abuse investigations which could be described as "putting the paramount interest of the children first".

10.   Reporting Child Abuse and Neglect

Unlike 47 of the States of the USA, the law in England does not provide for the compulsory reporting of child abuse. The idea of a reporting law was discussed by the DHSS *Review of Child Care Law* but the working party decided against such a proposal. (1985) para.12(4)). There is therefore no legal duty laid upon members of the public to report suspicions or knowledge of incidents of child abuse. Nevertheless, every encouragement is given to the public to ensure that if they provide such information their anonymity will be protected. As Lord Diplock pointed out in *D v NSPCC* [1977] 1 All ER 589, HL, the private promise of confidentiality must yield to the general public interest that in the administration of justice truth will out, unless by reason of the character of the information or the relationship of the recipient to the informant, a more important public interest is served by protecting the information or the identity of the informant from disclosure in a court of law. Their Lordships concluded in this case that the public interest of ensuring the protection of children was greater than the public interest in ensuring that the whole truth be told, and it thus refused to allow the disclosure of any details relating to the original informant in the particular case.

It also has to be said, however, that the different professional groups working with children, whilst not subjected to any mandatory reporting law as such, may nevertheless find their own professional association's guidance seeks to impose such a duty upon them. For example, the standards committee of the British Medical Council in November 1987 expressed the view that if a doctor has reason for believing that a child is being physically or sexually abused, not only is it permissible for the doctor to disclose information to a third party, but it is also his duty to do so (see *Diagnosis of Child Sexual Abuse: Guidance for Doctors* (1988), DHSS at p.12).

Similar guidance also exists for senior nurses, health visitors and midwives (see DOH *Child Protection – Guidance for Senior Nurses, Health Visitors and Midwives* HMSO 1992), and

Report of the
National
Commission of
Inquiry into the
Prevention of
Child Abuse

although the 1992 Guidance does not make a duty to disclose explicit, it is nevertheless implicit throughout the document wherever it discusses the relevant actions of nurses, health visitors and midwives in responding to suspicions about child abuse. That document makes reference at para.13.2 to the United Kingdom Central Council's "Code of Professional Conduct for the Nurse, Midwife and Health Visitor" and to the advisory paper on confidentiality published in April 1987. There the advice is rather more explicit in that it states "in all cases where the practitioner deliberately discloses or withholds information in what s/he thinks is the public interest, s/he must be able to justify the decision. These situations can be particularly stressful, especially where vulnerable groups are concerned as disclosure may mean the involvement of a third party as in the case of children or the mentally handicapped. Practitioners should always take the opportunity to discuss the matter fully with other practitioners (not only or necessarily fellow nurses, midwives and health visitors), and if appropriate to consult with a professional organisation before making a decision. There will often be ramifications that these are best explored before a final decision as whether to withhold or disclose information is made". It will be noted that such advice falls some way short of the stringent duty advised in the Guidance for Doctors.

Given their key involvement, it is even more surprising to find a very cautious stance adopted by the British Association for Social Workers in 1986 in their Code of Ethics for Social Work. This states, as a principle of practice, that social workers will "recognise that information clearly entrusted for one purpose should not be used for another purpose without sanction. They will respect the privacy of clients and others with whom they come into contact and confidential information gained in their relationships with them. They will divulge such information only with the consent of the client (or informant) except where there is clear evidence of serious danger to the client, worker, other persons or the community or in other circumstances judged exceptional on the basis of professional consideration and consultation". (BASW 1986). Department of Health Guidance on the other hand specifically aimed at social services, is rather more direct in its approach. Thus guidance on the issue of confidentiality is to be found in a Department of Health circular to local authority social services departments (LAC (88) 17) headed "Personal Social Services: Confidentiality of Personal Information". The approach in that document is admirably summed up at para.3.15 of *Working Together*. It states there that "in child protection work the degree of confidentiality will be governed by the need to protect the child. Social workers and others working with the child and family must make clear to those providing information that confidentiality *may not* be maintained if the withholding of the information will prejudice the welfare of a child".

Other staff, particularly in the education service, may also be deemed to be in the front line as far as initial identification and referral processes in child abuse cases are concerned. Local education authorities all over the country have, in compliance with local ACPC guidelines, issued education staff with an explanation of the new law and the new procedures which may flow from the referral of a case of suspected child abuse but large numbers of teachers in the public sector report little or no knowledge of the new Act or procedures.

Their general view is that they would try to refer the matter to the head teacher, or if there is one, to the teacher with responsibility for liaison with social services over child protection matters. Whilst LEAs are responsible for staff in the education service, such as teachers,

*Report of the
National
Commission of
Inquiry into the
Prevention of
Child Abuse*

education welfare officers, educational psychologists and youth workers, they have no responsibility for the private sector. This instead falls on social services departments, who should ensure that educational establishments, not maintained by the LEA, are aware of the local inter-agency procedures, and the governing bodies/proprietors of these establishments should ensure that appropriate procedures are in place, seeking advice as necessary from social services. It is obviously advisable that for all educational establishments, procedures should also cover circumstances where a member of staff is accused of suspected abuse. (See new DfEE Circular 11/95 Misconduct of Teachers and Workers with Children and Young Persons Working Together under the Children Act 1989). The DfEE have now issued a 27 page Circular entitled **Protecting Children from Abuse: The Role of the Education Service** (Circular 10/95) which emphasis that all teachers should be alert to signs of abuse and know to whom they should report any concerns or suspicions. The Circular also stresses that certain members of staff should be given responsibility for child protection matters in all schools and colleges. As *Working Together* states, "the key element essential to ensuring that proper procedures are followed in each educational establishment, is that the head teacher or another senior member of staff should be designated as having responsibility for liaising with social services and other relevant agencies in cases of child abuse. Furthermore for establishments maintained by them, LEAs should keep up to date lists of designated staff and ensure that these staff receive appropriate training and support." (*Working Together* (DOH) 1991, para.4.37).

314

It is perhaps unfortunate that in the period leading up to the implementation of the Children Act and indeed following implementation up to the present time, few education authorities in England and Wales had actually engaged in training upon the implications of the Children Act 1989 either generally or particularly in relation to child protection work. Staff in educational establishments often feel extremely vulnerable because of their ignorance on what they rightly deem to be a very important subject. Many teachers have reported being totally unaware of the existence of DfEE Circulars 10 and 11/95. Whilst the materials for the national curriculum now include modules within each of the key stages relevant to children keeping themselves safe and having relevant education in matters of personal relationships and development, many teachers feel that they are engaged in teaching such areas of the curriculum without themselves having the necessary background knowledge to act in cases where there may be a need to refer concerns about possible child abuse to a relevant agency. These criticisms have all been raised in addition by staff in day nurseries and nursery schools and further by registered child minders.

Probation Officers may also have concerns about possible child abuse in cases in which they become involved, either as a result of their responsibility for the supervision of offenders including those convicted of offences against children, or even more likely, in the performance of their role as court welfare officers in proceedings involving family relationship breakdown (s.7 CA 1989). Through their work in preparing reports for courts, they may well turn up concerns about whether a child is suffering or likely to suffer significant harm. In non-urgent cases they may refer their concerns back to court and the court is then able under s.37 CA 1989, to direct a local authority to conduct an investigation into the child's circumstances to see whether or not it is necessary to take proceedings for a care or supervision order. In urgent cases, the probation service must notify social services of their concerns, and social services will then be under a duty to make enquiries and to take

*Report of the
National
Commission of
Inquiry into the
Prevention of
Child Abuse*

such action as may be necessary. Of relevance also to this issue of reporting is the fact that arrangements exist to ensure that when offenders convicted of offences against children are discharged from prison, probation services inform the local authority in the area in which the discharged prisoner plans to reside. This allows the social services department to make enquiries and to take action where it is believed that there may be danger to children residing at the same address. In many parts of the country, it is now the case that pre-release case conferences will be held involving probation and social services, where the prisoner is believed to constitute a danger to children living in a particular family. This should provide the forum in which appropriate arrangements can be agreed in order to safeguard and protect the relevant children. Where prisoners are being released from psychiatric units it may be appropriate to hold such a case conference at the psychiatric unit and to involve not only staff from the unit but those who may be involved in community psychiatric support.

As far as police reporting of concerns about child abuse is concerned, this stems from their primary duty to protect members of the community and to bring offenders to justice. As will be seen in the following paragraphs, the police have special powers to take action in emergencies, but where they have concerns about the possibility of child abuse which is of a non urgent nature, then they would be expected to notify such concerns to social services.

It should be noted that what has been said about the duties of the different agencies in respect of reporting concerns about particular children, applies with equal force to later stages in the child protection process such as investigation and assessment.

315

Finally, whilst reporting of concerns about child abuse may come from any of the professionals in any of the agencies already discussed, and may come through to a social services department, the police or the NSPCC, referrals may also come from members of the public, or those working with children and families who are not accustomed to dealing with child protection matters. *Working Together* points out that "all referrals whatever their origin, must be taken seriously and must be considered with an open mind which does not prejudge the situation. The statutory agencies must ensure that people know how to refer to them, and they must facilitate the making of referrals and the prompt and appropriate action in response to expressions of concern. It is important in all these cases that the public and professionals are free to refer to the child protection agencies without fear that this will lead to uncoordinated and/or premature action." ((1991) para.5.11.1). As events in Cleveland, Rochdale and the Orkneys have demonstrated, a balance needs to be struck between taking action designed to protect the child from abuse whilst at the same time protecting him or her and the family from the harm caused by unnecessary intervention.

While much of this part has focused on the nature of adults involved in reporting allegations of child abuse or of children revealing that they are the subject of child abuse, the issue of reporting becomes once again more difficult when it is the case that children are making allegations against those supposedly in positions of care in respect of them. This, most notably, involves the situation when children make allegations against teachers in their schools or, when in the care of the local authority, they make allegations against care staff. Children as well as teachers and care staff need to know that such allegations will be dealt with in a proper fashion.Guidance in respect of local authority social services investigating allegations made against their own staff was contained within the volumes of guidance

*Report of the
National
Commission of
Inquiry into the
Prevention of
Child Abuse*

issued pursuant to the 1989 Act. Problems concerning allegations made against teachers have given rise to a considerable cause for concern and in England and Wales various of the unions and teacher organisations collaborated together with employers generally and formed a working group on allegations of physical and sexual abuse against teachers. A major conference was held involving inter-agency representation, as a result of which there was overwhelming support for national model guidance on best practice and procedures. Model guidance was indeed produced and was the subject of extensive inter-agency consultation resulting finally in new advice issued by the Department for Education and Employment in DfEE Circular 10/95. The DfEE Circular recommended that the agreed model guidance be sent to all schools and it is understood that a copy is now in every school though little or no training has been provided on its contents and many staff are unaware of its existence.

Somewhat disturbingly, however, the National Union of Teachers seems to have taken on board the lesson given out by the tabloid newspapers in respect to **Child Protection – Messages from Research**. In a letter to the author's co-researcher on a project on allegations against teachers, the General Secretary of the National Union of Teachers has commented that

> *considerable review of LEA procedures has taken place over the last year and many LEAs have now adopted the recommended models set out in DfEE Circular 10/95.* **At the same time, as you will know, there has been from the Department of Health an emphasis on preventative work on child protection following its concern over the resources spent on investigations many of which are unproductive.** *These factors have contributed to a changing emphasis and the Union's concerns are not what they once were. The changing emphasis to preventive work has been reflected in the rise in the number of allegations being held and, although it may be too early to be sure, a falling in the number of* **heavy handed investigations** *(author's emphasis is added).*

Unfortunately, for those of us who engage in a careful and analytical reading of **Child Protection – Messages from Research** this is not the message which we should be taking away from that document. There are, throughout the document, acknowledgements that there are many serious cases in which child abuse investigations are indeed warranted and that an early response to suspicions of child abuse, or identification of child abuse is absolutely critical. If those advising such a key professional group involved at the cutting edge of the identification of child abuse and neglect are taking away such a distorted message from that document this Commission has just cause to be extremely concerned.

As well as allegations of abuse being made against teachers, there have continued to be a great many serious allegations of abuse made by children who have been made the subject of care orders, who have been accommodated by local authorities, or who have been locked up in local authority secure units or Young Offender institutions. Nobody would like to think of Pindown happening again but where do we fear it happening? Do we only get worried if it may be happening in ordinary LA children's home and do we share the concerns in the same way if we are told very clearly that it is happening to the difficult problem children in society. **Banged Up, Beaten Up and Cutting Up,** Helena Kennedy QC's Report for the Howard League for Penal Reform revealed appalling levels of daily violence against children and young people in Secure Units and Young Offender Institutions. She reports one manager of a Secure Unit stating that 90% of the children in his unit have been abused and then they are locked up because they have become difficult and engaged in criminal behaviour whereupon they are subjected to even more abuse in the institutions.

Report of the
National
Commission of
Inquiry into the
Prevention of
Child Abuse

11.   Responding to Child Abuse and Neglect

As was noted earlier in **Pt.9**, the law is not seen as a universal panacea for dealing with the problem of child abuse and moving in with full blown legal investigations may also not be warranted. Much will depend on the critical building of partnerships with parents where families are already known to social services and where such children may well be on the local Child Protection Register.In most cases, if there is a new trigger for a cause for concern about a particular child, the concerned professional will make checks with other involved agencies and professionals and as a matter of routine will check the Child Protection Register if they are not already aware of the fact that the child is on such a register. As was noted earlier in **Pt.4** with regard to the law on safeguarding and promoting children's welfare, part III of the 1989 Act was particularly crucial in elevating the principle of prevention to a position of central importance in the work of all agencies concerned the protection of children and the positive promotion of their health and welfare. What has emerged in the 1989 Act, therefore, is a recognition of the point made by the Inter-Departmental Review of Child Care Law (1985, DHSS), that prevention was an inadequate term to describe the purpose of local authority provision for families with children . The Review indicated that there were two main aims of such provisions: to provide family support to help parents bring up their children; and to seek to prevent admission to care or **court proceedings** except where this is in the best interest of the child (author's emphasis added).

317

The provisions in section 17 and Sch.2 part I of the 1989 Act incorporate the recommendations of the Review and introduced a very positive model of prevention in the first instance, or prevention following on incidents giving rise to a cause for concern. Local authorities are now required to produce their Children's Services Plans and a number of research studies have shown the benefits of the notion of family support and prevention (see J.Gibbon, S. Thorpe and P.Wilkinson – **Family Support and Prevention: Studies in Local Areas** [1990, HMSO]) and see also **Paternalism or Partnership? a family involvement in the child protection process,** by Thorburn, Lewis and Shemings [University of East Anglia] HMSO (1995). A whole range of services can thus be provided by local authorities or by local authorities working together with voluntary organisations as the 1989 Act positively encourages. (see section 27). There is a great deal of recognition in the Act and DOH guidance that local authorities must also provide services to children with disabilities in their area so as to minimise the effect of their disabilities and to give such children the opportunities to lead lives that are as normal as possible. (Sch.2 Pt.1 para 6)

Thus, whilst the response of preventive work was certainly important under the previous law, the provisions in the 1989 Act have elevated the principle of prevention as a response to the top of local authorities' child protection agendas. But with a shortage of resources and with social workers often dealing with crises one may ask the question as to whether despite the principle being at the top the practice is there also?

Report of the
National
Commission of
Inquiry into the
Prevention of
Child Abuse

The problem would appear to be that an undue burden is placed upon local authorities to provide the services under part III of the 1989 Act. This burden falls particularly on social services and although section 27 provides social services with the ability to request help from a range of other authorities within the local area, such as local housing authorities, local education authorities, health authorities, and health service trusts such a request need only be complied with if it is compatible with the other authority's statutory functions and does not unduly prejudice the discharge of those functions. As the DOH guidance states, social services will, on occasion, turn to the education authority for assistance in meeting the duties placed on social services departments in respect of family support (**The Children Act 1989 – Guidance and Regulations, Volume 2: Family Support, Day Care and Education Provision for Young Children** at para. 1.13). The type of service envisaged here might include the services of an educational psychologist or speech therapist where efforts are being made to mitigate the effects of possible child abuse or neglect. The guidance goes on to state that the local authority carries the principal responsibility for co-ordinating and providing services for children in need, although in some cases its services will be supportive of other key agencies. Local authorities and other relevant agencies remain responsible for decisions about their own service provision or legal and administrative issues assigned to them. They should, however, seek out and have available the best relevant help from other agencies. Similarly they must "be available and prepared to contribute to the work of other key agencies in meeting the legitimate needs of children and their families" (para 1.14).

Thus, it can be seen that the elevation of the prevention principle as a response represented by the enactment of part III of the 1989 Act should have meant that the provision of day nursery places, playgroup places, child minding facilities, family aids, family centres, respite care, short holidays and access to various educational and health facilities, would all have been considered and that some would have been used before resort made is to legal action through such means as care proceedings.

It is implicit in such guidance that the task of all professionals working within the child protection arena should, therefore, be to provide services to help to maintain the child in the family, provided always that to do so is consistent with the child's welfare. This not only accords with part III of the 1989 Act but also with the UN Convention on the Rights of the Child. The legislative support for the principle of prevention as a response represented by the enactment of part III serves only to reinforce many examples of good practice carried on by a range of professionals prior to the enactment of the 1989 Act. What the Act, of course, **fails** to address is the issue of **resources**. Thus, whilst many professionals would see prevention as the **best response**, the reality with regard to implementation of the Children Act in England and Wales is that it has been seriously under-resourced and this has presented a range of difficulties for all professionals concerned with responding to the problem of the prevention of child abuse and neglect.

12. Investigation of Child Abuse and Neglect

It has already been pointed out above that different professionals may, at various stages in a child's life, be the ones most exposed to the chance that they will identify and then have to report further on their fears or suspicions about child abuse and neglect. Many of the guidelines which are in place emphasise getting in touch with social services and only rarely

Report of the
National
Commission of
Inquiry into the
Prevention of
Child Abuse

will it be the case that the police will be called in first. This may, however, arise where police have been called in by members of the public or family members related to the victim in relation to some sort of suspected physical injury or even an incident of domestic violence. The police may also be involved where there is an issue of **suspected** child abuse and, as **Working Together** emphasises, a great deal of work has been put into establishing joint working procedures and joint training particularly with regard to the issue of joint investigations in child abuse cases. (See **Fig.2** in Appendix).

Despite huge steps forward in the co-operation achieved between the professionals involved, particularly between police and social services, there is still evidence of professional concerns about the limits of the respective professionals' involvement in the work which they do in investigating child abuse.

By **s47** of the 1989 Act, where a local authority receives information that a child who lives or is found in its area, is subject to an emergency protection order or is in police protection, or it has reasonable cause to suspect that a child in its area is suffering or likely to suffer **significant harm**, the authority must make or cause to be made such enquiries as it considers necessary. The purpose of such enquiries is to enable the local authority social services department to determined whether it should take any action to safeguard or prevent the child's welfare. It should also be remembered that a local authority may receive information about the possibility of a child suffering or being likely to suffer **significant harm**, via a Court Welfare Officer engaged in providing a report to the court in family proceedings, under the 1989 Act, or the local authority may receive a direction from the court itself to conduct an investigation as to whether there is a need to institute care or supervision proceedings under **s37** of the 1989 Act.

319

The duty placed on the local authority to investigate in cases of suspected child abuse is the same, no matter where that abuse has occurred or by whom it has been perpetrated. Thus, whilst **additional** special procedures may be invoked where children are abused in residential settings, outside the family home, in foster placements or in schools, the first duty upon the local authority is to engage in an investigation under **s47**, which may well include taking steps to involve the police (see **Working Together**, paras. 5.19 – 5.24.5).

This is certainly the case if, at any point in the early stages of the investigation by social services or perhaps the NSPCC if it becomes apparent that there is the possibility of a criminal offence having been committed against the child. It may be the case, of course, that the police have been involved in some way either in the initial referral or in the early stages of investigation following referral, but it is essential that there is an early strategy discussion between police and social services in order to plan the investigation properly and, in particular the role of each agency and the extent of joint investigations (see **Fig.2** and for the background of such strategy discussions see N. Parton **Co-ordination Management and Assessment in Governing the Family** [1991, MacMillan 1995] Ch.5, especially at pp.127 – 129). It is the responsibility of the agency receiving the referral to initiate this and, throughout the early stages of the investigation, both police and social services must keep in mind that it may be necessary to invoke civil child protection proceedings or criminal proceedings, or both, against the perpetrator. Interviewing the child victim or the child or adult perpetrator must be conducted in accordance with the established codes of practice

*Report of the
National
Commission of
Inquiry into the
Prevention of
Child Abuse*

and current case law. As far as interviewing child victims are concerned the **Memorandum of Good Practice** on video recorded interviews with child witnesses for criminal proceedings (Home Office and DOH, HMSO 1992) should be followed wherever such interviews are being video recorded. Early problems associated with using the Memorandum, which followed on the recommendations of the Pigot Committee, have been identified and there are repeated calls for all the recommendations of the Pigot Committee to be implemented as early as possible in order to improve all aspects of the criminal justice system when responding to the problems posed by the perpetration of abuse on child victims.

Despite many excellent examples of police and social services working together in joint investigations and on interviewing together pursuant to the **Memorandum of Good Practice,** it is apparent that there are still concerns even now about the way in which such video recorded interviews are conducted and the outcomes generally for child victims in the criminal justice process.(See **The Child, the Court and the Video – A study of the implementation of the Memorandum of Good Practice on video interviewing of child witnesses** (Social Services Inspectorate 1994)) Whilst the police and social services may conduct as rigorous an investigation as possible and pursue this through to pressing for prosecution by the Crown Prosecution Service who then ultimately take the case to court, there remains very considerable concern that knowledge of the problems which child witnesses will face in the criminal justice process actually encourage adult perpetrators to believe that they have a good chance with "getting away with it". This whole area of the law is one which needs considerable further research with regard to the impact which the current process has on children's willingness to reveal child abuse through to the widespread belief of perpetrators that "children are never going to be believed".

The provisions in s47 of the 1989 Act which go on to deal with processing the investigation by social services, provide that enquiries must, in particular, be directed towards establishing whether they should make any application to the court or exercise any of their other powers under the 1989 Act, which could include any of the measures described in Part 5 above (the details of s47 can be ascertained by looking at Part 5).

Many of the problems previously associated with obtaining access to children have now largely disappeared as a result of the implementation of Pt.V of the 1989 Act.

In general, it is clearly desirable that agencies work in partnership with parents in order to ensure that suspicions about potential child abuse or neglect are allayed. Where parents refuse to co-operate, and this extends to denying access, then there are measures such as the use of S.46 of the 1989 Act or S.47 in conjunction with S.48 that enable access to be gained to a child's home, if need be, by force. (See **Pt.5** of this document).

Where there is no problem about actually obtaining access to the child but the parent is reluctant to allow the child to be examined or assessed, medically or otherwise, then S.43 may provide a remedy by the use of the Child Assessment Order. Evidence thus far available (see Children Act Advisory Committee Annual Reports 1992, 1993 and 1994) would suggest that the mere fact that a Child Assessment Order can potentially be used is sufficient without it actually requiring to be used. (See **Part 5** of this document).

As far as the investigation of child abuse is concerned and the subsequent initiation of any proceedings in civil law, it would appear to be the case that the 1989 Act has effected a substantial overhaul of the system and that the range of professionals working within the system believe it to be working well. Certainly the legal provisions are there which can ensure the protection of children. The only factor which mitigates against their use in all circumstances of child abuse and neglect is the lack of resources, principally the number of social workers available to adequately to resource the prevention of child abuse and neglect and the protection of children from abuse and neglect.

13. Legal Processes

a) Recent Changes in The Criminal Justice system

A number of points as to the conflicts posed by the differing demands of the civil child protection process and the criminal offence investigation process have already been noted. Although, as a result of the **Pigot Committee Report**, a number of changes were made to the criminal justice system dealing with the problem of difficulties faced by child witnesses, it nevertheless has to be noted that the criminal justice system has a long way to go before it can effectively be described as contributing to the prevention of child abuse and neglect. At the moment the suspicion is that it **contributes** to child abuse and neglect.

The Criminal Justice Act 1988 provided for the reception of evidence by television link in certain cases in order to reduce the stressful effects of a court appearance upon child witnesses in alleged child abuse cases and the reforms effected by the Criminal Justice Act 1991 have meant that English courts have used video and tape recorded evidence with increasing frequency.

321

Since 5 January 1989, under s.32 CJA 1988, evidence can be given in the normal way, but witnesses can be allowed to testify from a room outside the actual courtroom. Section 32(1) also allows evidence to be given by satellite link where a witness (of any age or in any type of case) is outside the U.K.

The Criminal Justice Act 1991 took the Criminal Justice Act 1988 reforms even further in the realm of video or live television links and has made admissible (in most cases) pre-recorded interviews with child witnesses in place of live evidence – in – chief. A new s.32(A) has been inserted into CJA 1988. A video recording is admissible only where:

(i)   *The child is not the accused;*

(ii)   *The child is available for cross-examination (assuming the proceedings get that far);* and

(iii)   *Rules of court requiring disclosure of the circumstances in which the recording was made, have been properly complied with.*

A video recorded interview is admissible at all stages of trials at the Crown Court and in the youth courts for those sexual offences and offences of violence and cruelty to which the provision of s.32 apply. Where any particular court does not possess live link facilities, the hearing can be moved to a court which does, even if that involves going outside the area for which the court acts. Live television links are available to any young person who has to be

Report of the
National
Commission of
Inquiry into the
Prevention of
Child Abuse

cross-examined following the admission of video recorded evidence. A video recording of an interview between an adult and a child who is not the accused, or one of the accused (the child witness), is admissible if it relates to any matter in issue in the proceedings.

The recording of an earlier investigative interview with a child victim/witness is not admissible as a matter of course. It has first to be shown to a judge who has the power to declare it inadmissible in certain designated circumstances and if it is felt that it should be excluded in the interests of justice. Thus, before the recording may be given in evidence, leave of court must be obtained and, under s.32(A)(3)(a), this will not be granted if

(1) *The child witness will not be available for cross-examination,*

(2) *Any rule of court requiring disclosure of the circumstances in which the recording was made has not been complied with to the court's satisfaction,*

or

(3) *The court is of the opinion, having regard to all the circumstances of the case, that, in the interests of justice, the recording ought not to be admitted.*

The court is allowed to exclude only that part of a statement which it is not in the interests of justice to admit, but, under s.32(A)(4) the court is asked to consider whether any prejudice to the accused, or one of the accused, might result by showing the whole or most of the whole of the recorded interview. The construction of the provisions indicates that all three conditions must be satisfied before leave can be given.

Once such a recording has been admitted, the child should not be examined in chief on any matters covered in the recording, although cross-examination of the child on other matters not covered in the recording is permitted, and this may be done through the live video link (s.32(A)(5). Any statement (which may include drawings and models since statement includes any representation of fact, whether made in words or otherwise (s.32(9)) disclosed in such a recording shall be treated as if given by the child in all testimony in the witness box. Thus, it shall not be regarded as hearsay simply because it is a recording. However, under s.32(A)(6)(b), any statement made in a recording by a witness will not corroborate any other evidence given by that witness.

Under the third condition in s.32(A)(3)(a), the video recording may be ruled out if it is not in the interests of justice to view it. The tape would, therefore, need to be of sufficient clarity in sound and picture quality in order for the court to view it prima facie viewable (see the **Memorandum of Good Practice**). The most obvious cases warranting exclusion might be where there are inadequacies in testimony amounting to evidence insufficient to satisfy a criminal prosecution, or the inclusion of inadmissible materials such as hearsay narrated by the child, or allegations of similar offences which have not been the subject of charges and which would not be admissible under the similar fact rule (see Birch D **Children's Evidence** (1992) **Crime Law Review** 267 at p.271).

Section 32(A) applies to the trial of offences covered by s.32 CJA 1988 in the Crown Court or youth court and in appeals therefrom, including a reference by the Attorney General.

Therefore, in certain cases, the child may still be called as a witness and may have to undergo the trauma and ordeal of cross-examination in open court. Amendments moved in the

Report of the
National
Commission of
Inquiry into the
Prevention of
Child Abuse

House of Lords (on the basis of recommendations by the Pigot Committee Report) to allow the prosecution to have the right to apply for a child witness to be examined and cross-examined at a **pre-trial out of court hearing** which would be video-recorded and shown to the court did not survive. Two main objections were taken to this form of pre-trial examination:

(1) It was said to be impractical, unrealistic and logistically difficult to prepare cross examination, particularly if it was supposed to be carried out long before the trial and especially if it meant that the child would not be recalled, even if new material were discovered;

(2) That if the child could be recalled for cross-examination at any time during the trial, this may prove to be even more stressful to the child and may prolong the agony and distress of the whole occasion for the child.

b) Supporting Children appearing as Witnesses – Reviewing Video Testimony and Witness Support Schemes

Nevertheless, one should not be too critical of the advances which the CJA 1988 and the CJA 1991 represent. There is, however, a crucial issue which needs to be borne in mind with regard to video testimony. It was, indeed, one which caused some vexation on the occasion of a joint professional dialogue between police, social services and the judiciary held at the **Centre for the Study of the Child, the Family and the Law** at the University of Liverpool .
The problem turned out to be one easily solved and was indeed solved by the judge giving judicial perspectives on the problems of children's video evidence. Social workers were concerned that children often could not remember, as they approached the day of their video link evidence in court, what they had said on the original video recording. Where a prosecution was actually being held between six and twelve months after the original events and, bearing in mind, a child's sense of time may differ considerably from the adult's sense of time, then social workers wished to know whether children could be allowed to see their video testimony again prior to the date of the hearing. The judge indicated that there was absolutely no problem with this and that children should be informed that they have **the right** to ask to see their video testimony although he would not advise this being done on the day of the hearing or even the day before, but perhaps two or three days earlier. It was apparent that neither the police nor the Crown Prosecution Service had ever thought to advise social services looking after children in such circumstances, that such was the case but, there again, social workers had never thought to ask. Since it is noticeable that the recent Court User's Charter makes only the briefest references to children or to children as witnesses, then it would be advisable for such information to be set out clearly for children somewhere. This could be done via the excellent **Child Witness Pack**, produced by the Home Office, Department of Health, Childline, NSPCC and the Calouste Gulbenkian Foundation.

It is, however, become apparent that not everyone working with child witnesses is even aware of the **Child Witness Pack**. The pack consists of the following items:

"Your Child is a Witness – Information and Advise for Parents and Carers";

"Let's get ready for Court – an Activity Book for Child Witnesses Aged 5-9";

Report of the
National
Commission of
Inquiry into the
Prevention of
Child Abuse

and "Tell me More about Court – a Book for Young Witnesses Aged 10-15".

These materials were all produced by Joyce Plotnikoff of the Institute of Judicial Administration at the University of Birmingham. Additional guidance to children with regard to reviewing video testimony should now be included within this pack and the material and guidance constantly updated in the light of children's experiences in the court system. Unfortunately, this has not, so far, been done.

In addition, it is clear that a great deal more needs to be done to support child witnesses. There have been one or two specialist witness support schemes operating in England and Wales for the support of child witnesses but these are by no means wide-spread and many of them suffer for lack of funding. In Merseyside, the police Child Protection Co-ordinator had had to obtain special police authority funding in order to allow the continuance of a Child Witness Support Scheme at the Liverpool Crown Court. Such schemes are seen to be vital in supporting child witnesses and thus in securing convictions for perpetrators of child abuse. Such schemes should be widely established all over England and Wales if children are to have any confidence at all in the Criminal Justice system.

c)   The relationship between the Criminal and Civil Justice Systems

Information about the Criminal Justice System as a whole and about the relationship between criminal prosecutions and civil child protection proceedings is not readily available to children who are the victims of child abuse and neglect. Children and young people themselves feel that greater care should be taken to explain the different purposes of the two systems, since many feel betrayed and personally to blame if a criminal prosecution fails to result in a conviction because their evidence has been called into question. Basic explanations that the standards of proof in criminal trials and in civil proceedings are different can often do wonders for the child. On the other hand, there are still major problems for the child and sometimes an appalling lack of judicial sensitivity to the problems which children will face at the conclusion of criminal and civil proceedings where their evidence appears not to have been believed, (see quotes from **Re H and R** [1996] 1FLR 80 HL). In civil child protection proceedings there will often be, in England and Wales at least, a special representative of the child's interests known as a **guardian *ad litem*. (For an explanation of the qualifications of such people – see below). The guardian *ad litem*** will explain to the child what goes on in court and will endeavour to explain the whole process. There is no such special representative for the child who has to experience the criminal justice system. This is because the child is not seen as a party to the proceedings. Where there are no special child witness support schemes in operation the child will often only have the support of the non-abusing parent if the child is still living within the family or, where the child has been removed, the support of social workers. In such situations, social workers have not been trained to deal with the problems raised by the intricacies of the criminal justice system. Given that there will be cases where the child has to appear in court, or has to undergo cross examination, the child will only be able to fully participate if she or he is prepared for the process and provided with support throughout. The appointment of a **guardian *ad litem*** for child witnesses in criminal cases involving the prosecution of the alleged perpetrator might well do a great deal to improve the chances of successful convictions in cases where proceedings are taken. It might also serve to encourage children and, more particularly, young people who, having heard of the experiences of other children, via the media or other means, feel understandably reluctant to subject themselves to a process in which, at the end of the day, they may neither be believed nor protected. There is still a great deal more that could be done by critical amendments to the criminal justice system itself in order to prevent children suffering abuse and neglect. (see Morgan J and William's J **Child Witnesses and the Legal Process** 1992 Journal of Social Welfare and Family Law p.484 – 496.)

As noted above, in civil child protection proceedings the child will have the benefit where they are a party to the proceedings and the court believes that it is necessary to safeguard the child's interests, of having a **guardian *ad litem*** appointed, who is usually an experienced independent social worker or probation officer.

In addition to the guardian ad litem, the child involved in civil child protection proceedings in England and Wales will also have the benefit of a solicitor who, will be instructed throughout the case by the guardian ad litem where the child is young but, where the child is older then s/he is able to give instructions direct to the solicitor. This unique system of the dual representation of the child by a solicitor representing to the court what the child wants and by a guardian ad litem whose duty it is to safeguard the best interest of the child for the court is one which is unique and which other jurisdictions are now considering copying. (See recent Child Law Conferences in Germany and Israel). It has been considerably strengthened by the provisions in the 1989 Act and the relevant rules of court.

Given that there are real risks to children involved in parental divorces or the breakdown of parental relationships, where parents may reach agreements which arguably are not in their child's best interests, it has been proposed that they too should have the protection of a special Children's Officer who would be available in family hearing centres to co-ordinate the provision of information, consultation and where appropriate representation for children caught up in proceedings and who may wish to consider taking some steps through the courts in order to prevent the development of a potentially abusive situation. In this area, children are particularly concerned about the impact on their own social development posed by the agreements reached between parents where no resort is made to court, (see amendments to the Family Law Bill (tabled by IRCHIN) supported by all the major children's organisations and the Family Law Bill (Briefing Paper prepared by IRCHIN (Independent Representation for Children in Need, December, January and February 1996).

d. The problem of Domestic Violence

The law on domestic violence, especially as it relates to children needs, much more attention. (See **Part 7**). Hopefully, some reform of this area of the law will be achieved by the enactment of the Family Law Act 1996 for England and Wales and, particularly, the enactment of the amendments to s44 and s38 of the 1989 Act, which provide for local authorities and others to seek the addition of an **exclusion requirement** to emergency protection orders and interim care orders (see Sch.6 Family Law Act 1996). The Act has now been passed and although it is unlikely to be implemented until 1998 at the earliest, the provisions on divorce contained within the Act contain some worrying features for partners and children suffering from domestic violence. Thus, the drive towards family mediation prior to filing for divorce and the extended cooling off period may entail greater risk and

*Report of the
National
Commission of
Inquiry into the
Prevention of
Child Abuse*

Report of the
National
Commission of
Inquiry into the
Prevention of
Child Abuse

distress for weak, abused partners and potentially for their children. The privatisation of child abuse in this sphere of the law is another cause for concern which could justify further research and investigation.

Conclusions on Legal Processes

Just as Marshall identified was, the case with Scotland, far greater consideration needs to be given to the rules of evidence and procedure in criminal cases involving children as witnesses against perpetrators of child abuse and neglect. Attention should be given to incorporating far more references to children in the newly published Court Users Charter and amendments to the Child Witness Pack should also be considered to give relevant information to children, particularly involving the use of video testimony and their opportunity to re-view it. Attention should also be given to the unimplemented recommendations of the **Pigot Report** since the current provisions on children as witnesses in the criminal justice system are seen as a direct contributing factor to the continued prevalence of child abuse and neglect, not only in families, but also in institutional settings.

In accordance with the work of Morgan and William's (cited above) consideration should be given to expanding the role of guardian ad litem currently available in civil child protection proceedings to allow the appointment of such a guardian in criminal proceedings.

As far as civil child protection proceedings are concerned, it has already been noted that the Booth Report indicates that delay in children's cases is becoming an increasing problem in the public law arena and thus, most particularly, in civil child protection cases. Despite the provision in **S.1 (2)** that delay will be presumed to be prejudicial to children's welfare delay is becoming an increasing problem. (see **Pt.3** above). Increased powers should be given to the judiciary to speed up civil child protection cases.

The issue of delay is also one which should concern those administering the criminal justice system. Delays in the criminal justice system in bringing cases involving child abuse to court means that therapeutic work with children can be delayed until the process is complete although the admission of video testimony has had some beneficial affect in ameliorating this problem. It is suggested that fast-tracking of cases involving abuse and neglect of children should be more closely monitored, as the evidence would tend to suggest that, if anything, these cases are taking longer to get to disposition than normal cases. (see **Prosecuting Child Abuse: an Evaluation of the Government's Speedy Progress Policy** by Plotnikoff J. and Woolfson R.(1995) Blackstone)

14. Outcomes for Children

As has been identified throughout the course of this initial position paper, the law in England and Wales now contains a much wider range of powers and responsibilities providing for the protection of children and for the investigation of situations in which children can be said to be at risk, than was previously the case. The 1989 Act is, however, not free from a number of criticisms and as was stated in **One Scandal Too Many – The case for the Comprehensive Protection of Children in all Settings** (report to the Calouste Gulbenkian Foundation, London 1993).

Report of the
National
Commission of
Inquiry into the
Prevention of
Child Abuse

"It is clear that, whatever the intention, the provisions afforded for the protection of children by the law and current policies and practice in all settings are far from adequate".

As repeated scandals involving child abuse in institutional settings in both England and Wales have shown, (see most recently the situation in Clwyd, North Wales) and the recent report of Helena Kennedy Q.C. for the Howard League, children who are placed in protective care may well be at risk of abuse equal to or greater than that from which they were removed.

It would still appear to be the case that children do not possess confidence in systems which are put in place to protect them. If having suffered from abuse in the home they are then placed in institutional settings where they are further abused, we can have little cause to be surprised. It was naively asserted by the Minister of State at the time of the implementation of the Children Act that **s.26**, the provision allowing children to make representations using new complaints procedures, would adequately safeguard against the sort of practice that had gone on in Pindown. Yet such was manifestly not the case and children have continued to be abused within the system.

When children do seize the initiative and actually complain to the police, the criminal justice system offers them little opportunity for protection and exposes them to the trauma of the adversarial dynamics inherent in the English criminal justice system. It is submitted that a proper balance has yet to be struck within the criminal justice system between the interests and safety of our children and the interests of the accused.

15. Specific Areas of Concern

a. *the legitimisation of violence against children*

One of the most frequently asked questions by children and young people at Seminars in the Centre for the Study of the Child, the Family and the Law at the University of Liverpool has been that with regard to the issue of parents being allowed to hit their children. Children perceive the differential way in which the law views assaults on adults and assaults on children as essentially unjust. They do not believe that the availability of the defence of reasonable chastisement or proper punishment can possibly be justified. As my own ten year old son put it "how do you decide what is reasonable in this context?". How do you teach children that bullying and assaulting other children is wrong if you allow parents and teachers constantly to assault and to bully? The essential denial to children of a voice in their own education system (see Education[no.2] Act 1988) is a devaluing of their position and means that teachers and head teachers have no obligation to listen to children and that children are constantly subject to the whim and discretion of individual adults who are not seen to be controlled in any way in terms of what they can say to children and young people.

b. *A Legal Definition of Parental Responsibilities*

There can be no justification for the now existing discrepancy between the Children (Scotland) Act 1995 and the provisions of the Children Act 1989 and the Children (Northern Ireland) Act 1995 with regard to the definition which has been given to the issue

Report of the
National
Commission of
Inquiry into the
Prevention of
Child Abuse

of parental responsibility. Whilst the definition provided in the Scottish Act is to be welcomed as representing a marked advance on that contained in the Children Act 1989 for England and Wales, it is suggested that a unified definition for all the U.K. jurisdictions could go much further and would be extremely useful not only for parents but also for children.

c.   Taking into Account the Wishes and Views of Children

The Children (Scotland) Act 1995 provides that families should take into account the views of their children where they are of sufficient age and understanding to hold such views. There is no such similar requirement in England or Northern Ireland and there is, therefore, another discrepancy between children in England, Wales and Northern Ireland and children in Scotland.

It should be noted that in this respect also the Children (Northern Ireland) Order 1995 mirrors exactly the provisions of the 1989 Children Act for England and Wales and thus, incomprehensibly, Scottish children are to be the only ones to benefit from a greater respect accorded to their position by the law.

Enactments giving children greater responsibility within the education system, such as the restoration of the provision allowing for pupil governors in schools might give children some self respect, as well as responsibility and the knowledge that they could have some impact in an area which critically effects them throughout most of their childhood. The potential for Schools Councils has been recognised in a number of parts of the United Kingdom and the value in such councils in reducing abuse by children on other children has been felt to be very considerable. (See Annual Report of Schools Councils U.K. [Schools Councils U.K. 1995])

d.   Reform of the Criminal Justice System

Much has been said about the need for reform in the criminal justice system specifically with regard to the issues of delays, the giving of evidence by children in criminal cases, support of such children by a witness support scheme and the possible introduction into the criminal process of a guardian ad litem. Further urgent consideration should now be given to the implementation of recommendations originally contained in the Pigot Committee Report.

e)   Implementation of the UN Convention on Children's Rights

A great deal more needs to be done to inform the children of the United Kingdom generally about the United Nations Convention on the Rights of the Child. Very many children do not even know of its existence and, even when they do, have been concerned that so little of our law in reality appears to conform with the demands contained within its Articles. It is, therefore, the case that those few children who do know of its existence view it as a collection of manifesto rights and not as real rights . Nevertheless, professionals and parents should do all that they can to make the terms of the Convention a reality.

As United Nations Secretary-General Javier Perez de Cuellar stated during the drafting of the UN Convention on the Rights of the Child:

Report of the
National
Commission of
Inquiry into the
Prevention of
Child Abuse

"the way society treats its children reflects not only its qualities of compassion and protective caring, but also its sense of justice, its commitment to the future and its urge to enhance the human condition for coming generations".

16. Key Recommendations

i. Key Recommendations regarding the current law in England, Wales and Northern Ireland

o Incorporation of the principles of the United Nations Convention on the Rights of the Child and the European Convention on the Exercise of Children's Rights into all United Kingdom legislation.

o Clarify the legislative provisions across all UK jurisdictions on parental responsibilities towards children. The current inadequate provisions in the law for England, Wales and Northern Ireland and even the limited provisions in Scotland do not guide parents on the reasonable standards of care which they should be providing to their children. The law in England, Wales and Northern Ireland tends to focus on a negative issue, viz that of significant harm, but fails to lay down standards of proper care to which reference can be made. Whilst the Scottish legislation does go a little further in seeking to explain what parents should do, this is, as previously noted, a limited provision and does not provide parents with the clear guidance which many of them are now seeking.

o The law on physical punishment of children should be clarified so that children are made subject to the same protection under the criminal law as adults. The mixed messages which are conveyed to children by the current ambivalence of the law are not defensible and the provisions in section 1(7) of the Children and Young Persons Act 1933 should be repealed.

o Bare legal provisions which provide children with rights, but which do not provide them with access to relevant information, advice, consultation and representation are mere theoretical rights and do not guarantee children protection from abuse in its many different guises. This is, particularly, the case with regard to children involved in parental divorce or relationship breakdown and is also the case with regard to representations or complaints procedures made available to children under the children's legislation, in England and Wales (see the provisions of Section 26 (3) Children Act 1989), and for Northern Ireland (see the provisions of Article 45 (3) Children) Northern Ireland Order 1995.

o Steps should be taken to make both the civil and criminal justice system more accessible to, and comprehensible by, children who may be involved as witnesses. Consideration should be given to extending the guardian ad litem provisions to the criminal justice system in order to support child witnesses in serious cases and more generally there should be an extension of child witness support schemes and the necessary resources should be made available.

o There needs to be a recognition by central government that the huge range of additional duties cast upon local authority social services, by the provision of legislation such as the Children Act 1989, cannot be sustained without the proper level of input of additional resources into local authority budgets. Forcing local authorities to choose between one type of service for one group of children and another type of service for another group

*Report of the
National
Commission of
Inquiry into the
Prevention of
Child Abuse*

simply means a process of circular accounting whereby one service is deprived of support in order to resource another. In extreme cases this has meant the closing down of schemes designed to keep children off the streets and out of trouble in order to support the system of support for children who are disabled and who need particularly expensive services. If so many problems are to be solved then there has to be a decision by Central Government that adequate resources will be made available.

○ Much more has to done to give children confidence in the system's ability to respond to their concerns. The message given out by professionals, across the system, and indeed by the criminal justice system itself is that if a child does find the courage to speak out, this will not necessarily mean that a successful prosecution will result nor more importantly that a safe outcome for the child is guaranteed. Children have to be given more information and assurance about their continued safety to enable them to appreciate that it is still important that they should speak out even if the criminal prosecution of those responsible for abuse committed upon them may not always follow, or where it does, will not always be successful.

○ Children in the United Kingdom need to be much better informed about the general provisions of the law affecting them and about the implications of the United Nations Convention on the rights of the child. This document focuses not only on children's entitlements, interests and claims to be protected, but also on their own abilities to become responsible citizens and to be involved in their communities. The legislation in the United Kingdom should focus much more upon the appropriate responsibilities which can be given to children in order that they may grow into more confident human beings understanding the laws which impact upon them for the benefit not only of the individual child but for children generally.

ii. A New Children's Code

○ All of the key elements in the United Nations Convention on the rights of the child should be translated into the laws of the different UK jurisdictions. It should be noted however that some of the articles of the United Nations Convention are couched in very general terms and therefore are not easily transferable into specific legal provisions. Nevertheless, if the UK Government is to demonstrate its commitment to the children for whom it is responsible then many of the provisions of the UN Convention need to be specifically included and implemented through UK statutory provisions. Article 12 concerning the child's right to express their opinion and to have that opinion taken into account in any matter or procedure affecting the child, would demand express implementation across the whole range of social, welfare, health and educational provisions which exist with regard to children. In order for this to be achieved consideration must be given to a complete new Children's Code and to the institution of the office of a Children's Rights Commissioner or Ombudsman. Such a Commissioner or Ombudsman would be able to act across all boundaries and, in implementing the Children's Code across all Government departments, would be able to ensure a uniformity of approach which is currently lacking across all UK legislation and jurisdictions.

○ The UK Government must recognise that if we are to turn children and young people into the responsible citizens of tomorrow, which it so obviously desires, we have to show that we respect all the provisions of the United Nations Convention on the Rights of the Child and, most particularly, to fulfilling the aims of education set out in Article 29(1)d which states that:

> "*the education of a child shall be directed to the preparation of the child for responsible life in a free society, in the spirit of understanding, peace, tolerance, equality of sexes, and friendship among all peoples, ethnic, national and religious groups and persons of indigenous origin*".

There are many provisions of UK law which do not promote the cause of children becoming responsible citizens in their own right, nor which encourage children to take responsibility for themselves, for each other, and for other people in their communities.

o In order to produce the recommended Children's Code there should be a complete overhaul of civil and criminal law as it impacts upon children which would have a massive impact not only on children but also on the lives of all people who participate in society in the UK today. Legislative instances of the disenfranchisement of children such as the repeal of the provisions on pupil governors enacted in the education (No. 2) Act 1988, send very negative messages towards those whom society, as a whole, would wish to encourage to adopt greater responsibility. One of the key principles of a society which is trying to eradicate child abuse and neglect should be that the people who are most affected by the problem have the opportunity to express their views and much more needs to be done through UK law to recognise that children are people and, as such, should be accorded respect for their views. Education law in the UK has effectively denied children and young people any role in their schools and thus importantly the UK has denied them their voice and it is thus not surprising that many children and young people find it extremely difficult when faced with abuse and neglect, whether in child care institutions, foster care or their own families or in schools, to press forward with any concerns about such treatment meted out to them in these settings.

331

o A proper Children's Code cannot possibly just concern itself with provisions relating to civil law. One of the problems repeatedly faced in the UK has been the confusion wrought by successive pieces of legislation concerning children which seem to be at odds with each other. Thus the UK as a body of people has never sorted out our attitudes to children who offend nor what can be done to remedy this situation. Are we to punish them or to treat them? Do we see them as depraved or deprived? Should we be more understanding or less? Should we be punishing more or less? All of these questions must be answered on the basis of full and properly researched information.

o When dealing with the issue of the perpetration of child abuse and neglect it is again important to realise that the criminal and civil justice systems cannot really be separated out and the same is true when dealing with the children themselves either as victims or as perpetrators. It is important that we device a clear coherent policy with regard to the position of children and young people in our society and the way in which they are treated.

o It is recommended that an independent but centrally funded Office for a Children's Rights Commissioner, situated at some distance from the offices of central government, should be provided and it is possible that the model of the French Education System in providing for pupil representation right up to Government Ministry Level could be followed in ensuring that the voices of children are actually heard at all important levels.

Report of the
National
Commission of
Inquiry into the
Prevention of
Child Abuse

The UK government should recognise children and young people as being a valuable resource for the future and should encourage them to think not only of their rights but also of their responsibilities. To succeed in this, however, the UK government must show that adults in the UK of whom members of the government are obviously the foremost and most public representatives are first capable of acting responsibly towards the children and young people in their care.

○ Finally, difficult questions have to be addressed with regard to the issue of resources and the preparedness of central government to expend the necessary amounts of money in order to achieve the right level of services and provisions designed to ensure a real reduction in the amount of abuse and neglect faced by children and young people in British Society as we head towards the 21st Century.

Report of the
National
Commission of
Inquiry into the
Prevention of
Child Abuse

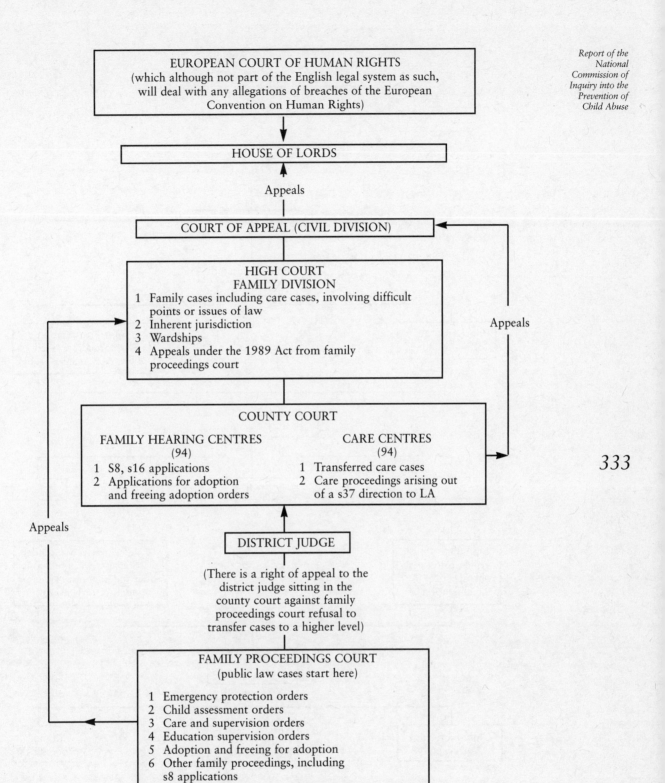

EUROPEAN COURT OF HUMAN RIGHTS
(which although not part of the English legal system as such,
will deal with any allegations of breaches of the European
Convention on Human Rights)

HOUSE OF LORDS

Appeals

COURT OF APPEAL (CIVIL DIVISION)

HIGH COURT
FAMILY DIVISION

1 Family cases including care cases, involving difficult
   points or issues of law
2 Inherent jurisdiction
3 Wardships
4 Appeals under the 1989 Act from family
   proceedings court

Appeals

COUNTY COURT

FAMILY HEARING CENTRES
(94)

1 S8, s16 applications
2 Applications for adoption
   and freeing adoption orders

CARE CENTRES
(94)

1 Transferred care cases
2 Care proceedings arising out
   of a s37 direction to LA

333

DISTRICT JUDGE

(There is a right of appeal to the
district judge sitting in the
county court against family
proceedings court refusal to
transfer cases to a higher level)

Appeals

FAMILY PROCEEDINGS COURT
(public law cases start here)

1 Emergency protection orders
2 Child assessment orders
3 Care and supervision orders
4 Education supervision orders
5 Adoption and freeing for adoption
6 Other family proceedings, including
   s8 applications

Figure 1: Court Structure Diagram

Report of the
National
Commission of
Inquiry into the
Prevention of
Child Abuse

Child Abuse

334

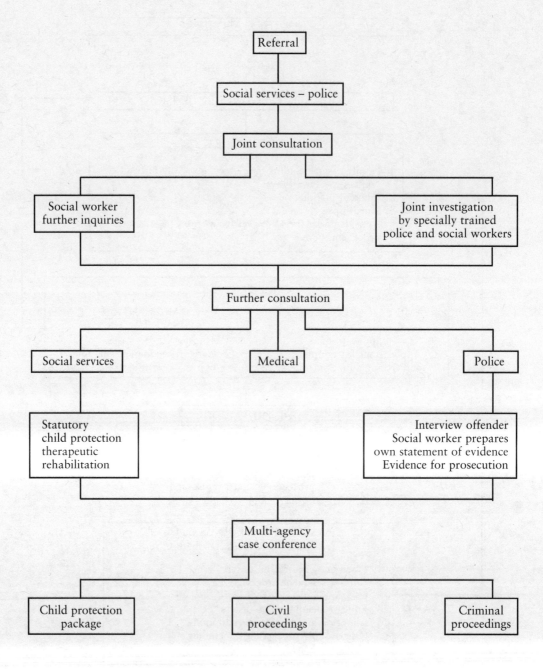

Figure 2: A working model demonstrating police and social services involvement in a child abuse case

*Report of the
National
Commission of
Inquiry into the
Prevention of
Child Abuse*

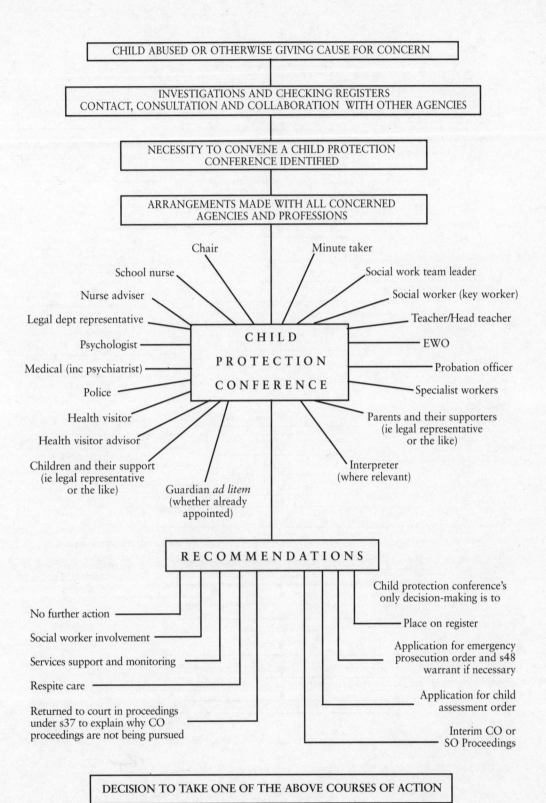

335

*Figure 3: Steps leading to child protection conference and the making of
recommendations for further action in child abuse cases*

Report of the
National
Commission of
Inquiry into the
Prevention of
Child Abuse

Civil Proceedings

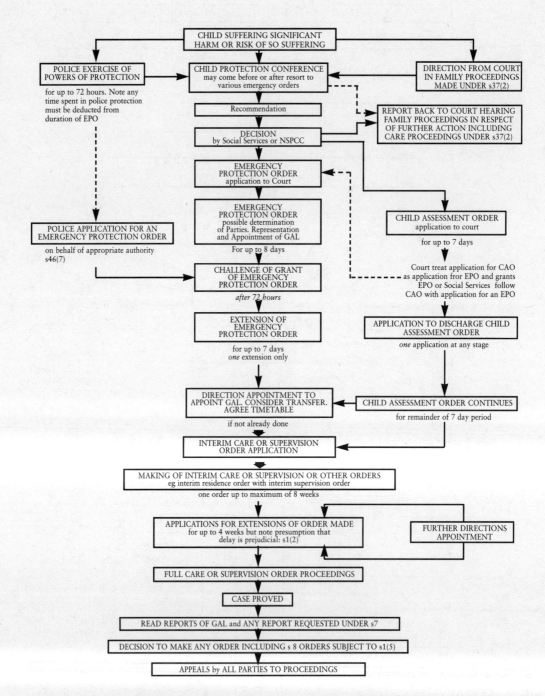

336

Figure 4: *Steps leading to the making of orders in respect of abused children under the Children Act 1989*

Responsibilities for the Prevention of Child Abuse

The prevention of child abuse is *everyone's* responsibility. If *anyone* has a concern about the wellbeing or safety of a child and they feel that it is not being dealt with they should take action. The appropriate action will depend on the particular circumstances but might include: asking the parent or carer if there is a problem; offering advice, help or support; and, if there are still concerns, contacting a professional or agency which can intervene, for example, a health visitor, doctor, police, social services, or NSPCC. While some individuals and agencies have specific responsibilities, described below, these should not be seen as detracting from the responsibilities which everyone should exercise.

Responsibilities for the Prevention of Child Abuse

	Role and Responsibilities	Needs	Action Plan	Note/Comment
Children & Young People	* To tell a trusted and reliable adult when they are unhappy or have concerns about themselves or friends * Self-protection, when they have sufficient understanding * To take responsibility for decisions when they have sufficient understanding	* Adequate living conditions * Basic physical care * Affection * Security * Stimulation and learning * Guidance and control * Responsibility * Independence * Active promotion of self esteem * Promotion of general emotional health	* Research into children's thinking and their worlds * Promotion of a greater understanding of children's needs by all adults * Change culture surrounding children * Personal and social education provision in schools from an early age * Implement UN Convention on Children's Rights	* Needs of children vary * Responsibility for child abuse should not rest with children but society as a whole * Not all children can "self" protect * All adults need to learn how to listen to children and be aware of signs of abuse
Parents/carers	* To have prime responsibility for the care of their children and meeting their needs * To provide protection * To seek help when things go wrong	* Adequate living conditions * Advice and information * Support in times of stress * Respite and relief from their caring role * Learning and skills development * Time for themselves * Non-abusing parents will have extra, particular needs	* The development of a nationwide network of non-stigmatising, accessible support services * Parenting education to be available to all parents * Education on alternatives to physical punishment * Measures to tackle childhood poverty and discrimination	* The family unit may take different forms with different needs * Children's and parents' needs will differ and possibly conflict * Bringing up children is probably the most difficult and challenging job we undertake * It is a lifetime commitment * It affects future generations * It is the "only job for which no training is provided"
Other family members	* To provide support to parents/carers and their children * To contribute as members of the family to the development of children	* Understanding of children and parents and their needs * If they are dependants, they may have extra needs * Grandparents' rights in relation to the children eg access * Understanding who is important in the child's family network	* Inter generational support to be encouraged * Support for parents of young children who are also caring for other dependants	* Children value grandparents * Parents turn to their parents and other relatives for advice * Other family members may not be in a position to offer support * Parenting styles change between generations * There may be conflicts between generations * Other family members may be potential abusers

	Role and Responsibilities	Needs	Action Plan	Note/Comment
Neighbours and friends	* To provide support to parents eg babysitting, practical help * To be vigilant about the well-being of all children * If they have persistent concerns which are unresolved, to report them	* Understanding of children's needs * Knowledge of when to intervene * Knowledge of to whom concerns should be reported * Understanding who is important to the child	* Change culture so that the care of children becomes everyone's responsibility * Public education on the needs of children and what steps to take when there are concerns about a child * Greater awareness of children's networks in the community	* The "professionalisation" of responses to child abuse means that neighbours are less willing to intervene * Neighbours fear being accused of interfering and of "getting it wrong" * Unsympathetic responses from professionals have been reported by neighbours
Offenders	* To take responsibility for their behaviour * To seek help when they are in danger of offending * When appropriate, to learn parenting skills	* To understand the impact of their behaviour on children * Knowledge of sources of support * Information about treatment and their effects	* Improved conviction rate for offences against children * Treatment services to be developed and available to all who need them * National helpline for offenders * Development of a national register of offenders and an effective system for vetting all staff and volunteers who work with children * Research on effectiveness of treatments	* The prevention of child abuse requires the rigorous control of sex offenders and their behaviour * There needs to be improved understanding of patterns of offending behaviour
Community groups: Religious organisations; Black and minority ethnic groups; Youth groups; Community/ neighbourhood groups; Tenants and Residents Associations; Women's groups; WI; Campaigning Groups.	* To provide support to members and their families * To provide information on sources of help * To make referrals as appropriate * To select carefully volunteers and paid staff working in contact with children * To campaign for improved provision * To build confidence and skills to move forward	* Knowledge of children's needs * Knowledge of child abuse, indications, and local child protection procedures * Resources to function and access to information * Some groups may need support from professionals	* Effective recruitment and vetting systems to be developed * Volunteer schemes might be developed to support families and to help prevent the abuse of children * While the informality of groups should not be jeopardised, statutory agencies should provide support and ensure that a safe environment is provided * All professionals to develop outreach approach to their work * Review local resources	* This sector contains a wealth of untapped experience * Religious organisations are providing a range of services to families * Many groups may provide direct services to children * Anyone can set up an association and club they should be checked carefully * Members of community groups may condone abusive behaviour * Ethnic minority groups may be undersupported

339

	Role and Responsibilities	Needs	Action Plan	Note/Comment
Self-help groups: Mothers; Parents of abused children; Survivors; Disability and special needs, etc	* To provide support to members * To meet specific needs * To campaign for improved provision * When necessary, to refer to outside agencies * To build confidence, self esteem, and skills	* To know when to seek external help * To link with professional networks, as necessary * Knowledge of child abuse and local procedures * Individual members may need support to enable them to participate in the group * Help with organisation, including resources * To contribute to policy, provision, and practice developments	* Need to learn from the experience of self-help groups, including strategies for individual self-help, and apply lessons to wider community * Need to support self-help initiatives * Where appropriate self-help initiatives to be financially supported * National support to be given to self-help initiatives, as appropriate	* Self-help groups may be more accessible than more "official" groups * Some individuals may be so traumatised that a group cannot help * Some groups run direct services, eg helplines * The transience of some groups may leave members vulnerable * Groups are not static and membership changes over time
Helplines: ChildLine; NSPCC Line; Parentline; Survivors' lines; Stepfamily Line; Lines in response to specific needs eg institutional abuse; etc	* To provide sensitive advice, information, and counselling * When appropriate, to make referrals to other agencies	* Accurate, current information * Knowledge of children's needs, child abuse and child protection procedures * Resources to meet the demand for services * Understanding of risks and ability to communicate them	* Action should be taken to ensure the effective funding of a national, 24-hour helpline for parents. * A national 24-hour helpline for survivors of child abuse should be established * Consideration to be given to the effective regulation of helplines * Implementation of the Telephone Helplines Association guidelines	* Helplines may be the first point of contact for children, family members and others with concerns * High level of unmet demand for helpline services * Helplines need to liaise closely with statutory agencies

	Role and Responsibilities	Needs	Action Plan	Note/Comment
Voluntary organisations: **1. Children and families organisations** Barnardos; Children's Society; NCH; NSPCC; Save the Children; Newpin, Homestart, etc	* To provide support to children and families through a range of services * To refer to other agencies, as appropriate, including child protection concerns * To campaign for improved provision * To involve parents/children	* Understanding of children's needs * Understanding of child abuse and child protection procedures * Effective staff and volunteer recruitment and selection * Liaison with statutory and other agencies	*In relation to all parts of the voluntary sector:* * Improve co-ordination both within the sector and with statutory agencies * Voluntary groups to participate in children's service planning * All voluntary agencies to develop understanding of child abuse and child protection procedures	*In relation to all parts of the voluntary sector:* * Voluntary organisations may be working independently or in partnership with other agencies * The sector is very varied, ranging from large national organisations to small local groups * Funding arrangements vary from own fundraising efforts to dependence on statutory funds
2. Meeting specialist needs Disability, health, housing, etc.	* To provide specialist services in response to special needs * To refer to other agencies, as appropriate, including child protection concerns * To campaign for improved provision.	* Understanding of children's needs * Knowledge of child abuse and child protection procedures * To differentiate between children's and adults' needs	* Children's charities to consider the images of children which they use for fundraising purposes * In contract and marketplace culture, funding needs of smaller groups to be considered	* The voluntary sector may have the capacity to develop innovative services * Voluntary groups may be more accessible than statutory services
3. General and umbrella groups Councils of voluntary service; CAB; Volunteer Bureaux; etc	* To support service-providing organisations * To provide advice and information * To recruit volunteers * To develop services * May provide direct services * To campaign for improved provision	* Understanding of children's needs and child protection procedures * Effective staff and volunteer recruitment and vetting		

	Role and Responsibilities	Needs	Action Plan	Note/Comment
Local authority services *Social services/ social work*	* To lead on children's services planning * To provide family support and day care * To provide social work support * To take lead role in child protection/ investigative duty * To provide residential care * To ensure the maintenance of standards in registered homes and services * To contribute to local authority general provision for children and families	* Understanding of child development and children's needs * Understanding of families and how to work with them * Resources to be allocated for family support * Strategic planning and joint agency and professional working * Staff development support and training * Feedback from young people and families on their experiences	* Children's services planning to become effective mechanism for developing preventive services * Priority to be given to prevention * ACPCs to develop an integrated approach to prevention * Child protection to be refocused to be a positive experience * Guidance on child protection procedures to be revised * Deployment of staff to be considered * Training and support needs to be met * Residential care to be developed as a positive option and to be rigorously regulated	* Social services is the lead agency in response to child abuse. Consideration must be given to how responsibility for the care of children can be extended to all professionals and members of the community
Education	* To identify possible cases of child abuse and to respond in accordance with child protection procedures * To set example of good behaviour * To provide family-life education, including sex education * To respond to bullying * To provide youth services * To provide adult education	* All teachers need to be able to recognise possible signs of abuse * All teachers need an understanding of child protection procedures	* Child protection procedures to be implemented in all schools * Family-life education to be provided in all schools * Teacher training to cover child abuse * Parental involvement in deciding policies and practices in response to child abuse * Resources to be available to enable teachers to participate in child protection procedures	* Existing guidance is adequate but not being implemented
Housing	* To ensure the provision of family housing * To provide emergency accommodation to homeless families * To provide refuges for battered spouses and their children	* Understanding of how housing provision relates to wider social provision	* Increased provision of family housing * Increased provision of accommodation for young people, especially those leaving care * Provision of refuges/safe houses for runaways, many of whom have been abused	* Homelessness has increased in recent years
Leisure and recreation	* To provide recreational services eg sport, swimming * To provide safe play areas * To provide out-of-school/ holiday schemes	* Understanding of child protection procedures * Guidance on physical contact with children and young people	* Guidance on child protection to be developed by all sports authorities * All sports and leisure staff to receive training on child protection procedures * Out of school activities to be effectively regulated	* private and voluntary initiatives as well as those in the statutory sector need to be regulated.

Role and Responsibilities	Needs	Action Plan	Note/Comment
Residential and institutional care	* To provide high quality care * To meet the needs of the "whole" child * To provide a positive experience * To ensure successful transition out of care	* Effective training, management and support for staff * Improved pay and conditions	* Effective staff recruitment and selection * Development of career structure for residential care workers, backed with training * Residential care to be integrated into wider pattern of community services * Regular checks on wellbeing of all children and young people in institutional care to be conducted as a priority	* Despite repeated inquiries, the abuse of children in institutions continues to be a problem. This must be tackled as a priority.

343

	Role and Responsibilities	Needs	Action Plan	Note/Comment
Health Service *General practitioners*	* To provide primary health care in the community * To provide advice on children's needs * To make referrals to specialist services * To participate in local child protection procedures	* Education on child abuse and procedures, including handling of confidentiality * Understanding of the needs of survivors	* GPs to receive in-service training on child protection * Fundholders to purchase health visiting and other preventive services * Development of services based on general practice, eg counselling	* GP services are among the least stigmatising of all forms of provisions. This needs to be built upon
Health visitors	* To ensure that every child has the opportunity to reach his/her full physical, emotional and social potential * To provide preventive health care, including the prevention of child abuse * To promote positive parenting * To run services for parents eg drop-in centres; parent and toddler groups, etc * To undertake health checks and population profiling * To provide child protection in accordance with local procedures and make appropriate referrals * To promote public health, including campaigning for improved services to meet identified needs.	* The management of the health visiting services to be improved * Effective resourcing of a universal service to be addressed * Contribution of the health visitor to be recognised by other professionals	* Health visiting to be retained as a universal service * Management and deployment of health visitors to be resolved * Home visiting schemes, for vulnerable families to be developed * Vulnerability of babies to abuse to be addressed	* The health visitor is the community nurse with key responsibility for child protection * The health visiting service is valued by the public and has the potential to form a central part of a prevention strategy
Midwives	* To provide antenatal care * To provide education on parenting * To undertake health checks * To make child protection referrals * To participate in local child protection procedures	* Understanding of child abuse and child protection procedures	* Home visits prior to birth to identify vulnerability to abuse * Closer liaison between midwives and other professionals to be developed * Midwives to identify and refer cases of postnatal depression	* Midwives may not be sufficiently integrated into the child protection network * Postnatal depression is a "hidden epidemic".

	Role and Responsibilities	Needs	Action Plan	Note/Comment
School nurses	* To act as a focal point within the school in relation to health matters * To ensure that children are encouraged to take responsibility for their own health * To support teachers in the delivery of health education * To complement primary care services in early detection and management of ill health * To provide advice on health issues to children, parents, teachers, etc.	* Understanding of child abuse and procedures	* Liaison with other professions to be developed * Work between school nurses and teaching staff over delivery of personal and social education to be promoted	* Pilot projects indicate that school nurses can play a key role in advising children and in delivering the curriculum
Paediatricians	* To provide specialist child health service * To advise and support non-specialists on child health needs * To assess and diagnose child abuse	* Training in diagnosis of abuse	* Only experienced paediatricians to assess and diagnose child abuse	
Accident and emergency service	* To identify possible cases of child abuse * To make referrals to specialist services * To follow local procedures	* Better understanding of child abuse and procedures * Promote A & E staff as part of wider child protection team	* Training on child abuse and procedures	
Child and adolescent mental health services	* To identify possible cases of child abuse * To provide assessment of children's condition and needs * To provide treatment to abused children and their families * To provide assessment and treatment to abusers	* Recognition of long term possible effects of abuse and harm	* Treatment to be provided to all victims of abuse, at times when it is needed * Training and appointment of child psychotherapists to be increased	* Many children fail to receive the treatment they need
Adult and specialist services	* To provide specialist services * To make referral when there are child protection concerns relating to the patient * To recognise the needs of children related to an adult being treated	* Understanding of children's needs * Understanding of child protection procedures	* Adult services to address the needs of children of adult patients and to make appropriate referrals	* Adult services may fail to recognise the needs of their patients' children * Adult services should recognise the needs of adolescent patients

	Role and Responsibilities	Needs	Action Plan	Note/Comment
Police	* To protect the community * To bring offenders to justice * To investigate allegations of child abuse * To undertake education on crime prevention and self-protection	* Understanding of children's needs * Close liaison between police and other agencies is essential * Police need to become more accessible to children and families	* Needs of children to underpin police response to child abuse * Consideration to be given to development of special investigation teams * Police response to domestic violence to be refined * Education provided by police on child abuse to be integrated with wider education to ensure consistent messages	* Training and practice in child protection has improved * There are concerns that in investigating cases of child abuse, the police's need to secure evidence predominates over the needs of children * The Memorandum of Good Practice on Interviewing Children has led to pressure on resources
Probation service	* To supervise offenders, including those with convictions against children * To inform the local authority when such offenders are discharged from prison * To provide treatment to offenders * For the courts, to supervise children following marital breakdown * To liaise with child care workers	* An understanding of the needs of children and responses to child abuse * Probation officers need to work with other professionals to meet the needs of the whole family * Training which includes social work	* To integrate probation work with offenders to the wider community response to child abuse * To develop multi-disciplinary responses to sex offenders * To work with male and female offenders who may have been abused	* The prevention of child abuse requires priority to be given to the treatment and control of offenders. The probation service has a key role * There are concerns at the removal of the social work content from probation officers' training * Increased resources are needed for treatment services
Legal professions	* To implement the law * To bring offenders to justice * To protect the innocent defendant	* Understanding of children's needs	* Legal practices to become child friendly and supportive of families * Reduce waiting times for cases coming to court * Implementation of Pigot proposals, including pre-trial hearings * In longer term, fundamental review of legal system to address how it can truly reflect children's needs and the UN Convention	* The legal system is a prime example of how our culture acts against children's interests

	Role and Responsibilities	Needs	Action Plan	Note/Comment
Employers	* To develop family-friendly employment practices * To provide flexible working arrangements * To make appropriate child care provision * To provide staff counselling	* Understanding of children's needs * Understanding of the benefits to employers of family-friendly policies * Understanding the composition of their workforce and their family responsibilities	* National policy for the promotion and implementation of family-friendly policies * Introduction of policies by individual employers	* Employment practices, and unemployment, have a major impact on family life
Trades unions	* To promote family-friendly employment policies and practices * To oppose use of exploitative child labour	* Understanding of children's needs and those of their parents	* Promotion of family-friendly practices as part of overall pay and conditions	* Employment practices have a major impact on family life
Media National and local: press; TV; radio; advertising	* To inform and educate * To entertain responsibly * To provide follow up advice and counselling * To represent appropriately children and their interests	* Accurate information on children and child abuse * Information on services which support children, parents, and families * Staff covering child abuse may need support and counselling	* Journalists' training to cover child abuse * Establishment of a proactive national organisation to provide informed comment/context on children's issues * Media to have a responsibility to consider the impact which coverage will have on individual children * All professionals, especially social services, need to develop a proactive approach to media	* Different parts of the media have different responses to children's issues and child abuse. While some parts respond positively and supportively there are some concerns about irresponsible coverage
Private and independent sector Child care services; Education; Health care; Leisure; Transport; etc	* To ensure that children's needs are identified and met within the service provided * To understand needs of children * To understand child protection procedures * To recruit effectively and vet all staff working with children	* Understanding of children's needs and child protection procedures	* Private sector services for children to be closely regulated * Services to follow local child protection procedures * Private sector needs to vet staff who work with children	* There are concerns that the deregulation of services may lead to children being put at risk * The independent sector needs to be involved in the development of children's services plans

	Role and Responsibilities	Needs	Action Plan	Note/Comment
National government: Dept of Health; DfEE; Home Office; Lord Chancellor's Department; Department of Environment; Dept of National Heritage; Welsh Office; Scottish Office; Northern Ireland Office; etc.	* To provide and promote co-ordination of a national framework and strategy to meet the overall needs of children * To consider the implications for children of all policies and legislation * To ensure that sufficient resources are available to meet children's needs * To take a lead in providing public education on the needs of children	* A proper understanding of the *overall* needs of children and how they can be met * An understanding of the needs of parents * An understanding of the dynamics of the community	* Appoint a Commissioner for Children * Appoint a Minister for Children * Enact laws that will implement and reflect the UN Convention on the Rights of the Child * Develop national public education to prevent child abuse and change the cultural framework in which children are treated	* The needs of children is the responsibility of a number of different government departments. This has led to poor liaison and co-ordination * In addition to the strategic action plan identified here, individual departments need to implement specific recommendations made in the Report.

National Commission: Survey Among Children and Young People: Overview

*Report of the
National
Commission of
Inquiry into the
Prevention of
Child Abuse*

As part of the Commission's consultation, around 1,000 children and young people filled in a questionnaire which focused on their attitudes to punishment and to adults and on how they get help when they are unhappy.

Main Points

- Nine in ten children believe that saying "Well done!" when children do the right thing, helps them behave better.

- Only three in ten think that smacking has a similarly positive effect. 67% believe smacking does *not* help children behave better.

- Most children feel that grown-ups are unpredictable. Only one in three believes the punishment they receive is fair 'most of the time'. The others feel it is only 'sometimes' or 'never' fair.

- Most children do not believe that adults generally listen to what they say. Around a half said they 'sometimes' and 8% that they 'never' listen.

- One in twelve children has a very negative impression (and probably experience) of adults. They believe that their punishment is never fair and that grown-ups never or only sometimes listen when children want to talk to them. This provides a very poor basis for personal and social development.

- What do children most want to change about grown-ups? Overwhelmingly they asked for more and better communication: more listening, greater understanding and support, more attention and more talking to children; and for less physical punishment.

*Report of the
National
Commission of
Inquiry into the
Prevention of
Child Abuse*

National Commission: Survey Among Children and Young People: Summary

1 Background

The Commission attaches importance to listening to children. This survey is part of its consultation process. The questions focused on the ways in which children seek help when they feel unhappy about something - at school and away from school - and their attitudes to punishment and to adults.

With the cooperation of youth groups and eight schools throughout the United Kingdom, around 1,000 children and young people filled in a questionnaire, which included some questions where the children filled in the answers in their own words. Of these, 985 were included in the main analysis and a sub-sample of 385 were specially coded and analysed in detail. The children ranged in age from 8 to 16, and just over half were girls.

The answers provide a useful reflection of the experiences and opinions of a large number of children. This summary covers only the main findings. Details of the project - including a copy of the questionnaire and the results - are available in the Commission archives.

2 Feeling Unhappy About Something: At School

Just over six in ten of the children in our sample (62%) said they had ever felt unhappy about something at school, with girls (at 69%) significantly more likely to admit this than boys (52%). It was the youngest and the oldest in our sample - the under 10s and the over 14s - who were most likely to report unhappiness.

The children described in their own words what had caused their unhappiness. Bullying was by far the most common single reason for being unhappy at school, mentioned by 28% of those who had ever felt unhappy. Bullying was most likely to be mentioned by the 9 - 10 year olds (at 39%).

School work was a much less common reason for unhappiness and, in contrast to bullying, was more of a problem among older children. It was quoted as the cause of unhappiness by around one in six of the 9 - 12s who had felt unhappy about something at school. This increased to one in three among the 13 / 14s and to one in two among those aged 15 or over.

Problems with friends - quarrels and exclusions from the group - were four times more likely to be mentioned by girls than boys.

Report of the
National
Commission of
Inquiry into the
Prevention of
Child Abuse

Table 1 *Reasons for Feeling Unhappy About Something at School*
based on those who have felt unhappy and were separately coded = 222

Being bullied	28%
Problems with work	14%
Being told off unfairly	14%
Quarrels with friends	11%
Being teased	8%
Exclusion from group of friends	4%
Loss of particular friend	4%
Doing badly	3%

3   Feeling unhappy about something *not* to do with school

Just over a half of the children said they had ever felt unhappy about something that was not to do with school (54%). Again, girls were more likely to admit to unhappiness than boys - 62% of girls compared with 44% of boys.

As with unhappiness at school, it was the youngest and the oldest in our sample - the under 10s and the over 14s - who were most likely to report unhappiness.

Describing in their own words what made them unhappy, the children mentioned a range of different reasons. Most were linked with one of three types of very personal experience:

○   loss - especially of family, but also pets or friends - through death or illness, changed family circumstances or moving away

○   conflict in the family or with friends

○   unfair punishment or bullying

351

Table 2 *Reasons for feeling unhappy about something not to do with school*
based on those who have felt unhappy and were separately coded = 193

Death in family	28%
Being bullied	10%
Relationship with friends	10%
Conflict in family	9%
Being told off/punished unfairly	8%
Loss of pet	8%
Problems with hobbies/holidays/sport	8%
Life in general	8%
Illness of family member/friend	6%
Quarrels with siblings	6%

*Report of the
National
Commission of
Inquiry into the
Prevention of
Child Abuse*

4   What did they do when they felt unhappy?

Most of them told someone - usually a parent or friend. 80% told someone about their unhappiness at school, and 76% when it was not to do with school.

Whom did they tell and how did it work out?

o Parents were the most popular choice of who to tell - for unhappiness at school and elsewhere, with friends at number two.

o Younger children were more likely to tell a parent, but older children confided in their friends more.

o Unhappiness at school was more likely to be discussed with a teacher than problems elsewhere. But even at school most children did not include teaching staff among those they would tell.

o In most cases the child felt that the person had listened carefully. In general they just wanted someone to listen.

o But when they did want action, the person they had told generally took the desired action.

It is therefore not surprising that most said they were glad they had told someone. Girls seem to be happier with telling than boys: irrespective of whether the unhappiness occurred at school or elsewhere, they were much more likely than boys to feel that their confidant listened carefully and more likely to be glad they had told someone.

Telling was, however, not necessarily seen as a good solution by everyone. Most of those who had kept their unhappiness to themselves did not wish they had told someone. However, a significant minority did wish they had shared their unhappiness - around one in fourteen of all the children who had felt unhappy. At the younger end - among the under 13s - a majority of those who did not tell wished they had told someone about their unhappiness at school. This underlines that more needs to be done to encourage younger children to talk about what is making them unhappy at school.

These answers show that although different numbers of children and, indeed, different children filled in their experience of what happened when they felt unhappy at school or away from school, what then happened was remarkably similar in the two situations. (Details are shown in Table A following this Summary)

5   Bullying

Bullying was by far the most common reason for feeling unhappy at school. In addition to the general questions about feeling unhappy, the children were asked to write in their own words what they would do if:

a   a friend was being bullied at school
b   they themselves were being bullied at school

Virtually all of them said they would either tell someone or do something. But what they would do would be very different depending on whether it was a friend or themselves who was being bullied.

*Report of the
National
Commission of
Inquiry into the
Prevention of
Child Abuse*

If they were the victim, most children - 76% - would tell someone - a teacher, parent or a friend; only a quarter said they would take some action, for example, by fighting back. But if a friend was being bullied, the children were as likely to say they would step in and try to do something to stop the bully as they were to involve someone else by telling. It seems to be OK to tell if you are the victim but not to tell on behalf of a friend.

Boys are more likely than girls to say they would fight. Older children are much more likely to try to sort out the bullying than younger children, who are more likely to tell.

Teachers are at the top of both lists as the person to tell. However, most children did *not* say they would tell a teacher if they or a friend were being bullied. They would find another way of trying to deal with it.

(Details are shown in Table B following this Summary)

6   ChildLine

Most children said they had heard of ChildLine - 85% overall, and among the 13+s, over 95%.

Most said they would not call ChildLine if they were unhappy about something (57%). However, 40% would call ChildLine, with younger children much more likely to say they would than older children.

To some extent this may reflect the nature of the problems that these children had experienced, and their understanding of what types of problem are most appropriately referred to ChildLine.

7   Attitudes to punishment and to grown-ups

In order to assess the children's opinions of punishments we asked: Do you think grown-ups can help children behave better by . . .

i   smacking them when they do the wrong thing?
ii   saying 'well done' when they do the right thing?

These children voted 2 : 1 against the effectiveness of smacking. Most did *not* believe that smacking children when they have done the wrong thing helps the children behave better. 67% said it does NOT help; 31% that it does. (The others were not sure.)

However, they believed even more strongly in the effectiveness of reinforcing good behaviour. Over nine in ten - 91% - said that for grown-ups to say 'well done' when children do the right thing does help children behave better. A small minority - 7% - did not think it helps.

A majority of the children were ambivalent about being told off and the punishments they received. Around one in three felt they were fair 'most of the time'. But 58% felt they were

Report of the
National
Commission of
Inquiry into the
Prevention of
Child Abuse

fair only 'sometimes'. And one in ten said they were never 'fair' - a view more common among the under 11s than in other age groups. (Other research indicates that children in this age group are more likely to be slapped and hit than older children.)

Those children who believed that when they are told off or punished it is fair 'most of the time' were particularly likely to think smacking can be effective. Whereas those children who believed their punishment is 'never' fair were especially likely to deny the effectiveness of smacking.

The ambivalence about the fairness of punishment was also reflected in their answers to the question: Do grown-ups listen when children want to talk to them? 38% said that adults listen 'most of the time'. Around a half that they 'sometimes' listen. And 8% felt that grown-ups 'never' listen.

Some of the children in the sample - one in five - had a very positive impression (and probably experience) of adults: they believed that grown-ups listen to children 'most of the time', *and* that when they are told off or punished it is fair 'most of the time'. These children seemed to feel fairly comfortable about adults. A larger number had an impression of rather less predictability. One in three said that adults listen only 'sometimes' and that punishment is fair only 'sometimes'.

At the extreme, this analysis identified a very small group of children with a very negative impression of adults. One in fifty (2%) said that punishment was never fair and also that adults never listened to children. A slightly larger group felt that their punishment was never fair and that grown-ups never or only sometimes listened when children wanted to talk to them - 6% of the children in the sample. In total, therefore, one in twelve of these children had impressions of adults which provide a very poor basis for personal and social development.

At the end of the session, the children answered the question: 'What is the thing you would most like to change about grown-ups?'.

Few said they would change nothing. The others mentioned a wide range of possible changes. Overwhelmingly, however, they asked for more positive behaviour and attitudes to children: to listen more (18%), greater understanding and more support (16%), be nicer and more friendly (16%), pay them more attention and talk to children more.

> Listen to us when we have something to say and not just ignore us much of the time.
>
> boy aged 11

> To sit and listen to what ever you have to say to them.
>
> boy aged 14

> Should try and see things from a child s point of view more often instead of an adult's point of view.
>
> girl aged 11

> Make them listen to what you are saying and to make them think that children are just the same as adults, just younger and smaller.
>
> girl aged 10

Report of the
National
Commission of
Inquiry into the
Prevention of
Child Abuse

Other children asked for less extreme treatment: be less bossy (11%), be less hypocritical and patronising (5%), and, specifically not to hit or smack children (6%)

Stop smacking children because it hurts. and for them to stop arguing.

girl aged 9

Stop smacking children, please.

girl aged 10

That they don t shout at us so much or slap so they leave marks where ever they hit us.

girl aged 10

355

Table A   *Telling: Summary of childrens response to unhappiness*

	Unhappiness at school	Unhappiness not to do with school
Based on those who've felt unhappy ...	606	534
	100%	100%
What did you do?		
nothing - kept it to myself	20%	24%
Do you wish you had told?		
Yes	7%	7%
No	11%	15%
told someone	*80%*	*76%*
mum/dad	48%	40%
friend	34%	37%
teacher	27%	8%
someone else	6%	10%
Do you think they listened carefully to you?		
Yes	65%	64%
No	14%	11%
Did you want that person to do something to help or just to listen?		
Do something	34%	30%
Just listen	46%	45%
Did they do what you wanted them to?		
Yes	22%	19%
Are you glad you told someone?		
Yes	71%	68%
No	6%	6%

Report of the
National
Commission of
Inquiry into the
Prevention of
Child Abuse

Table B   *Response to bullying*

	If person being bullied was:	
	a friend	me
Based on those separately coded	376	373
	100%	100%
Summary:		
Tell someone	56%	76%
Take some action	53%	28%
In detail:		
Tell:		
teacher	42%	40%
parent	4%	21%
friend	1%	14%
sibling	*%	3%
other specific person	4%	3%
someone (unspec)	7%	14%
Act:		
try to help/stop bully	21%	-
stick up for friend/self	14%	5%
talk to bullied friend	10%	-
get friend to get help	10%	-
fight bully	7%	12%
talk to bully	4%	2%
call for help	1%	2%
avoid school	-	1%
do something else	1%	6%

* = less than 0.5%.

The Commission thanks all the youth groups and schools who helped with this survey; Helen Fry who did most of the coding and Ariane Critchley who helped; and Finer Weston who generously donated the data processing.

The Portrayal of Young People on British Prime Time Television

*Report of the
National
Commission of
Inquiry into the
Prevention of
Child Abuse*

This pilot project was commissioned as the first detailed analysis of how young people (aged 17 or under) appear on UK prime time television - between 17.30 and midnight, (effectively excluding children's programmes). The Communications Research Group examined the output of the four UK terrestrial channels in the Central ITV region, in one week (5 - 11 May 1995). While the detail of the analysis is entirely determined by the programming in the 7 days covered, and cannot be generalised to TV output as a whole, it provides a basis against which future work may be compared.

In these 7 days of prime time TV:

○ Only 3 in 10 programmes included prominent children (for example, who spoke or were the focus of attention).

357

○ The 'harder' the programming, the fewer the prominent children or young people. They played a role in half of the fictional programmes but appeared as themselves in fewer than one in five factual programmes, and in only 15% of national news bulletins.

○ Different types of programme included children of very different ages. In fiction, 7 in 10 were aged 12 or over. In the factual programmes, over a half were primary or pre-school age.

○ Young people are generally portrayed in TV fiction in a positive context, displaying positive attitudes and behaviour.

○ Using a very broad definition of violence, young people were linked to violence (as aggressors, victims or witnesses) in 15% of fictional programmes, involving 28% of the prominent young people.

○ Abusive situations (persistent or continuing violence, neglect, emotional or sexual abuse.) were comparatively uncommon. One in twenty of the young people in fictional programmes was portrayed as a victim of abuse

○ Children appeared in just over 1 in 5 commercials. Most - 7 in 10 - were of primary or pre-school age, or babies.

This note summarises the main findings. A copy of the full report is available in the Commission archives.

*Report of the
National
Commission of
Inquiry into the
Prevention of
Child Abuse*

Summary

1   This pilot project was commissioned as the first detailed analysis of how young people (aged 17 or under) appear on UK prime time television - between 17.30 and midnight. (effectively excluding children's programmes). Funded by the Broadcasting Standards Council, Channel 4 Television, the Institute of Practitioners in Advertising and the Independent Television Commission it was intended as input to the National Commission of Inquiry into the Prevention of Child Abuse.

The Communications Research Group at the University of Aston examined the output of the four UK terrestrial channels in the Central ITV region, during prime time (defined as 17.30 to midnight), in one week (5 - 11 May 1995). They identified young people - who appeared to be aged 17 or under - and of those who made a contribution to the programme / trail / commercial recorded details of their personal characteristics and their roles, which could vary within one programme. In view of the National Commission's interest, violence which involved children and young people (in any way) was looked at as a particular issue in this analysis.

In a total of 165 hours of broadcast time, there were 319 programmes (115 fiction, 204 factual), 427 programme trails, and around 1,400 commercials.

Clearly the detail of the analysis is entirely determined by the programming in the 7 days covered, and cannot be generalised to TV output as a whole. However, it provides a basis against which future work may be compared.

2   How many TV programmes include young people?
3 in 10 TV programmes (95 of the 319) showed children or young people.

In these 95 programmes, 272 young people made 'prominent appearances' (ie spoke or were the focus of attention). These were evenly balanced between male and female, and one in eight was from an ethnic minority background. 3% had some disability, in most cases visible. In addition, a lot of young people appeared in the background in TV programmes - an estimated further four and a half thousand across the week. These have not been analysed in detail.

3   TV Fiction
Excluding background appearances, young people played a part in around a half of fiction programmes (52% - 60 programmes). 184 young people appeared in these 60 fictional programmes : one in three as a major character (ie : central to the storyline), one in four in a minor role (ie : with more than one speaking line but not central to the plot), and the rest (41%) in an incidental role (ie : they spoke but had very limited input into the programme with little or no character development).

There were few young children in this sample of TV prime time fiction. Seven in ten were aged 12 or over. The older the character, the more major the role. Most teenagers were in major roles; most younger children in minor or incidental roles. So, not only were younger children less common, they were also less prominent.

Report of the
National
Commission of
Inquiry into the
Prevention of
Child Abuse

Over six in ten films included a portrayal of young people, as did 56% of all drama programmes (including soap operas).

In general, young people were portrayed in a positive context: they were portrayed socialising with friends, usually in their own or someone else's home or at school. They received support (36%), or love (20%) from adults and negative attitudes to them were comparatively rare (with anger and aggression the most common - just over one in ten characters). Similarly, the young people generally displayed positive attitudes and behaviours (happiness - a third - and confidence, support, love - each at around one in five.). There was also a significant amount of rudeness/cheekiness and sulking (one in five), but disobedience and rebelliousness were comparatively rare.

In identifying both the positive and negative experience of the same young person, the analysis highlights the realistic representation in TV fiction of their complex experiences.

In this analysis, 'violence' was defined in a very broad way, to include verbal or physical aggression or a reference to it, and accidental harm or damage. Young people were linked to violence (as aggressors, victims or witnesses) in 15% of fictional programmes. This included 28% - 51 - of the 184 young people. Their role was mainly as victims of violence (37% of the roles portrayed by young people) or as witnesses to physical violence (39%). One quarter of roles, however, were as aggressor, much of it in fights and scuffs between children. Verbal violence was less common.

Abusive situations - defined as persistent or continuing violence, neglect and emotional or sexual abuse - were rarer, involving 8% of the young people. One in twenty of the young people in fictional programmes was the victim of abuse. One in ten used bad language and one in eight heard bad language used by others.

4 TV Factual Programmes

Young people appeared in 17% (35) of factual programmes (ie as 'themselves/real people' not acting a part). In these 35 programmes there were 88 young people. This contrasts with the widespread presence of young people in fictional TV programmes.

For example, there were young people in 15% of national news bulletins, 17% of serious factual programmes, and 22% of light entertainment participation programmes. The more serious the programming, the fewer the young people. Moreover, these percentages may well overstate a 'normal' rate of appearance, as one in three of these young people appeared in programmes about VE Day or World War ll, which may not be typical of TV factual output. (The sample period included the VE Day celebrations and commemorations.)

All were interviewees or contestants, most commonly in a minor / vox pop role (four in ten). One in three was a more in depth or targeted interviewee., and 11% were the subject of the story.

They were, on average, considerably younger than children in TV fiction. Over a half were primary or pre-school age. Girls outnumbered boys.

359

*Report of the
National
Commission of
Inquiry into the
Prevention of
Child Abuse*

In general, because the young people had a straight informational role, and made short appearances, there are few details about their characteristics. Violence and distress were comparatively uncommon.

5   TV Programme Trails

Of the 427 trails, 22% (95) showed 118 young people. Around a half were used to enhance the potential appeal of the programme.

The ages of young people in programme trails was broadly similar to the ages of young people in the programmes. Trails did not seem to show the violence with which young people were associated in programmes. Physical violence was uncommon, as was verbal violence.

However, unlike the generally positive context for young people in TV programmes, the trails (not necessarily for the same programmes) showed rather negative attitudes by young people - rudeness / cheek or fear (each around one in five) and distress / tears (one in seven). This may reflect a tendency to show the more dramatic scenes in trails for a programme.

6   Advertisements

Of the 1,400 or so commercials, just over one in five - 317 - showed 1,207 young people, mainly as background characters. Excluding repeats, this included 96 different commercials.

Young people were featured in commercials for a broad range of products and services : food and drink, durables, financial services etc.

There are clear differences in the ages of young people used to advertise different products or services. Babies featured mainly in commercials for financial services. Pre-school children were found in commercials for travel and consumer goods, but rarely for confectionery, with which teenagers were particularly associated.

Children in commercials were much younger than those in TV programmes and trails. Of the 250 prominent characters (including repeats), nearly seven in ten were primary, pre-school or babies. Comparatively few were teenagers.

The Communications Research Group has agreed this summary. Further information about this study is available from the Communications Research Group at the University of Aston on 0121 359 0844.

The Media: Response to Broadcasting Support Services Helplines following Programmes on Child Abuse

*Report of the
National
Commission of
Inquiry into the
Prevention of
Child Abuse*

Broadcasting Support Services offers a range of programme support services for viewers and listeners, including telephone support lines and supply of printed material. The cost is generally met by the programme maker, broadcaster, or, on occasions, a third party funder (for example, a government agency or charitable foundation).

This analysis covers the response handled by BSS[1] to 27 programmes on all four terrestrial channels and BBC Radio about child abuse between 1985 and 1994. The programmes covered a range of issues around child abuse - from cases of sexual abuse to false memory syndrome, to the treatment of persistent offenders - targeted at specific groups as well as a general public. Most of the programmes were seen nationally but some were only shown in part of the country on that date.

The telephone service provided varied: from a conversation with a personal adviser which may last half an hour or more, to a 3-minute dial-and-listen; available from a few hours to several days. The decision on the nature and scope of the service ideally reflects the information and support needed in relation to the subject. However, realistically it may depend very much on the likely cost of the service in relation to the programme budget. Most of the telephone services provided are free to the caller to ensure equal opportunity of access and anonymity on sensitive topics (no call charges on telephone bills).

Main Points

1   Each programme attracted a response. The size varied with the medium (TV more than radio), the coverage (national more than Wales-only), the type of support (dial and listen more than personal consultation), the topic and the target. The numbers range widely: from 3,833 calls to a dial and listen service open for 48 hours in November 1991, following a US TV movie *Mary Jane Harper Cried Last Night*. The other extreme is 15 calls to a 2 hour service following a 1994 programme *A Suitable Case for Treatment* about Usk prison, only broadcast in Wales on BBC2. Thirteen of these were long calls from perpetrators.

2   These numbers do not reflect the full demand.

In addition to calls which were answered, BT frequently reported blocked lines. In some cases many thousands remain unanswered. Following *Suggestions of Abuse* (June 1994), 196 callers spoke to advisers. But BT estimated that 32,904 calls did not get through. This may represent 4,000 callers, since callers will try between 8 and 10 times before giving up. But it could represent considerably more than that. In addition, and much harder to quantify, are the many calls to other, non-trailed helplines, which occur following such programmes, and which are reported informally.

*Report of the
National
Commission of
Inquiry into the
Prevention of
Child Abuse*

3 People who need help or want information respond very quickly. In 12 minutes following *The Boys from St Vincent*, 158 called the dial and listen line. This underlines the importance of the possibility of providing an immediate response by telephone than a slower response by post, for example.

4 It is clear that the programmes and support lines are very effectively reaching and helping the right people. Around a half of those who responded to *Secrets of the Coach* had been sexually abused in sport. Most who responded to *Unspeakable Acts* had been abused by women. It was mostly parents of abused children who responded to *Acceptable Risks?* And other programmes received response from other adults who were abused as children.

5 Moreover, the media seems to have reached people who would otherwise not have disclosed about their experience. Of those who spoke to a personal adviser, around a half said that they had never before spoken about it , and / or felt that they had not been believed.

6 There is no evidence from this analysis of any reduction over time in the numbers contacting the help lines, or of viewer / listener fatigue.

7 There is however evidence in the BSS reports, of concern by the Advisers that the lines are not available for long enough and that there are not enough - or in some places, any - support services to meet the huge potential demand, especially outside populated areas.

A copy of the detailed analysis is available in the Commission archives.

References

1 This summary has been agreed by Broadcasting Support Services.

Portrayal of Child Sexual Abuse in Brookside

*Report of the
National
Commission of
Inquiry into the
Prevention of
Child Abuse*

by Lesley Henderson, Glasgow Media Group

This summary addresses the portrayal of child sexual abuse in television fiction. In particular, it explores audience reception of the "Jordache Story" within the Channel Four soap opera, *Brookside*. It focuses upon the incest storyline and highlights issues raised in a series of focus group discussions conducted between June 1993 and June 1994.

Summary of Findings

Twelve focus group discussions were conducted to explore people's views on the inclusion of child sexual abuse in TV fiction and the portrayal of incest by Channel 4 *Brookside*. A total of 69 people took part in the survey, 56 of whom also completed a questionnaire. Nine of the groups had no obvious knowledge about the issue of child sexual abuse and three groups involved people who had direct experience from working in this area or having been sexually abused themselves.

1. Most respondents felt that child sexual abuse should be portrayed in TV fiction; a few thought that it *should not* be and some were unsure. This was linked to the participants' age and personal experience. Older research participants were less likely to believe that the soap opera format should deal with the topic whereas younger participants, those who worked with survivors or were survivors themselves, all believed that this topic *should* be tackled in soap opera.

2. Reasons for thinking child sexual abuse *should* be portrayed were that it would: increase public awareness of the issue; reduce isolation for children in an abusive situation; correct misconceptions about sexual abuse and fulfil the remit of soap opera as reflecting "real life".

3. Reasons for thinking it *should not* be portrayed or being unsure were as follows: fear of children "getting ideas" and making false allegations; fear of destroying childhood innocence, seeing soaps as appropriate only for "entertainment".

4. Research participants praised the portrayal of child sexual abuse in *Brookside* for:
    o   taking on a difficult and important topic.
    o   handling abuse scenes with sensitivity.
    o   showing child sexual abuse as perpetrated by a known family member as opposed to "stranger danger".
    o   illustrating the power dynamics within a family.
    o   making the link between physical and sexual abuse.
    o   portraying the way in which abusers silence victims.
    o   reinforcing the idea that young people do not provoke and cannot be held responsible for abuse.

*Report of the
National
Commission of
Inquiry into the
Prevention of
Child Abuse*

○ the strong character of "Beth Jordache" who illustrated that abuse victims do not, by definition, become future abusers or are "scarred for life".

○ the character of "Rachel Jordache" who elicited an understanding of the complex emotions which are felt by young people towards their abuser (denial/ love/ guilt/ loyalty).

○ helping to provide a framework for making sense of abusive experiences.

5. On the other hand, some research participants criticised the portrayal of child sexual abuse *Brookside* for:

○ taking on a sensational topic and airing inappropriate scenes of abuse.

○ seeming to imply that lesbianism was a direct and inevitable result of sexual abuse.

○ resolving the situation by killing the abuser. This added substantially to viewer enjoyment but allowed no positive portrayal of outside agency intervention. For example this decision was criticised because it missed an opportunity to portray police or social services work in a way which might help people in similar "real life" circumstances to consider their options.

6. There were some key differences in audience reception of specific themes and characters in *Brookside* which were linked to their personal or professional experiences. For example:

○ Participants with no special knowledge of child sexual abuse perceived "Trevor Jordache" as a stereotypical "psycho". In contrast, those with experience of the issue saw Trevor's abusive behaviour as motivated by the desire for power and wish to control his family.

○ Participants with no special knowledge of the issue thought that the combined physical and sexual abuse perpetrated by "Trevor" was unrealistic and exaggerated. Whereas those with experience praised the links made between physical and sexual abuse as reflecting reality.

○ Participants with no special knowledge of the issue believed, in theory, that "abusers can be anyone" yet resisted a more realistic soap portrayal of an abuser. The source of this belief rested on their fears about personal safety. If abusers are characterised as "ordinary men" rather than "monsters" then who could you trust?

○ Participants with no special knowledge of the issue accepted, in theory, that "any child" can be at risk from abuse yet resisted the idea that children whom they knew personally may be at risk.

○ Some participants *without* experience of abuse believed that a "normal" childhood could be damaged by knowledge about sex abuse. This reflects fears that if information is available to young people it could corrupt childhood innocence. Some also thought that soap operas might contribute to children making false allegations. Participants *with* experience of sexual abuse challenged such views and believed that information helps keep children safe and children rarely make false accusations.

○ Participants *without* experience of sexual abuse believed that a mother would always "know" that her children were being abused and could protect against abuse. This significantly reduced sympathy and credibility for the character of "Mandy Jordache". By contrast, participants *with* experience of child sexual abuse

*Report of the
National
Commission of
Inquiry into the
Prevention of
Child Abuse*

praised her portrayal for it's realistic characterisation of a "battered wife" living in isolation.

○ Those without experience of sexual absque believed that soap operas should not portray negative realities about child sexual abuse, for example, a child disclosing and not being believed. Most participants who worked in this area however believed that realism rather than idealism should be portrayed. This study supports, therefore, the findings of the study of *Women Viewing Violence* (Schlesinger, et. al 1992) which found that those who have experienced physical and sexual violence want the "reality" of this experience to be represented by media.

Conclusion

Fictional drama has a role to play in increasing awareness about child sexual abuse. This study reveals that *Brookside's* child sexual abuse storyline communicated complex and important messages about the issue. Key moments in the storyline, such as "Trevor's" rape of "Rachel", made a profound and lasting impact upon research participants. People could recall imagery and reproduce dialogue from this scene almost word for word many months after the episode had been transmitted. In particular the sustained portrayal of "victims" coping with their abuse drew praise and, for those themselves who had been sexually abused, the characterisation of "Beth" and "Rachel Jordache" as "survivors" rather than victims provided realistic and sympathetic figures with whom they could identify.

365

Brookside's sexual abuse storyline provided a crucial opportunity to tackle pervasive experience in the field. However, research participants who had no special knowledge of domestic or sexual abuse, were confused and frustrated by some aspects of the story. For example, "Mandy's" perceived failure to protect her daughters from abuse and herself from physical violence. This was seen as "collusion". Although *Brookside* viewers acknowledged her feelings of guilt and helplessness, blame was implicit. This suggests that *Brookside* successfully confronted some myths about "victim blame" but not others. In particular, it failed to challenge much of the mother-blaming which surrounds discussions of child sexual abuse.

Similarly, the portrayal of "Trevor Jordache", was praised by "special knowledge " participants as successfully demonstrating the power and control exerted by abusers. However, it failed to make an impact upon the preconceptions of most "general population" participants. Strongly held beliefs about abusers as simply "evil" or "mad" were reinforced by Trevor's characterisation as unpredictable and volatile.

The *Brookside* incest storyline increased knowledge and understandings about the language, reality and effects of abuse. This study however identifies some important areas of audience resistance. Many of the research participants believed that a mother would always know if her child was being abused; that they themselves would take swift action against an abuser and that abusers are identifiable. *Brookside's* apparent failure to communicate more problematic experiences of the mother's position or why men abuse is, in part, connected to powerful constructions of motherhood and reflects the dearth of debate in wider media about abuser's motivations (Kitzinger and Skidmore, 1995b). However it may also be a problem with the *Brookside* text. For example "Trevor" was introduced to *Brookside* as an

*Report of the
National
Commission of
Inquiry into the
Prevention of
Child Abuse*

external and short term character with no prior history. If abuse had been perpetrated by a regular, long term figure in the soap, viewers would have perhaps engaged more fully with debates around why abuse happens and how it may be prevented. As it was, "Trevor" was more easily sidelined as a mentally disturbed "monster" thus removing the threat posed by "ordinary" men.

The study highlights the deep anxieties which the subject of sexual abuse provokes. In some respects, people are unwilling to confront these fears. The soap genre is one which focuses primarily on the minutiae of everyday life and sexual violence against women and children as a pervasive reality in our society. By addressing the difficult topic of child sexual abuse *Brookside* illustrates how a traditionally "entertainment" genre can be used to enhance knowledge and understanding about a social problem.

Note: The Role of Fiction as a Medium for Social Issues

○ Fiction reaches larger audiences than factual programmes. The average weekly audience for the soap opera *Brookside* (C4) is 10–11 million viewers.

○ Fictional output can reach different audiences from news and documentaries. The soap opera *Brookside* (C4) attracts an audience which is predominantly aged between 15–34 years [BARB figures]. Helplines for *The Jordache Story,* a condensed version of the incest/domestic violence storyline, (TX: C4, 2.10.94, 1800–1900) attracted an unusually high level of calls from children (13%). This was perhaps due to the early transmission time as the programme was broadcast within Channel 4's Children's *'Look Who's Talking'.* In addition, the story was narrated by 'Beth Jordache', a teenage character with whom many young survivors identify.

○ Surveys indicate that soap operas are a key source of information about social problems for young people. For exmple, one study found that for two out of three children, soap operas were their main source of information about HIV/AIDS rather than parents or teachers (Barnardo's, 1993).

○ Fictional accounts generate a high level of debate through other media outlets. Factual reports are often 'hooked' to fictional storyline features in the press and actors are interviewed across a range of media formats which reach diverse audiences. The actors involved in the 'Jordache' storyline were interviewed in factual television, press features and youth magazines. Additional audiences may be reached by videos and books released by soap opera productions. *The Journals of Beth Jordache* provides a fictional diary account of the character's emotional response to her abuse.

○ Soap operas rely on audience responses to key players in the storyline. Viewers are extremely loyal to regular characters. Whether audiences respond to characters with sympathy or indeed hostility the narrative itself is structured to maximise engagement. Fictional accounts of social problems can elicit powerful audience responses whether or not they have direct experience of the issue.

*Report of the
National
Commission of
Inquiry into the
Prevention of
Child Abuse*

○ Specific fictional programmes have been responsible for children disclosing abuse and also for helping people to 'name' past experiences as abusive. Helpline reports for fictional programmes indicate a significant number of calls from adult survivors of abuse and also from children in an abusive situation.

○ Fictional portrayals of social problems are used currently by agencies involved in prevention and rehabilitation work. Domestic violence scenes portrayed in *Brookside* have been used by police and women's organisations to facilitate discussion of emotive issues.

○ Factual media is bound by legal and ethical restrictions which cover, for example, anonymity of victims. In fiction audiences can see and hear the 'abuser' and the 'victim'.

○ The soap opera format allows long term treatment of social problems in which complex issues can be played out, e.g. ambiguities concerning 'collusive' mothers and victims' conflicting feelings of guilt/love towards their abuser.

This report has been produced for the National Commission of Inquiry into the Prevention of Child Abuse on behalf of Channel Four. A more extensive study by the author explores the production, content and audience reception of child sexual abuse as framed within fictional television, including soaps, plays, police and hospital drama series.

Full details are available from Lesley Henderson, Glasgow University Media Group, 0141 330 6680.

Report of the
National
Commission of
Inquiry into the
Prevention of
Child Abuse

The Child Protection System - a note

1.   This Appendix briefly describes the "child protection system" by which professionals take action following a report that a child may have been abused. These notes may usefully be read in conjunction with the appendices on the law (Appendix 10 and Appendix 11). For a more detailed discussion readers are advised to consult the government guidance.

A Referral

2.   Anyone - a member of the public or a professional - who is worried that a child is in danger from abuse can report their concerns to the social services or social work department, police, or the NSPCC. The law requires that when a referral has been made there must be an *investigation* to ascertain the facts and to decide whether the child is in danger of abuse or neglect.

The Investigation

3.   If the professionals believe the child is at risk of harm which is **'significant'** they will start an investigation. Investigations are carried out by police and social workers, either working together or independently. The government guidance requires that "during a child protection investigation the child and those personally and professionally connected with the child must be interviewed." The investigation could last for several weeks and involve a number of meetings.

A Child Protection Conference

4.   At some stage of the investigation a **child protection conference** will usually be arranged. This meeting is held because one or more professionals want to discuss their worries about the child with the parents and other professionals. This meeting may be attended by people from a range of agencies - usually the health visitor, the police, the education social worker, the child's doctor, and the parent's doctor, and the teacher or head teacher. Other professionals who know the child may also be invited. Both parents and children are now encouraged to attend the child protection case conference.

5.   The conference makes recommendations to individual agencies about what actions they should take. It is for each individual agency to decide whether or not to carry out the recommendations although they usually do so.

6.   Decisions taken by the conference include: whether the child's name should be put on the **child protection register** and under which category of abuse; how the parents or carers will be told about the decision to register the child and what plans have been made to protect the child; who the **keyworker** will be (the professional who will carry the main responsibility

*Report of the
National
Commission of
Inquiry into the
Prevention of
Child Abuse*

for the case between child protection case conferences and make sure that the plan agreed at the conference is carried out).

7.   The conference can make recommendations to individual agencies about all sorts of things. The most common ones are:

○   if the child is placed on the register, the **child protection plan** which is the help which should be provided to the child and his or her family.

○   whether the police should investigate to see if a criminal offence has been committed.

○   whether the child's health should be investigated further.

○   whether, with the parents' agreement, the child should leave home for a while, by being "accommodated" by the local authority.

○   whether a legal action should be taken by social services or the NSPCC. This could be applying for a court order.

9.   Government guidance states that a **written agreement** should be made between the parents and the professionals about what the problem is and what will be done to improve things.

The Child Protection Register

369

10.   The child protection register lists the names of all children in the area that a child protection case conference has decided are at risk of abuse or neglect and need a joint plan to protect them in future.

11.   The register is looked after by a **custodian** who is usually a senior member of the social services department. Professionals can ask the custodian to find out if the names of children they are concerned about are on the register.

12.   If a child's name is on the register the joint plan will have to be reviewed at least every six months. Government guidance does not state that a child's name has to be on the register for any particular length of time. The guidance states that "for de-registration to occur all members of the review conference must be satisfied that the abuse or risk of abuse (either the original or any other) is no longer present or is no longer of a level to warrant registration."

13.   The decision to de-register a child does not mean that there is necessarily no longer a need to provide services to the child and the family.

The Area Child Protection Committee

14.   The government's guidance on child protection is contained in *Working Together*. The detail of this guidance may vary from area to area. That detail, and its interpretation will be decided by the **area child protection committee (ACPC)** or **child protection committee (CPC)** as they are known in Scotland. The ACPC is a group of senior managers or professionals from each of the key agencies with an interest in child protection: social services, NSPCC, health service managers, medical and psychiatric services, nursing, general practitioners, the education department, teacher representative, police, probation

Report of the
National
Commission of
Inquiry into the
Prevention of
Child Abuse

service, and armed services (where appropriate). The ACPC usually covers the same area as the local authority.

15.   Each ACPC will decide its guidelines about: what child abuse is; the initial investigation; the running of child protection conferences; planning help for the child and family; reviews of cases and taking children off the register; how much children and parents participate in the procedures.

16.   Each ACPC should have a programme of work to develop and keep under review local joint working and policies and procedures.

Community Care/National Commission Survey of Social Workers' Attitudes

*Report of the
National
Commission of
Inquiry into the
Prevention of
Child Abuse*

Background

These results[1] are based on a survey undertaken jointly by the National Commission and Community Care magazine during April and May 1995. 3,600 self completion questionnaires were mailed to a randomly selected sample of social workers on the Community Care reader list, with responsibility for working with children. 1,306 usable questionnaires were returned before the closing date, a response rate of 36%.

This paper summarises the main findings. Further information about this research - including a copy of the questionnaire and tabulations - are available in the Commission archives.

The Sample

Everyone in the sample had experience of dealing with child abuse cases - either in their current work or in the past. The vast majority worked in the statutory sector (92%) and three in four in a local area social services team. Most (74%) worked with children and families only, and one in five with other client groups also.

Most were experienced social workers. Nearly six in ten (58%) had worked in social care for ten years or more. The average age was 41, with a wide spread around this. 62% were female.

Community Care reader lists contain an accurate cross section of the social worker population. These results reflect the views of a large number of involved and interested workers in this field, and as such represent an important input into the work of the Commission.

Key Findings On Social Workers' Views

o Social workers believe there have been some improvements over the past 10 years; for example, in interagency relationships, in the management of suspicions, in user friendliness, and in increased public awareness and willingness to take action. However, the overall context for child abuse work is unpromising, with continuing widespread denial of the full extent of abuse.

o On balance, many of the present arrangements for protection are thought to work well and achieve their aims. These tend to be at the harder end of their work : investigation, protection of children on register, and preventing serious abuse. Arrangements work less well at the softer end of protection and in prevention.

o The balance between protection and prevention work has swung too much to protection; seven in ten think there should be more emphasis on prevention . This would

Report of the
National
Commission of
Inquiry into the
Prevention of
Child Abuse

take social work back to former practice : seven in ten believe that social workers now do *less* preventive work than 10 years ago.

○ Most of the sample believe that social workers *should* be involved in all activities surrounding child abuse.

○ An overwhelming majority - 86% - felt that their social work qualifying training did NOT prepare them sufficiently for work in child abuse prevention.

○ There was widespread support for a special qualification in child protection.

○ There is clear evidence of a high level of stress. A significant minority - 16% - felt frustrated and over-stressed by child abuse work and would prefer to change their job . 62% say they more often find the work frustrating or stressful than satisfying, but on balance are prepared to stay with it.

Main Results

A. General Impressions About Child Abuse

1   Overall, there is no consensus among these social workers about which types of abuse are most and which least common. Based on their own professional experience, there is a wide spread of views. Just under a half - 46% - put emotional abuse at number one, but most thought one of the other categories of abuse was the most common - physical (25%), neglect . (17%), or sexual (14%).

Order of Occurrence Type of Abuse
% who said ... was most common, second, third, least

	most	second	third	least
emotional	46%	19%	16%	16%
physical	25%	25%	33%	14%
neglect	17%	27%	24%	29%
sexual	14%	28%	23%	31%

2   There is also some difference of opinion about trends over the past ten years. For each type of abuse, most believe that there is more or the same amount. Few think there is less. But emotional abuse and sexual abuse stand out as most likely to be seen as increasing (by two in five), with virtually no-one seeing a decrease.

Trends

Compared with ten years age, there is ...

	more	same	less	more/less
emotional	42%	43%	1%	+41
sexual	40%	46%	1%	+40
neglect	29%	47%	10%	+19
physical	21%	52%	16%	+ 5

3   These social workers are clear that a range of factors contribute to child abuse. On a scale from 'considerably', 'to some extent', 'slightly', to 'not at all', five factors were very

*Report of the
National
Commission of
Inquiry into the
Prevention of
Child Abuse*

widely regarded (by at least three in four) as contributing to abuse, at least to some extent: abuse suffered by the perpetrator, poverty, unemployment, bad housing and ignorance about child development. In comparison, some of the factors which get a lot of public and media attention - including the media itself, single parent families and social work practice - are not widely considered to be significant factors.

Factors contributing to child abuse

	Significantly	Significantly OR to some extent
abuse suffered by perpetrator	39%	92%
poverty	35%	85%
ignorance about child development	28%	74%
unemployment	27%	78%
bad housing	26%	78%
social norms and opinions	15%	58%
racism	14%	59%
residential care	11%	56%
violence on TV and films	8%	53%
single parent families	4%	33%
social work practice	3%	33%

Note: The list also included 'violence towards children', which emerged as top: 83% significantly and 95% at least to some extent.

4   There is general agreement that the overall context for child abuse work is unpromising : 84% agree that society denies the full extent of abuse. Most people are thought not to want to get involved with child abuse and would not report their suspicions. In view of the factors thought to contribute to abuse, it is hardly surprising that three in four social workers agree that child protection social workers are expected to deal with the effects of social disadvantage. The media was criticised - for denying the full extent of child abuse (59%); for being unhelpful in the prevention of child abuse (76%); and for not giving am accurate impression about the prevalence of abuse.

B.   Activities, Training and Support

5   Most in the sample were involved in a range of child protection activities. Eight in ten undertook assessment work, nearly as many family support, and seven in ten said they did investigations. Treatment, training, work with people who have been abused, and staff supervision were each undertaken by a quarter to just under a half.

6   One in two had a first degree, and eight in ten a CQSW. An overwhelming majority - 86% - felt that their social work qualifying training did NOT prepare them sufficiently for work in child abuse prevention.

7   Most had received special training in aspects of child abuse : eight in ten had received training in detection / investigation, two in three in interviewing suspected cases of abuse, 45% in treatment / therapy and 42% in family support.

Report of the
National
Commission of
Inquiry into the
Prevention of
Child Abuse

There was widespread support for a special qualification in child protection. (77% thought it would be a 'benefit to the child protection service'.)

8   The performance of managers was, on balance, judged favourably in most aspects - though the balance was that they performed 'fairly well' rather than 'very well' on: access to senior child protection staff, to senior mangers, to supervision, support, further training, keeping you informed on law and guidance, ensuring varied tasks and allocating caseloads - though for the last four functions, significant minorities (at least one in four) judged management performance 'fairly' or 'very bad'. It was only on evaluating the success of practice that managers were, on balance, thought to do badly.

C.   Social Workers and Their Work

9   Most social workers are confident that they can prevent child abuse in their job. (Nearly eight in ten) There is, however, ambivalence about working in child protection and clear evidence of a high level of stress. 22% find the work very satisfying and would not consider changing to another job. Many more, however - 62% - 'more often find the work frustrating or stressful than satisfying, but on balance are prepared to stay with it'. And a significant minority - 16% - went further; they felt 'frustrated and over-stressed by child abuse work and would prefer to change their job'.

10   These social workers define the social work role quite widely. There is a virtual consensus that social workers *should* be involved in all activities surrounding child abuse (that is, all those listed on the questionnaire) - from family support, to investigation and work with victims/survivors and with young abusers.

11 On investigations, for example, there is strong resistance to the idea that specially trained police officers should do investigations and leave family support to social workers. (eight in ten reject the idea) Six in ten think that 'specialist multi-agency teams' should be mainly responsible for investigations. One in three, however, want social workers to take the lead.

12   What do social workers feel about the effectiveness of the current system and practice?

There is general agreement that there have been changes and that some things have improved over the past 10 years : interagency relationships are more constructive (77% agree); the management of suspicions is better (70%); child protection is more user friendly (56%); the public is less tolerant of abuse (44% agree versus 22% disagree) and more likely to report suspected abuse (60%); helplines have empowered children (64%).

13   On balance, social workers feel that many of the present arrangements for protection work well and achieve their aims. These tend to be at the harder end of their work : investigation, protection of children on register, and preventing serious abuse - for each three times as many think they work well as think they work badly.

There is less agreement about the extent to which present arrangement work at the softer end of protection and in prevention. On supporting families under stress, preventing less serious abuse - the margin is much less, but, on balance, social workers think the arrangements work well. On work with victims / survivors, and with abusers,and protecting children not on the register, opinion is finely balanced.

The balance is definitely that arrangements do NOT work in preventing re-offending, nor do they promote public awareness. And there are widespread specific fears that the introduction of purchaser - service contracts will NOT help prevent abuse

*Report of the
National
Commission of
Inquiry into the
Prevention of
Child Abuse*

14   They expressed widespread support for certain aspects of the current system:

○   they reject the idea that child protection registers are ineffective and should be abolished (63% against, 9% in favour);

○   they disagree that child abuse investigations are given too high a priority by social services departments (61% disagree versus 21% agree);

○   they disagree on balance with the Audit Commission contention that 'large numbers of families are investigated inappropriately, when there has been no child abuse' (49% v 23% agree).

15   On the balance between protection and prevention work, it is generally believed that the balance has swung too much to protection; seven in ten think there should be more emphasis on 'prevention'. This would take social work back to former practice : seven in ten believe that social workers now do *less* preventive work than 10 years ago; only one in six believes they do more.

16   Many are, therefore, unhappy with social workers' current role. The level of resources is seen as an important but not the only problem.

375

○   Nearly one in two disagreed that the 'only problem with social work and child protection is the lack of resources', but three in ten agreed.

However, this does not mean that social workers are satisfied with the current level of resources. 'More resources' was the most common single recommendation made spontaneously by these social workers to the Commission. Made by 22%, it is nearly three times the number making the second most common suggestion - 'more / better training'.

○   While 28% supported a reallocation of resources from child protection to family support, 36% did not. The others did not express a view.

On the question of whether there is too much emphasis on professional procedures in work with children, opinion was balanced - 37% agreed and 44% disagreed.

17   Some possible changes, however, received widespread support, and reflect areas of dissatisfaction with current practice:

○   There should be more sharing of experiences between agencies about child protection (91%)

○   Family centres should be open to a wider community than they are now (82%)

○   ACPCs should have responsibility for prevention as well as protection (83%)

○   A system which emphasised therapeutic work and behaviour change in dealing with perpetrators would better help children than our current system based on detection and punishment (71%)

*Report of the
National
Commission of
Inquiry into the
Prevention of
Child Abuse*

D. Personal Experience and Views About Children

18   One in three said they consider they were abused as a child : 22% emotionally, 12% physically, 11% sexually and 4% by neglect. (7% refused to answer the question.) In the absence of comparable information based on a general sample of adults, it is not possible to draw firm conclusions about the experience of social workers compared with other people. However, these figures are not out of line with a range of survey data, which suggests that social workers may be similar to other people in this respect.

19   A small minority - 6% said they had themselves abused a child. A much larger percentage - 43% - said they had come close to it. Most - seven in ten - were or had been parent or primary carer of a child; the vast majority of these (87%) agreed that this experience had affected their views about child abuse.

20   Some of the questions in this survey were the same as a recent NSPCC survey among adults (Creighton and Russell), so broad comparisons can be made.

○   Social workers are more tolerant of children than other adults.

Among social workers only 45% think children are less well behaved than when they themselves were a child, and 52% believe children are about the same.

In the population as a whole, the balance of opinion is very different : 72% think children are less well-behaved and 26% that they are the same. Hardly anyone in either sample believes children are now *better* behaved than in their own childhood.

○   The vast majority of social workers agree that certain actions are sometimes justified as punishments: denying privileges (96%), shouting and screaming (63%), smacking with an open hand (60%).

But most are opposed to many forms of punishment included in the questionnaire: forcing to miss a meal, isolation, warning about fear figures, silence, verbal threats, swearing/verbal abuse, shaking a young child, and physical violence.

○   The majority of social workers (60%) think that hitting with an open hand is justified in certain circumstances. They are, therefore, *less* in favour of physical punishment than other adults, of whom eight in ten think it is sometimes justified.

One in two social workers believes that physical punishment is never an effective method of disciplining a child, and 44% that it is only occasionally effective. Two in five believe that it always or often leads to injury of the child. (There are no comparable figures for the general population.)

The Commission acknowledges the support and contribution of *Community Care* in the conduct and analysis of this survey.

References

Creighton S and Russell N : Voices from Childhood : A survey of childhood experiences and attitudes to child rearing among adults in the United Kingdom NSPCC 1995

---

[1] Community Care has seen and agreed this summary.

Acknowledgements

*Report of the
National
Commission of
Inquiry into the
Prevention of
Child Abuse*

The Commission wishes to express its gratitude to the many individuals and organisations who have helped and supported its work and apologise for the inevitable and inadvertent omissions to the following list.

Commission Secretariat

Christopher Cloke, (Secretary to the Commission)

Sarah King, (Research Assistant)

Henrietta Bond and Jude Tavanyar, (Press Managers)

Fenella Davidson, (PA/Administrator)

Katharine Peake, (Secretary)

We are particularly grateful to Pam Mills for her invaluable help and advice with the work of the Commission.

For Providing Meeting Rooms and Refreshments for Commission Meetings

Allen & Overy, 1 New Change, London EC4

British Paediatric Association, Regents Park, London.

Channel 4 Television, Horseferry Road, London SW1

Denton Hall, 5 Chancery Lane, London EC4

Focus, 84 Baker Street, W1

Harrisons & Crosfield, 1 Great Tower Street, London EC3

Llandough Hospital Trust, Penlan Road, Penarth, Cardiff

NSPCC, 42 Curtain Road, London EC2

Publicis Ltd. 82 Baker Street, London, W1

Saatchi & Saatchi Advertising, 80 Charlotte Street, London W1

Thorn EMI plc, 4 Tenterden Street, London W1

For Professional Advice, Consultation and Assistance

All Party Parliamentary Group for Children

All Party Parliamentary Group for Parents

Luci Allen, NSPCC Child Protection Helpline

Avebury Publishers and Jens Qvortrup, for use of the title "Childhood Matters"

Keith Bilton

Martin Brader, International Computers Ltd

Robert Carter

Pat Cawson

Sue Chambers

Jill Coffin, Staffordshire Social Services Department

Report of the
National
Commission of
Inquiry into the
Prevention of
Child Abuse

Sue Creighton

Alma Erlich

Mike Hames

Pauline Hardiker

Jeanne le Bars

Alan Lotinga, Assistant Director, Central Service, Staffordshire County Council

NCH Action for Children for Claire Sparks' time

NSPCC Helpline counsellors

Jane Naish, Royal College of Nursing

Phillip Noyes, NSPCC

Terry Philpot and *Community Care*

Esther Rantzen

Peter Saunders

Claire Sparks

Wendy Stainton-Rogers

Corrine Wattam

Catriona Williams

Clare Woodward

For Support with projects about the media

Broadcasting Standards Council

Broadcasting Support Services

Channel 4 Television

Communication Research Group

Glasgow Media Group

Independent Television Commission

Institute of Practitioners in Advertising

For Advice on the Work-Home Reality material

Austin Knight, Recruitment Consultancy, UK

Business in the Community, London

British Quality Foundation, London

Care for the Family, Cardiff

CBI, London

Demos, London

Employers for Childcare, UK

Equal Opportunities Commissin, Manchester

European Network "Families and Work", France

Exploring Parenthood, London

Families and Work Institute, New York

Family Policy Studies Centre, London

Industrial Relations Unit, University of Warwick

Institute of Directors, UK

National Children's Bureau, London

*Report of the
National
Commission of
Inquiry into the
Prevention of
Child Abuse*

National Institute of Social Work, London

New Ways To Work, London

One Plus One, London

Opportunity 2000, UK

Parents at Work, London

Policy Studies Institute, London

The BT Forum, UK

The Industrial Society, London

UK Committee for UNICEF, London

Whirlpool Foundation, Michigan, USA

Women Returners' Network, London

Working for Childcare, London

For attending Advice Columnists meeting

Lola Borg (*More*)

Annie Brabham (*Singled Out*)

Jane Butterworth (*News of the World*)

Sue Cook (*Sun*)

Gill Cox (*Woman's Realm)*

Jenny Firth-Cozens (*Good Housekeeping*)

Donna Dawson (*Company*)

Suzie Hayman (*Woman's Own*)

Barbara Jacobs (*My Guy*)

Tricia Kreitman (*Mizz, Chat*)

Anne Lovell (*Bella*)

Patricia Mansfield (*Take a Break*)

Denise Robertson (*This Morning*)

Celia Taylor (*Me*)

For attending Legal Meeting

Professor Christina Lyon (Dean, Faculty of Law, Liverpool University)

Kathleen Marshall (Solicitor, Gulbenkian Fellow in Children's Rights, Glasgow University)

Ackroyd, William (Association of Lawyers for Children)

Baine, Ouaine (Senior Psychologist, Strathclyde Regional Council)

Bull, Professor Ray (Dept of Psychology, University of Portsmouth)

De Cruz, Professor Peter (Department of Law, University of Staffordshire)

Gallagher, Greg (Principal Child Protection Officer, Strathclyde RC)

Hodgkin, Rachel (National Children's Bureau)

Hoyal, Jane (Barrister)

Hunt, Philip

Joel-Esam, Barbara (Solicitor, NSPCC)

Lawson, Miss E A, QC, (Family Law Bar Association)

Mellor, Anne (Psychologist, Birmingham Child Witness Support)

Newell, Peter (EPOCH)

del Priore, Christina (Royal Hospital for Sick Children, Yorkhill, Glasgow)

Report of the
National
Commission of
Inquiry into the
Prevention of
Child Abuse

Richardson, Vanessa (Local Authority Solicitor, Devon)

White, Richard (Solicitor, White & Sherwin)

Members of Parliament interviewed

The Rt Hon Michael Alison (Con: Selby)

David Alton (Lib Dem: Liverpool Mossley Hill)

David Amess (Con: Basildon)

Hilary Armstrong (Lab: Durham North West)

Peter Bottomley (Con: Eltham)

Julian Brazier TD (Con: Canterbury)

David Chidgey (Lib Dem: Eastleigh)

Malcolm Chisholm (Lab: Edinburgh Leith)

David Congdon (Con: Croydon North East)

Robin Corbett (Lab: Birmingham, Erdington)

Jean Corston (Lab: Bristol East)

Frank Field (Lab: Birkenhead)

Maria Fyfe (Lab: Glasgow Maryhill)

Neil Gerrard (Lab: Walthamstow)

Llin Golding (Lab: Newcastle-under-Lyme)

Bernie Grant (Lab: Tottenham)

Win Griffiths (Lab: Bridgend)

Margaret Hodge MBE (Lab: Barking)

Kevin Hughes (Lab: Doncaster North)

Nigel Jones (Lib Dem: Cheltenham)

Joan Lestor (Lab: Eccles)

Elfyn Llwyd (Pl C: Meirionnydd Nant Conwy)

Alun Michael (Lab: Cardiff South and Penarth)

Rhodri Morgan (Lab: Cardiff West)

Bill Olner (Lab: Nuneaton)

Elizabeth Peacock (Con: Batley and Spen)

Marion Roe (Con: Broxbourne)

Allan Rogers (Lab: Rhondda)

Clive Soley (Lab: Hammersmith)

Peter Thurnham (Con: Bolton North East)

The Rt Hon the Lord Archer of Sandwell QC

Baroness Faithfull OBE

Lord Graham of Edmonton

Lady Kinloss

Lady Lockwood

Lord Northbourne

Baroness Seccombe

For attending Newspaper Editors/Journalists Meetings

Christena Appleyard (*The Times*)

David Brindle (*The Guardian*)

*Report of the
National
Commission of
Inquiry into the
Prevention of
Child Abuse*

Sharon Collins (*Sunday People*)

Eileen Fairweather (*Evening Standard*)

Roy Greenslade

Mark Palmer (*Daily Express*)

Marjorie Proops (*Daily Mirror*)

Sarah Sands (*Daily Telegraph*)

Neil Wallis (*The Sun*)

For attending Meeting on the Role of Education

Christine Atkinson (NSPCC)

Jill Clemerson (Health Visitors Association)

Enid Colmer (Enfield Child Guidance)

Liz Cowley (Early Years Unit, NCB)

Erica De'Ath (Stepfamily)

Tom Dyson (Gwent Educational Psychology Service)

Michelle Elliott (Kidscape)

David Harrison (Mentors in Schools)

Elizabeth Hartley-Brewer

Carol Hayden (SSRIU, University of Portsmouth)

Eileen Hayes (NSPCC)

Gareth James (National Association of Head Teachers)

Kay Jenkins (National Union of Teachers)

David Knight (Schools Outreach)

Polly Lowe (OFSTED) observer

Diana Margetts (Protective Behaviours)

Christine Prideaux (Colfox School)

Caroline Ray (Sex Education Forum NCB)

Gillian Sage (Association of Teachers and Lecturers)

Anne Schonveld (Community Education Development Centre)

Judith Stone (National Early Years Network)

Hadrian Southorn (National Association of Governors and Managers)

Kathleen Taylor (Department of Health) observer

Priscilla Webster (Tayside Regional Council Educational Department)

Ivor Widdison (Council of LEAs)

Deborah Woolley (Department of Education) observer

John Werner (former Head Teacher)

381

For help with the making of the Commission's video "Survivors Speak"

All those who appeared personally on the video

Louise Rainbow

David McCormick

Channel Four Television

Report of the
National
Commission of
Inquiry into the
Prevention of
Child Abuse

For help with the making of the Commission's video for the launch of its Report

Sainsbury's, New Cross Gate, London SE14

Colgaen, Valerie, The City Literary Institute, London WC2

Hackney Film Unit, Mr John Hardy

Michael Jempeji

Beryl Karney

Susan Harwich

Giles Webb

Joanne O'Brien

Letherby and Christopher, Richmond Park, Surrey

Worlds Apart (kitemakers) London SW8, Jeremy Pilkington

David Ward, NSPCC

For Support with Projects and Suveys Among Children and Adults

Community Care, Polly Neate

Finer Weston

Irene Levine, Hackney Children's Rights Unit

Millwood Brown, Lucie Rolli and Linda Free

Peagram Walters Market Research Group, Sue Chambers

Schools and Youth Groups who participated in the Commission's survey